JEAN SEATON

Carnage and the Media

*The Making and Breaking of News
about Violence*

ALLEN LANE
an imprint of
PENGUIN BOOKS

ALLEN LANE

Published by the Penguin Group
Penguin Books Ltd, 80 Strand, London WC2R ORL, England
Penguin Group (USA) Inc., 375 Hudson Street, New York, New York 10014, USA
Penguin Group (Canada), 90 Eglinton Avenue East, Suite 700, Toronto, Ontario, Canada M4P 2Y3
(a division of Pearson Penguin Canada Inc.)
Penguin Ireland, 25 St Stephen's Green, Dublin 2, Ireland (a division of Penguin Books Ltd)
Penguin Group (Australia), 250 Camberwell Road,
Camberwell, Victoria 3124, Australia (a division of Pearson Australia Group Pty Ltd)
Penguin Books India Pvt Ltd, 11 Community Centre,
Panchsheel Park, New Delhi – 110 017, India
Penguin Group (NZ), cnr Airborne and Rosedale Roads, Albany,
Auckland 1310, New Zealand (a division of Pearson New Zealand Ltd)
Penguin Books (South Africa) (Pty) Ltd, 24 Sturdee Avenue,
Rosebank 2196, South Africa

Penguin Books Ltd, Registered Offices: 80 Strand, London WC2R ORL, England

www.penguin.com

First published 2005
1

Copyright © Jean Seaton, 2005

Set in 9.75/13pt PostScript Linotype Sabon
Typeset by Rowland Phototypesetting Ltd, Bury St Edmunds, Suffolk
Printed in Great Britain by Clays Ltd, St Ives plc

A CIP catalogue record for this book is available from the British Library

ISBN 0–713–99706–0

For
Ben Pimlott
Daniel, Nathaniel and Seth Pimlott

Contents

Acknowledgements   ix
Picture Acknowledgements   xiii
Introduction   xv

1   Blood in the High Street   1
2   Filth   29
3   Reality Violence for Fun: The Roman Games   49
4   Suffering is Good for You   80
5   Painful News   102
6   Wars and Sentimental Education   133
7   Do We All Feel the Same?   151
8   Bad Death is Good News   182
9   Media Memorials   203
10   Moved to Tears   230
11   Global Compassion   261

Conclusion: All the News That's Fit to Enjoy   287

Notes   297
Bibliography   324
Index   345

Acknowledgements

News is ultimately an editorial process. If it is done well, it keeps us honest and safe as well as absorbed. If it is done badly, instead of fun it may lead to corroding triviality, as well as ignorance and danger. We ought to bother about it more.

Penguin, I have found, has a gold-standard editorial process. I have been immensely privileged to have been dealt with so professionally by such a wonderful machine. Stuart Proffit is the ideal and inspiring publisher, authoritative, fastidious and ambitious. I am nearly as proud of being published by him as he is of baby Alice. Liz Friend-Smith has been delightfully enthusiastic and impressively capable at all times. My patient, eagle-eyed (and at times puzzled) editor, Bob Davenport, has been a treasure. All the errors are mine, but I am extremely grateful for Penguin's tireless attempts to save me from worse pitfalls, and for the heady purposiveness of being carried along as a minor part of such an intelligent enterprise.

Pip Lewis and Emma Brown of Edifice – charming knightesses – rode to my assistance with marvellous picture research and professional wisdom. I am indebted to them both.

The Arts and Humanities Research Board awarded me a grant for a visit to Russia, for which I am most grateful. Many people helped me over this trip, and shared their experienced understanding with me. I must express my gratitude especially to Sir Roderick Braithwaite, the late Sir Frank Cooper, Bill Thompson, Arkady Osgovsky, Alexei Pankin, Yvegeny Kiselov, Sergei Parkhomenko, Michael Berger and Iena Nemirovokskaya, among others. I also visited Romania, Hungary and Poland and met journalists from Serbia under the auspices of the British Association for Central and Eastern Europe, and am most grateful for these opportunities to see at first hand how media systems operate under different political pressures. Judith Herrin helped me imaginatively at an early stage, and Dr Kirsty Thompson and Dr Anu Rau at University College Hospital assisted me in many ways. I am sure I have made many mistakes, but not for want of expert advice, for which I am particularly grateful.

I owe a special debt to the many journalists with whom I have discussed aspects of this book, and would particularly like to thank Jonathan Burke, Nick Gowing, Sir Max Hastings, Mark Latey, Anatol Lieven, John Lloyd, David Loyn, Ron Neil, Quentin Peel and Vaughan Smith. In different ways discussions with Nick Cohen, Mark Damazar, Timothy Garton Ash, David Goodhart, Isabel Hilton, Donald MacIntyre, Peter Riddle, Francis Wheen and many others have all contributed to my ideas. A good deal of journalism has also flowed through my kitchen over the years. I have spent much time listening to many other journalists ponder their craft. They all have their own passionately held ideas about their work, and many will not agree with my approach, but all this book is really proposing is that news is so important that we ought to find richer ways of discussing it.

You cannot write books without libraries and archives. I am grateful to Jackie Kavenagh at the BBC Written Archive, that Aladdin's cave, for much assistance. I am especially indebted, however, to the British Library, a kind of socialist Utopia (to borrow a phrase) where nice, kind people find books for you. Both are lovely places.

Another stimulant to the book has been work (also funded by the AHRB on the official history of the BBC in the 1980s. Impartiality and objectivity are not easy to define or sustain, and scrutinizing how the BBC defended and elaborated them in a challenging climate has been an object lesson in how values that matter need intelligent institutions and the resources to care for them. I am very grateful for the acumen of Suzanne Franks, Daniel Day and Heather Sutherland, my colleagues on the project. Anthony McNicholas has brought his formidable research skills, integrity, great kindness and strength of character to supporting me in every conceivable way. I am particularly indebted to him.

Numerous audiences at numerous seminars have given me the benefit of their views. I have presented parts of the book at the BBC, Birkbeck College, Bristol University, Cambridge University, the Campaign for Press and Broadcasting Freedom, the Freedom Forum, Goldsmiths' College, the Institute of Historical Research, LSE, the *Political Quarterly*, Queen Mary's College, the Reuters programme in Oxford (twice), and Sussex and Stirling universities among others. I have organised and taken part in seminars that have shaped my thoughts in discussion with many journalists, broadcasters, policy-makers and politicians – and enjoyed myself.

Something magical happened to me when I started to work in the Department of Communications at the University of Westminster. It represents everything that a university should be. Nick Garnham set us all a demanding standard; Steven Barnett, David Hendy, Colin Sparks, Roza Tsagarousianou, Annette Hill, Sally Feldman, Peter Goodwin, Winston Mano, Daya Thussu and other colleagues have been an unfailing source of ideas. The book has also been shaped by the nods, frowns and interest (and its glazed absence) of the students I have taught, and I am particularly aware of the excitement of teaching generations of outstanding Ph.D. students. I am indebted to them all.

I must thank Reeva Charles and Edna Pellet, who, while running a happy, hectic and productive office for my husband, also helped me (in the flat upstairs) with computers and much else, with their habitual charm and efficiency.

Jenny Hartley read an early draft and took the kind of perceptive, witty interest that sets you back to work with relish. Everything is always brighter in Jenny's company. John Lloyd brought his customary searching intelligence and generosity to the chapters he helped me with. James Curran and Paddy Scannell sweetly read the whole manuscript, and their expert and shrewd comments invaluably altered the form of the book. Peter Hennessey read the nearly final version and threw himself at encouraging me and improving it with his characteristic brio. Jan Daley deftly lifted my spirits at a key point. Tony Wright MP sent me back one last time to the manuscript – a bit severely I thought, but of course he was right, and it was a great help. Finally, I commandeered everybody on a holiday in Norfolk as proof-readers and proof-readers' assistants, and thank them all. None of them is responsible for what I have written, but I am extremely grateful for their time and attention and interest. Many thanks.

Recently so many people have acted with countless acts of grace that I can only say what a difference it has made to us, and thank them all. Our friends Rodney Barker, Chris and Nicola Beauman, Bambina and Robert Carnwath, Catherine Crowther, James Curran, Gillian Darley, Danny Eilenberg, Lexi Douglas, John and Catherine Geives, Jenny and Nick Hartley, Genevieve Herr, Michael Horowitz, Margaret Hung, Peggy Pyke-Leese and Helen Roberts have given us much comfort and pleasure. However, it is to my family I owe most, and Anne Pimlott Baker, Jane Pimlott, Carin Pimlott, and Andrew Seaton and Helen Potts have been marvellous. At home, Lucy Schejbalova has been a tower of strength.

Daniel, Nathaniel and Seth Pimlott, my children, are the audience I most fear and would most like to please. From an early age they have been Olympic disputers, mordant humorists and sceptical idealists. They are decent. They are magnificent. They have kept me going.

My deepest debt, which I explore daily, is to my husband, Ben Pimlott, dearest comrade. This book, like everything else I have ever done, was the product of the utterly absorbing conversation (and constant argument) that arched over all our lives together. Ben found my voice and nurtured thought like a tender gardener – but a ruthlessly demanding one as well. He had an alarming capacity to concentrate (as well, of course, as to idle), was an enemy of cant, and believed fiercely in the power of sound judgement, clearly expressed, to make things better. While I cannot claim such qualities for this book, it was inspired and shaped by his loving encouragement, uniquely independent mind, teasing, and boundless energy. One of the last things we did together, before he died, was work on it, blissfully, in his hospital room.

It is dedicated to him and our sons, all my darlings, with love.

Picture Acknowledgements

The author and publisher are grateful to the following for permission to reproduce the images on the following pages:

p. 3, copyright © The Barnes Foundation, Merion, Pennsylvania, USA, Bridgeman Art Library © DACS 2005; p. 7, author's own; p. 9, Museum of London; pp. 12, 23, 63, 78, 143, 234, copyright © EMPICS/PA; p. 21, Kobal Collection; pp. 22, 44, John Frost Newspapers; p. 24, Advertising Archives; pp. 27, 75, 104 (top), copyright © Reuters/Corbis; p. 30, AP Photo/John D. McHugh; p. 33, copyright © Philippe Petit-Mars/Corbis; pp. 35, 93, 268, copyright © Bettman/Corbis; pp. 36, 37, Mary Evans Picture Library; pp. 38, 205, copyright © Corbis; p. 40, Illustrated London News Picture Library; pp. 54, 57, 69, 91, 106 (top and bottom right), 206, 207, 264, Bridgeman Art Library; pp. 61, 66, 106 (bottom left), The Art Archive/Dagli Orti; pp. 73, 79, copyright © 1990, Photo Scala, Florence; p. 100, Guardian Newspapers Ltd/Dan Chung; p. 104 (bottom), copyright © Russell Boyce/Reuters/Corbis; p. 115 (top), copyright © Archivo Iconografico S.A./Corbis; pp. 115 (bottom), 166, 239, copyright © Peter Turnley/Corbis; p. 123, The Art Archive/National Gallery of Art Washington/Joseph Martin; p. 131, copyright © Bettman/Corbis; p. 135, copyright © Ralph-Finn Hestoft/Corbis SABA; p. 139, copyright © Christophe Calais/In Visu/Corbis; p. 146, copyright © Alain Nogues/Corbis Sygma; p. 153, The Archive of the Panoramic Museum of the Battle of Stalingrad, Volgograd (Arkhiv Muzeya Panorami Stalingradskoy Bitvi); p. 156, copyright © France Keyser/Corbis; p. 179, copyright © NTV/Via Reuters TV/Reuters/Corbis; p. 184, copyright © Jones Jon/Corbis Sygma; p. 194, copyright © Bazuki Muhammad/Reuters/Corbis; p. 197, copyright BBC; p. 199, PA Photos; pp. 208, 209, Edifice; p. 211, AFP/Getty Images; p. 215. Express/Getty Images; p. 216, copyright © Chris Steele-Perkins/Magnum Photos; p. 227, copyright © Mastrullo Giuseppe/Corbis Sygma; p. 228, copyright © Western Mail & Echo; pp. 236, 262, copyright © Hulton-Deutsch

Collection/Corbis; p. 242. copyright © Alexander Demianchuk/Reuters/ Corbis; p. 251, copyright © Mark M. Lawrence Photography/Corbis; p. 266, copyright © Antoine Serra/In Visu/Corbis; p. 270, copyright © Tim Graham/Corbis; p. 274, AP Photo/Karel Prinsloo; p. 275, AP Photo/SABC/ APTN; p. 285, copyright © David Turnley/Corbis.

Every effort has been made to contact copyright holders. The publishers will be glad to make good in future printings any errors or omissions brought to their attention.

Introduction

This book is about vicarious horror. In particular, it is about how news of terrible events is made and consumed.

'News' is so continuous and ubiquitous that we take it for granted. Good news, bad news, sports news, celebrity news – all are part of our daily fare, the background music of the lives of virtually all of us. When we get up, news sets the agenda for what is going to happen, and as we go to bed it recaps and reflects on what has occurred. News brings ghastly surprises and tragic predicaments into homes and workplaces. Few aspects of life are more familiar than news. Partly for this reason, we seldom inspect the psychology that inspires it, the conventions that frame it, and the ways in which it adapts to historical changes. Yet the economic structures that support it and the pattern of news that is produced are neither inevitable nor accidental; as much as any feature of modern living, they are the product of past events. News has won freedoms and privileges as a democratic necessity, but we have few means of assessing, or even discussing, how it uses or abuses the rights it has accumulated. News makes history and is part of it. Indeed, it is the argument of this book that news is not merely a core part of our culture – as important as religion used to be, until the twentieth century. It is also an artistic form that reflects, and for better or worse shapes, that culture to an extent that we do not appreciate, animating our collective experience.

There is a dilemma. If we have little news and few images of an unfolding tragedy – for example of the victims of a foreign dictator – we may fail to act either in our own interests or in those of its victims. On the other hand, the avid consumption of news of gruesome events, justified on the grounds of freedom of expression, frequently panders to dark aspects of the collective psyche. Rationalist's tool or sanctified voyeuristic pornography? The paradox that news is *necessarily* both is something this book will seek to unravel.

Rationality and pornography are of course not opposites. Indeed, in the case of news the two are linked. Thus the unique hold that news has on the public imagination is the claim to reality: namely, that news describes events that really have occurred, and that have been revealed and guaranteed by rational procedures. Yet – as we all know – it is possible to be economical, or prolix, with the truth. News must also engage and please its audience. The actual shape of news as it is delivered depends on many factors. The gathering and presentation of modern news require great efforts of organization and selection. These in turn reflect, and help to mould, public tastes and preferences. 'Violent' news is a particular case in point, both because interest in violence is universal, but also because the nature of that interest – and hence how people like violence served up – has varied widely. Violent news can be awesome. Yet at times we read about and watch events of epoch-making importance unmoved. Sometimes the world is shocked by the plight of a single wild animal; at other times it passes over genocide with indifference. At times news is the vehicle for bellicose propaganda; at other times it responds to public anxiety or complacency by retreating into sentimentality or trivia.

This book focuses on the historical, cultural and economic strands that bring us our daily portion of printed and electronic pain, concentrating on violent news that has a claim to political significance. It inspects the special features of violence on television and on the printed page: the emotional charge of bringing mundane lives face to face with disrupted ones. It draws attention to the taken-for-granted proximity of domestic security on one side of the television screen and the harshest suffering on the other.

The power of such juxtaposition – pain and comfort – is not new. Indeed, it was familiar as a literary device to the ancients. Homer famously made tragedy more poignant by emphasizing the fragile nature of domesticity. In the *Iliad*, the poet describes the Trojan hero Hector in his civilian guise as 'the guardian of chaste wives and little children'. Hector's wife, Andromache, unaware that Achilles has killed her husband and is desecrating his body outside the walls of Troy, dashes about the house in preparation for the warrior's return. She busies herself in wifely concern, dealing with emotional and material things:

> Her voice rang through the house calling her bright-haired maidens
> To draw the great tripod to the fire that there might be
> A hot bath for Hector upon his return from combat.
> Foolish one! She knew not yet how far from hot baths
> The arm of Achilles had felled him –
> Because of the green-eyed Athena.[1]

It is through just such a prism of ordinariness that modern spectators observe the misfortunes of others, while preparing their own hot baths. But do they watch in a mood more open to the claims of others because of their own safety? Or are they more indifferent because they feel safe themselves? In both the ancient and the modern cases, the audience is discomforted and excited by the thought 'Perhaps my own sense of security is an illusion.' Modern news, like classical tragedy, engages emotions and relates horror through the audience's own experience. The most effective news causes a frisson: 'This, or something like it, could be happening to me.'

⌐Indeed, news is not just about external events. It is about placing ourselves in the world – understanding ourselves in the context of the fate of others. At the same time, news is a commodity: it has to be chosen, processed, manufactured, advertised, distributed and sold. As such, it is subject to cultural and market pressures, and – like any other retailed product – its form and nature continually evolve. That there is a public interest in news being well made – that democratic values depend on news that is comprehensive and aspires to truthfulness – is only one relatively minor influence on how the news is actually put together. Modern news varies in quality, depending on many factors. Some news is high-minded. Some is routine and weary, or technically proficient while pandering to the image of the world that audiences are judged to prefer. Much titillates appetites or comforts and confirms prejudices. All news has to compete with other, more easily pleasing, louder, less complex, sources of amusement.

Whatever its dominant quality, news has one universal characteristic. ⌐For news to perform any function at all, it has to attract attention, which means that it has to entertain. However responsible and representative of democratic realities news may seek to be, it fails if it doesn't keep its audiences. Entertaining the public is not a good or a bad thing: it is a news necessity. What is entertainment? Behind the need to catch and hold attention lies a familiar if disconcerting reality. From a production point of view, bad news is good news, while good news is generally dull. People want news that shocks. They like to be disturbed, frightened and disgusted – up to a point.

News is so much a part of life in a free society that it responds to and helps to shape every aspect of the political process. A free press is not only a defining feature of democracy. It is impossible to imagine a properly functioning parliament or effective political parties without one. The relationship is not so much interdependent as integral. Styles of news cannot be conceived except within the context of such integration. The media and the democratic process are not different things, vying against each other across a fence. Yet changes in the ownership, control and financing of the organizations which produce news, which have immense implications for democratic politics – altering the whole shape of political parties, reducing the power of Parliament, setting political agendas – go largely unnoticed. Meanwhile news is expensive and often not very profitable, and this has an impact on its coverage of politics. One aim of this book is to ask questions about this core of politics-and-the-media which we take for granted.

The debate is not about how the news has allegedly been 'dumbed down'. The view that news has simply been degraded depends on what the historian Michael Schudson has called 'retrospective wishful thinking', the summoning up of a mythic golden age.[2] The counter-argument that news is getting better (because there is more of it) also misses the point that the news media are in a constant state of flux, buffeted by competing pressures to deliver audiences, to make profits, to calculate the significance of events, to adapt to their ever-shifting role in public and private lives. Yet although news is continually changing, this does not mean that we should not judge it. Arguably the news we get today is not only more widely distributed, but also faster, slicker, more professionally produced – and more entertaining – than ever before. Print and broadcast news are now often accessed by the Internet, and these established sources (which are still dominant) can be supplemented by the competing online views of the groups and individuals who are the subject of the news, enabling consumers to update stories and to cross-check facts and opinions in a way that was previously inconceivable.[3]

One of the most important recent developments has been the phenomenon of 'breaking news' taking place before the audiences' eyes. It has always been a central ambition of news organizations to carry news to audiences as swiftly as possible; today real-time news eliminates the time gap altogether, and the public is given a carefully engineered but literal window on to events. Meanwhile, those journalists who seek to provide understanding, objectivity and interpretation have to accommodate to the new temporal chemistry. Rumours are floated more easily in the new world of breaking news – there is less time to check them, and the news agenda drives ruthlessly forward with little concern for the relative importance of stories, except as fodder for the next bulletin. Many journalists work in news organizations with scant interest in objective news. News fidgets and often lies in order to keep stories moving fast.

The social and cultural conditions in which reporting takes place are one important determinant of the news we get. Other determinants are economic: how news is paid for, owned, regulated and distributed; what rivals it faces in new sources of information and amusement. The untidy

realities of the news now vie with cheaper, more predictable, more gratify-
ing and less anxiety-provoking stimuli. News may have become universal,
but in those societies where it is politically most secure it is nevertheless
under great pressure – losing its privileged positions in the schedules, losing
circulation, and suffering cuts to its budgets because all over the world
'deregulatory' policies have stripped away audiences. 'Objective' news is
under threat as a commodity as well as as an ideal.

At the same time, news and politics act together in the ever-shifting
theatre of social values. News is not *just* about the marketplace. It is also
about the parameters that audiences set. Yet another aim of this book is to
show how radically our expectations of what is acceptable evolve – and
how changing assumptions have influenced our consumption of non-fiction
carnage. There is always a tension between a 'Whig' theory of values,
according to which contemporary preferences are assumed to be superior
to those held in the past, and an alternative, pessimistic, narrative of moral
decline. According to the first theory, modern Western societies are more
tender-hearted than their predecessors, yet less squeamish. That is to say, an
increase in human sympathy has been combined with a more matter-of-fact
attitude towards the representation of bloodshed. Thus, according to the
optimistic theory, television can display the human debris of disasters and
battlefields and arouse an audience's compassion and indignation without
offending against canons of public taste.

Arguably, however, the picture is more complicated than either the optimistic or the pessimistic theory allows. Another book could assess the
kaleidoscopic changes in Western values since 1945. One of the arguments
of this one is that the representation of misery has its own history, which
is disconcertingly independent of the history of misery itself. At the same
time it seeks to examine how people who are increasingly comfortable and
well-protected accommodate to what happens to others less fortunate than
themselves. Values swirl in bewildering confusion, and it is important to
recognize the speed of change – and also the ways in which change influences
and is influenced by news and the process of producing it. Have sensitivities
become more acute? Does what we once found unacceptable no longer
bother us – or are we more fastidious than we were? Is the search for
immediacy in the news, and action on the ground, a kind of lust? This book
approaches such questions by looking at shifting news values – the editorial
instincts which handle, sift and grade information before decisions are
taken about what counts as 'news'. These values are determined not by
evidence, or importance, but by likely impact. The book argues that the
way in which 'violent' news is constructed and consumed owes much

to traditions of which news-gatherers, news-purveyors and audiences are oblivious. It suggests that modern news is only the latest manifestation of the long history of the public representation of cruelty.

It also suggests that the public theatre of torment that news has become has generally involved a tension. The history of the representation of suffering has never been simply about reporting facts. Portrayals of violence cannot all be reduced to descriptions of the unprovoked infliction of suffering by oppressors upon the oppressed. Thus it is a suggestion of this book that 'violent news' in its political form often involves a stage for martyrs as well as for persecutors.

Attitudes have evolved: representations that were previously unacceptable are now considered socially justifiable. On the whole, we believe that our willingness to witness suffering is to our credit. It is not merely that our knowledge of their pain may be useful to those subjected to it: we like to believe that there is virtue in frankly confronting a difficult subject. Such attitudes contrast with mid-twentieth-century coyness, but we should consider whether they are actually new. In fact there are cycles: the twenty-first-century view seems to hark back to a historic belief in the instructiveness of harsh reality. Being a spectator may sometimes bring out the best in us – and echo a long, even ancient, tradition of bearing witness – so that the task of the news is to catch our attention with accounts of events that will test our mettle.

At the same time, the ubiquity of news can be seen as an instrument helping us to deal with personal crises. Social historians have claimed that death is the 'last taboo', arguing that rituals surrounding the 'normal' death of ordinary citizens have become impoverished. Whatever may be said of this proposition, it is notable that (reflecting unchanging public preference) journalism has focused on the 'abnormal' death – of the murder, accident, disaster or war victim. In doing so, the news has invented new rituals. The reports of these dramatic deaths are contemporary ceremonies that are universally understood – and which sometimes endow the undeserved death of humble commoners with emotional and, even more critically, political weight.

Are these rituals and habits producing a common, even global, way of experiencing the world? There has been a huge increase in interest in the human-rights debate – and a parallel rise in the number of campaigning organizations dedicated to monitoring abuses of internationally agreed standards. Has this debate been influenced by spectatorship? Societies with sharply contrasting religiously inspired attitudes towards pictorial representation nevertheless all unhesitatingly watch the news (which can only represent reality). Do global news rituals produce common feelings? For reasons that are partly technological, partly cultural, the form of news has become internationally homogenized. Are we moving to an era of global news values? Is one of these values the urge to foment, around particular events, a worldwide concerned attention? As we have noted, the media are not marginal to the way in which we understand and respond emotionally to the world. Should we therefore conclude that everyone in the global village will end up 'empathizing' about the same things?

In this book it is argued that public emotions are *not* universal, that they continue to be refracted through the grasp that people have of their own interests and situations. When we see others reacting differently, we need to ask why they do so. Political calculation still calibrates feeling. By looking at how Russia – a nation and society with a different history of suffering – has dealt with a recent conflict and a humanitarian crisis, we can better appreciate the relationship of feeling to understanding. The problem is not one of evoking sympathy, it is more stark: how do societies have trustworthy accounts of their conditions?

News has to simplify events and create consumer fun out of them. Ideally it does so without trivializing what it describes. This poses a challenge. In an attempt to meet it, the press has to fit in with our mental furniture. People think in narratives. The news therefore has to create chronicles that dovetail unexpected historical realities with the stories that people understand. The discipline of producing stories is central to news. Competition for the attention of readers and viewers is intense. So is the pressure to fit events into well-understood frameworks. Sometimes the result is that stories are shaped to create dramas with satisfyingly predictable resolutions, imposing reassuringly familiar patterns of violence, disaster and catastrophe in a way that actually masks the reality.

Meanwhile the many pressures on news-making that push it towards pleasing us affect coverage of even the worst disasters: newsmen hunt for pigeon-holes in which to place a story, however unprecedented that story may be. Thus on 11 September 2001 CNN ran its story of the destruction of the World Trade Center under the headline 'America Under Attack!' On the next day this had changed to 'America Strikes Back!' – it was as if the viewing public were witnessing a series of episodes in a blockbuster movie in which the United States faced a familiar enemy. The end was summoned up before the beginning had been properly registered.

Of course, all the things that go under the banner of news are not the same. A distinction might be made between good, serious, passionate and principled reporting and semi-fiction, exploitation and sensation. Such a distinction is acutely important to the quality of public life. However, this book is not about such a distinction, at least in the first instance. Rather it is about news – 'all the news that's fit to print' – as a cultural product. The argument is not about the power of the media as modern necromancers, but about news as a part of our social structure.

Helping us sympathize with suffering people by demonstrating how like us they are is one of the difficult tasks that news performs. Sympathy is directed at something outside ourselves. It is also a way of stimulating action on behalf of others. Eliciting empathy, however, can also be a good way of selling the news – because it involves using our feelings about ourselves. 'With justice,' as the political philosopher John Rawls has put it, 'we require not only common principles but sufficient ways of applying them in particular cases so that the final ordering of conflicting claims can be defined . . . we do this by seeing others and ourselves in the same way.'[4] Yet, however appealing empathy may be, there is a self-reflective aspect to it that risks telling audiences more about how they like to think of themselves than about the tough things they need to know. In sum, empathy makes us feel good, even when we feel bad. By contrast, the news we need has to deal in the real world of grey, confused reality, in which the actions of good people may have dire consequences, and unattractive people may be the only ones available to help. At the same time, in a harsh commercial climate the press, broadcasting and Internet news may be too anxious about our sensibilities – because they underestimate the public appetite for reality, or are worried about the market consequences of difficult stories. News is expensive to produce. Inevitably, the news also demonizes and canonizes in a way that disturbs reality. As well as making people empathetic, it frequently seeks to do the opposite: drawing focused attention to the ways in which people differ from each other.

Yet we need news, and news values are vital. News bridges the gap between complex events and the busy, preoccupied, bored, self-indulgent, ignorant public. News has to put events in order, relate them to each other, and attract our attention to them – and it does so through news values. News values simplify complicated things and concentrate our wavering attention. But news increasingly has to package difficult – even unresolvable – problems as if we already know about them, and as if answers are quick and simple. What we need to understand is how the interests of various groups and nations are distinct – and different from ours. Such realism and toleration of difference are far more strenuous than empathy. We need to come to terms with the way in which decisions we have made sometimes make things worse, but also with how 'good enough' decisions can improve

– if not solve – things. If the news is forced to push reality into shapes that we find unthreatening, or pleasing, it may fail to alert us to dangers that we need to appreciate realistically. We need to be more aware of how journalists and the institutions that produce news come under strain as they adapt to markets and audiences. It is not enough to moralize about what news 'ought' to be. Nor is what is at stake a matter simply of principle. Coming to terms with what is happening and being able as societies to have some common discussion of what affects us based on a relatively objective understanding of events are not luxuries. They are practical matters vital to our survival as citizens who can make choices in a complex world.

When terrorist bombs ripped London and Londoners' lives apart on 7 July 2005, everyone turned to the net, to broadcasts and to the press to find out what was happening. But, in a technological and cultural revolution that had been gathering pace for a decade, those closest to the events also became reporters, using their mobile phones to capture wrenchingly immediate images from inside the disaster. Like those of any front-line eyewitness, their reports were simultaneously exact representations of what they could see and partial, because limited by their inability to take into account anything of the wider situation beyond their own harrowing experience. The remarkable composed attempts to record horror were a testament to the belief in the enduring value of telling the story of an event as a way to exercise some control and to regain some kind of authority in the most harrowing of circumstances: to record an event is to become a witness, which is to be a kind of editor, and thus an active shaper of the story of what happened and less merely a victim. Yet these images were as commanding as they were only because they were true. In fact, although they took us deeper into the tragedy, we remained spectators.

A little later, as the familiar frenzy of a major news story developed, with traffic islands commandeered for tribes of foreign journalists and their satellite dishes, there were the usual (and usually unreported) stories of unscrupulous journalists driven by the hunger for sensational images impeding the security and medical staff attempting to deal with the consequences of the bombs. If you were at the heart of the event then reliable estimates and a scrupulous caution were a comfort, because closer to the truth. But for more distant spectators it was just another story which had to painted in shouting colours to attract attention. The next week, almost unremarked, suicide bombers deliberately blew up a crowd of children in Iraq. News as usual then. Yet, without news that is careful of us, how can we judge our situation and know where we are?

I

Blood in the High Street

Until the invention of television, the most familiar display of carnage was in the high street. Butchery has many guises. For me it meant a shop. My first memories of bloodshed are of my family's way of life. Long, smooth and cream-coloured, greasy and flecked with fluttering rose-petal shreds of flesh and streaks of blood, the great fresh bones were stacked in a corner of the yard. It was only if they were splintered or shattered that the inner, crisper, whiter bone showed through. There were bins of craggy, difficult-to-understand bones: joints, hips and shoulders. There were racks of ribs: unlike other bones, these were pink, porous and rough when they were cut through – like bloody Maltesers. The concrete floor was treacherously slippery to walk on, and ran down to a reeking sump in the centre that had to be cleaned out regularly. Mahogany stains patchworked the walls. The yard smelt sour and fetid. On Tuesdays the great tubs of fat were tipped into a copper and boiled up. The fat began hard and smooth, like marble, and then – disconcertingly – melted into grainy soup. Finally, as the heat mounted, it became a viciously hot, reeking liquid that spat like a snake. It scared people, and was treated with respect. The yard itself was overhung by tall buildings on three sides, with a high wall on the other. It was a damp, dark, sickly place where the sun never reached. Metal pails of water were always being thrown over it, sloshing down the walls, and bubbling dark red into the dank drain.

I remember carcasses. Dead bodies were the aesthetic I grew up with. The butcher's yard was not strange or barbaric to me. It was my territory, part of the map of my sense of myself that I carried in my head. On long hot Sunday afternoons I would fight fierce battles from the top of the back wall, defending it against marauding children who swarmed up the embankment behind it.

The yard had pails of chicken innards – pink viscous loops of gut, slimy, sometimes gleaming with partly formed yellow eggs. There were strange gizzards, neatly etched in parallel ridges on the inside, which spilled grit when they were cut. It was puzzling that birds ate stones. There were also bowls of liver, carefully set aside – soft, slippery, voluptuous, precious, but sometimes stained and spoilt with bitter acid-green bile.

Bloodshed was not just business: it defined who we were. It was the source not only of my twice-yearly two new pairs of shoes (one everyday and one best) and my smocked dresses, but also of familial pride, of my feeling part of a benign order. Later my attitude changed. As an adolescent, I am ashamed to say, I found aspects of butchery embarrassing, not because it was barbarous, but because I had become a snob. As an adult, I have some ambivalence about butchers' shops: I experience a mixture of professional interest in the quality of meat, an unsqueamish willingness to deal with it and a strong preference for seeing it cut properly in front of me (and a distaste for tidy, vacuum-packed supermarket meat), and an occasional flash of vivid unease at the spectacle of corpses. Most people, of course, find nothing repellent or bothering about meat. Yet people who know the inside of butchers' shops are one step closer to the reality of 'butchering' that makes carnivorous living possible.

Meat provides a good metaphor: my sense that what seems natural at one time can at other times seem the opposite can be generalized. The history of human sensibilities shows that they are inconstant, adaptable to religion, philosophy, custom and culture. In the scales of human disgust, there are few fixed weights. My own perceptions of meat have helped me to realize – for example when I turn on a television set – the malleability of public shock. To some extent, shockability depends on how you are brought up. The borderline between revulsion and prurience is as fine as the line between fastidiousness at the sight of animal flesh and liking to eat it. A similar narrow line perhaps separates enjoyment of a documentary about the Second World War and grief at news of a terrorist outrage. Or – to put it in a media context – we believe ourselves more refined and civilized than previous generations, yet we simultaneously allow ourselves to be unashamedly fascinated by televised murder most horrid, without the restraints that used to exist.

Values change, even those we regard as part of our identity. In my own case, the intimacy I once had with blood and carcasses, and my closeness to the consequences of approved death, has become distanced from me. But recognizing the malleability of some at least of one's values is perhaps salutary in a wider way. We need to be alert not just to the fact that values alter (it would, of course, be surprising if they did not) but also to the direction in which they are evolving – and their meaning in the context of the times. News may reflect and reinforce values. Alternatively it can remould them, and fundamentally change their weight and direction.

Rabbit by Soutine captures how a rabbit looked to me as a child. The notion of being 'thick-skinned' has a different meaning after you have skinned something.

Bloodshed is partly skill and habit. I acquired butchery skills under supervision, and exercised them proudly. I was taught how to gut chickens when I was about four or five. I felt it was rather an adult accomplishment. To prepare a chicken you would put your hand up inside it and, grasping all you could find, gently but firmly twist and pull until the whole glutinous mess came away, leaving the clean cathedral of the body. I was pleased to be able to do it so professionally, and I would beadily watch to see if someone would buy one of 'my' chickens in the shop afterwards.

In the mid-1950s my family's relative prosperity was based on unrationed rabbits. My father sold about 500 a week, and as a small child, before I started school, I learned how to skin them – standing on a special box to raise me up to the high, scrubbed marble counter. Some things you don't forget. I rediscovered my prowess with rabbits when as a young mother I learned the art of taking a new baby out of a Babygro – babies and rabbits both have delicate rounded muscles, and relaxed joints that will gently bend.

Possibly there are modern parents who would object to a five-year-old learning how to flay a bunny. I remember it as a helpful, independent skill that I was proud of – but one with a disconcerting side to it. To skin a rabbit, you cut firmly but cleanly around the neck and down the breastbone (as the skin had a value, you needed to be careful not to damage it). Then, in as smooth and simple a movement as you can manage, you peel the skin back around the body, slipping the leg joints forward and then back, so that the pelt pulls neatly off the flesh. Then, with the skin inside out, someone chops off the rabbit's paws with a clean blow. There was also the skinning of the heads, with their blue milky eyes that stared reproachfully. As I say, as a little girl I enjoyed skinning rabbits. Yet it certainly had an impact on my unconscious. I still have vivid flashback images of conducting rabbit autopsies as a child. The notion of being 'thick-skinned' has a different meaning after you have skinned something.

My father taught me to gut and to skin because they were tasks small enough for a child to manage safely but big enough to be proud of. I understood that they had to be done well and carefully. But I was under no illusion about where I stood in the pecking order of butchering jobs. As well as rabbits, my father's shop was also full of great, heroic sculptural carcasses. Huge sides of beef were the most important material for bravado butchers' performances. They would be slung up on hooks (the leg end being conveniently provided with a hole torn above the ankle) near the front of the shop, to show the aristocracy of meat that we dealt in. My gentle, pet-loving father would also go to work on the taut, orange carcasses of sheep. Stiff and headless, they looked as if they were caught in a frozen leap. With his razor knife he would – almost balletically – dive into the marble mountain of yellow fat and dark purple beef, or smoothly cut around a lamb's shoulder. Only when he cut it would the flesh show red, glossy and juicy. There was something very different about the dry, hard exterior and the glistening cut meat. And then there would be the saw, as the huge architecture of ribs and limbs was demolished into joints. Cutting was serious. It was one of the bases of a respectable, profitable trade. Cutting joints to show off the meat as the public wanted it was a building block of success. Good flesh was good publicity. It was a skill my father taught others, a source of pride.

There was also a conspiratorial family interest in choice meat. Occasionally there were veal kidneys to be eaten; more often there were fine pieces of steak or pork, or gentle rolling slabs of liver. The sculpting of meat was also related to private pleasure. At home, meat defined a meal. Within a carcass our own family hierarchy of prized cuts sometimes differed from public preferences. What my father valued was 'juicy' meat. Thus he would say that 'people' preferred leg of lamb, but as a butcher he knew that the cheaper shoulder was better to eat. He did not like meat that ate

My grandfather and father's butcher's shop, 52 Lavender Hill, Battersea, 1936.
I grew up above it during the late 1950s, by which time health regulations had
forbidden the display of meat outside the shop.

'tight', or was too lean. Similarly, 'people' valued 'tenderness', but for
my father 'tender' and 'sweet' were opposites. There was a clandestine
superiority in all of these values. My father thought that chewing did you
no harm. He believed in flesh marbled with fat. In those days, fat was an
asset. Dad believed in how fat tasted, and he regarded fat as a sign of
plenty. Fat kept your hands soft, and was a protection against the endless
washing and scrubbing in the shop. Above all, he thought that meat was
good for you.

The king of carcasses was always beef. My father loved to look at it, to
eat it and to sell it. Visits to relatives were always accompanied by bleeding
packages that would be discreetly but admiringly unwrapped. When my
mother disappeared into hospital to have my brother, my father cooked us
both steak and fried eggs every night. Then he cooked steak for her – to
build her up – when she came home. My brother's first food was baby rice
flavoured with a little juice from a steak. On birthdays, anniversaries and

the infrequent occasions on which people outside the family ate with us, roast beef was served. On my twenty-first birthday an express parcel arrived at university including a bunch of fresh violets, dewy in damp newspaper, a book on Leonardo da Vinci, a new dress, a bar of fragrant soap shaped like a lemon, and a carefully wrapped, party-sized fillet of beef.

Beef was about more than profit. It was about stability and patriotism. When I was growing up, beef and Britishness had long been linked, just as meat in general had been associated with strength and virility.[1] In common parlance (and in the language of the mass media) a 'meaty' story was one that was strong, interesting, sensational – to be approached with a metaphorical licking of lips. Even today, if a newspaper story is too thin it may need to be 'beefed up'. In the same way a 'full-blooded' story is powerful, convincing, what it ought to be.

The language of consumption is often a useful give-away: what seems normal at any given time frequently contains ritual and unacknowledged symbolism. My family revolved around carcasses, but it did so because of a society that gave the eating and contemplation of livestock a special place. Breeding cattle for beef became a British obsession in the eighteenth century. It was then that there emerged an elite band of aristocratic breeders who were preoccupied with producing cattle which had pure bloodlines. At one level the ambition to breed hardier, healthier livestock was a rational one, and provided a key element in the agricultural revolution. At another level it was fetishistic: breeders became interested in bloodline as an end in itself. Thus the search for purity of heredity usurped the utilitarian purpose of breeding. The contest ceased to be about the economic or stock value of the beasts that were bred. Instead, breeders competed to produce ever purer bloodlines, and consequently bred prize cattle that became so fat that they could hardly walk, so inbred that recessive features emerged, so strangely shaped that they could barely get up from the ground. According to the food historian Harriet Ritvo, 'the heady atmosphere of excited purpose that stirred patrons of breeding came to exist quite apart from the breeding for taste and use of stockmen.'[2] At the annual sheep-shearing dinner held by Coke of Holkham (the great Norfolk agricultural improver) the assembled breeders drank to 'the constitution of the King, breeding and all its branches and a fine fleece and a fat carcass'.[3]

In toasting their achievements, the elite of the livestock breeders were also celebrating a national characteristic and quality. However, the public also admired the huge, square-shouldered cattle produced by the breeders' obsession. Prize-winning cattle were a popular subject of prints sold to an

The British prime minister Anthony Eden, in retirement,
with his prize-winning bull, Avon Priam.

admiring public, and prize cattle were exhibited all over the country in special moving exhibition cars. 'Comet', the famous bull that won first prize in the 1802 Smithfield show, spent the next six years touring the country being exhibited, and was finally sold for an astronomical 1,000 guineas. Such a price represented Comet's star value, which far exceeded the money that could be made from using him for breeding, let alone the value of his carcass as beef. In 1820 the Duke of Bedford claimed that 'the only true object of the farmer is to profit, not by high prices but by grand products.'[4] In the twentieth century, breeding remained an upper-class fascination. When Sir Anthony Eden resigned as prime minister after Suez, he took up cattle-breeding, and exported prize-winning semen all over the world.[5]

Aztecs ate the hearts of their victims. British aristocrats contented themselves with the buttocks of their prize cattle. In the eighteenth century, society hostesses would frequently buy the 'famous' meat from prize-winning cattle to be served at their dinners, not because of its flavour but for what it represented: an image of Britain's greatness. Contemplating the prize beasts, the British public marvelled at the grandeur of those important enough to consume it. 'To see the whole beast,' according to one report on Comet, 'is to see a feast fit for kings. And every Englishman's right!'[6] To some extent, beef-obsession was universal. The French social analyst Pierre Bourdieu commented that 'red beef meat, the nourishing food par-excellence, strong and strong-making, giving vigour, blood and health, is the dish for men in many societies.'[7] However, in Britain it had pride of place, as part of the national inheritance.

The economic and cultural historian Fernand Braudel points out that meat-eating took off in Britain during the eighteenth century – against a general European decline. The Spanish ambassador, reporting home about London in 1752, observed that 'more meat is sold in a month in London than is eaten in the whole of Spain during a year.'[8] In his picture *O! The Roast Beef of Old England* William Hogarth depicts a quarter of beef as the very emblem of British freedom. Carried outside the forbidding walls of Calais, imprisoning the unfree French inside, the quarter of beef is bathed in a bright light representing all the freedoms and nobility of British life.

Today there is a question mark over the consumption of beef, partly because of CJD, but also because of a growing culture of vegetarianism. There is also concern about the sustainability of cattle farming. Until recently, however, lack of meat in a diet was taken as an index of deprivation. Thus, in a pre-war survey of the food situation in Britain in 1939, written to help the government plan for the coming war, the author pointed out that '20–25% of the population are existing on diets deficient in every respect . . . but the fact that meat is too expensive for these families to eat is the most pertinent fact.'[9] In the months preceding the Second World War the eminent social reformer Richard Titmuss proposed a radical scheme for improving and managing the national diet. In his report he observed that 'It takes as long, said one rural sage, to rear a bullock as it does to build a battleship . . . and they may be more equal parts of the war effort than is yet recognized.'[10]

Similarly, in the 1950s the historian Eric Hobsbawm intervened decisively in a debate about how to assess the evidence for a rise (or fall) in working-class living standards over the nineteenth century. He identified meat-consumption statistics as the key variable, and, 'without too much hesitation', used the number of cattle and sheep brought to Smithfield as the best available indicator.[11] Meat-eating was repeatedly seen as the most potent index defining plenty – and want.

8

Calais Gate, or O! The Roast Beef of Old England, *William Hogarth. The artist was arrested while drawing the gate in Calais. The picture, and then the very successful print made from it, used beef as a symbol of English patriotic xenophobia.*

My father's career as a butcher – from the 1920s until the 1960s – spanned a period of great change in the consumption of meat. Over the nineteenth century, as the urban population grew, later work showed that there had been a slow, steady rise in recorded meat consumption – from 86.3 lb per head per year in 1830 (when my great-great-grandfather was a drover, herding cattle into Fulham) to 126.9 lb per head in 1914[12] (by which time my grandfather had bought the family shop in Battersea). Meat consumption declined to 110.0 lb per head in the economically depressed inter-war years, but was boosted in 1937–40 by government intervention.[13] The experience of the First World War had shown, according to another official report, *The Urban Working Class Diet*, that if rationing was not to lead to inflated prices 'intervention in the supply' of meat should be taken 'before and not after shortages have occurred and prices started to rise'.[14] The Food Defence Committee started to prepare for the possibility of war in 1936. Meat wholesalers soon realized that the allocation of supplies would be made on the share of the market held at the start of rationing. So they cut prices – and profit margins – in order to secure larger market shares. For my grandfather and father in the retail trade this was a good time. The war itself changed that, and the ration for meat was reduced to 100 lb per person. It fell even lower during post-war austerity: by 1948 it was down to 87 lb per person a year (one factor that gave the unrationed rabbits their importance in the calculations of a family butcher).

Meat rationing remained until 1954 (and I spent most of the rest of the 1950s using an apparently inexhaustible supply of brown ration cards stacked in the shop parlour to draw on – drawing paper remained a special treat for far longer). After its abolition, meat consumption climbed steadily, until by the mid-1960s people in Britain were eating over 150 lb a year – and a great deal more poultry than ever before. Nevertheless, beef retained its hierarchical pre-eminence, a reminder of other social distinctions. 'The proportion of animal protein was higher in the diet of the south of England than in the north,' explained a 1964 food report, 'and beef consumption was higher in London than anywhere else in the nation.'[15]

My father would have dismissed any suggestion that his pleasure in meat was based on 'symbolism'. He liked meat because as far as he was concerned it was good for you. Yet he would not have denied its place in the food hierarchy, something different from its nutritional value. The truth is that people have often consumed 'symbolically' or for reasons not articulated. In the words of the American anthropologist Marshall Sahlins, 'Apparently innocent food tastes are guilty of bearing much social meaning.'[16]

In the twenty-first century, food symbolism retains its grip. The consumer society, however, is ripe with other commodities – eagerly and unthinkingly gobbled up – that are as important for their role in reinforcing norms as for any other function. The arts, sport and education are richer in symbolism than is commonly appreciated. So too is journalism. It is a thesis of this book that public consumption of the media is as much determined by cultural symbols as is the consumption of food. Contemporary media consumption is extensively researched for commercial purposes; nevertheless it is also often treated as something that tells us much about ourselves. Corporations selling newspapers and television programmes, mobile phones and computer games and magazines conduct endless, restless research into audience preferences and behaviour. Indeed, understanding consumers' tastes and habits is almost the most important thing they do. Although there is no 'standard of nutrition' against which to assess media consumption, public-service broadcasting is often discussed in terms of efforts to secure a 'balanced diet' of programmes for audiences.

Media consumption – what newspaper you read, what programme you tune into, what music you download, what games you play – is often treated as a casual preference. In fact, as with most other consumer choices, powerful social factors are involved: media producers are well aware that the public 'choice' of newspapers, television programmes and Internet sites is linked to age, sex, class and ethnic origin. Nevertheless, coverage of great international events or fashionable programmes can attract cross-cultural, cross-class and global audiences. Often, however, watching a particular TV programme or channel or buying a particular paper binds us into the sociability of belonging to a particular group. Broadcasting, throughout its history, has created communities. It also defines us to ourselves. Thus our 'own' diet of stories, preferred tone of address and entertainment is at least as symbolically revealing as the meat we choose or don't choose to eat.

When I was a child my father used to take me to the Royal Smithfield Show, a relic of the great breeder obsessions of earlier times. At this show, live cattle would be competitively exhibited. On the third day the cattle were slaughtered and shown again as carcasses. Neither of us particularly liked the atmosphere of doomed prizedom that surrounded the huge, docile beasts. More important, in my father's case, was an uneasy sense of marginality: the show was posh, and my father was cagey around posh. But the shows did reassert the idea of the grand and generous nature of British beef.

In our home, everyone ate meat, on principle. There was no gender divide, with some foods thought to be suitable for men and others for women. However, there were mythic fables of our uncles and grandfather who had reputedly eaten large steaks for breakfast. I was brought up to hold in awe the gargantuan scale of the pre-war, pre-rationing, successful-petit-bourgeois male appetite. In the early 1950s, the choice that had been available to those with cash in the 1930s still seemed like a Hollywood fantasy. Such opulent indulgence had, we all knew, long gone. 'Before the war' (that fabulous time) my parents had gone out to dances and dinners, even worn evening clothes (my mother's blue silk shoes were still in her wardrobe to prove it). None of that happened any more. There were other clear divides. The fact that my mother never worked in the shop was considered a mark of social advance. By contrast, my long-dead grandmother had always scrubbed and served alongside the men. My father thought she had had a miserable, exhausting life, and was proud that my mother did none of this. Men cut the meat in the shop, and my father carved it (with a good deal of ceremony) at home.

Our own media consumption was, of course, as symbolic as our food. The newspapers that littered our tables were mostly out of the Beaverbrook stable. They reflected a maverick, anti-establishment conservatism that distrusted government and was proudly quick-witted and independent. The newspapers were avidly consumed by both my parents, and they would read out bits to each other over their morning and afternoon cups of tea. My father liked to suspect that governments were up to no good, and my mother liked to be shocked by crime. Like clockwork we went, all together, to the local public library on Wednesdays and to the Boots private library

The King is dead. Long live the news. People gather at the end of Fleet Street to read about the death of George VI in 1952.

on every other Friday. You never caught my father reading fiction. Just as red meat was seen as something particularly for the men, news – non-fiction – has historically had the same status. Politics and world events have been for the gentlemen alone, and until very recently the ladies discreetly withdrew from the dinner table so that the gentlemen could discuss such topics. One of the key problems identified with contemporary news, especially political news, is that it is often seen as too masculine, potentially excluding the new emancipated and commercially imperative female audiences.

There is a long history of 'rational' news, information and discussion being seen as 'masculine', in contrast to what are seen as the 'feminine' aspects of contemporary journalism, emphasizing the human-interest sides of reporting. Thus it has been argued that in the last generation newspaper stories started to depend more on personalities, and the news began to look for a more intimate mode of address. One study suggests that women *are* interested in news – but only if it 'related to them'. Those questioned said they had no interest in international economics because it had 'no experiential bearing' on their lives.[17] Another indicates a shift in news policy such that 'news should offer audiences opportunities to identify with events and personalities ... and the transformations of news-readers' hitherto serious mode of address into a more personal and intimate style': emphasizing emotional and entertainment values opened up a new women's terrain of 'feminine intimacy' in the news.[18] 'Intimization' should not be dismissed – it can be a good way of leading people into stories. Nevertheless, the contrast is with what has come to be seen as impersonal, linear, 'masculine' news. There is also the issue of whether this represents what Richard Sennett, in *The Fall of the Public Man*, called a contemporary 'tyranny of intimacy' that tends to translate political affairs into psychological ones.[19] The contemporary convention by which many interviews begin with the question 'How do you feel?' is no more than a habit, and one that often does little to illuminate reality.

Is 'taste' an expression of audience preferences, or can it be manufactured? The physical sense of taste, like smell, is not something that words or pictures can easily describe: it resists representation. Despite both writing and television making increasingly sophisticated attempts to communicate how food strikes the senses, accounts of taste are elusive. However, tastes in taste change, and this can be quantified objectively: over the twentieth century, preferences for meat steadily shifted from a taste for the strong flavours of older animals and well-hung meat, to the weaker flavour of contemporary meat. Moreover, the chemical mimicking of taste and smell has become a big business.

'Taste' is also a symbolic expression of power, and the preference for some kinds of taste in meat may be simply explained by wealth and aspiration – just like preferences for different media goods. Bourdieu in the 1980s described what seemed to him the simple opposition between powerful tastes and powerless ones: 'the taste of the senior executive or professional defines the popular tastes by negation, as the taste for the heavy, the fat, the coarse, the strong – by tending towards the light, the refined, the delicate.'[20]

According to such a theory, pale, unbloody, delicately flavoured meat was substituted for stronger flavours as more people became wealthy enough to be mobile in their tastes. Public preferences will often choose food for symbolic, not nutritional, purposes – preferring white bread as being more refined than the nutritionally superior wholemeal, or turning to sweet foods for comfort. While this account is persuasive, and the structure of its argument lies behind much cultural criticism, it is too simple.

Has the taste for news been influenced by comparable shifts? If disturbing stories are often described as 'strong meat', part of the implication is that they are hard to digest or even to face up to. But when we consider arguments about 'taste' in the media products there are contradictory views. The first is that public tastes have become weaker: that the public like 'blander' stories.[21] The second argues that, on the contrary, the public like or need to have their attention caught by more vigorous, violent imagery – in this account they have to have stronger flavours for their interest to be excited.[22] However, a narrative of deceit or corruption informs both of these versions of the movement in public tastes. The argument is that the tastes exhibited are not 'natural', but are a product or a symptom of other forces. Thus 'stronger', more realistic reports of distressing events are seen as corruptingly and unnecessarily graphic, while it is simultaneously argued that the media are becoming insipidly more similar in their accounts of the world. It is difficult to hold on to the idea that, while there are few 'natural' tastes, they often express genuine interests and yet can also be helped to form by more – or less – responsible media choices.

The way in which changes in taste occur may be illustrated by the story of how the shift in preference for flavour developed. Changes in what the public wanted in meat were caused by a complicated interaction between market pressures, technological advances and consumer choice. It was definitely not simply a shift in what consumers 'liked'. A report on meat consumption between 1910 and 1940 commented that 'joints from two-year-old sheep that had been popular before 1914 would have been rejected in the 1920s because of their size, dark colour and strong flavour.'[23] Such an account explains change in taste preferences firmly in terms of consumer choices. Indeed, like media consumption, 'taste' is of course also an issue of income and, more than that, of class identity. This is the aspect high-lighted by Bourdieu, writing of a more food-centred French culture in the 1950s and '60s, when he argues that the lower-class taste for more 'coarse, filling, bloody food' was a genuine preference – as well as a rational response to fewer resources.[24] He also frequently suggests that 'insipid taste' is a characteristic of all 'wide-audience' products that seek to appeal to as many different tastes as possible (although his interpretation takes the form of a classically romanticized argument about the 'robust vigour' of working-class preference, in contrast to the 'effete' discrimination of the upper classes), while reinforcing the point that what people choose to consume is not just economically determined.[25]

The situation in the media is more complex. Since the 1970s there has been a slow rise in the circulation of the quality press in the United Kingdom (against a background of steady fall in overall newspaper consumption). This increase has largely been at the expense of the ailing 'middlebrow' and middle-market press. (The only exception to this trend is the rapid growth in circulation of the *Daily Mail*. This paper has not only become immensely successful with readers, but it is, as Polly Toynbee put it, 'the newspaper all journalists read first'.)[26] Yet, according to the Bourdieu prescription, this rise in readers' aspirations should be accompanied by a preference for news that is less highly coloured than the strong journalism that defines the tabloid press. But it would be difficult to describe present-day media content as more 'bland' than in the past. In fact consumer 'taste' is certainly only one variable in a rich cultural mix.

Thus, even in such an intimate area as the flavours that people appreciate in the food they eat, changes in commercial conditions exert an almost irresistible but imperceptible influence on what are experienced as private preferences. In turn producers of commodities often experience public tastes at a particular point as elusive and independent when trying to provide customers with what they want. Nevertheless, consumer preferences are, at least in part, in fact determined by the impact of long-term structural changes in the industries whose products consumers devour. Thus the shift towards weaker flavours in meat cannot, on closer examination, be explained simply by consumer aspiration towards tastes that are perceived as representing greater refinement, as Bourdieu argues. Consumers' tastes were not merely freely expressed: they were influenced and constrained by other factors of which individuals would hardly have been aware. Many of these factors were quite independent of the 'tastes' of consumers. Thus by 1910 the proportion of frozen meat consumed in the UK had increased steadily to nearly 20 per cent.[27] This meat was nearly all imported from abroad, and was cheaper than home produce. The freezing and transportation of meat, especially given the relatively crude processing of the period, tended to damage the cell structure of the flesh, and essential flavouring oils were lost. Thus imported frozen meat tasted less distinct, and people became more familiar with a blander flavour. This was not the choice of aspiration, but rather of economy. But it influenced expectations in turn.

Another factor which affects the flavour of meat independently of consumers is the age at which animals are slaughtered. This is in turn determined by the value of the animals in different markets. Thus, until the 1970s, sheep were seen both as wool-producers and as carcasses destined for the table. Wool-producing animals were valuable for several years, as they produced regular shearings. However, better breeding meant that animals came to be specialized primarily as wool- or meat-producers. Animals reared primarily for meat were slaughtered as early as possible when they reached full size. Indeed, improved feeding regimes and the growing use of growth hormones in the post-Second World War period were designed to arrive as economically as possible at the fullest-grown carcass. So there has been a steady decline in the age at which slaughter takes place – and younger animals taste much milder. In 1927, when my father was a young butcher, sheep were slaughtered at three or four years of age, after several wool shearings. Now they are usually slaughtered before they are one year old.[28]

Another way in which taste has been weakened is through changes in the management of the carcass. In order to develop the most complex flavour, meat needs to be 'hung' for ten to fourteen days, to allow a controlled process of decay to start. However, hanging meat occupies expensive space. Hence there has also been a steady decline in the amount of time for which beef is hung – from fourteen days to just over four. A largely economic change has been justified misleadingly as 'bringing fresher meat more quickly to market' and 'reducing the time in travel and cold storage'.[29] The effect has been to alter flavour, and in turn the public's expectation of flavour. There has also been a decline in the distance that cattle walk before slaughter, with the result that the meat does not taste as strong. 'There are 60% less essential oils in the meat of stall-reared pigs in comparison to free-range animals,' according to a recent report, 'but it is not clear that the public actually like the enhanced flavour of the outdoor reared meat, which is also tougher.'[30] Such factors subtly alter what consumers expect – and prefer. They alter the parameters of public taste.

Consumption patterns are never settled. The view that the public likes meat of any particular kind needs to be qualified. 'Meat' is a relative term. It is as much a concept as a substance. Public taste is almost infinitely malleable – shaped by producers, advertisers and culture. Thus in the last 100 years there have been oscillations that have not simply been related to budgets. By 1930, for example, the British public's overwhelming preference, despite an increase in the amount of meat eaten, was for 'joints of the kind that supplied smaller families with two meals'.[31] This was the product both of a downwards drift in family size and of changes in the role of cooking in family life. By 2000 the butchering of carcasses had altered: chops and steaks were more important, and even joints were being demolished for single portions of meat – 'single or double portions of meat account for over 70% of all packaged raw meat products sold.'[32] People cooked less and cooked fast. Much of the meat that consumers ate at the beginning of the twenty-first century was contained in pre-prepared and cooked food. From 1959 until the method came to be more carefully regulated in the late 1990s because of the BSE crisis, much of the processed meat was 'recovered' – that is, it was made up of mechanically flaked bone and gristle that had been reconstituted, with added water to increase the weight. Thus a good deal of the meat that the public was eating was hardly meat at all. Today up to 40 per cent of steak pies and up to 30 per cent of ham, bacon and poultry products is still composed of water added in the course of manufacture.[33] Meanwhile, a whole industrial subculture of flavour enhancement has developed alongside the industrialization of food. Much meat now has flavours that are believed to offend the public removed from it. My father sold meat to be cooked. His successors do so decreasingly: raw meat continues to decline as a proportion of the retail market. However, the consumption of two flavouring ingredients, salt and sugar, has risen steadily. In 1914 the British public ate 1.1 lb of salt per person per year; by 2000 they were eating nearly 6 lb. Sugar consumption had risen from 7.9 lb to 105 lb in the same period.[34] Meat manufacturers spend forty times more on flavouring agents than they do on preservatives. It is estimated that everyone in Britain eats about 4 lb of flavouring and flavour neutralizers in meat products every year.[35]

Public taste in meat (like public taste in music, clothes or television) is not separable from other aspects of living; it is, in sum, ideological. At the same time, whatever the additional flavours we have added to our meat, the factors which contribute to the 'meatiness' of it have diminished and there has instead been a rise in other features. Indeed, since the 1960s the most desired characteristics of meat, according to public-opinion surveys, are that it should be 'tender' and that it should be 'bright'.[36] The consumer preference for 'easy to cut and easy to chew' meat has led to an elaborate technology that injects animals with tenderizer, before slaughter, and then treats the meat with 'aerosol needles' which inject water right into the flesh.

Why did the late twentieth century see a decline in 'meatiness'? Part of the answer is that people prefer not to be reminded too sharply of the actual processes – slaughter, butchery – that fill their plates and stomachs. Is the same true of public taste in political and social ideas and images?

Style in stories is usually explained as a response to sovereign consumer demand. But it is, of course, also influenced by profitability, changing demographics, and changing technological limitations and possibilities. Class and taste are closely related in the media, with readership patterns in the press and viewing preferences and habits still rigidly stratified, though in increasingly complicated ways.

Is news like meat? Has taste shifted across the spectrum of consumption consistently in one direction, towards more artificially 'flavoured' processed stories? Arguably, doctored food is paralleled by doctored reality. Thus stories are in key respects now always part of a relevant family of stories already familiar to the members of a given society. For an event to be judged newsworthy, as the sociologist Michael Gurevitch has argued, 'it must be enclosed in narrative frameworks that are already familiar and recognizable by newsmen as well as audiences.'[37] This processing of novelty through the filter of the familiar is one of the most powerful – and sometimes misleading – aspects of the packaging of events. However urgent the hunt for giving audiences what they want, the media are also part of a long-term sculpting of public preferences.

However, another aspect of the marketing of meat also helps to reveal some of the ways in which taste may shift more generally. Indeed, it is hard to believe that meat-selling is not itself subject to some pressures which are exerted by media representations. Thus not only has flavour (or perhaps 'original' flavour) decreased in meat, but some aspects of the visual presentation of meat have become increasingly important.

Why do we like both our news and our meat to be 'bright'? There are illuminating comparisons to be made between various contemporary ways of dealing with blood. Consuming meat seems very remote from consuming news and entertainment. In one way, however, they are the same: what is consumed is frequently red, raw and bloody. In both of them a sanguinary element has the power to attract and entertain, but also to shock and make the observer feel uncomfortable. In meat, the distinction is between redness and pools of blood. Redness is desirable; liquid blood is not. Ideally, blood neither flows nor clots in the presentation of flesh as meat. Carcasses are drained of blood after they are slaughtered (or during slaughter in the case of ritually approved meats). Blood in butchers' shops trickles, oozes and smears. Blood that appears in places selling meat is a mistake, a leaking error to be cleaned away. Sawdust on the floor in old shops and clean packaging in supermarkets play the same role, absorbing and hiding the distressing reminders of the body that the meat once was. Thus the supermarket chains issue butchers and packers with strict codes about the packaging and presentation of meat; 'No blood should be visible in any packet. This is a priority,' reads one.[38]

Guidelines about the portrayal of blood in news programmes are also very clear. 'Blood and disturbing pictures must be excluded,' cautions one BBC memo. 'We are here to show news, not gore.'[39] During the war in Iraq in 2003 a controversy developed over the display of Coalition soldiers' blood. In 2004, as gruesome images of hostages being murdered became available, the controversy grew. Some newspapers have clear ethical codes which require photographs to be reproduced faithfully, and which prohibit the use of technology 'to enhance or change images in any misleading way'.[40] But this requirement is harder to police when all images arrive electronically. In any case, public taste – in news, as in selling meat – has been on the move. In a content analysis of front-page quality newspapers comparing pictures on the front of *The Times*, the *Daily Telegraph* and *The Guardian* in three months in 1980, 'blood' or pictures with blood clearly apparent occurred only twice. By 1990 this had increased to eleven times. By contrast, a similar examination in 2000 revealed nearly two dozen pictures with blood – including several top-fold pictures (the key image intended to attract purchasers) of people lying dead in great pools of blood.[41] Perhaps 2000 was simply a more violent year. Perhaps colour printing had got cheaper and advertising revenues more buoyant and so there was more money to spend on colour front pages, while the circulation war had got fiercer. There may be a number of contributing causes. Nevertheless, the increase is startling. Bloodiness is also a feature of news about distant places rather than familiar or near-at-hand ones.

Yet if the presence of blood itself is fiercely controlled in the contemporary butchery trade, other aspects of bloodiness have been visually enhanced in the industry. The role of cutting – as we have seen – was to display the red meat of a joint. 'If meat does not *look* right it does not taste right . . .' commented a meat-industry report in 1957, 'and increasing efforts must secure that it looks just like the housewife imagines it should.'[42] This meant cutting joints freshly. As more meat was purchased from supermarkets and more meat was sold already packaged from abattoirs, more intrusive industrial solutions to stabilizing meat (to look 'just like the housewife imagines it should') were adopted. Thus artificial colouring was added first to meat products like sausages, and later (from the mid-1980s) to whole meat joints. The most commonly used additive was Red 2G, a coal-tar derivative, because, unlike cochineal (a natural additive), 'it stays stable under light, and also the red is more similar to blood in hue.'[43] Marks &

Spencer took an early stand in 1982 – deciding to use only cochineal, because it was a natural product. Similarly, packed meat, covered in cling-film or plastic, will usually have nitrogen, carbon dioxide or carbon monoxide pumped into the packages as they are closed, to preserve the meat and enhance the red colour. The use of strip fluorescent lighting has a similar colour-enhancing effect.

All these procedures secure the brightness and the visibility of the colour. Indeed, the cosmetic removal of blood itself, combined with the display of its effects, has become an increasingly important part of butchery. In 1965 the *Meat Trader* announced that 'a real revolution in packaging meat has arrived, the paper napkin. Placed under meat it absorbs all unsightly blood – but displays the meat against a vivid, white, wholesome background. It makes the meat look brighter!'[44] The colour of meat is seen as indicating something fresh, tasty and desirable. Consumers judge by colour. However, bright redness is not – as we believe it to be – an indication of freshness. Before meat is cut, the cells are purple. After a brief exposure to air they turn bright red, and they remain so for two or three hours, before reverting to the original purple.

If meat retailers are preoccupied by physical colour, so – in the most literal sense – are retailers of news. Presenting and withholding blood is a media phenomenon as well. Pictures of the genocide in Rwanda in 1994 and the war in Kosovo in 1996 were composed and cropped to centre on blood. In the autumn of 2001 pictures of a dead Taliban fighter, whose body looked eerily intact, displayed the pool of blood he lay in from different angles. In some newspapers the redness of pictures is exaggerated by filters. Tabloids favour scarlet red, while *The Guardian* prefers a deeper and more solemn hue. Beyond the meat and news industries, guidelines about the fictional representation of blood have also been subject to change. Is 'news' blood influenced by changing mores around 'entertainment' blood – the gore that features in fiction? Why do we like our meat redder? Are all these different aspects influenced by a separate shift in the understanding and meaning of the colour in blood?

A history can be constructed of blood effects in the film industry. Such representation moved from the improvisation of the early black-and-white days, using ingredients available in the kitchen – flour and water, food-colouring, black treacle, chocolate cake mix – to industrially produced ranges of cosmetic products including 'thick, thin, flowing, fresh, stale, glistening, dull, granular, smooth' bloods,[45] all in a variety of colours. Professionals even comment that the blood effects are key to a movie's tone. 'Before splashing out on a lot of blood,' warns one American manual,

There have also been changes in the use of blood in the movies. In one extreme example, Quentin Tarantino's Reservoir Dogs, *the central character, played by Tim Roth, lies in a puddle of his own blood for most of the film.*

'remember that blood design comes first, and consider the effects as part of the whole impact of the movie. If they are not in keeping with the meaning of the movie they will be wrong.'[46] 'Choosing the colour of the blood will fix the colour for the film,' it continues. 'Get it too dark and an overly serious note may be struck.'[47] Many of the make-up manuals are concerned that blood effects 'should not tip over into humour – unless that is what is called for'.[48] One of them adds, 'Don't apply heavy, outmoded, copious effects . . . unless that is what you are really trying to create.'[49] The argument is that blood effects have to fit an aesthetic – not that they have to mimic reality.

Blood and blood coloration were one of the first topics in *The Standardization of Motion Picture Make-up*, an authoritative report produced by Max Factor in January 1937.[50] Similarly, a report on a 1963 symposium on special effects in the *Journal of the Society of Motion Picture Engineers* concluded 'Blood and blood effects have to be used increasingly.'[51] More recently, in 1995, the special-effects veteran Vincent Kehoe, looking back over a career in make-up, commented, 'I think we have seen blood used more apparently realistically, yet always more voluminously over my career. Less is more they say. But in blood effects the less is getting more all the

SUNDAY TELEGRAPH

No. 1400 | MARCH 20, 1988 | Price 45p | FINAL

Murdered by the mob

These shocking pictures convey the horror of yesterday's murders. Right: A priest attempts mouth-to-mouth resuscitation. Seconds later he was pushed aside for the man to be shot in cold blood. Above: One of the victims, gun in hand, seconds before he was dragged from the car

Two soldiers lynched by funeral thugs

by Walter Ellis, in Belfast, Robert Porter and Simon O'Dwyer-Russell

The killing streets of Belfast — p23

TWO BRITISH soldiers were murdered yesterday by a lynch mob which only seconds before had been part of the funeral cortege solemnly mourning the death of Kevin Brady, the IRA man killed in Wednesday's shooting at Belfast's Milltown cemetery.

Early today the Army named the murdered men as Cpl David Howes, 23, and single, from Northampton, and Cpl Derek Wood, 24, single, from Carshalton, Surrey. Both belonged to the Royal Corps of Signals.

The two soldiers were on duty, the Royal Ulster Constabulary said. "Three persons are being questioned by police."

The IRA, admitting the killings by the Belfast Brigade, claimed last night the men had been identified as members of the SAS by equipment and documentation before being shot. The Army denied this and said they were radio technicians.

An RUC spokesman said the murders were "an obscenity committed by depraved and perverted people".

Mrs Thatcher described the killings as an act of "appalling savagery". She said: "There seem to be no depths to which these people will not sink."

It appears that when challenged by Republican funeral stewards the men, in civilian clothes, refused to identify themselves and tried to drive away.

The incident occurred after the funeral cortege had left the church. As the hearse carrying the coffin draped in the Irish tricolour drove away, a struggle appeared to develop, after which a silver Volkswagen Passat, an unmarked car used by the military, reversed at high speed with squealing tyres out of a side street.

It skidded to a halt, moved sharply forward and was then blocked by a black cab which drove across its path.

Immediately a mob of youths wearing jeans and anoraks engulfed the car, clambering on to the bonnet and roof, kicking body panels and pummelling the closed side windows and windscreen. One balding, sandy-haired man climbed on to the roof and systematically smashed at the windscreen with a wheel-brace.

A youth wearing a blue anorak punched a hole through the front passenger window with his fist.

> 'An obscenity committed by depraved and perverted people'

The crowd had by now become a frenzied lynch mob, screaming for blood. There were repeated attempts to pull the car's front-seat passenger through the shattered window and on to the road.

Moments later there was the muffled thud of a pistol shot which sounded as though it came from inside the car.

For a moment the crowd scattered in alarm before closing in for the final assault. The baying mob dragged its victims from the car.

On-the-spot reports told of the two men being stripped to their underpants, systematically tortured and brutally beaten with concrete posts before being shot dead.

According to Army sources the two men had been repairing radios at North Howard Street police station and were en route to their Lisburn headquarters.

"They were not required to do anything during that journey and were supposed to be miles from the spot where they were killed," said a senior Army source. He denied they were engaged in surveillance, and insisted the Army had not yet established why they were near the Brady funeral.

"Had the soldiers been on a surveillance job, they would have had considerable back-up in the vicinity and been in radio contact. As it was, they had no radios and it took several minutes for the security forces to realise what had happened."

Earlier an Army spokesman had said: "It is normal for soldiers in transit to travel in plain clothes and civilian vehicles and it is not unusual for them to carry personal protection weapons."

An explanation that they were "lost or had decided on their own initiative to venture near the funeral" is unlikely to satisfy ministers.

Mr Gerry Adams, president of Sinn Fein, the political wing of the Provisional IRA, said the presence of the soldiers at the funeral "bore all the hallmarks of an official British Army dirty-tricks operation".

The brutal murders have called into question the current RUC and Army policy of holding back uniformed patrols from IRA funerals. Mr Tom King, the Ulster Secretary, ordered an immediate inquiry.

Although both soldiers would have been armed with 9mm Browning pistols, only one shot was fired by them during the

Continued on p2

'A priest was pushed away ...the man was shot again'

THIS is the picture which shows a Catholic priest desperately trying to save a young British soldier by giving him the kiss of life. Seconds later the priest was bundled aside by a masked gunman who pumped a final, fatal bullet into the soldier's head.

Witnesses to the murder of the two soldiers on the streets of West Belfast showed little remorse yesterday—even at a sight as bloody and sickening as Ireland has ever known.

Lynch law reigned. One 20-year-old onlooker said: "The two men inside were dragged out, stripped and beaten.

"Masked men then took over and dragged the men off and took them to the PD Club ("People's Defence", an Andersonstown community club) where they were beaten again till they were lying covered in blood. Then they were shot."

by Walter Ellis in Belfast

The final hate-filled episode of revenge against the two soldiers came on waste ground alongside the club in a scene of unbelievable barbarism.

Another man, in the club at the time, saw the two men lying on the ground in their underpants, covered in blood.

"One still looked to be alive and a priest from St Agnes's tried to revive him. He was giving mouth-to-mouth resuscitation when a masked man pumped a second shot into him from close up to put him out of his misery."

A group of about 10 onlookers were witnesses to this scene, and several photographs were taken of the bodies.

Witnesses generally insist that the silver-grey car had appeared to be about to ram the hearse, despite the fact that television pictures show the car reversing at speed in an apparent effort to avoid the approaching crowd.

The incident took place opposite Casement Park Gaelic football ground, and the initial beating of the two soldiers took place in a culvert immediately beside the ground.

The beatings given to the two men were horrifically violent. The men were stripped of their clothes within seconds, and concrete posts were used against their defenceless bodies.

Within minutes a large convoy of RUC and Army Land Rovers roared into the area and set up a cordon along a 200-yard section of the main road.

By this time, however, the bodies had been taken to the nearby community club, where the final shootings took place.

Police and soldiers saturated the area and forced all shops to close. Local people were indignant at this, but appeared generally satisfied that justice had been meted out to two men who they clearly believe were undercover agents.

Waite 'alive, but operated on after accident'

by David Blundy in Washington

MR TERRY WAITE, the Archbishop of Canterbury's special envoy, is alive but was involved in an "accident" some months ago, after which he needed an operation.

His captors, the radical Shi'ite group led by Imad Mugniyeh, are treating Mr Waite not as a British humanitarian but as an envoy of the United States.

They believe, although there is little evidence to support it, that he was closely linked with Lt-Col Oliver North, the former member of the National Security Council, and with Vice-President Bush. The captors are also convinced that the Americans will do a deal for Mr Waite.

Details of Mr Waite's capture and the identity of his kidnappers were disclosed for the first time last week by a Lebanese who played a key role in the investigation into his disappearance. He asked that his name should not be used because his family is still in Lebanon. The British Government has received no word of Mr Waite and his kidnappers have made no demands.

For three days after his capture Mr Waite was in a house in the southern suburbs of Beirut and was in frequent contact by telephone with the American Embassy in Lebanon.

The source said that Mr Waite was "not really a hostage" during this period. He was driven around the southern suburbs and, although under guard, visited people in the area.

He was spotted by members of the Druze militia who had served as his bodyguard. Without difficulty they found the house he was staying in, tapped the phone and monitored his calls to the American Embassy.

The Druze, headed by the Lebanese warlord Walid Jumblatt, also considered a military rescue. "But it would have meant a major battle with Hezbollah, and the Druze did not feel they had the full backing of the Americans for this," said the source.

After three days of semi-captivity the negotiations broke down and Mr Waite became a fully-fledged hostage. He has not been seen since.

When Mr Waite arrived in Beirut in January, 1987, for his final attempt to gain the release of the American hostages, he seemed, according to this Lebanese source, different, more nervous than he had been on his previous visits.

"He was not the same Terry. I sensed there was something wrong," he said. From evidence produced by the investigation after his kidnapping, this is not surprising.

Imad Mugniyeh is a rising star of the Hezbollah (Party of God) movement, which has strong links to Iran but is under the direct command in Lebanon of its spiritual leader, Sheik Fadlallah. One of Mugniyeh's relatives was imprisoned by the Kuwaitis for carrying out bombing attacks.

The Mugniyeh family believed that Mr Waite had the power through his United States connections to do two things: to negotiate the release of Shi'ite prisoners held in Kuwait—including Mugniyeh's relative—and to provide weapons for Hezbollah.

There is no evidence that Mr Waite promised to fulfil, or even discussed, either demand, but in the atmosphere of rumour and paranoia in Beirut this is what the Mugniyehs believed.

The arms were not part of the secret United States deal with Iran.

Shortly after his kidnap the Mugniyehs' paranoia really blossomed, according to the Lebanese source. They suspected that Mr Waite had been sent to Beirut as a scout to find the American hostages, a mission that would be followed swiftly by a United States rescue attempt.

INSIDE

MURIEL SPARK TALKS TO JOHN MORTIMER
Magazine

THE RETIRING DUKE OF EDINBURGH?
Wheatcroft's week
Page 15

ST MUGG AT 85, BY RICHARD INGRAMS
Page 14

WITNESS TO STALIN'S SHOW TRIAL
Fitzroy Maclean
Page 13

HOMES v THE GREEN BELT
Paul Barker
Page 6

Peregrine Worsthorne ... 22
Geoffrey Wheatcroft ... 15
Albany by Kenneth Rose 10
Mary Kenny ... 21
Oliver Pritchett ... 10
Arthur Marshall ... 22
Auberon Waugh ... 22

Art	17	Media	16
Ballet	18	Motoring	40
Books	16	Music	19
Bridge	17	Nature	10
Chess	8	Personal	44
Cinema	17	Property	42-43
City	24-34	Radio	18
Collecting	18	Sport	45-48
Crossword	44	Television	18
Drink	21	TV Choice	18
Elimination	8	Theatre	17
Fashion	21	Topic	17
Food	20	Travel	36
Gardening	20	Weather	2
Letters	11	Women	20-21

Today's Broadcasting 48

Blood has become a more prominent feature of news pictures. In the 1980s (opposite) it was a shocking exception. By the late 1990s (above) it was routine.

time.'[52] Thus there have been distinct changes in the representation of blood in fiction as well as in reporting.

There is another history of human blood, separate from its symbolic representation – yet surely linked. The collection of blood and its shipment into war zones is always a clear indication that battle is expected – and is consequently kept secret. The Second World War, it has been argued, 'decisively altered blood's cultural significance from the "mother liquid of all health and disease" to a strategic resource, devoid of mystical overtones, yet essential to human enterprise'.[53] Nevertheless, blood has retained moral as well as therapeutic considerations. Richard Titmuss, in his famous *The Gift Relationship: From Human Blood to Social Policy*, published in 1970, compared the quality of blood in the British transfusion system, where blood is given voluntarily, to that in the United States, which at that time

A Cold War American advert, 1952. The organization of blood supply and donation reflects different nations' images of blood. It is practical but also symbolic.

depended largely on blood that was 'donated' in return for money. The British voluntary-donation system emphasized community spirit and altruism. At the same time, giving rather than selling blood also meant that the blood medically available was of a far better quality. The British system attracted donors from the entire social spectrum. By contrast, the American system found it hard to find donors, encouraged the wastage of blood, and, above all, produced blood that was more often infected, because a high proportion of blood-sellers were destitute. 'The commercialization of blood and donor relationships,' wrote Titmuss, 'represses the expression of altruism, erodes the sense of community, lowers scientific standards, limits both personal and professional freedom . . . [and] places immense social costs on those least able to bear them – the poor and the sick . . . The redistribution of blood . . . from the poor to the rich appears to be one of the dominant effects of the American blood system.'[54] As Titmuss pointed out, the attributes of blood donors required by an efficient service are 'consistency, regularity, responsibility and honesty',[55] because blood supply is a bureaucratic response to a series of crises. However, Titmuss also saw the organization of blood supply as something that reveals social reality and social organization in a peculiarly telling way. Thus, more recently, in some nations, like France, the symbolic pride in the nation's 'good blood' actually impeded rational policy in the face of new threats to the blood supply. 'Viewing blood products in the context of national pride, they failed to act when it became tainted. On the other hand, viewing blood as nothing more than a commodity led to the recent abuses and pollution of blood products,' concluded one writer.[56]

Blood banks reflect the composition of donating groups. The 'science' of transfusion has always been saturated with problems caused by social and political differences. Recently, infections have repeatedly found their way into national blood pools. This has been a consequence both of new infections emerging undetected – first hepatitis, then Aids, then CJD, which have all been transmitted through blood products – and also of the development of new treatments. Thus the discovery of life-saving blood-plasma products, requiring the pooling of ever-larger numbers of donations, has also caused new difficulties. The challenges in managing blood are concerned with the identification of difficult-to-detect tiny groups of donors with new blood problems which pose a lethal threat to the entire stock, just as in the modern 'war on terrorism' the problem is to identify the small groups of hostile agents who are difficult to isolate from the surrounding population. Ever since the early days of transfusion it has been observed that the safest blood comes from the smallest pool of donors. As many blood products cause immune reactions in long-term patients, blood platelets, for example, are now occasionally collected from a single donor and transfused to a single recipient, as this at least reduces the reaction. This is an effective practice and an inspiring idea, linking the donor's gift to the individual recipient, but of course the result is even more expensive.[57] Attempts to develop a synthetic – and consequently pathogen-free – blood, together with the increased costs associated with testing blood, have increased the price exorbitantly: safe blood is increasingly too expensive for many societies.

How do doctors think of blood now? How does their professional under-standing relate to other ways of thinking about it? Blood may be less prominent in how individuals think of themselves than it used to be, in part because it has been medicalized and rendered less mysterious. The rise of genetics has also meant that blood and heredity are now separated. In the past there were 'bloodlines' and 'blood feuds', and blood itself was seen more directly as the carrier of social and individual identity. Yet blood is still unpredictable and vital. A surgeon, perhaps surprisingly, commented, 'Blood is what we most fear in any operation. Blood always means trouble.'[58] A disease of the blood, such as leukaemia, is 'everywhere in the body' from the onset – none of the usual metaphors of speed of transmission or spread that are part of the pathology of related diseases are apt. If you ask haematology specialists to talk of blood they still think first of transfusions of whole blood. But blood to them is also a series of numbers – the fluctuating and deviating indices of its different constituents, monitored daily and registered on computer readings. Blood, like universities and health departments, is subject to a kind of accountancy, because this is how computers assess quality. In a leukaemia ward, much hangs on the daily expectation of how many neutrophils, or command cells, a patient has. While much of the assessment of blood is now done by machines which alert doctors to abnormalities in counts, nevertheless a visual scrutiny is the next stage. Doctors still judge blood pathology by looking at cells. Soon, expensive new technology will permit them to understand the genetic make-up of both normal and malignant cells and to target (or at least to understand more subtly) those which may be more susceptible to treatment. So doctors get deeper and deeper into the interior micro-life of blood cells, understanding the particularity more complexly. Blood, like other forms of matter, is developing an infinite interior. Yet what is most feared is the haemorrhage – blood flowing in anarchy.

It is, in sum, hard to overstate the symbolism, and the angst, surrounding blood – in literature, in news reporting, in food, and in every part of daily life. Blood is about religion and sacrifice. It is no accident that its colour is also the colour of radicalism. Socialism is termed 'red', and so was the most powerful army of the left in history. The symbolic role of the willingness to spill its own blood has always been part of a community's identification of itself as a cohesive group. Even the milk-and-water social democracy of the British Labour Party boasted a historic anthem, 'The Red Flag', which tells proudly of socialist martyrs and triumphantly rang out, 'Their hearts' blood dyed its every fold.' Certainly video games, films, television and the news all dwell on displaying blood, and, although this is often perceived as

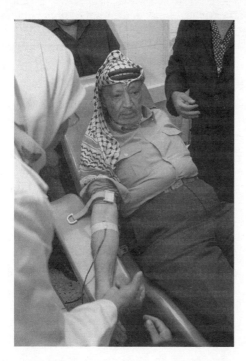

In a domestic propaganda gesture, the Palestinian president Yasser Arafat donates blood in Gaza, 12 September 2001, for the victims of 9/11.

an issue of almost abstract violence, in fact these images also relate to feelings about communities which spectators identify with.

In *Blood Sacrifice and the Nation*, Carolyn Marvin argues that 'enduring groups' are those 'whose members will shed blood in their defence. To join an enduring group is to commit to a system of organized violence. This lesson is difficult and repugnant.' As an anthropologist, she observes that the strength of these commitments can be measured in terms of the difficulties encountered in admitting them in everyday discussion. 'Our refusal to recognize the contribution of violence to the creation and maintenance of enduring groups,' she argues, 'is the taboo at work.'[59] Marvin maintains that the willing 'blood sacrifice' of soldiers in wars in the name of the totemic 'flag' is the defining feature of the American civic religion of nationalism. Such an anthropological view also suggests that, for example, wars are effective as totemic mobilizers, not despite but precisely because of the casualties they cause. Popular cultural representations of violence and blood can thus be interpreted as commemorating and reiterating this central national fact of the nation's capacity to sacrifice willing victims.

Indeed, pictures of blood are highly charged political statements. When the World Trade Center was attacked in September 2001 there were almost no pictures of the victims' body parts or blood. The blood of the wounded and dead was too close to home to be bearable, and images were tightly controlled. In addition, 'home' was a powerful news-manufacturing nation. There was both an official attempt to manage images of chaos and disorder and also a more powerful instinctive sense on the streets that the disaster was too huge for the kind of voyeurism that is so common in contemporary media accounts of lesser or more distant disasters. Nevertheless, as the Palestinian leader Yasser Arafat intuitively recognized, blood was a response with great symbolic weight in the immediate aftermath. Soon after the attack he was seen on television all over the world donating blood, in effect arguing for American interest in the Palestinian cause as he did so. At the same time, pictures of New Yorkers queuing to donate blood were both a practical and a symbolically powerful demonstration of shared community with the victims.

Tastes are disconcertingly malleable. Many factors contribute to the movement of values over time – but few of them are apparent to the public, who internalize new standards and regard them as normal and right. News polices values, but it also makes them, and, while it reflects the tastes of communities, it also constructs them. Thus images of blood – the real blood of the news and the meat industry, but also the symbolic blood of entertainment – are related across a far wider area of social contexts than we might have expected. Indeed, all images of bloodshed transcend the boundaries between physical and cerebral consumption. What we find appropriate, what we find pleasing and what we just take for granted in how we deal with blood are linked. The old newsroom adage 'if it bleeds it leads' remains true.

2

Filth

News needs bloodshed. Where blood is spilt, wrong-doing is not far away – and news thrives on misbehaviour. Bloodshed also excites public curiosity and horror in itself. Blood is a symbol as well as a physical manifestation, and it commands our imaginations partly because it sustains life and partly because it stands for violent death. Blood is the colour of action, health, destruction and finality. News needs blood – and the disorder and nuisance its appearance in the wrong places implies – in order to display its cleansing morality.

As a child, I was interested in the colour and presence of blood. The only thing I hated about my father's trade was the stench that, in summer, rose from the yard on the days before the bone men came. If the weather was warm you could catch the scent of the shop from the other side of the main road on the way home from school. The smell was sweet and pungent, and hung thickly in the air around the shop and crept into our home above it. Along with the smell there were the visible signs of putrescence – maggots, flies and rotting. My father was at his most irritable if the bone men were late: it was a bad advertisement for the shop.

In fact a butcher's shop was a place of contradiction. If decay was one smell I vividly recall, another was that of bleachy pails of water, designed to catch decay and halt it in its tracks. There was also the wet, woody odour of scrubbed blocks and scoured floors. After the shop shut, everything was ferociously washed and burnished. Daily scraping of the blood-saturated surfaces of the wooden meat blocks had worn them into a moonscape of hollows. When he was cleaning the shop, my father was transformed into a fierce matron or fanatical housewife, excavating hidden pockets of dirt with knives, and often on his knees, scrubbing. Some of his stories were about what he saw as a permanent struggle between good and evil, cleanliness and its opposite. Casting himself as St George, he would describe the ceaseless battle against the dragon of decay. I always found one tale especially affecting – about how, 'before the war', just as they had finished cleaning up, around ten at night, a pail of dirty water was knocked over. Apparently my normally long-suffering grandmother burst into exhausted tears at the prospect of having to scour the shop all over again. After the daily scrub-out, bloodstained dirty clothes were boiled in a copper in a milky, seething mass. When the public and the meat were gone and the scrubbing was completed, the shop became a cool, chilly, glinting place, with a scoured white floor and neat stacks of clean paper to wrap the meat in. It was like a hospital, or a morgue. My father's aprons – stiff and shining white from the laundry – were folded in the parlour. All of him shone with a kind of buffed wholesomeness.

A nineteenth-century child's model butcher's shop. Until recently, being a butcher was a proud, petit-bourgeois trade. Journalists are also entrepreneurial traders, in the market for news.

Butchers are allowed to deal in blood in order to feed us. Slaughtering turns animals into meat by removing their blood. Butchery is about an endless cycle of seeing blood spilt and eliminating the consequences. News – at least in the imagination of the public, but also for some journalists – offers a similar pattern: it does not create bloodshed, but it identifies it and – as the crusading fourth estate – seeks to clear up the mess. News deals with polluting disorders all the time, yet it remains morally pristine because its role is to cleanse them. Indeed, so vital to the existence of the news is the disorderly filth it hygienically removes that sometimes there isn't enough of the real stuff conveniently around. In such circumstances news resorts to producing the dirt needed to keep its campaigning reputation in good order.

Indeed, the production of a news story, particularly one involving death or injury, can often be seen as a morality play – in which outrage, grief, anger and the search for culprits all have their parts. Even everyday politics yields a satisfying harvest of destruction: a clerk to a parliamentary select committee commented that one good and critical report it produced was picked up and given a lot of publicity by the press, but he added, 'They only ran with it because the minister in charge was already wounded. They sensed they could make a kill.'[1] The press got its kill: the minister resigned.

How does the news transform corrupt decay into seemly order? By exposing it – making it public – but most critically by ordering it, fitting the unshapely chaos of events into a tidy, known format. The imposition of narrative explanation transforms threatening chaos into a system of remediable human errors. News may alarm us, but once events are turned into news the public is reassured that something is being done about them. It is this purifying role of the story that legitimates journalists and the news. As dragon-tamers, they deal in corruption but remain untainted by it.

It has often seemed to me that there is a stark analogy between my father and his preoccupations and the modern purveyors of print and broadcast news. Both butchers and newsmen to begin with like their product raw and fresh – and abhor staleness and decay. News, like meat, is a fragile, transitory commodity, with a peculiarly short shelf-life. Both meat and news are subject to a variety of processing technologies. Meat is cooked, refrigerated, salted; news is researched, amended, ordered and updated. The best news is 'hot' – which can mean warm from the kill or, alternatively, subject to the processes of editorial heating; that is to say it may have just happened or it may have happened long ago but be current. Those who handle meat and news are ever-conscious of the ticking clock – the need to take stock, replace the old with the new, clean the boards.

Journalists, like butchers, are people who seem to get their hands dirty in a trade that is simultaneously seen as necessary and regarded with unease. Like butchery, journalism is seen to perform a publicly vital function, though often motivated by the desire to make a profit. There are many kinds of journalism. But, however distant in intention, they share a broad sense of what is sellable. Two kinds of news-reporting are apparently contradictory: journalism driven by the desire to unearth new information for the public benefit, and 'yellow' journalism, designed to entertain and titillate. Some journalism is described as 'muckraking', scooped from the filthy gutter of Fleet Street, a location geographically close to the original meat market of Smithfield. Other journalism claims to be providing the 'first draft of history' in the 'papers of record'. These kinds of journalism have more in common than is at first apparent. For example, both regard themselves as purifying, having a moral voice that seeks to root out wrongs and cauterize the rotten. Higher journalism is seen – and regards itself – as forensic and precise, like a surgeon's knife. Observers have described the function of the media as that of policing boundaries – exposing deviance. This is as true of the tabloid press and 'infotainment' television documentaries as of the broadsheets. The tone is exculpatory. Upmarket newspapers and public-service radio and television programmes are often accused by commercial rivals of a moralistic, 'auntie', approach. Yet a distinguishing feature of tabloid news is a passion for guilt and the invocation of a moral community of victims or the outraged. Judgement and condemnation are essential to tabloids – whose coverage of public affairs, indeed, often offers little else. Thus Ian Connell has observed that, while television constructs celebrity reputations, the popular press, by contrast, tends to attack them and thus performs 'a kind of cultural police work'.[2] Even the most entertainment-driven stories claim a moral imperative as well.

News and journalism have always done more than register facts. The key skill in journalism is that of 'recognizing a story' and shaping it in a way that distinguishes between victims and perpetrators. News is never morally neutral: commodifying quotidian events into narratives nearly always implies some kind of judgement. The creation of a narrative, of course, involves simplification and selection – with a moral edge. A common way of turning all events into a more exciting, more newsworthy story is by imbuing them with conflict. News is inherently melodramatic in style: even when it claims neutrality, there is a search for what 'should be done'.

'Dirt,' observes the anthropologist Mary Douglas, 'is essentially disorder. There is no such thing as absolute dirt: it exists in the eye of the beholder.'[3] In this respect the impure is also useful and comforting, for it delineates the dangerous territory outside order, and throws into sharp relief the proper limits of that which is ordered. News is indeed concerned with edges and limits, but eliminating disorder is not negative. News is constantly poised on the same cusp as my father fighting the incipient danger of decay in his shop: ever seeking to make form out of formlessness. As Douglas also observed, 'Dirt is never a unique, isolated event. Where there is dirt there is a system.'[4]

Butchery has a daily, repetitive pattern – a constant rolling uphill of Sisyphus' stone. So has the news. Public events have no stopping point or

News searches out scandals partly because it needs them. In doing so it evokes a moral community (which by implication it is part of) to condemn those guilty of misdemeanours. Home Secretary David Blunkett reaches for the Prime Minister's hand, Wednesday 1 December 2004, during the scandal about the visa for his son's nanny. He resigned shortly afterwards.

pause. More significantly, the news has to fill the pages and bulletins regularly as a commercial imperative. News is – and characterizes itself as – a daily, ever-repeated battle against scandal, misbehaviour, internal or external threats to stability, events beyond the control of legitimate authorities, bad luck and disasters. It is always in favour of an ordered universe. Even on days when the rough-and-tumble seems to slacken, the ritual aspect of news-ordering is still important. Above all, the whole process of journalism – the acts of journalists, the routine of the production of news, the commercial pressures, the stories into which events are put – transforms disordered violence into ordered violence, because the story has to make sense.

At the same time, news produces scandal as well as passively describing it, because the presses and the schedules need it. Thus we need to ask not only whether news stories about violence reflect reality, but also what social and political forces their interpretations of reality support. To say simply that violence sells – pandering 'to the lowest common denominator in audience taste'[5] – is incomplete. It ignores the more important question of what role violent news performs for those who undoubtedly have a taste for it, and why the presentation of news about violent events is contained within such ritualized conventions. One of the 'purifying' roles of news-reporting is to separate out the details that can be served up and expressed from those that would bore, upset or be felt inappropriate by the audience. News is in this way part of a fundamental and continual social reconstruction. This is not necessarily damaging – responsible news exercises a duty of care on behalf of audiences. But it should not blind us to how the news also alters over time. After all, some threats are objectively more serious than others, and news is one way we calibrate threat.

News and journalism can deal in dangerous and corrupting material because by displaying it they begin to clean it up. Journalists are like butchers in this sense: they cut and shape raw meat in order to sell it. They may have to sell it to an editor first, but ultimately they sell it to the public. Some of the authority of journalism comes from its key democratic role (even in – or especially in – those organs that seem least democratically directed), and some of its authority comes from the accumulated sense that journalists are, or have been, willing to take risks to bring the news to audiences. In a more general way, this authority is derived from the perception that journalism deals with threats. All journalism, however venal or deceitful, draws legitimacy from the exemplary notion of a battling fourth estate which exposes dangers and protects civilization by taking risks.

Dealing with threatening disorder and with the necessary but unpleasant aspects of communal life is also a source of marginality. Although the role of the press varies from country to country, public attitudes towards journalists everywhere are often ambivalent. At some times and in some places, journalists seem heroic figures. While the UK public trusts the broadcast journalists it is familiar with and who work within the framework of public-service impartiality (although the public may be barely aware of what makes the difference), it has come increasingly to distrust others – for example those who work for some tabloids. Since the 1980s, journalists (along with politicians) have been viewed as increasingly unreliable, but recently evidence has begun to show that audiences make realistic discriminations between different kinds of journalist.[6] Audiences who pruriently enjoy scurrilous attacks on public figures are uneasily aware of the arbitrariness and distastefulness of some journalism. There is also a reservation (although still a mild one) about journalism which does not merely report but also incites and sets up scandalous events, harrying the innocent and invading privacy.

A group of paparazzi photographers, 2003.

Journalists are turned to as defenders of liberty. But they are also contaminated by what they deal in and how it is obtained. Compared with other high-street trades, butchery has often been regarded with caution and unease. Fictional tales – Sweeney Todd, Chabrol's *Le boucher* – feed on a primitive feeling derived from butchers' historic status as slaughterers who bear some of the opprobrium of killing. Linguistic ambiguity reflects a social ambivalence surrounding the word 'butcher'. Thus a dictionary reference of 1657 describes butchers as 'greasy, bloody, slaughtering, merciless, pitiless, crude, rude, grim, harsh, stern and surly',[7] while in 1716 the poet John Grey warned Londoners to 'Shun the surly butcher's greasy tray, / Butchers whose hands are dyed with blood's foul stain, / And who are always foremost in the hangman's train.'[8] Until 1857, butchers were not allowed to serve on juries in capital-offence cases, because they were seen as having

The Power of the Press *by Thomas Nast. The cartoonist shows a journalist crushing men with a printing press.*

an 'inherently cruel inclination'.[9] Butchers were marginal partly because of what they did, and partly because it was believed they were made callous by it: their trade corrupted their sensibilities. As the daughter of someone supposedly of inherently cruel inclinations, I remember feeling vulnerable in the playground and on the street: I was always being taunted as 'butcher girl' and 'bloody miss'. Taunts work only if the general view is that they hit a mark. The mild bullying worked because I was simultaneously seen as stuck-up and above myself as a shopkeeper's offspring and dirty because of the meat that my father traded in.

Similar suspicions attend some kinds of journalism – 'newshound' has connotations of hunting, dismembering and killing. Just as meat-eaters are wary of butchers, tabloid-readers simultaneously buy and enjoy candid shots of the famous and condemn the paparazzi who take them, are shocked

A 1889 cartoon from Punch: *a newshound scents his prey.*

by atrocity stories and photos in war and doubt the motives of those who provide them. Butchers have also historically had an uncertain place in cities – depended upon, yet derided. As the anthropologist Jack Goody comments, the authorities were continually worried about the security of meat supplies.[10] However, this anxiety was accompanied by an attempt to limit and define the nuisance that meat markets could create. The territorial limits of Smithfield Market, the main meat market in London, were repeatedly redrawn, and slaughtering and trading elsewhere were prohibited in an attempt to regulate the problem.[11] The conflict between the need to have fresh meat for consumers and the offence caused by the stinking waste the butchers produced marked out the trade as a particular nuisance. A similar process can be seen at work in the news of violent and disturbing material: there is hunger for some aspects of the product, but anxiety about its consequences.

Like that of journalists, the status of butchers has fluctuated: indeed, the public standings of Grub Street and of butchery at times seem to have gone hand in hand (up in war, down in peace). In the case of meat, the separation of the slaughtering and the butchering of carcasses changed the picture. Smithfield was turned into the grand and cavernous space, with its wrought-iron-and-red-brick respectability, that my father took me into when I was a child. In the early and middle years of the twentieth century butchers were

Smithfield Market, as it looked when my grandfather 'walked' it in 1895. It was a regular, and thrilling, treat to be taken there as a small child.

usually self-employed entrepreneurs – part of the army of petit-bourgeois shopkeepers who characterized urban life but who have since become scarce. Since the 1980s there have been more souvenir shops in Britain than butchers.[12] In the early post-war period, the growth of chains of butchers' shops heralded a tight control over the whole market by the supermarkets, from slaughtering to selling. My father was a dinosaur. Like many other small businesses, butchers briefly flourished in 'affluent' Britain, but their position was always compromised by what they traded in and by shifts in consumer habits. Today the sale of meat in the UK is dominated by five supermarket chains, which together sell 86 per cent of all meat consumed. In these chains, the industrialization of the management of the carcass is advanced. As a result, the ambiguity of butchers' social position has disappeared, as butchers have become the invisible, deskilled, employees of giant corporations.

Indeed, the continual removal from public view of the processes that produce meat is an important aspect of the industrialization of meat – mirrored in journalism, which also goes to considerable lengths to shield its practices from public scrutiny. Did these processes develop to satisfy public squeamishness, or did they help create it? Historians have noted that in pre-Christian societies animal slaughter was typically treated reverentially, as a sacrifice. It was done in public, and was well understood. According to one view, it was Christianity, by substituting in Christ a human in place of an animal sacrifice, which secularized and brutalized animal slaughter. 'In the great civilizations of antiquity,' the historian James Serpell suggests, 'slaughterers and butchers had unusual status. They were almost invariably priests.'[13] According to Serpell, the ritual aspects of early slaughter had the distinctive feature of showing a public respect for the animals. By contrast, contemporary slaughtering practice is designed to distance consumers from the reality of the acts that are performed on their behalf and from the processes that produce the neatly prepared portions of flesh that they eat. Indeed, the meat-producing industry (like the media) can also be seen as a set of procedures that has been developed to protect customers from the potentially disturbing reality of what they consume.

This insulation of the community can take many social and territorial forms. In the USA the harsh realities of the meat industry were originally concentrated in the stockyards of Chicago and Cincinnati, 'hog capital of the United States'. The meat industry was the model for the modern industrial factory process. Thus Henry Ford commented that 'the whole idea for a moving assembly line came from the overhead trolley the Chicago packers used in dressing beef.'[14] Later, industrial sociologists were content to describe the 'modern, utilitarian and scientific practices' of the car assembly line. They were more reserved about its origin in beef disassembly. Upton Sinclair described the horror of the Chicago killing sheds and their dehumanizing brutalization of those impoverished immigrants who were forced to work in them in his path-breaking novel *The Jungle*.[15] Slaughterhouse pay was low, and union organization was violently repressed. Not much has changed: the American habit of employing impoverished immigrants in slaughtering continues, and the work is still perilous, with the number of injuries over three times greater than the national industrial average – and significantly higher than in Europe.[16]

In 1900, slaughterhouses in the UK were also urban. There were the huge sites at Birkenhead (where the majority of livestock imports from Ireland and America were landed) and Southampton (which dealt with imports from Australia and Argentina). In London, where livestock was brought up the Thames, there were a large number of small slaughterhouses. Until 1933, over half of butchers' shops in Britain did their own slaughtering. The Humane Slaughter Act of that year (which introduced the requirement that animals be electrically stunned before slaughter) was one

Sheep disassembly line in a Chicago slaughterhouse, 1893.

factor in the move towards larger, more industrialized slaughterhouses. By the end of the century, slaughtering had moved decisively out of cities into rural areas, while the impact of EU legislation was driving it into ever-larger industrialized packing stations. The pattern is similar to that in the United States, where, according to one report, meat packers search out declining rural communities in which to site slaughterhouses. They do this because the supply of labour is likely to be depressed, cheap and non-unionized, and also because there is less chance of well-organized complaints about the pollution and nuisances the processes produce.[17]

Thus a steady removal from public consciousness has occurred, distancing people who would prefer not to know or see or be aware of the processes that produce what they consume. Indeed, there are striking similarities between the industrialized process of slaughtering animals for meat and the depiction of violent acts as news. In meat production the key moment is that of death. 'Slaughtering' has been broken down into component parts, making it harder to pinpoint who exactly is the executioner. One worker stuns the animal; the next slits its throat. The senseless beast is then carried forward on a rail while the blood is drained away. Neither the stunner nor the slitter 'kills' the animal – nor is the precise moment of death identifiable. Thus is the burden of responsibility spread. In a similar way, distancing is a key part of the industrial process of modern news production, which seeks to present 'reality' while deflecting attention from the ways in which the impression of reality is obtained. Would we eat meat with such enthusiasm if we had to kill the animals ourselves? Perhaps we would, but we might be more concerned with the propriety of how slaughtering was carried out. James Serpell and James Rifkin argue that our entire relationship with the animal world is based on distancing through the mechanisms of detachment, concealment and misrepresentation. 'To ease their consciences about eating meat,' comments Rifkin, campaigning presenter of a new militant interpretation, 'modern man and woman have created a set of barriers designed to distance themselves as much as possible from the animals they eat.'[18] But many with direct scientific experience have noticed a similar phenomenon: 'Just as we have to depersonalize human opponents in wartime,' according to the Nobel Prize-winning scientist Miriam Rothschild, 'so we have to create a void between ourselves and the animals on which we inflict pain and misery for profit.'[19] Undoubtedly there is common ground between 'hiding' the slaughtering process that leads to meat on our table and 'hiding' the media process that leads to suitably entertaining, informing and pleasantly horrifying images in the news. The steady removal of abattoirs from city to rural sites has been driven by commerical forces rather than public sensibility. The equivalent is true of the separation from sources of modern 'processed' reporting.

I am not at all sure how my stubborn, hard-working and sentimental father felt about slaughtering. He had a great respect – amounting to awe – for good meat, well dead. But I doubt that he would have been prepared to slaughter animals himself. Just as much as his customers, he was distanced. No doubt his father and his father's father (both butchers) would have felt differently. The point is generational as much as temperamental. In an oral history of the east-London district of Walthamstow, collected in the 1980s, an elderly lady recalled how, as a little girl of five or six, she 'used to stand by the door and watch the slaughtering – quite happy you know. It was just something which didn't bother me at all in those days. It never upset me.' An old gentleman was even more positive. 'Word would get around,' he recalled, 'perhaps when we got out of church from Bible class, there would be sheep grazing – and we would go up there and stand outside the slaughterhouse. I was fascinated to see it all.' Another chipped in: 'I was only a nipper really, over't Whipps Cross, I used to enjoy myself with slaughtering over there. It was a bit of fun then.' Others remembered being initiated as fourteen-year-old slaughterers by drinking a cup of fresh, warm blood. It seemed pretty odd now, one acknowledged, 'but that's how it was.'[20] None of these elderly people had been turned into monsters by their childhood experiences. Their memories merely reflected the values and needs of a different age.

Like butchers, journalists and other news-producers have acquired some of the unique features of marginality. Reporters and their employers present themselves as objective purveyors of truth, but are frequently seen as the opposite: propagandists for special interests. The best-known insult was Stanley Baldwin's thrust at the popular-press magnates of the 1930s, when he likened them to prostitutes. 'What the proprietorship of these newspapers is aiming at is power, and power without responsibility,' he declared, 'the prerogative of the harlot throughout the ages.'[21] Although the notions of 'independence' and 'impartiality' as values in public-service journalism place reporting in a taut and ambivalent relationship to established power and authority, they are not shared throughout the media. The profession can have a positive image – reinforced by the pivotal role it is seen as having in democracy. Yet, while acknowledged as indispensable, journalism is simultaneously reviled. Obviously, there are many different journalisms, and their role varies from nation to nation (as well as from age to age). A reporter working for *The Guardian*, a liberal-left newspaper run as a not-for-profit news trust, or the *Financial Times*, where accuracy is at a premium, is perceived differently from a zoom-lens photographer commissioned to catch images of celebrities off guard. In general, however, journalists are placed on the edge of respectability.

Of course, as many classic sociologists have pointed out, marginality brings its own insights and strengths. The Marxist Georg Lukács argued that the organized working class had a privileged viewpoint, combining the experience of being under all the other classes with the external and independent understanding provided by a political party, while the liberal Karl Mannheim also suggested that the marginal 'outsider' had special insights as a social observer. Similarly Edward Shils, in his work on the external status of the intellectual, and recently Eric Hobsbawm, in exploring the advantages of 'being at an angle to history' in his autobiography, have both explored the positive advantages of social marginality for a critical and comprehensive understanding of society.[22]

Michael Schudson has argued that 'objectivity' 'became an ideal in journalism precisely when the impossibility of overcoming the subjectivities of presenting the news was widely accepted. Criticism of the "myth" of objectivity has been a contrapuntal accompaniment to the enunciation of objectivity from the beginning.'[23] The idea that journalists are often really at the service of the economic interest of the press and not of any public value (and that this is also demonstrated by venality) arose in the 1850s. It started at the point when the press began to be organized for profit. Different kinds of journalism, however, relate to profit in different ways. Accuracy is really the prime source of profit for only a fragment of the news industry: the big news agencies (whose core business is financial news, and who still sell the majority of their product to businesses) sell uninflected news; the public-service news-providers have to attempt accuracy because of regulation; and some quality newspapers still sell their reliability. Most other news-providers make their money in quite different ways.

If news has to display its capacity to cleanse the system of pollution by telling properly constructed stories, can any distinction be made between kinds of journalism? The process of journalism painstakingly reconstructs the course and nature of dismaying events. However, even if this process is important, it does not in itself guarantee accurate journalism – let alone the responsible kind. 'Quality' journalism attempts to make sense of unfolding stories as clearly as possible. Like a scientific observation, this can be done only by using reflective knowledge that is historical in form. This kind of journalism needs curiosity – and expertise. It needs local familiarity with the context of events. However, such exercises are relatively slow, expensive and cautious, constrained by the obduracy of the pattern into which facts are fitted. Journalism in this mode is a realist form, driven by a powerful sense of a 'truth' or a reality that has to be explored.

It is, of course, much easier simply to make up disorders. Although this has always been a temptation, the pressures in this direction have recently grown stronger. It is important to recognize that the distortion happens not at the level of fact, but rather at the level of the story. There are few structures in journalism that ask whether the narrative is the true one, and perfectly satisfactory disorders (satisfactory in the sense of filling pages and attracting audiences) can be constructed by turning accurate facts into inaccurate stories. The emphasis of journalism on 'facts' is uncomfortably both necessary and misleading. 'Facts' are relatively easy to identify; interpreting them is where the risk generally lies. The key is always the marketplace. The problem is that the news the public needs most frequently fails to find audiences (or attract advertising) – and hence fails to generate the profit required to make it financially worthwhile. Like butchers, objective journalists may become evolutionarily obsolete.

Thus, 'being a reporter' has altered, and goes on changing. Conventions are ever on the move, and scorn for journalists has also shifted ground. Reporters writing of the atrocities during the conflict in the Balkans in the 1880s stirred public disquiet at the massacres, and helped fuel opposition to them. Their vivid eyewitness reports shocked the world (and doubled their newspapers' circulations). Many of the leading journalists of the time were ardently Nonconformist in religious outlook; their writing was part

43

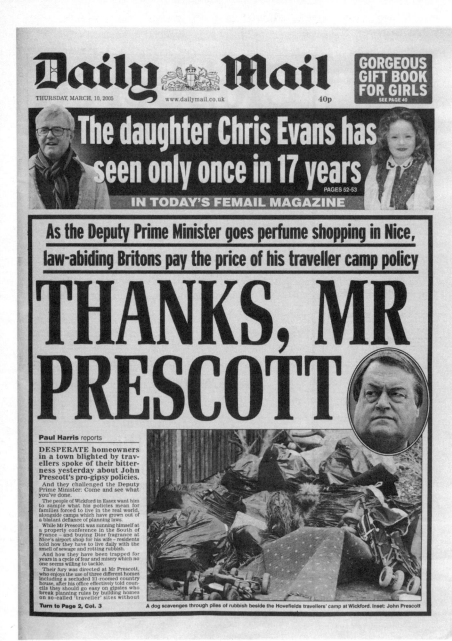

Front page of the Daily Mail, *a newspaper whose capacity to set the news agenda is much discussed. News can claim to be untainted by the corrupting disorders it deals in, because by exposing them it starts to clean them up.*

of an enduring radical principle of duty and salvation that underlies much of the best reporting.

It is interesting to note that these same campaigners cheerfully returned home with bags of victims' skulls and other gory souvenirs. One journalist even displayed a trophy skull over his garden gate in a London suburb.[24] Sensibilities alter: it is hard to imagine such behaviour now. Journalists' styles alter as well. Thus the demeanour of Allied reporting in the Second World War was understated, austere and laconic. The BBC consciously strove to be dignified, calm and information-driven, rather than emotional. For example, Richard Dimbleby's famous 1945 broadcast from the liberation of Belsen was rerecorded, held up and questioned because the broadcaster's feelings were supposedly too clear: his breaking voice broke the contemporary rules of sangfroid.

Feelings alter, but so do the expectations that produce and judge them. While some Battersea people found butchers' shops offensive, my father remained impervious. So far from seeing any clash of values, he found in his work the basis of his own sense of worth. Butchers, he never tired of saying, had a code of honour: in Smithfield Market 'a man's word was his bond.' Just as he saw his steady commercial success in the early 1950s as a vindication, so he regarded his subsequent business failure as his own private, unshirkable, responsibility. This reflects the degree to which people like to feel that they are moral agents: the best journalists often see themselves as small traders, craft producers, selling news in the shifting market of the newsroom or the wire.

As much the victims of changing industrial practices and customer whim as my father, journalists are caught up in the maelstrom of what is happening to their industry, whether they understand it or not. Economic change is often experienced by individuals as a private indignity, but the nature of the industrial pressures on news is something about which there is little public discussion – least of all by journalists. When the subject does come up it is through the fiercely protectionist inter-media conflict. Middle-market papers expose the salacious practices of competitors; quality broadsheets sneer at each other's reporting; the press exposes the scandals of documentary-makers, and so on.

Sometimes it goes further. Thus in the 1980s there was a sustained attack on the BBC by the Murdoch-owned press at a time when the Corporation posed the main threat to a Murdoch enterprise, Sky TV. In America during the 1980s and '90s broadcasting deregulation led to a swift collapse in the size, market share and authority of the main national public-service broadcasters, while the closure of the majority of public-service cable stations was combined with a fierce consolidation of local press markets into increasingly large press monopolies. In the UK the deregulation of broadcasting in the 1990s meant that Independent Television News (a commercial news-producer whose combination of public-service obligation and market-driven competitiveness had made it the most innovative British broadcasting news organization) was almost destroyed as its budgets and secure schedules were removed.[25] The huge change of deregulation has been accompanied by a major increase in other kinds of information and entertainment, an explosion in the number of channels, and the emergence of video games and the Internet. Many of these changes were not inevitable, and all were the consequences of clear political choices – whose effects have often been subsequently bewailed by politicians who have found themselves with less airtime and almost no secure press platforms as the terrain and purpose of journalism have altered. Despite a proliferation of media pages in the press, all of which of course exist to attract advertising in the burgeoning media industries, longer- and larger-scale developments in the media are rarely considered. The public knows very little of what interests its news serves – or of how news is made. A public apparently eager for revelations about politicians' families might nevertheless be shocked by just how large are the proportions of some newspapers' budgets devoted to 'chequebook' journalism in pursuit of such stories.

Is what we could call the Whig theory of delicacy right? Are we more tender-hearted than we used to be, or just more squeamish? We think of ourselves as more sensitive and caring than our forebears. We lead more comfortable lives than most people at most times in history, and imagine that an increase in leisure and resources has enhanced our appreciation of the misfortunes of others: a sense of moral advance is a necessary part of a belief in progress. Rhetoric and action have accompanied discussions of human rights, and recent decades have also seen highlighted debate about animal rights as well, stimulated by media attention, crystallizing or shifting public opinion.

There is an alternative view of contemporary sensibility, in which the media are also seen as key agents. According to this view, things have gone from bad to worse. Tales of moral corruption and a corrosive coarsening of public taste are located in discussions about media sensationalism. Indeed, because the culture of news affects public opinion, the idea of a sensation-driven news has a political as well as a cultural resonance. Our sensibilities are one thing; more important is the danger that our political system may be altered by the strong flavours of market-driven journalism. According

46

to this view, public tastes are manufactured largely, although not wholly, in pursuit of profit or ideology. As a consequence the public miscalculates risks because of the distorted prominence given to some issues by the media, and policy-makers respond inappropriately to media phantoms rather than to real problems.

A great deal of persuasive work on the media has been concerned to demonstrate how routinized news is, how transitory reality is ordered by barely perceptible influences. Thus the silent authority of the interests of owners, or the pressure of advertising revenue, or the discreet but powerful impact of the choice of editor and the selection of journalist, determines news over time more effectively than the flow of events. Such accounts have been concerned to show how the industrial structures of the press and broadcasting have subjected meaning to the routines and economic rationalities of production. News is a commodity with a price, and one that is produced and processed at regular times in predictable and reliable amounts. News, according to this powerful strand in thinking about communications, is a construction, not a series of events.

Yet such work, radical in its attempt to demystify the news, is nevertheless highly conservative in some of its assumptions. Thus the content of news is seen as irrelevant to the processes that make it. Yet such an approach often makes it impossible to assess changes in the quality of news processes. It also excludes any realistic judgement of how adequately news has responded to important historical change. Indeed, some of the most influential contemporary thinking has suggested that it is illegitimate to ask whether the quality of institutions has improved or declined. Michel Foucault argued that changes in institutional arrangements and ways of thought have all been driven by different accommodations with power.[26] What may look like an evolution in the ways of dealing with crime and punishment, or the fate of the ill, is from this perspective merely an alternative arrangement of the relationship between those groups with power and those without it. Consequently, questions about shifts over time hardly feature in such analyses.

News certainly represents justifications of power, but it also attempts to represent the flux of events. All too often it does this inadequately. The great submerged movements that affect people's lives profoundly find it hard to feature in news stories: the rise and fall of inflation; the structural changes in any society's industry; climate change; the impact of women's employment – all need longer time frames than the fidget of the news. Journalism is often part of such changes rather than a reflective analyst of them. Yet we also unwittingly carry overwhelming interpretations of historical movement in our understanding of events. After the First World War, it has often been observed, people were almost obsessively anxious about the danger of another conflict. Appeasers and rearmers were two faces of the same phenomenon. Eventually, the fear of another war crystallized into an expectation and then a sense of inevitability that helped to bring it about. Similarly, after the initial euphoria at the collapse of the Cold War, hedonism was combined with an uneasy waiting: a sense that another kind of danger must replace the one that had passed. The American anthropologist Vincent Crapanzano examined the phenomenon of waiting for a cataclysm in pre-democratic and segregated South Africa. 'In the very ordinary act of waiting', he suggested, men and women lose 'the capability of negating their identity so as to be imaginatively open to the complex and never very certain reality around them. Instead they close off: they create a kind of psychological apartheid.'[27] In these conditions there can be no real appreciation of the distinct reality of particular people or particular times. Such moods have provided overarching frameworks that percolate through many aspects of commentating and reporting. Has reporting been part of this kind of anxious retreat?

We seem recently to be becoming more sensitive, more anxious about some depictions of violence, while policy and opinion have at least at times been more likely to be moved by media images of suffering. Yet we also consume, in many different media, more varied images of pain – fictional pain, real pain; the big pains of peoples, and the pains of individuals. As a result, it could be argued, we are increasingly corrupted by mundane exposure to horrifying events. At the same time, the editorial choice of news items seems to be driven by a more relentless pursuit of titillatingly horrifying images. Journalism indicts disorder, accuses miscreants, exposes malpractice, and is justified by thus purifying the public space. But often it creates too much of the corruption it reveals – at the expense of ignoring more uncomfortable or intractable real threats and the problems of rational politics.

48

3

Reality Violence for Fun: The Roman Games

The violence we contemplate in the news is indisputably genuine. Disagreements about what caused it, what it means and what should be done about it are highly charged emotionally – and intensely political. Understanding how different groups interpret the brutal reality they consume is vital to resolving many conflicts. News violence is a compelling arena which brings together audiences and political actors (who attempt to manage the public responses to what has been displayed). But all these reactions depend on audiences attending to the news – and, indeed, appreciating it. Enjoying violence that is real is scarcely a new pastime. In fact it has a very long history. In the past, as in the present, it was ritualized. Watching people suffer was not enough. They needed to suffer in specific ways.

The Romans, in particular, regarded the sophisticated contemplation of pain as a mark of civilization, to be contrasted with the vulgar brutality of barbarians. They went to the games not to see people killed, but to see how they greeted their fortune. Today the games seem sadistic almost beyond belief – it is hard to think of any institution in the modern world that even approaches them in gratuitous brutality. One contemporary explanation of the games was that they 'inspired a glory in wounds and contempt for death'.[1] A modern explanation is that, in an empire torn apart by civil war, gladiatorial combat 'contained' violent death within reassuring bounds. The games created system out of chaos, offering a spectacle of ordered mastery over random horror. But in a more general way the entertainment provided a society which combined high mortality, fortuitous violence and civilized order with a sense of its own superiority – as well as demonstrations in how others dealt with terrible fate. Of course many Romans merely developed a taste for savage entertainment, and such urbane explanations of their habits seem close to an excuse rather than an explanation. Nevertheless, what is indisputable is that, as political institutions withered, the games grew in significance.

Like the Roman games, news is ritualized. While there is little or no actual dying on the news, there is an awful lot of death. In our comparatively safe Western societies we regularly observe death at a distance – comforted by the thought that it is remote from our own immediate experience. Although we have our news-violence edited and filtered, we draw pleasure from a voyeurism which, like the Romans, we regard as a mark of civilization – of our willingness and need through a free press to know what is going on in the world. We think it more civilized to be aware of others' disasters – and, of course, it is.

As with the Roman games, one role of the news – especially violent news – is to establish, in the name of audiences, order over threatening uncertainty. Another role is to display the consequences of disorder. It is no accident that news-gathering is most highly developed and news values are the most sophisticated in countries where the majority of citizens are secure, where most people will die in their beds, where the everyday experience of pain and discomfort demands immediate relief. It is also no coincidence that security in the rich societies which consume the most news – although taken for granted as a right – is nevertheless felt to be tentative. It is a truism that the safety of modern living is fragile – menaced by terrorism, ecological oblivion, disease, genetic experiment, global instability, technological complexity and human error. After a decade and a half of post-Communist nervousness, there is today a growing unease at a 'new world order' in which there is in fact no order. In a world of bewildering competitiveness and random messages, a sober framework of news gives reassurance, putting threats into perspective and showing how other people, elsewhere, do or do not cope with inordinate and overwhelming dangers.

Sometimes news exaggerates risk; at other times it lulls us when we ought to be worried. In either case audiences may conspire to accept only the more comfortable news. All news, however, seems to hold attention by providing a display which has two characteristics: that the events described or shown are real, and that a high proportion of them warn of risks to ourselves or others. Convincing us of reality, inspiring trust, is vital. News must entertain, yet key to entertainment, in the case of news, is credibility. Hence journalistic practices that guarantee the reality of what is shown are an important part of what makes the news of a violent event palatable and captivating. It is not merely that news is located on the edge of a massive entertainment industry, and so has to attract and hold on to audiences, by engaging them. The news offers dramas of strangers facing up to disasters that have befallen them. It shows other people being humiliated, despairing, in shameful and pitiable misery – in ways that keep us watching and that we enjoy. Are we, then, so different from the ancients? A rare contemporary critic of the Roman games, Tertullian, noted wryly that the contest in the arena was both a 'delight' for audiences and a solace. 'They found comfort for death,' he added, 'in murder.'[2]

It is a commonplace that, while we like to regard ourselves as civilized, we live in a violent age; yet it is less often considered that it may not be a contradiction at all, and that the record of the civilization from which our own is most directly descended, and from which so many of our values and priorities can be traced, suggests that an optimistic view of human nature as 'civilized' may be misplaced. Such a thought can be edged further: Graeco-Roman civilization, which ruled Europe, North Africa and the Middle East for half a millennium, included as a component part a culture of enjoyed cruelty which offers parallels with our own vicarious experience (principally through the mass media) of the violence we ostensibly deplore. One way to investigate the interplay between news-gatherers and news-consumers in the modern, violently civilized epoch may be to look at an equivalent interplay in a previous one. We, too, watch and read about deaths, and evidently enjoy doing so. News is full of real death, in whatever medium it is distributed; the more violent and bloody the events, the greater their news value.

It is important to underline the enduring popularity of the games. 'The Roman people,' observed Edward Gibbon in *The Decline and Fall of the Roman Empire*, 'still considered the Circus their home, their temple, and the seat of the republic. The impatient crowd rushed at the dawn of day to secure their places, and there were many who passed a sleepless and anxious night in the adjacent porticos.'[3] There they sat from morning to night, their eyes fixed, their hopes and fears aroused, their sense of what mattered in Roman society focused on the events in the arena. There were other things which entertained the Roman public – chariot races, drama and, in the late Empire, bawdy comedy – but earlier it had been death in the arena that was the most potent stimulant.

Many observers of contemporary mores see modern popular culture as an agent of decline. Indeed, the familiar narrative of entertainment as a corruption, debasing those who consume it as well as eroding the capacity of culture to deal with important issues, often brings in the example of the games as an illustrative starting point. In its modern form, the argument presents popular culture and the modern media as lethally seductive. Sometimes treated as an active cause of decay, sometimes as a passive symptom and consequence of it, violent entertainment has often been seen as insidiously undermining society from within. Gibbon was not the only writer to see the games as a symptom of decadence. 'When under the emperors,' wrote Giuseppe Mazzini, the great Italian nationalist, 'the old Romans asked for nothing but bread and circuses, they became the most abject race imaginable, and after submission to the ferocious tyranny of the emperors, they basely fell into slavery to the invading barbarians.'[4] The thought had already occurred to the early Christians, who were acutely conscious of the addictive power of the games. St Augustine tells the story of a man who hated the games and who, when taken there by his friends, kept his eyes shut – until he took one peep and became captivated: 'He saw blood and gulped down savagely, he drank in madness, drunk with the sight of blood. He was no longer the man who came there – but was one of the crowd.'[5] Eventually the Christians put a stop to the games. However, the moral linking of violent entertainment and social and economic decline is wrong. Rome was at its zenith as a world-defining empire when the games were at their height. Violent entertainment did not interfere with the growth of the Empire, or even its 'civilizing' role. Rather the games became the site of a transaction between the audience, their rulers and the performance that was a central institution in Roman life and civilization. Moreover, although many Roman critics thought that entertainment was bad for the public, they thought that the violent amusement of the games was good for it – it played an edifying role.

Of course, Roman cruelty is not unique. Historically, public killings – for retribution, religious propitiation, social control or the desire to exterminate populations – have been frequent, generally combined with an element of spectator satisfaction. What does make Roman society distinct is the organization of murder for the primary purpose of entertainment. Public pleasure was politically vital to the performance, and the games offered an arena for much besides judicial execution. It is this interweaving of politics, violence and amusement in a period of uncertain legitimacy that makes the games and contemporary news disconcertingly similar.

The penetration of the organization and performances of the arena into Roman life was so deep but became so alien to later tastes that the significance of the games has often been ignored. At best, they have been placed on the periphery of other, more respectable, aspects of the history of the Empire – but then amusement has generally been regarded as marginal to the mainstream of historical events. Even those who have been puzzled have not considered it necessary to amend their opinion of the success of a great civilization. The historian William Lecky, in his early-twentieth-century study of European morals, articulated what has remained the conventional view: that the games were a shameful mystery in an otherwise morally disciplined society. 'The gladiatorial games form, indeed, the one feature of Roman society which to the modern mind is almost inconceivable,' Lecky maintained. 'That not only men, but women in an advanced period of civilization – men and women who not only professed but very frequently acted on a high code of morals – should have made the carnage of men their habitual amusement, that all of this should have continued for centuries, with scarcely a protest, is one of the most startling facts in moral history.'[6]

What did the Romans troop out to see? Prisoners of war, condemned men and women, compelled to kill each other or be torn apart by beasts – which were themselves hunted and slaughtered by the thousand – as part of a carefully planned series of shows. The organization of these events required the most highly developed administrative system of which the Empire was capable. If Roman bureaucracy extended over a huge domain, so did the politics and commerce necessary to provide for the games. Some of what the Romans saw was theatrical, in the modern sense of extravagant fantasy. The core, however, was fantasy come to life: authentic suffering and death. Such bloody entertainment might be seen as aberrant, had it not so clearly been so normal and culturally central for many generations. Its relevance to our own time lies in that centrality, and the parallel between observation of violence contained within an arena and observation of violence contained within a newspaper or displayed on a television or computer screen. Not only is almost all information a kind of entertainment, but the information that entertains most today is precisely the kind which might also have pleased the palate of a classical audience. To understand our own taste for contained reality violence, often representing matters of genuine political significance, we need to look more closely at the ancient prototypes.

Literary and archaeological evidence suggests that the Roman games evolved out of an earlier Etruscan tradition of sacrificing prisoners of war to honour the dead. The contest held to mark the death and burial rites of the Greek hero Patroclus in the *Iliad* is an example of this kind of religious and military ceremony. In Rome, the ceremonial developed into the practice of offering a similar sacrifice to mark the death of an honoured citizen. In 264 BC the sons of a man called Brutus compelled three pairs of gladiators to fight to the death at their father's funeral. Following the Etruscan pattern, the Roman games started as solemn occasions, associated with funeral rites. They were redemptive sacrifices, expiatory offerings, at a time of stress, and at first they took place in a public place – the forum – where matters of importance were debated between citizens. However, although they were not originally purely for entertainment, the 'spectacle' element already existed. The games were first known as *munera* or gifts, and the idea of the games as gifts from the rich to the poor remained central to their organization and meaning throughout their history.

Semi-sacred elements lingered, but became increasingly shadowy. A great victory, the safe succession of another ruler, a threat overcome could prompt especially lavish displays – the greater the munificence, the more people killed – but the evolution was towards routine. The games also became more frequent, moving out of the forum into purpose-built arenas whose colossal scale helped to make them the most durable – as well as the most powerfully symbolic – monuments of Roman culture in many of the territories that once formed part of the Empire.

The Colosseum, in Rome, engraved in 1900 from a picture by Piranesi (1720–78). The games – like the news – combined politics, entertainment and violence in a gripping mass-spectator show.

'Going to the games' became a large part of what urban Romans did with their time. During the reign of Augustus (r. 27 BC–AD 14) there were 66 days of games a year; by the time of Marcus Aurelius (r. AD 161–80) this had risen to 125 days, and by the fourth century it had gone up to 175 days of regular shows – with an increasing number of special one-off imperial 'gifts' as well.[7] As the games increased in frequency and regularity, they also got larger. They started and finished at set times; the timetable of entertainment (with less interesting slaughters in the lunch break) was as considered and predictable as any television programme schedule, and was

54

composed with similar ends in view. Enjoyment was not universal; then as now, some of the intellectually snobbish regarded the pleasures of the masses with disdain. Seneca, who enjoyed the games on occasions but who sometimes preferred to work in his study on games days, described with irritation how his writing was interrupted by the thunderous applause that shook the empty city. Everyone, he said, was at the games: they always were. 'Nothing is so damaging to good character as indulgence at the games, for then it is vice steals subtly upon one through the avenue of pleasure. I mean the people become greedier, more ambitious, more corrupt and more cruel.'[8] Such an attitude, however, was rare.

Gladiatorial combat has provided the basis for several generations of Hollywood movies. Not only does it have a modern box-office appeal, it was the most enthusiastically appreciated manifestation of the games at the time. The special status of such events was marked by the frightful oath, the so-called *sacramentum gladiatorium*, which bound gladiators to endure being 'burnt by fire, shackled with chains, whipped with rods and killed with steel'.[9] It was a key part of their training, and audiences watched combats through the refracted understanding of what the oath meant for the gladiators' willingness to die: it supposedly transformed the performers' attitude to their work, giving them a contractual relationship with their own demise. Other victims were merely put to death; gladiators, by contrast, could – within the stark terms of their pledge – negotiate how they died. Thus the classical scholar Carlin Barton suggests that the oath turned 'an involuntary act into a voluntary one, and so, at the very moment he becomes a slave condemned to death, the gladiator becomes a free agent and a man with honour to uphold'.[10]

Gladiators were trained in special schools that combined savage discipline and dedicated professional care. Galen, the Roman physician who codified much early medical knowledge, began his career as a kind of sports doctor attached to a Roman gladiatorial school in Asia Minor. He claimed that his skill in dealing with wounds, and his views on diet and how to develop general well-being, reduced (unintended) gladiator mortality and taught him 'most quickly and most thoroughly' about the conditions of health. A number of jargon-ridden treatises were written about the training of gladiators. The problem of disciplining highly skilled, but futureless, fighters presented the organizers with a security problem which occasionally exploded: the famous Spartacus slave-rebellion (73 BC) was led by gladiators armed with stolen kitchen knives.

Gladiatorial games were expensive, because the bodies of the trained gladiators cost money to produce. So the fighters were not squandered, but often survived to develop 'form' and to fight in many shows. One notable gladiator survived fifty-two fights, but this was so exceptional that it became the stuff of fable. Nevertheless, despite the costs of training, gladiators were used lavishly. One event lasted 117 days, and displayed fights between 4,941 pairs of gladiators. Between AD 106 and 114, 23,000 gladiators fought in front of the emperor. The games became big business, hugely lucrative for promoters. But while gladiators had an ambiguous social status, being both despised and admired, the '*lanistae*' – the contractors who supplied gladiators, 'death's middlemen' – were always regarded as contemptible. To be forced to die fighting, or even to choose it, or to enjoy watching the show, was one thing, but to organize death for the amusement of others had a shady status, comparable to that of a boxing promoter today.

However, the 'bread and circuses' aspect of the games should not lead one to suppose that they were merely vulgar spectacles for the uneducated masses. Attendance at the games was, except for those very few aloof citizens like Seneca, virtually universal. Wealthy Romans even developed a taste for a few 'after-dinner' fights, which frequently resulted in deaths. The enjoyment of choreographed violence at home for amusement (as opposed to the mundane brutality dished out by some owners to slaves) became an aspect of conspicuous consumption. Cicero congratulated a rich friend after one evening's fun: 'What a fine troop you have bought! I hear your gladiators have been fighting splendidly and never limit themselves – they go right on till the end.'[11]

Public enjoyment of gladiatorial combats was complex, and the contract of the oath was fundamental to it. The point was to appreciate an appropriate, deserved, well-taken death. The combatants were carefully balanced. Lots were drawn in public to arrange who fought whom, to lessen the chances that the outcome of events could be fixed. The best fighters were the bravest and fiercest, who were also the bravest in the face of mortal danger. The most munificent shows, those most avidly appreciated, were the really profligate ones – the *munus sine missione* affairs – where, however brave, sprightly and eager the combatants, no mercy was permitted to those defeated. The gladiators who lost would (not might) die.

The exotic weaponry of successive waves of prisoners of war, compelled to fight with the arms they had borne when defeated, was also absorbed into the routines of the games and added an element of historical theatre to the displays. Thus the defeat of the Samnites by the Romans in a famous battle in 308 BC lived on in 'Samnite' gladiators, who carried long oblong

Battle between gladiators,
AD 320, *Rome.*
Gladiators were the
'stars' of ancient Rome,
adulated, reviled and
consumed by audiences.

shields and wore protection on their left leg as had the original defeated warriors. In time, 'Thracian' gladiators, with small round shields, and 'Gauls', with huge visored helmets, tridents and nets, also emerged as gladiatorial classics – illustrating, like a modern tabloid, high points in Roman imperialism. None of these differences was designed to improve the chances of survival of the competing fighters. Instead, the equipment was intended to enhance production values. Thus armour in imperial shows was often made of precious metals. When Juvenal deplores the 'ultimate scandal' of a Roman nobleman fighting as a gladiator, what heightens the social disgrace is that he performs as a half-naked *retiarius*, armed with a trident and a net, and is seen 'mincing of course, then running for his life all around the arena' in the least dignified gladiatorial style.[12]

A defeated gladiator had literally to offer his neck to his opponent, while the audience or the emperor could intervene to save or condemn. Cicero observed, 'We hate those weak and supplicant gladiators who ask for mercy.'[13] The bravery with which this moment was taken was the high point of the show, the emotional centre of the whole proceedings, with the crowd expectantly silent. The flow of blood that followed it was greeted with a roar of release. Victorious gladiators were crowned and given prizes, but the real goal of the performance was the moment of death – which was the consummation of the ritual.

Gladiators were stars: adulated, reviled and consumed by audiences. Tertullian, one of the Christian critics of the games to emerge towards the end of the Empire, wrote, 'The audience on the same occasion glorifies them and degrades them. The perversity of it! Yet they love those whom they punish: they belittle those whom they esteem. The art they glorify: the artist they debase.'[14] At first, as we have seen, gladiators were prisoners of war, or criminals sentenced to fight. Yet, although they were desperate outcasts, interest in them became so passionate as the games developed that they also became figures of a strange, doomed glamour. Such was the enchantment with gladiators that aristocratic and wealthy women took them as lovers. Roman matrons used to gossip about the attractions of rival fighters.[15] When the gladiator school in Pompeii was excavated in the 1960s, archaeologists discovered – along with the bodies of seventeen men, many in chains – the mummified remains of one sumptuously jewelled woman. Indeed, the position of gladiators became sufficiently ambiguous, and the rewards of success so appealing, that towards the end of the Empire some men (and even women) appear actively to have sought glory (and riches) in the arena – as a free choice. The French historian Paul Veyne estimates that by the late Empire nearly half of gladiators were born free men.[16] For the audience, of course, free will added an extra frisson. What was especially prized was a genuine fight: hence free men and later even nobles in financial distress were seen as providing a better performance than mere prisoners.

The imagery of gladiatorial combat appears everywhere in Roman life: on floors and mosaics, in paintings and on pots, in statues and reliefs. There are graffiti of gladiators in Pompeii, and a staple of museums of classical remains is the clay feeding-bottle for babies, decorated with gladiators. Then there are the images of cherub gladiators, little models of playful murder. Gladiators and their behaviour became what everyone talked about, and children imitated them in their play, much as they imitate contemporary TV heroes today. This role-playing was regarded benevolently, as an appropriate part of growing-up. Yet within this ubiquitous iconography there were hesitations, as if there was an undercurrent of official reservation, and indeed an attempt to keep the power of the games within limits. Thus no coins were ever issued with gladiators on them.[17]

If the gladiators' performances ideally represented control, deportment and rules, the wild animals that made up another component of the show were supposed to demonstrate the opposite: untamed ferocity. Yet nature was not enough: just as composure had to be produced by the gladiators, so wild anger had to be produced in the beasts. The role of the animal world was to provide a 'sincere' performance of fury. Martial's chilling poem *De spectaculis*, written to celebrate the opening of the Colosseum, is far more concerned with the performance of animals at the games than with their victims. There is little mention of gladiators, let alone of those who were treated as fodder for the beasts. In one stanza an antelope stops at the emperor's feet – and is left unharmed by the pursuing hounds. Martial observed that this demonstrated the emperor's powers, effective even over the wild beasts, 'sacred in their potency', the poem declares. 'Believe it. Wild animals never learned to lie.'[18]

The splendour of the show was judged by the exotic creatures displayed – and by their unbiddable wildness. An impressive variety of animals was used: lions, tigers, panthers, bison, crocodiles, hyenas, wild dogs, bears, strange 'bearded cows' (gnus), and on one occasion a kind of iceland fantasy, including seals and a polar bear. 'Wild beasts are hunted in the forests for gold,' wrote Petronius, 'and deepest Africa is searched to supply the monster whose teeth make him precious for giving men their deaths. Strange, ravening creatures are made and the padding tiger is carried in a gilded palace to drink human blood while the crowd applauds.'[19] In AD 275 four 'Lucanian cows' – elephants, so named after the region of Italy in which they had supposedly been captured from the Carthaginians – were displayed in the arena. Elephants became an expensive but regular part of the usual show. In one account, Martial describes the carefully trained creatures: the elephants he reported 'came in walking daintily, shaking their whole bodies in a sexy way, and wore brightly coloured dancing dresses'.[20] When live elephants became boring, public interest was restimulated by killing them.

Organizing the capture, transport, survival and eventual performance of wild animals from distant habitats meant harnessing the organizational resources of a great and scattered empire. The letters of a Roman called Symmachus throw light on the extent of the preparation involved. Symmachus starts preparing for games he intends to give for his sons (and which will thus secure his social position, and advance their political careers) two years in advance. He bullies, cajoles, pays and bribes officials in the most distant provinces; he arranges for shipments of dogs from Britain, lions from Africa, crocodiles from Egypt, and fierce bulls from Spain. Some of these creatures and their captors get shipwrecked on the way. Many die from other causes, and Symmachus is furious when, on the eve of the games, he has only a few 'mangy and weary cubs' to slaughter. The fifty crocodiles refuse to eat, and eventually only two prove worthy of display.[21]

Fierce 'wildness' was a key production value in the games, but one only very laboriously achieved. A recurrent problem, much lamented, was that after animals had been transported thousands of miles in cages, when let loose into the arena they lacked the vicious energy that people had come to see. Hence stage management was required to produce real rage. There were two ways of doing this – assuming that the animals were healthy enough to oblige. The first was machinery which propelled them into the arena at speed and spurred them on with pain and fear. A similar effect was achieved by the expedient of tying a bear and a bull together, or a man and a lion, and then letting them fight it out. However, paradoxically, the required appearance of wild, raw ferocity could sometimes be achieved only by training. Thus the lions that performed best were those familiar with the noise and light of the arena.

There was a contradiction. Training involved creating behaviour that was controllable and predictable – when the demand was for animal wildness that was, precisely, out of control. On the one hand, sentimental stories were told of how beasts recognized their captors – and even their victims. According to one famous tale, a slave called Androcles, condemned to be thrown to the beasts, was greeted affectionately in the arena by a lion whose wounded foot he had once treated in the wild. Seneca refers to 'familiar trainers' who put their hands and heads in lions' mouths and who trained tigers.[22] On the other hand, animal aggression was expected to be spontaneous. The emperor Claudius, who hated the games (but who was unable to stop them), ordered the destruction of a lion recognized to be a trained man-eater, on the grounds that the lion's highly popular homicidal performances were not fit for Romans to watch. Thus, although routines had to be carefully prepared, if the rehearsal was too evident a taboo was broken – convention required the appearance of genuine and spontaneous violence.

In Martial's writing, animals bear a moral weight that is denied to people. There is the lion that kills bulls but then 'retrieves' hares without harming them, and the ram and the lion who lie peacefully together. There are the animals that inspire pity. 'Yet for your sudden death,' Martial addresses a defeated lion, 'much consolation it will be to take with you, that people and senate mourn you.'[23] But these, paradoxically, were trained beasts – there was recognition that the fury was coached. 'The leopard bears a yoke upon its spotted neck,' wrote Martial, 'and the cruel tigress endures the whip . . . who would not think that these spectacles were the work of the

Man being eaten by a lion, El Djem. In order for the performance to 'come off', the animals had to be trained to seem 'wild'. In this example the bound victim is apparently being 'fed' to the lion.

gods?'[24] At times there was more discussion of the 'feelings' of animals in the arena than of the human victims. Plutarch, in a dialogue on the intelligence of animals, protests against forcing 'some to fight against their will and destroying others that by nature are unable to defend themselves'. He reminds the reader of the fable of the boy throwing stones at frogs: 'What was fun for him was no fun for them.'[25]

Notably absent, from almost every account of the games, is any mention of an emotion that today we would take for granted in some, at least, of the spectators: sympathy for men and women victims. When sympathy does appear, it is strictly reserved for animals. There is one rare account of an audience disturbed by the fate of victims in the arena – the elephants. On one occasion, an observer writes, 'the last day was for the slaughter of elephants . . . The mob showed much astonishment at them but no enjoyment. There was even an impulse of compassion, a feeling that the monsters had something human about them.'[26]

Killing beasts was also a way for emperors to demonstrate and maintain their sometimes fragile authority. This could take the form of slapstick too. The emperor Domitian shot two arrows into the head of an ostrich, so that the unfortunate beast was made to look like a deer, to the appreciative laughter of the crowd. Decapitating ostriches was thought especially funny, as the headless bodies cavorted around the arena for some time before collapsing; one emperor killed 300 of them in a single show. Gibbon, commenting on such practices, observed that killing bears was a heroic thing for an emperor to do when the beasts were dangerous, but politically hazardous when they were not. Such demonstrations were, he observed, 'ridiculous for the prince and oppressive for the people'.[27]

The third component in a day's show was the routine slaughter of criminals or prisoners of war – whoever was available – usually by each other. Untrained, inexpert, the victims would be forced into the arena and be goaded to fight until they were all dead – or finished off by the attendants. This was the noonday B film, and production budgets were small. The arena was often half empty. 'In the morning they throw men to the lions and beasts,' commented Seneca; 'at noon they throw them to the spectators.'[28] This was the least 'performative' of any of the shows, and was no more than what it appeared – a form of public execution.

Afternoon was the time for the main features, and frequently involved killing in an exotic, choreographed mode: the artistic presentation of the condemned dying in role. Real water, real boats, real men, real weapons, real bodies, real wounds, real death, real blood – all in the service of enjoyment. The day was judged particularly successful if the combatants, reluctant fighters at first, acquired a passionate involvement in the job in hand, and fought each other savagely. The object of the extravaganza was the production of authentic – not fantasy – conflict that was horrifyingly delectable.

What were the ratings? That the games met a genuine public demand is indicated not just by their evident popularity, but also by the effect they had on other kinds of entertainment. For several centuries the games existed alongside traditional forms of non-violent drama, which, however, seldom played to such full houses. In particular, the rise of the 'tragedy' of the games was accompanied by the demise of the theatrical tragedy. The emphasis in the theatre itself, according to the historian Martin Bieber, 'shifted from more serious drama and tragedy to increasingly vulgar comedies'.[29] Unable to compete with the tragedy of the games, theatre became more sensational, scatological, farcical and satirical.

Another popular way of adding entertainment value to slaughter was what the classical scholar Katherine Coleman has called 'fatal charades'. The condemned were dressed up and killed in the manner of a story.[30] One technique was to make the punishment appear to make a witty allusion to

We expect to be shown death routinely. The ratings vary.

the crime or the criminal. Thus when a bandit who came from the vicinity of Etna was brought to Rome to be killed, an elaborate Etna-shaped hill was built in the arena; when the hill artfully collapsed, it dropped the convict into a cage of animals. Another approach was to use familiar myths. Tertullian commented that he saw one victim 'burned to death in the "role" of Hercules', another castrated as Attis, while another – equipped with wings and dropped from a height – was forced to act out the fate of Icarus. On yet another occasion the mythical musician Orpheus was killed by 'one of the animals he failed to enchant by his playing'.[31] In part, classical fables merely provided the taken-for-granted framework of an event. Everyone knew the stories; everyone could pick up allusions to them.

Fable-based executions turned the arena into a place where religious narratives were exploited. However, the audience's relationship to the familiar stories was altered by showing condemned criminals in the role of gods. Tertullian pointed out the anomaly: 'Over human blood, over the polluting stains of capital punishment your gods dance, supplying themes and plots for the death of criminals.'[32] By reducing the myths to shows acted out by the most base in society, the myths themselves were devalued. Sometimes they were brutally reinterpreted. The fable of the seduction of Europa by a bull (who is really Zeus) was scarcely done justice by having a real live woman raped and killed by a real bull.

Illusion in the arena was assiduously fostered. Audiences (like those watching a modern horror movie) understood that the effects were simulated, judged them by their ambition and impact, and also rated them by their ability to provide a convincingly realistic impression. Special effects were used frequently in the more lavish and sophisticated games. Choirs and orchestras, trumpets and water organs were employed to heighten emotional and dramatic impact – not only to introduce and conclude games, but also to provide a musical commentary, rather like a film score today.

The audience for the games seems to have encompassed virtually everyone who was not in the ring – like cinema in the middle years of the twentieth century, and television at the end of it. All of Roman society – seated in strictly ordered blocks by status, with specially reserved seats for vestal virgins – turned out regularly, dressed in their best clothes, to watch and judge what the arena had to offer. Juvenal's satires refer to a woman who pawned everything she owned to hire dress and jewels to go to the games, while Martial wrote, 'What race is so remote, so barbarous, O Caesar, that no spectator from it is in your city?'[33] Such universal impact gave the games political centrality.

Like football on television or TV soaps today, the events of the arena provided the common coin of everyday conversation. 'How often will you find anyone who talks of nothing else at home,' commented Tacitus, 'and when you enter the lecture halls what else do you find the young men talking about?'[34] To go to the games was to be a part of Roman society. Beyond the audience there was the watching, knowing Empire – at once both a potential source for performance in the ring and a potential audience. The games were second only to Christianity as Rome's most important cultural export: any decent-sized administrative centre aspired to its own arena. 'In Syria the games first produced rather terror than pleasure,' comments Lecky, 'but the effete Syrians soon learnt to contemplate them with passionate enjoyment.'[35] Very few nations held out against the seduction of holding games; only the Greeks persistently disliked them. Indeed, to organize games marked you out as being within the Empire rather than outside it. To hold games meant that you watched them, rather than the unpalatable alternative – that you were what was watched: a part of the show.

Yet the line between the watching spectators and the watched victim shifted. As the demand for ever-bigger displays developed, the problem of the supply of arena-fodder (especially in the cheap 'just-for-slaughter' routines) became acute. One fall-back was petty criminals. A contemporary critic pointed out that service in the arena had almost become a kind of draft: any particular audience would contain people who were likely, in time, to become participants.[36] One celebrated example occurred when the emperer Nero, confronted by a boring display, spiced up the show by ordering that a section of the audience be thrown into the arena. If a piece of machinery failed, the carpenters were hauled out to die in the sand. Rulers sometimes tossed hecklers to the beasts. Imperial whimsicality could even be directed at the majority: once, Nero ordered that the huge blind in the Colosseum that protected the crowd from the searing sun should be drawn back and the exits be guarded, so that he could enjoy the spectacle of the entire audience tortured by the heat – and, in the process, demonstrate his absolute power over them.[37]

There was little concept of excess. To contemporary critics, 'cruelty' was not what happened in the ring, but what happened to the audience when the show was not good enough. Caligula displayed (and got away with) his contempt for the public by 'pitting feeble fighters against decrepit criminals, or staging comic duels between respectable householders who happened to be disabled in some way or another'.[38] At the same time, the arena provided an opportunity for political leaders to win support, by presenting themselves in a heroic light. Some emperors, such as Commodus, themselves took to the sand, in order to demonstrate their prowess by personally dispatching beasts and even fighting gladiators.

Becoming a part of the applauding, roaring crowd may have felt more necessary when one increasingly threatening alternative was to become the spectacle. Thus the arena became a microcosm: Roman society and its pressures were to be viewed there. Entertainment had functions which bound the society together, but which also illustrated the arbitrary terror, the bureaucratic process and the relative authority of different strata in Roman life.

Emperors and other members of the political elite were thus as much on show as the hapless victims, while some of the excitement was the product of a genuine tension about who was in charge of the outcome of the viewing. Just as in the modern news, some of the excitement came from the thrill of the unexpected. Emperors cared greatly about how their appearances at the games were regarded: Nero employed 'applauders' – in much the same way as modern television programmes employ people to warm up studio

The Emperor watching the games. Detail from a relief from the reign of Theodosis, AD 390. As other political institutions withered, the politics of 'real-life' entertainment became more important.

audiences – to cheer his arrival. This was because the games offered real political opportunities. The humblest, remarks Horace, 'could piss on your statue, or hiss you to your face at the games'.[39]

Gibbon remarked, 'We are obliged to confess that neither before nor since the time of the Romans so much art and expense have ever been lavished for the amusement of the people.'[40] This was partly because the success of the games came to be the basis for power. It was not merely that the gift of the games to the public was a necessary and often ruinously expensive condition of public office; it also provided the opportunity for advancement. An ambitious politician like Cicero became exercised by wrangles over the supply of panthers to the Roman circus not because he cared about the show in itself, or even about making a gesture, but because satisfying the public lust for games in an appropriate manner was an essential part of maintaining power. It was a quasi-political necessity.

Emperors 'gave' the games, which were organized and paid for by public officials. Together with supplying what came to be known as 'bread', but what was in fact a mechanism for controlling the price of food for Roman citizens, the games became the key way of consulting, attending to the wants of, and gaining the permission or assent of the people. Games became bigger, fuelled by ambition and by the way in which public expression of agreement was funnelled through them. By the end of the first century AD the scale of performance required in Rome to secure satisfaction had outgrown the simple space of the forum. Hence the Colosseum was built – an awesome structure with a 50,000 capacity, whose purpose was to deliver people to a performance, a performance to the audience, and consequently legitimacy to rulers. The construction of the Colosseum was seen as a major political development (AD 69–86).

With well-judged irony, Martial put his finger on a critical aspect of the games: the emperor and audience were together locked into a performance that obeyed strict rules, just as much as the notional 'actors' themselves. An emperor might personally be indifferent to the games or (like Claudius) strongly dislike them: but he was obliged to go on providing them. Those rulers who appear, in modern terms, to have been capriciously sadistic were often shrewd politicians successfully making points to a watching (in two senses) public. As Seneca put it, 'the people love an emperor who loves the games.'[41]

To spend more freely – to organize more extravagant, more original, bigger, stranger, gorier events than ever before – was both a way of maintaining authority and a means for new contenders to challenge it. Thus both the government of the Republic and later emperors sought repeatedly to control expenditure on the games by a series of (in their case) ineffective sumptuary laws that could be compared with necessary attempts in twentieth- or twenty-first-century democracy to control election expenditure. The Romans failed to limit costs because the games were so popular – and because they were increasingly vital politically as the more representative institutions of the Republic faded. Cicero suggested that the games became the only arena for securing legitimate public assent as other venues were closed during the arbitrary rule of the late republic. 'The judgement and the will of the Roman people,' he maintained, 'can be most clearly expressed in three places, public assemblies, elections but now, above all, in gladiatorial shows.'[42] The public amusement of citizens was in effect part of the Roman constitution.

It was not enough that emperors gave the shows: like gladiators, animals and victims, they had also to bear themselves well at them. Their conduct was scrutinized and interpreted, rather as the intentions of a totalitarian dictator can be inferred from nuances and gestures in the modern electronic media. But the relationship between the populace and the ruler was far more intimate than in any contemporary polity. In Rome, for about a quarter of each week the people 'lived with' the emperor at the games. The games were where the reality of power relations could be expressed and seen, with entertainment the instrument of their articulation. Certainly the crowd – each individual protectively submerged in the collectivity – expressed approval and disapproval not only of gladiators and displays, but also of the emperor and his decisions. The games, comments Veyne, 'were a cross between court ceremonial and a tête-à-tête between the emperor and his court of citizens'.[43] In this respect the increasing elaboration of the games (often seen in the narratives of cultural corruption as a simple matter of the inevitable growth of depraved public taste) had less to do with public appetites and more to do with the increasing insecurities of the political order.

The 'gift' of the games reciprocated the 'gift' of the people, which was not power but authority. Veyne argues that the emperor 'though sovereign by absolute right, has been made emperor by his subjects. Would they hesitate to take back the crown they had given?'[44] Controlling a huge empire without mechanisms for securing legitimacy increasingly led to an increase in violence, and, as legitimacy became more tenuous, rulers had to hit out at everyone, everywhere. Veyne argues that political tension explains the immense importance and the charged atmosphere of the games: within his sophisticated appraisal, the games become little more than an opportunity for the expression of political tension that only accidentally happens to take the form of amusement. But, as we have seen, public appreciation of the spectacle was inseparable from the political role of the games. Veyne misunderstands how far the requirements of producing an entertainment shaped political expression.

Another familiar explanation sees the rise of the games as a by-product of an economy in surplus. Thus Roland Auguet has argued that the provision of cheap food to citizens, to secure their quiescence, created the leisure that in turn stimulated demand for the games. Once idleness was given the stamp of approval, he suggests, it 'became a necessity to amuse the plebs, lest they should fall prey to moods dangerous to the totalitarian power which had just been set up'.[45] The Roman games can in this way be seen as an early example of a popular-culture opiate used to satisfy, distract, amuse or tranquillize – and hence, Auguet argues, degenerate the audience.

What is clear is that the significance of the games increased as other political institutions became more unstable. The sense that the world was topsy-turvy, that accident and arbitrary fate could be catastrophic, or that

Holding the attention of audiences at the games was central to their political purpose. Entertainment was the basis of politics.

'victory could be snatched from the mouth of a lion', became more intense as imperial power took root. Indeed, the gladiator offered a powerful metaphor for a polity increasingly at war with itself. For Seneca, the gladiator represented the 'still power of a man without hope', a man who battles not against a foreign enemy, but against 'his brother', with whom he has lived, trained and shared bread. 'We live our lives in the gladiatorial barricades,' Seneca commented of his society. 'We fight with the man with whom we share our drink.'[46]

Managing public opinion, by stimulating and satisfying the waxing hunger for increasingly exotic and dreadful spectacles, became an acute problem. 'The excellence of government,' observed Juvenal, 'is shown more by its concern for pastimes than by its concern for serious matters. Negligence it is true being far more prejudicial in the latter, but producing far more dissatisfaction in the former . . . [the] people are, all in all, less avid for money than they are for spectacles.' Juvenal went on to claim that, although the dole of bread satisfied individuals, 'Spectacles alone serve to satisfy the people as a whole.'[47]

Indeed, rather than seeing the arena as the agent of Roman civilization's decline, some scholars, like Peter Brown and Carlin Barton, have described it as a territory of powerfully pure imagery: a kind of moral centre in a society of unstable, compromised, unpredictably illegitimate politics.[48] It was not merely that 'giving' the games had political effects, or that what happened in the sand had political consequences, but rather that the very way of thinking about politics was saturated with ideas about the games. Some who watched these bloody entertainments, it has been argued, saw them as a model of propriety. In the arena, awesome discipline confronted savagery – contrasting with the unstable uncertainties of other late Roman institutions. According to this view, the Romans admired the games not because of their own degeneracy, but because of a need to hold on to political value in a brutal world.

In his book about later medieval penal systems, Michel Foucault suggests that the public display of punishment was an essential component of justice: the elaborate tortures that preceded execution were a way of incising on the body of the convicted criminal the elements of the indictment. 'The public execution,' he writes, 'is to be understood not only as a judicial but also a political ritual.' Thus for Foucault the penalty inflicted before death was 'that part of the crime that the punishment takes back as torture in order to display it in the full light of day'.[49] There were clearly aspects of this approach in the games.

The possibility always existed of a dispute between the audience's sense of what was proper and the official view of justice that was played out in the arena. On some occasions there was a space between the behaviour of those condemned and the satisfaction of the viewing citizens that could be exploited. Sometimes this meant that the crowd was more vengeful, demanding the swift dispatch of gladiators. Occasionally the crowd relented and urged clemency. Thus Foucault's argument that the role of public executions was to provide an opportunity to demonstrate social approval of punishment is persuasive up to a point. Yet such an explanation cannot account for the unique political and symbolic role of the performances. Nor does his account explain how the audience, both the present and active crowd and the wider, absent but knowing audience of the Empire, collaborated so intensely with the events in the arena. The 'theatre' of effects was designed to bring off a performance that they relished.

For Foucault, torture and the public execution and display of criminals allowed the law and its appropriateness to be seen and shown. However, although judicial torture before trial became increasingly common in the Roman Empire as a means of securing a confession or a conviction, it seldom took place in public. The legally tortured Roman citizen retained his civic persona: he was still a legal person. It is significant that Romans never illustrated legal torture, because the objects of torture retained a degree of humanity. By contrast, they were happy to depict those condemned to die in the arena, because they had lost all such status.

By the late Empire, the spectacle of the arena had become such a vital aspect of Roman society that it provided the dominant metaphysical language for thinking about collective life and individual experience: a prism through which people viewed themselves. It was on this basis that Christian martyrs successfully took control of the meaning of the arena away from the bemused Roman officials and used the emotional and political impact of the games for their own purposes. The Christian martyrs understood that to be seen to die in terror legitimized authority, but that to refuse to be frightened, to control the time and place of death, to die willingly, and to master the performance of death, constituted an attack on death itself, and became a challenging subversion. It was a battle about meaning, carried out through a performance. Through their exploitation of the meaning of the dominant entertainment the Christian martyrs unequivocally won the struggle for control of public opinion.

When a spectacle is so universally recognized, and its conventions become a way of seeing the world, managing performances becomes a very important political tool – and one that may escape the control of the event's organizers. Much the same, of course, can be said of the modern news media. News is now a widely recognized and powerful arena in which real events of considerable importance are played out – and as such it provides political opportunities to those who can use its conventions for their own ends. The modern public space of the news is an incendiary mix of real events, powerful emotions taken for granted and globally understood conventions which can be used to alter political outcomes. When the second plane flew into the World Trade Center, it appeared to do so a carefully calculated fifteen minutes after the first plane had hit the first tower. The suggestion has been made that this was planned, so that the first plane would attract the news cameras and the second would consequently be shown playing out its vengeance for the watching world. Whether or not this was so, there have been many examples of modern 'martyrs' emulating their early Christian predecessors by embracing death in a way that would command maximum attention. Suicide attacks timed for media attention are only one aspect of an increasingly gruesome array of executions and displays of atrocities whose main purpose is to influence public opinion (to horrify enemies or to stoke indignation) by an adroit manipulation of the shared conventions of the news.

The concept of the martyr – the word comes from the Greek word for 'witness' – did not acquire its religious meaning until the late first and early second centuries. Then, as now, martyrdom was a political as well as a religious act – in the Christian case, the product of the martyrs' relationship with the authorities and the audiences at the games. To be a martyr was to perform the familiar rituals of the arena while investing them with a new meaning and new consequences. Above all, it was a means of taking command of the theatre of politics of the arena.

In some ways the early Christian martyrs had in fact at first become peculiarly choice victims. Sent into the arena on high days and holidays, they were killed on the emperor's birthday, not so much as a warning, more as a treat. They were a celebratory, luxury good. At the same time, their notability was also a source of authority, and they exploited it. To the extent that they controlled the pace and nature of the process that led them finally to the arena, they negotiated the conditions of how they would die, constructed a performance out of it, and used that performance for their own political ends.

How did Christian martyrs snatch the meaning of the arena away from the control of the Roman authorities? Several vivid accounts of well-born Christians' martyrdom have survived. These intimate documents, while poignantly expressing the dilemmas of individuals, also fit a tight set of literary conventions. They combine first-hand diary accounts by the future martyrs of the road to martyrdom – their lives and the events leading up to death – with a detailed legal transcript of their interrogation by the authorities. The stories conclude with eyewitness accounts of the martyr's death, its manner and its impact on the audience and the Church. They start an entirely new genre, one exciting and dreadful to read, yet gratifyingly edifying at the same time. Martyrology was to become a dominant literary mode for hundreds of years.

A typical illustration of the new kind of narrative is provided by St Perpetua. A young Roman matron of good birth, whose devoted slave Felicitas (later also made a saint) voluntarily follows her into the arena, she records her dreams in captivity, and describes her affecting anxieties about her newborn child and concern for her father, who attempts to dissuade her from her chosen course. A clear image of a headstrong and courageous young woman emerges from her account. Condemned to die as a Christian, she appropriates the imagery of the games to explain her fate to herself: in one vivid dream, she sees Christ as the 'giver' of the performance she is to appear in, and God as the 'orchestrator', the producer, of the event. 'So much for what I did until the eve of the public spectacle,' she concludes her

St Perpetua, Ravenna. The saint's affecting account of her route to martyrdom was an example of the ways in which Christians appropriated – and transformed – the politics of the dominant entertainment medium (the games) for their own purposes.

diary. 'About what will happen at that spectacle let him who sees it write of it as he will.'[50]

St Perpetua's martyrdom was based on her principled adherence to the new religion, but it was evidently reluctant and consequently respected as authentic. She chose to die rather than recant her faith, and refused to enter the arena dressed up as a Roman goddess: she would not accept the fiction that she was other than what she was. Finally she was allowed to go in to meet her death, if not on her own terms, then at least not on those of the authorities: she entered naked, without the make-believe costume and (it is recorded) with milk still dripping from her breasts as she died. The crowd was allegedly horrified at the indignity.

In general, while a public trial ennobled the defendant, and a public execution debased the condemned, under some circumstances a public throwing to the beasts could be turned to the Christians', admittedly post-humous, advantage. Yet what is noticeable about both the martyrs' success-ful attempts to set terms for their entrance into the arena and the Roman authorities' usual eagerness to throw anyone into it is precisely a shared language of performance. Both knew that a terrible show had immense political and religious, as well as entertainment, impact, and both shared a

73

common perception of values to be exploited. 'Satisfactory' martyrs – satisfactory from both points of view at first – were properly reluctant yet stoically brave. Precisely because the Christians were not hardened criminals or foreigners, and were sufficiently adroit at controlling some of the meaning of the journey to the arena, what happened there had value, if not for them, then at least for their followers. Gibbon's explanation for the martyrs' behaviour was succinct and characteristically acid. 'The assurance of a lasting reputation upon earth,' he commented, 'a motive so congenial to the vanity of human nature, often served to animate the courage of the martyrs.'[51]

Indeed, it became such a powerful mechanism that complaints later began to be made that the Christians had become overenthusiastic martyrs. There are accounts of a perplexed Roman administrator in AD 180 in northern Africa being besieged by a 'pious mob, which encouraged the governor to do his duty and consign them all promptly to death'.[52] The governor sent a few of them off to the arena, but told the rest he was not going to oblige them, suggesting that if they were so eager to die they should jump off a cliff instead. St Hippolytus of Carthage, a non-martyr, remarked plaintively that the Church could not easily expect to expand if it 'continued to be known for the ostentation and voluntary death of its members'.[53] We find Tertullian enquiring sardonically how the imperial authority is to cope when half of Carthage presents itself eager for immolation, and Severus observing that the martyrs of the early Church 'desire death even more eagerly than the clergy desire a bishopric'.[54] The Church itself began to make a distinction between 'true martyrs', forced by circumstances not of their choosing to die in the arena, and illegitimate 'voluntary' martyrs. What was at issue was not merely the attrition of the Church caused by the eager stampede of would-be victims, or the authority of the ecclesiastical hierarchy, but rather control over the meaning of the deaths – and it was in the interest of the Church that these retained their powerful authenticity.

Much of what the Romans watched in the arena is familiar to us. Roman mosaics abound with images of detached or about-to-be detached body parts. Christians provided a further twist to the story, arising from their concern about resurrective reintegration – a familiar theme in twentieth-century cartoons and special effects, in which human beings (or animals) are sawn in two, dropped over cliffs, eaten by beasts, and somehow, in the next shot, miraculously restored to their own *status quo ante* selves. In *Jurassic Park*, a man is pulled apart by dinosaurs; though he does not reintegrate, the spectacle of human bisection, a Roman arena staple, has

Modern insurgents plan their martyrdoms with news in mind.

not lost its power to amuse. Contemporary audiences, viewing this scene for the first time, typically roar with laughter.

Indeed, in the early Church, a knotty theological problem was posed by the question of what happened to the disintegrated corpse on the Day of Judgement if the bits were dispersed or digested. 'Lord let me be the food of wild beasts, through whom it is possible to attain God,' prayed St Polonius, hopefully.[55] However, the view of resurrection as involving the revival of the physical body led to arcane disputes about the requisite condition of the resurrected corpse, and set off arguments that persisted for hundreds of years. Did you resurrect reassembled, or with all your parts still unattached to each other? Were you resurrected as you were on the day you died, or in your prime? Or perhaps resurrection implied restoration to a divine perfection. All of these were a matter of genuine concern (and are all vividly represented in subsequent Western art). Yet the disaggregation of the real body was seen as a route to greater perfection in resurrection.

How people, and animals, behaved in the games was central to many aspects of Roman life. The Christian martyrs managed to wrench the meaning of the games away first by colonizing conduct and consequently by altering the meaning of the events. However, Peter Brown suggests that this was particularly effective because of the Roman obsession with proper behaviour. Men who cheerfully patronized the carnage of the games, and who collaborated in imposing a savage penal system on the lower classes, were obsessively fastidious about exercising self-control in their relation-ships with others.

The highest ideal was studiously self-controlled benevolence. What was most desired was an 'awesome bearing'. Thus, so far from the brutality of the games corrupting the attitudes and behaviour of spectators – as the conventional narrative of the desensitizing impact of images of brutality demands – many Romans became increasingly fastidious about the impact of their manners on how they were seen by other people. They were constantly anxious that they would exhibit a 'womanly' lack of self-restraint. Social intercourse was governed by strict verbal decorum and a startlingly careful approach to every detail of gesture and behaviour. How to address friends, dependants and equals, how to speak in public, how to put forward arguments were all matters of intense debate. Brown points out that as the arena grew more deadly there was an anxious elaboration of the delicacies of comportment, summed up in the term *paideia* – the aim of conducting oneself with harmonious authority.[56] Men who took a keen delight in the excitement of the moment when animals and men in the arena really fought, when the stage-managed opportunity for fierceness was transformed from a performance to reality, were apparently terrified of losing their temper in a social situation.

In reality both the ferocity of the games and the delicacy of manners were the product of growing political fragility: it was a society in which 'the body was bravely held together for a short lifetime by the vivid soul of a well-born man.'[57] The desired equanimity of temperate self-control could all too easily be dissipated by unruly feelings. A sharp sense of the discipline necessary to sustain survival was also a response to the growing absence of legal restraint over the use of violence in the exercise of power. Violence extended throughout Roman society, till it lapped around the feet of even its most prominent citizens. The unpredictable brutality of the legal and political system was a quite separate phenomenon from the uncertainty of natural mortality. Thus violence was also the consequence of the instability of political legitimacy – it was becoming unclear where authority lay. Anger had become the critical component in the language of late Roman politics.

Indeed, the obsession with composure and bearing can be seen precisely as a desperate response to the endemic brutality. More than that, restrained

Seneca, above, was one of the few critics of the games. But most Romans did not believe that they were brutalized by the games. Some saw them as moral fables of self-control.

self-control in the face of arbitrary anger provided the only remedy against it. If decorum and discipline were the most highly prized values, assiduously pursued by training and demonstrated in how a citizen carried himself in public, then any breach of this self-discipline displayed in anger was to be despised, abhorred, regretted. If anger was a breach of manners and a humiliating error, then any decision made in anger was necessarily a mistake and reversible. Perhaps this partly explains what the audience wanted to see in performances at the games – both from the angry animals and from the desperate but controlled men. They wanted a display of stoic fortitude. The clash between threatening anger and its mastery by gladiators also partly explains why going to the games was so exciting and interesting – even a social and political imperative. Paradoxically, the threatening uncertainty and encroaching brutality of the political system produced in Romans an intense social fastidiousness. They were not simply brutalized by disorder. What does the experience of being witnesses to a daily portion of the world's disorder do to us?

Iraquis displaying the corpses of murdered American contractors, 2005. This image is 'just bearable', however horrifying, because the pain is in the past and because of the double focus of the picture. But it is above all a complex political image.

The arena and its amusements were central to ancient Roman society, just as the modern media of entertainment, with the news as a component, are central to life today. Values, metaphors, politics and dissent flowed through them both, and were in turn formed by their public display. The recurring idea that pleasure corrupts, that entertainment may foster individual and collective perversion, derives from subsequent historical accounts of the Roman games. The idea that entertainment may be addictive and fatally distract a whole, powerful, society from its proper objects started there – partly because of Christian perspectives. The very real problem of the hunger for ever greater spectacle, more extreme and lavish entertainment and a steady escalation in impact in order to satisfy jaded tastes is demonstrated by the arena. Although what happened there was an artifice, the deaths were genuine and (by our standards) grotesquely cruel. But the consumption and attitudes of spectators to what they saw was also profoundly political. It cannot be dismissed as an unfortunate deviation from more august interests – watching the games was too central to Roman institutions, and Romans consumed their savage entertainments as citizens, as well as as spectators enjoying the gruesome fun.

Just like the Roman games, the modern news works very hard to exhibit what audiences will appreciate – authentic performances of real events, many of which provide terrifying spectacles of shocking violence. These can be appallingly gripping. The ways in which they are interpreted confer political legitimacy, and can move public opinion. Modern 'witnessing' is as complex as its ancient antecedents.[58] In a world where democratic institutions seem to command less interest and scant respect, the power of the news to provide legitimacy has increased – just at the point when its authority and the security of how it is made are threatened. The political impact of the news is enhanced because, although news has to entertain audiences, and although it may not exercise its power responsibly, even the most sensationalist, exploitative news about the most tawdry affairs addresses those that consume it as political participants. When the Romans went to the games, one reason why they enjoyed what they saw was that the arena provided the space in which a genuine struggle for political power took place – superimposed on the savagery of bloody conflict in the sand. As other sources of political legitimacy were lost or destroyed, political power was increasingly pulled through the damaging mould of entertainment at the games. Contemporary news also combines amusement and politics against a background of uncertain political legitimacy.

The awesome emotional and political authority of the games was then captured and turned upside down by the conspicuous resolution of the Christian martyrs, who instinctively understood how to undermine the meaning of what had become a dominant way of understanding the world and how to use it to build a new institution. The Roman authorities failed to comprehend how the cruel spectacle was subverted. If the media provide a new, global, arena, do we understand how the theatre of modern news cruelty is understood and used – and for whose political purposes?

4

Suffering is Good for You

Officially, the suffering we watch on television news, read about in papers and take note of on Internet sites is not for entertainment. It is supposed to be instructive and transformative. Ostensibly it is intended to induce compassion, even to lead to social change by galvanizing action. Thus it may benefit the recipients of our attention, the sufferers. But, quite apart from this justification, we certainly believe that our collective recognition of the real condition of others through its depiction on the news is good for us. While the private voyeurism of the crowds and traffic jams that congeal around road accidents is disapproved of because we know that the fascination – even if we share it – is ghoulish, our public voyeurisms carry no such opprobrium. On the contrary, they are endowed with virtue. Disputes about the images of pain are really arguments about the power of that public virtue. When we do something as casual as watching a news tragedy unfolding on television, we are part of a long historical tradition of contemplating pain – for self-improvement. The media may be novel, but the experience is the product of a deep-rooted and unacknowledged heritage. Any contemporary image of pain is seen both within the context of recent images and in a longer-term powerful tradition.

Some media accounts of suffering jolt complacency and bring about change. Where do such images come from? How do they do it? What is it that they do? The ability of the news to bend audiences to compassion and indignation is taken for granted, yet it is important and puzzling. The indifference, turning away and confusion which greet some accounts are equally important, just as the indulgent lack of proportion in responding to other images is yet another aspect of the same issue. The problem is to recognize the processes at work, on both image-deliverers and image-consumers.

The suffering (or lack of it) in the news is usually regarded as a reflection of the 'reality' of events. The wretchedness we actually see is cut and edited very carefully to make it bearable (and also, perhaps, in accordance with an important sense of propriety). Of course other traditions using the images for other purposes in other cultures also cut and edit images to highlight anguish – so that the same event seen through the lens of the BBC or al-Jazeera, or in a terrorist propaganda video, will look different – but all the accounts will have been constructed. Media organizations put together the suffering we see by a complicated process that includes thinking carefully about what we would like to see – and what they want to do with us.

The underlying assumption of much recent criticism of the news is that if only the public could inspect the unedited horror of events this would alter its response to the needs of others: greater knowledge would mean greater action. Graphic depictions of dreadful realities are accorded a kind of moral equivalence with freedom of expression. But such a view needs qualification: not only are viewers and readers resistant to images and stories of want and misery, advertisers, proprietors and the commercial interests which manage most of the media (and consequently editors) are concerned with maximizing commercial success and are thus also increasingly hostile to much disturbing material – particularly that which poses uncomfortable problems. Unless, that is, it is presented in ways which satisfy audiences' appetite for sensationalism. However, well-made news also respects those whose images it uses as well as those it addresses, and editing images can also be a positive part of establishing a civilizing reverence for human tragedy. Unfortunately, it is also simply not the case that knowledge of misery in itself prompts compassion or action. Even more unsettling is the perception that witnessing suffering can produce anger and injustice as well as virtuous responses.

Nevertheless, the idea that a clear understanding of the true condition of those who endure injustice will prompt a remedy has been a potent, and at times very effective, force. For example, the campaigning organization Amnesty International has since its foundation in 1961 always sought to end political oppression and torture by bringing injustices and abuses to public notice. The novelty of Amnesty's approach, however, was that it would take up only those cases for which it was possible to produce secure evidence that would meet the media's criteria of accuracy. Amnesty needed more than information: it required media-angled knowledge. Thus the organization's founder, Peter Benenson, argued early in Amnesty's history that 'the most rapid way of bringing relief to prisoners of conscience is publicity, especially publicity among their fellow citizens.'[1] By contrast, the Red Cross works differently, reporting in private to governments and seeking 'to establish a knowledgeable dialogue with administrations'.[2] From the start Amnesty's success was built on scrupulous research that established the evidence for stories of injustice and atrocity. 'The success of Amnesty,' observed one critic, 'depends on how sharply and powerfully it is possible to rally public opinion – but it always has its sights firmly fixed on the media.'[3] Campaigns had to be accurate and politically impartial. The public mobilization of knowledge was combined with, and reinforced by, personal crusading, in which local groups adopted individual victims.[4] The organization has succeeded because it has understood that disseminating knowledge of abuse was insufficient to prompt remedy by itself, but that stories established and presented within dominant media conventions could produce relief.

Amnesty was one of the founding organizations in what has now developed into an impressive human-rights community – what John Lloyd called 'a modern fifth estate of politics, with a purchase on every story'.[5] These new pressure groups have varied forms of organization and aims, and operate at different levels of the international political system. At the same time, although discussions of human rights sometimes refer to law and legal changes, and sometimes to a more general philosophy, for many of the organizations the media are seen as central to the process of remedy. In the words of Human Rights Watch, an influential and authoritative international monitoring and pressure group, 'We investigate and expose human rights violations and hold abusers accountable . . . we enlist the international community through publicity to end abusive practices and respect international human rights law.'[6] Indeed, the recent exposure of atrocities has often been seen as changing the future behaviour of potential oppressors; in these circumstances public exposure is a precondition for restraint. Thus one report on a 1998 massacre in Afghanistan concluded, 'These events represent the latest chapter in Afghanistan's history of revenge killing. Because every group has its scores to settle, a thorough investigation and exposure of the event represents the first step towards breaking the cycle of violence.'[7] This report was concerned with the redemptive impact of stark information about reality not on the international community, but as the precondition for improvement in the domestic conditions in a war-torn country itself.

But is the process so simple internationally? Such a view of the media's relation to suffering assumes a direct correspondence between images and consequent intervention: that the media merely have to show or speak the reality of what is happening for an adequate remedy to follow. Many campaigning organizations have sophisticated ideas about how they have to bring pressure to bear to lead to political changes and how they use the media as part of this pressure. Nevertheless, versions of a crude mechanism of image-prompted response underlie much public and political argument about how the media work. But such an explanation does not address the problem of all the social meanings that terrible events carry. In particular, events are often more complicated than they look when reduced to the clichés of journalism. Each war or catastrophe is the product of determinate political and social processes and decisions – it is unique. In addition, each event is filtered through the fashions and obsessions of the media of the moment, and subject to the long-term alterations in the politics and recourses that the media bring to bear on understanding events. Then there is what the media believe their audiences to be interested in. And we, the spectators, contemplate images of hurt in the context of a long history of conventions and expectations that is rarely explored.

Everyone, of course, acknowledges that media organizations sieve and select, and do not merely reflect an unvarnished 'truth'. Where they play to our prejudices, however, we are less conscious of their emotional and ethical intervention. We may be even less prepared to accept how our response to tragedy is refracted through interests, politics and habit. In a period of rapidly changing values, the media reinvent and analyse beliefs relentlessly. The anthropologist Clifford Geertz explored how values have to be continually remade, and how they are embodied in almost every aspect of cultural life. Thus he wrote, 'Classical quartets, still lifes and cockfights are not merely reflections of pre-existing sensibilities, they are positive agents in the organization and maintenance of a sensibility.'[8] Geertz, however, was concerned with enduring values – and how they are maintained. By contrast, while the media often conservatively reinforce existing values, they also lead changes in them. It is their capacity to shift, not merely reflect, ideals that, if exercised irresponsibly (and it often is), is so threatening.

All news, irrespective of the technology of delivery, and however person-ally selected, is a collective product. It is produced and consumed out of a relationship to a convention. If it is not, it is merely information – which is different from news. The news we get is a product of the practices and pressure of the news industry. The process of manufacture, however, is not merely in the hands of the industry itself: it also interacts with consumers, and is shaped by what we feel – and what we feel it is appropriate to feel. Yet again, the media do not merely 'reflect' feelings. At the very least, the press and broadcasting may reinforce them in the way that Geertz describes.[9] So far from being a minor impact, such reinforcement helps to define the social context in which events are observed. In any case, the reinforcement of feelings (in particular) is a very powerful thing to do: defusing feelings sells fewer copies, yet it is what is often necessary for rational political solutions to gain support.

The reporting and representation of calamity and pain did not, of course, spring up suddenly with the growth of the modern mass media. Nor is inspecting others' real pain for a variety of purposes new. As we have seen, controlled brutality, designed for both an immediate and a distant audience, played a central part in classical civilization. The contemplation of it, moreover, lies at the heart of the religion that is Rome's legatee. Thus it is pertinent to observe the central role of Roman executions – and other state-devised torments – in Christianity, the Christian tradition and Western culture. It is not just the repertoire of images that the religion so lavishly provided us with that is important; it is the attitude towards them – how they should be used – which has also left an inheritance. Indeed, as the role of images, rather than words, has become increasingly dominant in news because of the power and reach of television, understanding the origins of the ways in which suffering has been portrayed has become more important. So, in part, considering the development of the Christian representation of suffering reveals how much our own media rely on ancient traditions. In addition, when we think about how the media shape and respond to suffering – when various forms of distress occupy such a prominent place in news agendas – the evolution of Christian preoccupations with representing pain provides an illuminating analogy. Showing pain is almost never neutral – it always has purposes, and is part of arguments and strategies.

In particular, Christian art often elaborates the notion of suffering as a route to salvation. This has produced a particular attitude not just to suffering, but also to the continuing role of contemplating images in the news. Of course, modern, secular news has many origins. Nevertheless its depictions of pain draw directly on the idea of vicarious pain as an avenue to perfectibility. In medieval art, images, not just of Christ's Passion, but also of the lives of the martyrs and saints, were created in the belief that representation had a direct purchase on the beholder. Great art was impelled by the urgency of the task of making the tales of the Christian canon immediate to beholders. Paintings were also a way of recording great historical events. The key purpose – to which the art attended – was to make these exemplary incidents personally affecting to those who observed them. Looking at the pictures turned viewers into eyewitnesses of events. In this way pictures brought news of the Passion to later viewers and made the events live again. It is important to note that religious imagery was not merely the *representation* of the suffering of saints: it could be seen as the thing itself. A long tradition of holy iconography included many examples of images of the Virgin that wept real tears, and of thorns that produced real blood. Often art was concerned to make arguments, and it was frequently used as part of power struggles over ideological and doctrinal interpretation. Modulating emotional response was a vital part of these functions as well, just as modulating the public's emotional response to news of atrocities and violence is acutely political today.

Modern news photography and television (like modern reporting) draw directly or indirectly on this tradition. In some cultures – Islamic, Judaic – pictorial imagery has played a small or only recent part. In Western culture, by contrast, there is an unbroken tradition from Graeco-Roman imagery to the refinements of the Renaissance and the Enlightenment through to the birth of photography that has seen physical representation as simultaneously instructive, uplifting and entertaining. Thus, if one task of painting was to make a direct connection between important events and individual medieval citizens, so news and current events have a notably similar object. Their job is not merely to bring distant events to the attention of viewers and readers, but, however implicitly, to argue why attention to them matters. Great pictures survive because, however specific or narrow their content, they address general truths about human experience. Journalism is by definition ephemeral. Nevertheless, a combination of specificity and generalization is also inherent in all good journalism. Journalism also deals with general truths about human experience, but through the unfolding of discrete, individual events. Effective journalism is committed to the unique flow of specific happenings. Yet this antipathy to generalization should not obscure the very general purposes of journalism and of the news as a whole. Indeed, one of the defining features of news journalism – as distinct from some of the other media contents it is related to – is that it deals with what it claims is important. In various ways the suffering of others may always make such a claim.

Christianity is based on an image of exceptional pain: Christ crucified. This act of torturing to death has been extolled as the moment that transformed human history. No other major religion has had such a horrible, and mundane, visual idea at its heart. Its centrality to Christianity has perpetuated the Roman cultural fascination with suffering, adding a corollary – redemption. Torment became key to spiritual survival.

The notion of salvation through Christ's agency has been the focus of Christian mysticism for two thousand years. Until recently, the Passion of Christ was so much part of the mental furniture in Western societies that it was hard to grasp its peculiarity in the context of other cultures. Even today, in the world's great art galleries the public wanders unquestioningly past portrayals of torture which in any other context would be censored as pornographic, or in bad taste. The peculiarity of giving Christ's suffering such a central position in a new religion may be highlighted by contrasting it with another freely chosen, model death – that of the Greek philosopher Socrates. Like Jesus, the Greek philosopher was also a teacher who provided an enduring example of independent thought. Socrates was finally forced to take poison after being convicted of being a danger to the state when he denied the value of death (and consequently questioned the nature of the gods). Throughout Socrates' discussion of his impending death, he considered the different options that he faced and the meaning of his actions. 'I suggest, gentlemen,' he addresses the jury, 'that the difficulty is not so much to escape death; the real difficulty is to escape from wickedness, which is much more fleet of foot.'[10] Yet, despite the careful consideration of the meaning of his choice of death, a vivid eyewitness account of the death itself as the poison moves through his body, and an affecting description of his courage, neither Socrates nor his disciples dwell on the means of his death. Recent classical scholarship has suggested that he chose poison to avoid a more public and painful execution – and that this seemed a logical choice.[11] But the mechanics of how he dies are not the source of the meaning of his death for Socrates. Indeed, his tone throughout his defence is one of witty truculence. He finishes with a flourish of defiance: 'Well, now it is time to be off, I to die and you to live; but which of us has the happier prospect is unknown to anyone but God.'[12] His claims for attention and respect certainly do not depend on the details of the actual death itself – although they do depend on the bravery of choosing to die rather than recant. By contrast, Christianity had at its very centre *how* Christ died – requiring for its significance the precise description of an unpleasant kind of death.

Such a focus on the suffering of Christ was not immediate. Early Christians had reservations about depicting such a shameful and degrading act of Roman execution. The earliest Christian images do not represent Christ's death itself at all; even the cross was not, at first, used as a symbol. As we have seen in the last chapter, Christian martyrs came to exercise power by their willingness to endure suffering. The audience's response to such theatre was also at the heart of the new religion: Christian martyrdom was about display. 'When I watched the Christian standing fearless in the face of death and of every other thing that was considered dreadful,' wrote Tertullian, 'I realized the impossibility of living in sinful pleasure.'[13] However, although written accounts of the deaths of martyrs were an important and persuasive contemporary response to the arena, contemporary Christians produced no visual record of the deaths.

Suffering in Christian theology derived its authority from the Scriptures: 'for so persecuted they the prophets which were before you' (Matthew 5:12). Thus Christianity offered an interpretation of suffering that endowed it with purpose: 'We must through much tribulation enter into the kingdom of God' (Acts 14:22). In a similar way, contemporary suffering is often seen as purposeful – if it is disseminated for an effect. If suffering is written about, seen, acknowledged to be real, then it is regarded as having a purchase on the world. One role of important contemporary suffering is to reveal itself in order that it may be relieved. But for early Christians, as Tertullian observed, 'Human and bodily infirmities are not a punishment but a militia, a school of discipline . . . How fair a spectacle for God to see when a Christian stands face to face with pain.'[14] Thus suffering and torture are at the centre of Christianity both as a discipline that Christ, the embodied God, underwent for us and as an ordeal which, following his example, the martyrs were prepared to emulate. Nevertheless, the centrality of this suffering to the new religion was a separate issue from *depicting* such misery.

Christianity was only one of a number of competing mystery religions that arose in the Roman Empire at the same period. Does its unique relationship to affliction explain its overwhelming victory over its rivals – in a dominant culture that placed such an emphasis on public executions? Many other factors influenced the outcome. However, Christianity did provide a vehicle for relating to, and expressing, what could be called the interests of the suffering. This has had an enduring impact. Themes involving pain and redemption are an abiding feature of the modern media. When crusading, campaigning (and commercially successful) journalism began to remake the press in the late nineteenth century, many of the most significant journalists were devout Nonconformists, often with a missionary zeal to redress wrongs perpetrated against the weak and defenceless. The first owner of the *Washington Post* in America was a Congregationalist. A Nonconformist started the *Manchester Guardian* – now run by the Scott Trust, which remains governed by a code of principles that obliges it to consider its responsibilities as well as profit. The BBC was given its public-service tone by a devout, proselytizing and self-punishing Presbyterian. All these men belonged to Churches which place a high value on campaigning on behalf of those in need, and on obligations towards truth. Even today's secular journalists often owe more than they realize to a highly committed reporting tradition. Nonconformists have been in the vanguard of probing journalism since the nineteenth century. However, their ambitions were also focused on popular and commercial success, and their principles were intertwined with their business acumen. 'Speaking to many,' as Reith put it, 'is better than speaking to few. And it is doing God's work.'[15]

To understand the Christian influence on the 'reporting' image and narrative, it is important to appreciate that, for believers, Christ's suffering and resurrection were seen not as fable, but as historical fact. Thus, attention to detail and accuracy – 'bearing witness' – had a special importance. The validity of the evidence for the existence of a real historical Christ continues to be challenged and strenuously debated. What matters is that Christianity claims that he did – in reality – live, and that the events described in the Gospels really took place. Thus the images showed verifiable events. Drawing on the evangelical tradition of revealed truth, modern news reporting similarly claims its attention to substantiated evidence as the basis for its validity. There is of course a difference in that for Christians, in the end, after all the evidence has been considered, belief is a matter of faith, whereas journalism is not. Nevertheless, while reality is the first claim of journalism, it can at times also be the first claim of belief.

Christianity also led the way in creating a new kind of sense of being a person, albeit one in a direct line of descent from its Judaic origin. By emphasizing Christ's suffering, and extolling the value of suffering in the lives of his followers, it helped create a new kind of 'suffering subjectivity'. People defined themselves and claimed importance because of what they endured, not despite it. The authority of affliction remains an important – if disputed – aspect of the subjects of the news.

Nevertheless, the origins of 'suffering subjectivity' were constituted by two rather separate developments. The first was a new way of thinking about health. The second was the emergence of a novel kind of privately consumed literature. The classicist Judith Perkins has argued that, as Christianity itself was emerging, 'narratives from different points of view – medicine, Christian martyr literature – brought into cultural consciousness a representation of the self as a body in pain, a suffering body'.[16] Romans had begun not only to feel their pains and maladies, but to find words to describe them, and to be intrigued by what their ailments might tell them about their own condition. Christianity meanwhile depended on an emerging sense of the inner life of the sufferer which also produced a pervasive tool for taking the belief into the interests and experiences of oppressed groups. What made Christianity unique, however, was that these 'suffering subjects' formed the basis for the establishment of a new, and extraordinarily powerful, institution in the form of the Church. In this way the images and stories which formed the basis of so much great Christian art were also playing a part in the development of what came to be a massively unavoidable institution, which penetrated every aspect of personal and political life for many centuries.

During the first three hundred years after Christianity was founded, during the persecutions, there were very few images of pain and suffering. This was because the new idea associated with the new sect was that Christians were able to overcome their torments. The emphasis was on the story after pain stopped – the Resurrection. Just because suffering occurred, people did not look at images of it. Even the narrative accounts provided in the Gospels were austere. Thus the existence of suffering and even its importance to the Church do not explain why people began to contemplate suffering. We have to look elsewhere for the emergence of the image of suffering. We now consume many more images of pain in the media than in the past. This may – or may not – reflect changes in the amount of suffering. But in any case we have to ask why the increase has come about.

On the one hand the form and content of the news are derived from origins it hardly knows, let alone acknowledges; while on the other there are enduring remnants of religiously derived attitudes in the media handling of events. The early Christians established the idea that contemplating images of suffering, torture and mutilation was good for the observer – and, indeed, good for society as a whole. The news, too, touches on enduring human predicaments. Usually the contemporary debate on the impact of media images is about their bad effects. Yet there are categories of image that we believe have important and often valuable social effects. And we are not imagining this. Pictures of suffering often have a powerful effect on people, and have many kinds of result – perhaps compassion in the case of the innocent victims of a disaster; perhaps a change in political opinion in the case of victims of a military conflict. Western news practices have developed out of a secular culture which is nevertheless littered with the ethical elements of religion. There are some continuities that are hardly ever even recognized. These may be at the level of values, but there are also powerful visual conventions that merit examination. At the very simplest, the composition of images plunders the motifs invented by Christian art. But the attitude which we bring to the assessment of real events is more complicated than is allowed by our necessarily shallow everyday acceptance of them as part of life.

Early Christian image-making was at first restricted by Judaic hostility to representation. In particular, the second of the Ten Commandments – 'Thou shalt not make unto thee any graven image . . . Thou shalt not bow down thyself to them, nor serve them' (Exodus 20:4–5) – seemed to prohibit representing Christ. Moreover, the Gospels contained no description of Jesus's physical person. Nevertheless, even the earliest representations of something Christlike – not portraits, but symbolic references – in the cata-combs involved a relationship to a past, and a reordering of a future. They were also attempts to disguise the sect, from fear of persecution. The early image of the shepherd, sheep on shoulder, found throughout the very early Church – in which the sheep is the cared for, symbolizing Christ's tender care for his followers – is itself derived from other sculptures and pictures of the period. This key part of Christian iconography is derived from the calf-bearer motif found frequently on Roman temples.[17] Yet there is a fundamental transformation in the reuse of the familiar motif. While the original images represent a votive offerer carrying a sacrificial animal to the temple, the Christian 'Good Shepherd' is himself the sacrifice on behalf of the lamb he carries. Christ was also referred to indirectly in a visual pun. Thus the sign of a fish was used, because the Greek initial letters of the phrase Jesus Christ Son of God combine to form the Greek word for 'fish', reminding the faithful of baptismal water and of the disciples becoming 'fishers of men' (Mark 1:17), and so on. Such symbols, and the words they were associated with, inspired great devotion. It was the combination of real pictorial presence with the respect and mystery of symbolism that was to provide Christian imagery with such authority.

It was only later, after the first wave of persecutions had come to an end, that detailed pictures depicting the suffering of Jesus and the exquisite pain of the martyred saints began to emerge. Thus looking at martyrs skewered, severed and dissected was the product neither of the suffering itself nor even of proximity to the reality of the events, but rather of changes in the meaning and interpretation of what happened. It was in part propaganda. Looking at pain was the product of a change in the point of the suffering: it was not a simple mirror-like reflection of a familiar, dreadful process.

Western art has carried with it a long shadow of the role of the icons – the venerated images created by Byzantine Christianity in the Eastern Christian Empire. In this tradition the image has its own presence and authority. Nevertheless, images are also surrogates for what they represent. They stand in place of something else with varying degrees of direct reference. In a similar way, a modern news item is as subtly created, conventionally made part of a market in images as were the great medieval paintings.

Proximity to suffering does not necessarily produce vivid depictions of it. Early Christians, closer to the persecution, did not picture Christ on the cross but produced images that referred to him metaphorically as 'The Good Shepherd'. Early Christian marble, Museo Cristiano Lateranese, Rome.

News is, of course, often crude, often conservative, containing a large number of items that are rarely important in themselves. Nevertheless, the whole flow of production and the institutions which support news and

91

which depend in part on it are hugely influential. Like the art of the Christian religion, news provided by the modern media is a product of a cultural knowledge, and is similarly designed to influence how the world is seen. News, like art, can inspire awe and dread. Despite the limitations of its production – the technological and commercial determinations which make it – it may also aspire to teach us what we need to know.

Indeed, Christian imagery and the news share a relationship to truth. They do not merely represent reality: they also claim to be guarantors of the veracity of the events they depict. There may be elements of fantasy or imagination, and both are conventionalized, yet they claim a special relationship with the real. Both forms were apparently driven by – among other things – a compulsion towards realism. In contemporary secular society the authority of the genuinely verified reality is challenged by various techniques of simulation. But films, pictures, video games pose a threat to the unique claim of the real only because they mimic it convincingly.

Images have at times exercised a disruptive influence on understanding. The art historian Hans Belting, in *Likeness and Presence: A History of the Image before the Era of Art*, referring to early Christian representations, contends that 'Whenever images threatened to gain undue influence within the church, theologians have sought to strip them of their power.'[18] His argument was concerned with very early depictions, but the battle over who controls public understanding continues. Images can command authority. A dispute over the impact of what is shown, as opposed to how it is described, is a familiar part of arguments about, for example, television. The simple assumption that the pictures dominate interpretation was challenged by a number of critics who argued that the 'meaning' of news images was in fact established (even on television) by the words that were used to frame the pictures – not by the pictures themselves.[19] Such views were reinforced by the observation that many images can be read by spectators in many different ways. It was argued that it was not so much the pictures but the context in which the words set them that established meaning. Indeed, images neither can be explained nor can explain themselves. A picture of a tired, frightened fighter may be of someone for whom we should feel pity (exhausted, heroic) or of someone whose tiredness we celebrate (he is on the losing side, the side we are against), or we may observe his fear through an impartial eye, as evidence of a situation (the Americans/Russians claim to be winning – but are they really?). Our viewing may be tinged with pity – or not. Indeed, much of the swiftly evolving paraphernalia of modern politics and its concern with images is really a by-product of the damage that the image can do. Politicians, governments and causes are increasingly

A picture of an exhausted soldier may be interpreted in different ways by different spectators, who may feel pity or relief or, more impartially, see it as evidence of the progress of a conflict.

anxious to engineer acceptance for their interpretation of the meaning of images.

At the same time, images are also often difficult to control by words. What an image says can be startlingly at odds with what it is intended to communicate. Images, suggested Belting, 'lend themselves equally to being displayed and venerated and to being discarded and destroyed . . . Images function specifically to elicit public displays of loyalty or disloyalty.'[20]

To what extent do we now perceive victims that we see in the media as effective human agents? To some extent this may depend on how far we see them as unique individuals. Again, it may be helpful to consider the evolution of images of the most celebrated victim of all. The portrait image of Christ that we all recognize did not emerge into a dominating position until the fourth century. It was the product of a combination of circumstances. There was no written description, yet at a particular point the long face, the beard, the dark flowing hair became a fixed and familiar presence. Its emergence was not a visual accident, but the expression of a changing conception of the nature of Christ and Christianity and the conventions that were available. In context, all the many different versions of a Christ image were identifiable as such. They are presented as having the appearance of a real and distinct person. Christ, like a modern news story, acquired a face.

Another aspect of this gathering power of the portrait-like image of Christ was that it was provided with uniquely authentic origins: that is, it was claimed to be a real representation, not an imaginary one. According to legend, St Veronica compassionately gave Christ a cloth to wipe his face with on the road to Calvary, and this cloth was imprinted with his likeness when he returned it to her. The cloth, held in the Vatican, and then reproduced innumerable times, was treated with great respect and was given the power to grant 'indulgences' – the paid-for remission of sins. A similarly 'authentic' rival image, the so-called Mandylion, emerged in the Byzantine Empire and came to play an important part in the ceremonial and beliefs of the Russian Orthodox Church.

Both of these images had an enhanced status because they were 'not made by human hands'. They were regarded with awe because – like photographs – they directly reproduced, or purported to reproduce, the living Christ. Such an imprint of Jesus's face (it was claimed), like the camera, could not lie. Their supposed authority depended not on the skill of a craftsman but on a direct contact with Christ himself. One popular set of images shows the saint herself holding up the cloth with the holy features printed on to it. 'By her presence,' argued one commentator, 'she both identifies the image, and, as the relic's first owner, provides proof of its age and origin.'[21] The presence of the saint helped secure the historical specificity of the image, and because the image was 'real' it wielded special powers.

When it emerged, the new image of a recognizable Christ depicted him in his kingly, magisterial role as the Son of God. Although his history was of suffering, it is the triumph over pain that is seen as the proper aspect for contemplation. The images reflected his role as God made flesh, as a masterful figure. Thus the early – and hugely influential – portrayals of Jesus in early mosaics show Christ in a recognizable form, but as a king and great leader, certainly not as a man in torment. It was an imagery that owed something to ancient images of Zeus. Although there were allusions to the Passion on the cross, the humiliated suffering of Christ was not portrayed directly. But this image also evolved.

A great deal of theological energy was expended by the pre-medieval Church on the purpose of images: not only on what was depicted, but also on how they were to be used and the powers they contained. Indeed, the emergence of apparently realistic portraits of Christ was itself both a pro-

Dürer, Sudarium of
St Veronica, *1511,*
Nuremberg. St Veronica
holds up the cloth with
the 'true' image of
Christ's face, imprinted
on it by him on the way
to Calvary.

duct of and in turn directed a theological emphasis on Christ's humanity
as opposed to his divinity. It was proper and permissible to show Jesus as
he appeared, it was argued, because he was a real man as well as a divine
presence. Depicting his reality consequently broke none of the biblical
injunctions against representing the divine.[22]

Icons produced in the workshops of the Byzantine court had a unique
power as images. They gave rise to a distinct aesthetic tradition, but were
also later to have a direct impact on the emergence of a new Western
tradition and sensibility. Their most important aspect was the way in which
they were used, especially the deep interest taken in the nature of their
powers. Many of the most important and influential icons were held to
have an especially privileged relationship to the subjects they depicted.
Thus 'true icons' were said to have been images 'taken' from the genuine
and holy originals. For example, a particularly important and powerful
image was one of the Virgin and Child widely believed to have been painted
by St Luke himself. Its supposed authenticity endowed it with great power.

Icons were used in two quite different ways in Byzantine life. One use
was public and imperial, the other was private and devotional. Icons were

seen as mediators – devices for speaking for supplicants in a way which would enhance the efficacy of the supplicants' words. At the same time, they were not mere microphones enhancing the impact of a supplicant's message, nor simply editors choosing some appeals for special attention. Rather, they endowed the communications with the independent power that they themselves wielded. Icons were regarded as precious because of the belief that the divine would attend to them (and consequently to appeals channelled through them) more carefully on account of their unique and fine nature. They were effective because they were authoritative. Thus some were believed to have miraculous powers – even to bring victory in war, for which purpose they were used officially as insignia on arms. Indeed, the added virtue provided by the image of the saintly subject of a holy icon was so highly regarded that even images of still-living patriarchs could possess a magical power. It was the form and quality of the icon that provided the access to the divine. Nor did such a superstition disappear with the fall of Constantinople. In countries where the Orthodox tradition survives, icons still produce an intense emotional response.[23]

Icons were also used in an intimate and personal way. Their capacity to amplify and stimulate prayer was independent of the human institutions of the Church, thus the use of icons provided a direct access to the divine that disposed with the need for a church or a liturgy. The historian Judith Herrin has argued that the belief in communication with the Deity through icons became central to the religious experience of disempowered groups. 'In the privacy of their homes,' she writes, 'women set up their icons and poured out their distress and gratitude to the figures, whom they came to know in a very personal way.'[24] Indeed, the existence of such images that people believed they could speak to played a part in the growth of an internal dialogue of devotion.

Iconoclasm was a reaction to a perceived credulity. Yet it also testified to the sensitive and prominent role that images had assumed. Concern about infringing the second commandment was serious enough, but anxieties about the impact of the icons were made acute by the tense politics of the seventh century AD and the inextricable involvement of images in these struggles. The prolonged attack on Byzantine power as the Empire faltered led to a rejection of the sacred images. Herrin has argued that, as a new military resistance to the successes of Islam developed, Byzantine rulers like Constantine V – hero, leader, emperor, and theologian of iconoclasm – responded to Islamic prohibitions on imagery by emphasizing that the only true image of Christ was in the Eucharist. 'Under his victorious campaigning,' she adds, 'a highly successful integration of religion and politics proved long-lasting.'[25] But much of the argument about the real circumstances of the time was carried out through a passionate discussion of the role of images.

Nevertheless, private devotion to the icons – based on what Herrin has called 'the holy person's power of intercession and the personal nature of the prayer, a relationship between the worshippers and worshipped that did away with any ecclesiastical intervention'[26] – was so important that devotees took great risks to hide and protect the holy images from the image-breakers. Icons were protected in a kind of underground movement of devoted women for whom the personal efficacy of the images still held. They continued, it has been argued, to offer devotees an enduring source of comfort and strength.[27]

Iconoclastic hostility to images combined two complementary beliefs. On the one hand there was a powerful sense of the revealed diabolical inefficacy of the previously revered Christian images that had so manifestly failed to protect the Empire and the city. On the other, there was anxiety about and dread of the magical influence of the pagan Roman remains that littered the iconoclasts' world, whose origins had become so mysterious. By the eighth century, Greek and Roman statuary was part of a lost art – but one that inspired dread: so real did the images appear that, according to a contemporary account, one empress, Euphyne, ordered a statue to be flogged. The hidden power or meaning which was presumed to lurk in these pagan statues was viewed with fear and uncertainty. 'Don't trust ancient statues – especially Greek ones' was a view reflecting the belief that the classical remains could bewitch and harm spectators. In one much-discussed example, a guide was showing a visiting cleric the local ancient statuary. As the guide looked up, one 'small and squat but very heavy' statue toppled from its plinth and killed him. In the ensuing panic, the statue was drowned in the river, everyone took refuge in the church, the cleric blamed divine providence, and eventually the emperor ordered that the statue be retrieved and buried outside the city.[28] Statues were felt to be able to lure believers into idolatrous worship and indecent thoughts: virtually the whole city, complained St Jerome, was filled with naked women on plinths. Iconoclasm lived in a world rustling with meanings and threats, many of which had to do with the powers of images.[29] The attempt to understand them came to be seen as a necessary condition of avoiding their bewitchment.

Classical images of Zeus, Aphrodite or Pan were idealized and generalized. They never claimed the status of a portrait of a god. Christian images, by contrast, were claimed with growing urgency to represent the 'real', 'true', saint or martyr. They thus introduced a new impetus to the understanding of the uniqueness of individuals. Paradoxically, the icono-clasts' objections to images gave added charge to the production of true depictions. The image of Christ hence crystallized into many different and yet unified portraits of a distinct and recognizable person. Nevertheless, this unique person looked distant and perfect in the images.

Indeed, the nature of Christ's embodiment caused an important rift in the theological case against images. For while God, it was agreed, was insubstantial, Christ had been made man. As both God and man, he was knowable, and hence could be portrayed. Underlying the iconoclastic attack on images was a powerful theological dispute about the relationship of images to the reality they represented. Christ said to Philip, 'He that hath seen me hath seen the Father' (John 14:9). The sacred primacy of sight is also emphasized in St Paul's First Epistle to the Corinthians (1 Corinthians 13:12): 'For now we see through a glass, darkly; but then face to face: now I know in part; but then shall I know even as also I am known.' The anxiety was that there would be slippage between the image and the reality. Origen, a third-century cleric, had put the case against representation succinctly. 'Men,' he commented, 'tend soon to believe that statues are God. They believe what they see. God alone is not any kind of matter.'[30]

In the ninth century the defenders of icons began to make an even more powerful case for the images. Indeed, the text 'And the Word was made flesh, and dwelt among us' (John 1:14) became central to a new argument about images and divinity. The proposal was that Christ was not a copy of God, nor was he less than the Father.[31] The 'word is not "like" God, he is God' argued one pro-icon bishop.[32] According to this view, the notion of an 'image' loses all connotation of inferiority and the Son is the same as, equal to, not superseded by, the Father. Representations were not inferior but could be godlike. Thus the elaboration of a theological belief justified Christian art. Through contemplating the images of the invisible God, wrote St Basil, 'We are lifted up to the glory of the Father to whom belong both the imprint, the Son, and the printing block, the Holy Spirit.'[33] Indeed, the devotion to images always depended on the assumption of the close relationship of the image to its prototype. Cyril Mango argued that it was this relationship that formed the most important basis for worship.[34] The relationship of the image to the original was consequently a continuing issue. The eventual defeat of the iconoclasts led to a theological shift which emphasized the embodied Christ even more.

Iconoclasm was defeated by an alternative interpretation of the role of images – and a change in politics. The emperor Leontius (r. 695–8), an early articulator of this position, argued that no one believed that the images actually were God; rather, they reminded the viewers and worshippers of the divine, and consequently made the audience feel reverence. 'We do not say to the cross, nor to the icons of the saints, "You are my God,"' he claimed. 'For they are not gods, but open books that remind us of God and of his honour.'[35] The faithful, explained another defender of the icons, 'are guided and led up to the divine in their own way, and some are led towards God by these images'.[36] Pope Gregory I (r. 590–604) commented that 'images are the books of the illiterate', more valuable than words. 'They stir the spirit more strongly to compassion.'[37] John of Damascus (676–749) wrote that pictures 'bring us the Passion of Christ simply and without adornment'. The uneducated, he argued, 'would hardly be able to understand the Passion. But the sacred images not only embroider the Passion and delineate it in greater detail, but also they demonstrate with greater breadth and clarity the miracles and prodigies that Christ performed.' The cross, he concluded, 'is a symbol of the Passion and it only hints at the manner in which he who suffered bore the Passion'.[38] However, as Herrin argues powerfully, it was a succession of empresses who used the full power of the Byzantine state to get their way and protect icons. The defenders of images argued that pictures were persuasive, and elaborated meaning for audiences whose knowledge or beliefs were not well developed. So images were defended on the grounds of their impact and the privileged access they afforded to the truth of belief. But the success of iconophiles had immense consequences for the whole Western tradition of representation and the rational attempt to apprehend reality.

What did images do for those who consumed them? The idea that they spoke for the audience and had a special purchase on God's mercy and understanding varied in intensity but was an important aspect of the seventh- and eighth-century debate about images. When the Eastern Empire was sacked, in 1204, and icons began for the first time to be taken to Italy, brought with them were ways of looking at and using them. The emotional and spiritual intensity with which they were regarded brought a new aspect to making and consuming images. The art historian Kurt Weitzmann argues that with the final ending of iconoclasm, in 843, there was not merely a huge revival in religious imagery but a surge in a new liturgical employment of images, which were subsequently used far more in public worship than before.[39] The Byzantine Empire was reduced to one medieval state among many, but it was nevertheless a vital protector of the Hellenic tradition and its promotion of figurative realism. Great ideological and political consequences flowed from the settlement of the dispute about the power of images in their favour.

Iraqis flee Basra, 30 March 2003. Such pictures intercede on behalf of suffering with public opinion rather than God.

So pictures listened to the faithful and acted as a kind of spiritual megaphone to the heavens. The heavens might listen more because the image was louder, but they were also expected to be more concerned, more interested, more touched, more moved to mercy, more likely to intervene, even more likely to perform miracles. Images might thus articulate the needs and longings of those that used them. This was a two-way relationship: God, 'pleased by what he saw', was called on to express his mercy. The dwelling on the images was supposed to transform believers, and the subjects of the images – the saints and martyrs – were, because of their pain and holiness, in a special position to intercede for the faithful.

The intercessionary powers of the icons, whether dependent on human skill or divine inspiration, have a modern equivalent. Modern news is also an intermediary. Most people in NGOs campaigning around disasters and everyone in situations of oppression – whether it is a famine or a war – understand that well. Journalism projects pain, and can amplify it. It chooses afflictions – through a complex variety of procedures – and then articulates and edits them. Indeed, the editing process is designed to present suffering in an acceptable but appropriately affecting register, with considerable precision. At the same time, like early Christian Byzantine iconography, the news and its accompanying imagery of destruction are expected to heal, change and bring relief. The horror of what is seen is legitimated by the purposes it is displayed for. Christian art devoted to the image of the suffering Jesus, and to the pain of the saints and martyrs, was intended to inspire the supplicant, who in turn would use the imagery to intensify his supplication. In both cases – ancient and modern – authenticity is an issue. The modern news team use photography in much the same way as the devotees of St Veronica used her cloth: to prove their case, and enhance the power of their persuasion. There is a direct line of descent between this ancient imagery and modern media, although there are many other influences on the press and broadcasting we make and consume. Just as the dominant imagery elaborating suffering of the early Christian period developed, so have the modern media sculpted great new monuments of suffering in the news – and, just like our predecessors, we think it virtuous to contemplate them.

5

Painful News

News communicates pain. Many news stories, from reports of the large tragedies of wars and disasters to accounts of the 'minor' pains of humiliated celebrities, involve shaping suffering into forms that audiences can comprehend. Sometimes the object of the story is to move audiences to pity; at others it enables audiences to share a self-righteous pleasure at the spectacle of deserved shame. But news is always hunting for more pain to display. Journalists, editors and photographers search for new and convincing ways of expressing pain that strike the right note with audiences.

We are often cautious about accepting the reality of the pain we observe, because it is hard to comprehend. While we dismiss the claims of some who suffer because we believe they have committed misdemeanours so they deserve what they get (or perhaps we think those in public positions are fair game for a little sport), nevertheless there is some suffering that it is hard to ignore, because it seems to make demands on us. How suffering affects us depends on how it is communicated. Yet the communication of pain is never neutral: it inevitably implies an argument that demands a response. Audiences are often suspicious of the motives both of those expressing pain and of those shaping it, because audiences know that an appeal is being made to them. Consequently, in order to communicate pain convincingly, the news has to legitimate the calls it makes on observers. It does this by describing the reality of pain, and by putting competing pains in a hierarchy. Articulating arresting narratives of suffering requires scrupulous attention to fact, and considerable ingenuity.

If news-producers are successful in communicating a pain tellingly, they produce some of the most highly valued news: images and accounts of events that linger in their audience's memory, define historical moments, and occasionally have the power to alter the course of history. Communicating pain successfully is highly charged emotionally. Oddly enough, still photographs seem to have some of the greatest impact. Although they are often taken from film, it is as if memory works better with frozen images.

Nevertheless, the power of such iconic pictures always depends on the narrative context in which they appear, so that they sum up and make lucid a larger story. But such appeals also have to operate within contemporary expectations about pain.

At the same time, audiences easily weary of familiar images of suffering. They see many pictures of people in extreme conditions; they are apprised of pain in so many different countries and in so many different contexts. They get bored by long-running sagas of apparently irremediable misery – not least, perhaps, because news has little to say about things that have got better. Again we are reminded of the Roman games and the ingenuity of the emperors: communicating pain is constantly being reinvented in relation to audience interests. But it is not simply that the news has to find novel ways of representing pain: in doing so it reflects and fosters evolving attitudes towards the suffering of others, and provides a theatrical performance of individual and social responsibility. News does not do this in isolation: drama of many different kinds provides models as well. Medical knowledge determines what we expect of pain relief; the prevailing conditions of political settlements establish opportunities and limits to what appeals the public regard as legitimate – and so on. But while the news explores what will work creatively, it also influences what audiences perceive as a proper response to events.

How do you communicate pain? Why are we willing and eager to observe suffering at certain times, while at others we are more resistant to it? Attitudes towards pain mutate – and must surely determine the audience's experience of it. While news covers many other aspects of life, nevertheless it trades in pain the whole time – one of the defining features of news has come to be that somebody, somewhere, is suffering. Even the most minor conflict over the most trivial issue can be pushed to yield a measure of pain to someone. It is this that gives stories their savour – because at the very least conflict requires winners, and losers are uncomfortable.

Today we take it for granted that we will observe images of destruction, humiliation or violent death on a daily basis and with graphic intimacy. Those of us who have not had children die of terrible illnesses or want, who have never been to war, or seen the impact of an explosion on a body, have had little option but to contemplate such disasters visited on others. Much of what we have read or watched has not been fictional, but real events. We have observed suffering in a variety of moods – indignant, pitying, casual and even irritated. Though we have little choice in the matter, the fact is that the presentation of pain to the public can also fuel a demand. People may flinch from what they see, but sometimes they want

The news is always hunting for pains, large or small, and many groups have attempted to use this for their own advantage. Anti-hunt protester holds up a dead fox in London, 17 January 2001. Later, anti-hunt demonstrators dressed as foxes walk towards the High Court in London, 25 January 2005.

to see it. Such an impulse to spectatorship requires explanation, as it is universal to *Homo sapiens*.

No other species takes an equivalent interest in the misfortunes of its own members. Nevertheless, the interest has varied in intensity. In classical times it reached one kind of peak in the late Roman Empire, before being checked by the rise of Christianity. But then Christianity extolled another relationship to suffering. As we have seen, painters, patrons and early believers had not at first wished to contemplate Christ's agony;[1] it took several centuries for pictures dwelling explicitly on the Crucifixion to emerge. Furthermore, beyond the fact of the death, Christianity began to use pictures to linger over and dissect other kinds of distress. Indeed, it is key that the manifestation of such interest is not static. We need to understand how mobile the representation of suffering has been in order to appreciate its public role.

Art concerned with Christ's suffering produced a repertoire of images and attitudes which is still consciously – and unconsciously – called on by the media when they find ways of showing pain. Yet the original representation of this suffering developed through a fierce competition of interests. Battles over how the Christian experience ought to be represented were concerned with the distribution of power, and they reveal how making suffering visible is never easy – nor as simple in its effects as it would appear. In the contemporary media situation we are familiar with how fierce (and weighty) arguments about the representation of suffering can be – in the battles that develop for example over images of wounded allies, or the effects of displaying pictures of the dead bodies of Saddam Hussein's sons. But, in addition to such cases, all the little pains we consider – or ignore – help shape our collective sense of our obligation towards others. Thus, news (just like the artistic depiction of suffering) reflects and promotes how we think of ourselves, as well as what can be done in the world.

Early depictions of the Crucifixion showed Christ still alive, calm and masterful on the cross. Often he was shown with arms outstretched as if in radiant welcome rather than in pain. The historian Robin McCormack argues that such imagery then evolved into portraying Christ dead (but peaceful) on the cross. Later, more turbulent images emerge of Christ racked in torment.[2] Stylized depictions give way to vividly emotive ones. The image becomes more man-like, and the suffering is handled with increasing explicitness. In a variety of ways, a radical new interpretation of Christ's story was articulated and modified with a whole new pictorial vocabulary.

Changes in the images were related to theological changes – and also pointed to very different human possibilities. Early Christian images reflected the view that mankind had withdrawn itself from God by sinning. The fate of man's salvation was fought out between God and the Devil, but because man had sinned voluntarily God was unable to use his

It took time, and theological argument, for the image of Christ suffering to emerge. (left) Christ in majesty, fresco in San Climente, Tahull, Catalonia, c. 1123. Although not in pain, Christ has his instantly recognizable 'face'. (below left) Crucifixion, Daphni, Greece, c. 1198: Christ is on the cross and weary. (below right) A detail of Grünewald's Isenheim altarpiece, c. 1512–16: Christ in agony.

superior power simply to overpower evil. In the face of mankind's self-destructiveness, God was able to win man back to salvation only by superior strategy. Although in such a view of the world Jesus' incarnation was a matter of reverence, it was not central to the story of man's salvation. The earthly incidents of Christ's life, according to the medieval historian Richard Southern, were 'swallowed up in a drama enacted between Heaven and Hell'.[3]

Thus the new emphasis on the torment that Christ suffered in his mortal form also involved a profound ideological shift. It was not only Christ's humanity which was being accentuated, but also the different path to salvation that his reinterpreted role offered. The making of the new sensibility had many origins. First it required a novel sense of what it was to be a person. This was developed, it has been argued, by St Benedict among others, who demanded, 'Stir up our torpid mind, dispel the shadows which sin has cast on it . . . chew over in thought, taste in understanding, swallow in longing, consume and become one in overwhelming joy.'[4] Such views introduced a new subjective inner world of tumult and struggle. Faith was replaced as the principal aim in spiritual life by understanding. 'The urge to a greater measure of solitude, of introspection and self-knowledge . . . ran like fire through Europe,' Southern has argued.[5] Life was talked about among the educated as an exercise in endurance, and death as a quest.[6] The new emphasis on the humanity of Jesus and the refocusing on his centrality to salvation placed his torment at the heart of the Christian religion – and consequently images of it at the centre of the artistic endeavour.

The changing understanding of Christ's suffering, Hans Belting argues, produced in the twelfth and thirteenth centuries a particularly strange (yet at the time conventional) image of the Son of God: the half-length semi-naked, wounded corpse of a very realistically represented man. The dead body, Belting suggested, was bearable for viewers to contemplate only because what would usually have been seen as a repellent image was in fact seen as a body about to live again. At first such pictures were intended for a new kind of personal devotion, and consequently they were relatively small and portable. Contemplating them was part of a turning towards private piety, and an awakening interest in inner, solitary, tumultuous individual feeling. However, this development of a new inner life by medieval art also foreshadowed another, more public, art. One part of the revolutionary contribution of Giotto's great cycle of frescos in the Arena chapel, Padua, is the way in which the entire decoration of the chapel is intended to be displayed most completely from one (personal) point of view only. Although spread around a public place, the scenes from the life of Jesus are aimed at the

individual viewer, who has become the focus of the purpose of the art.[7]
Thus the new sensibility remade public spaces as well as private feelings.

The media – with the news at the heart of them – are the new public
spaces. Architecture still helps define and change ideas about the common
good. Forums, markets, cathedrals, parliaments and parks have all
reflected, embodied and shaped what a given society has felt to be in the
interests of its members. They were the places where people discussed
things, and where they were preached at as well. These kinds of public
space contributed to an individual's own sense of his or her place in a
society. The press and broadcasting are a modern equivalent of these manifestations and shapers of culture. They are, electronically, the public spaces
we share. When people phone or email their views on an issue (the BBC
gets about 50,000 emails a week, an American congressional committee
usually receives about 1,000,000, and a *Guardian* columnist about 200)
they are usually responding to events in the news. While many broadcasters
simply encourage the expression of – and use – the most entertainingly
extreme opinions in this flood, others grapple with how to moderate and
judge all of the responses they are now inundated with. How to assess the
representativeness of such views, how to react to this communication, and
how to use the active participation it embodies is an urgent and unresolved
democratic problem. The danger is a shift to plebiscitary volatility; the
opportunity a greater public involvement in politics. But it is the news
agenda that sets off the cascade of views. News is both a tremendously
artful cultural form – one that is determined by the best, and the worst, of
contemporary society – and something that has helped mould individual
experience in the contemporary world. At the same time, like parliaments
and democratic institutions, the news is a public space in which ideas about
justice and competing ideas about what is good or bad struggle. Moreover,
just like the Church in the past, the media in which the news has to live
have their own interests.

Conventions for representing pain (and evoking empathy) have had to
be invented by the news media – just as they were in medieval art. Moreover,
they continually adapt to political and personal realities. The media always
produce and address audiences as communities as well as individual
listeners and spectators, and so ideals of collective action are also articulated
in programmes. The conventions that work successfully involve many
aspects of the viewers' social and intellectual lives as well as changes in
their sense of themselves.

An examination of shifts in the Christian depiction of suffering shows
how contemplating the painful experiences of other people, as edited and

shaped by the media of the day, is part of contemporary psychology. Suffering is potent, but used for changing purposes. The historical problem, which helps us understand the contemporary use of suffering in the news, is whether the image of the dead Christ, the *imago pietus*, existed before the piety it served or whether the piety was the product of the pictures – or, finally, whether the pictures were a response to a new need. One argument is that the private style of devotion seeped into public life, while another is that the emergence of these portable images – along with the books of hours and other written products aimed at the new public – was also a commercial response to a new market.[8] The new piety also required individuals and societies to dispose of their incomes in novel ways: the construction of medieval cathedrals commanded a far greater share of available wealth for collective purposes than any subsequent historical project. As Hans Belting has argued, 'works of art, no less than other goods and services, generally owe their existence to the interaction of demand and supply. They hope to find a buyer; they hope to meet an existing demand.'[9] A novel reconstruction of inner life worked within a market – just as contemporary media images have to.

It is important to realize that communicating pain is not simple, and that it evolves all the time. Thus the stress on the centrality of Christ's suffering was not arrived at fully explored. Suffering was not sufficient in itself: interpreting its meaning was the basis of major ambitions and projects, and its interpretation was hotly disputed in a period when the Church was the dominating international institution. Different aspects of the meaning of pain were developed and argued over in a range of theological and political disputes. The articulation of different pains and their interpretation changed medieval institutions. Such processes are also changing contemporary institutions.

A widespread movement developed which argued that Christ's humanity rather than his divine nature ought to be the basis of Christian worship – and which consequently put pain at the heart of belief. The teachings of St Bernard of Clairvaux (1090–1153) and St Francis of Assisi (1182–1226) were an especially persuasive part of this case. Their arguments were also part of attempts to reform, dominate and lead the Church – and the power and wealth it commanded. The discussion of Christ's humanity focused on the material form of his body. In terms of pictorial representation, this meant that images that precisely delineated the injuries done to Christ and his real human torment in undergoing them were emphasized. Indeed, there was a lingering on the one hand on the corporeal charm of the Christ-child's infant self, and on the other on the wounds to his adult body.

Painting was one way of representing Christ's human pain; another was the almost theatrical reliving of that suffering by mystics attempting to use their own experience to communicate to believers the extremity of his experience. Luddolph of Saxony, a thirteenth-century sage, captures some of the strange mood which produced the new imagery concerned with embodied pain (which we frequently ignore, seeing the pictures as 'art' – antiques stripped of meaning). 'I know now for sure *how* you are sweeter in the heart of one who loves you in the form of the flesh,' he wrote of the torment of Christ, 'it is sweeter to view you as dying on the tree, than as holding sway over the angels in heaven. It is more delightful to see you as a man, bearing every aspect of human nature.'[10] The aim of such views was to persuade adherents to adopt new institutional forms by refocusing the spiritual life of Christians through dwelling on pain. In the case of this medieval work, observing Christ's pain was believed to be comforting, providing solace for the afflicted, as well as an incentive to improvement. These views were also a powerful motor for the pursuit of more graphic and compelling depictions of suffering. The aim was not greater realism for its own sake. It was to render the sights more appealing and more shocking by heightening the impact on viewers.

Suffering also became part of a sophisticated visual propaganda – with wealthy patrons controlling the markets in images. What were the interests of the groups that kept most painters employed? Competing theological interpretations battled it out in art – but there was also competition for resources to fund new religious institutions. In Italy, one of the successful groups was the newly established Franciscan order, based on the holiness of its founding saint's stigmata. The new sensibility had patrons whose interests were involved, and institutions whose prospects were advanced by its advocacy. A change in style was to some extent an adaptation, on the part of working artists, of the functions assigned to the visual image by a given society. St Bonaventure (a Franciscan and propagandist for the order) wrote of St Francis, that 'the saint experienced none other than the pure love for the crucified one, transforming him into Christ so that finally he could cry out "I am crucified with Jesus Christ on the cross. I live, no not I, but Christ lives in me!"'[11] For Franciscans, the wounds of Christ's torture were of heightened significance because of the legitimacy that St Francis's own wounds gave the order. 'Among all the gifts which God bestowed on this humble and poor little man, St Francis, there was one special, and if I dare to say, unique privilege: that he bore on his body the stigmata of our lord Jesus Christ,' argued the politically astute Bonaventure in 1255, and, as he pointed out, Francis had no rivals in

St Francis receiving the stigmata, north Italian, 1470–80. The saint was the focus of a celebrity cult based on the legitimacy that this Christ-like affliction conferred on his order.

this peculiarly authoritative affliction (although others were to claim the stigmata later).[12]

St Francis became the focus of a celebrity cult, and of a theological split about the reality of the stigmata and their origin. Did St Francis, through his devotion and passion for Christ, produce his own suffering, as some sceptical non-Franciscan critics suggested? Or were the stigmata divine, imposed on the saint graciously by God? The art showing the saint and his affliction was a fundamental weapon in a bitter propaganda struggle for supremacy within the Church. However, the growing empathy with Christ's suffering that had developed between the end of the eleventh and the beginning of the thirteenth century was not restricted to the Franciscans.[13] It represented a change in the emotional climate. Nevertheless, for much of the later period the Franciscans were the dominant patrons, commissioning more art than other orders, and supervising the production of new crosses, altarpieces and narrative cycles which recast the story of the Passion in terms of suffering.

Depicting pain may involve a loss of dignity – just as pain itself tests the

Christ, Man of Sorrows, Netherlands, c. 1500. Pictures showing Christ's Passion, or even in this case dwelling on the instruments of his torture, were only 'bearable' because Christ was seen as about to live again after the Resurrection.

dignity of those who suffer it. The contemporary media can be ruthless in humiliating their subjects. Yet even the new interpretation of Christ's suffering as human that we have seen evolving had also depended on a novel reconception of the dignity of God. Jewish theologians had argued that the Incarnation, with all the implied indignity of Christ's shameful death, was incompatible with – and indeed an insult to – God's supreme nobility. Thus the real disgrace of Christ's humiliation had to be accepted and not diminished for the new sensibility to take hold. St Anselm, in the early twelfth century, had begun the work of reformulating the nature of the divine.[14] He argued that 'Unbelievers deride our simplicity, objecting that we do God an injury, and disgrace him when we assert that he descended to a woman's womb . . . not to mention many other things unbecoming to God – suffered weariness, hunger, thirst, scourging and death on the cross among them.'[15] However, the saint proposed, such views failed to acknowledge the honour that God bestowed on mankind by choosing to become human. Not only was suffering dignified and made 'Godlike' because God suffered it, but also this was part of God's plan to save mankind from its own sinfulness. The historian Anne Derbes has argued that there was a conscious manipulation of the whole story of the Passion, elaborating more and more painful and poignant moments in the journey.[16] The journey to Calvary was reimagined, and many pictures of the time emphasize Christ's voluntary decision to sacrifice himself. Thus the contemplation of Christ's simultaneously divine and human pain became the most powerful path to redemption: that is, the viewing of pain would transform the spectator – not merely compel compassion for the victim.

The emphasis on Christ's humanity produced profound changes in the repertoire of visual imagery.[17] By the fifteenth century, Catherine Walker Bynum suggests, 'theological attention was focused on the body of Christ (not in the contemporary sexualized sense) but in order to emphasize it as testimony of Christ's enfleshed humanity.'[18] Thus the French nun Marguerite of Oingt swooned with love over Christ's bleeding side, and received a vision in which she flowered like a tree in spring when watered by Christ, while her branches were named with the names of the five senses – a 'graphic illustration of the medieval conviction that those who love Christ should respond to all of his body with all of theirs'.[19] Indeed, some extraordinary images of the period depict the wounds he suffered, or the objects that inflicted the wounds, surreally separated from the body itself: turned into separate objects of veneration.[20]

There were also changes in the way in which those who witnessed Christ's suffering and the ordeals of the saints were depicted. In order to magnify the affective power of the suffering, these witnesses were increasingly shown as overcome by what they saw. Registering grief was by no means an exclusively female role, but women set very high standards for assessing the magnitude of the loss – a convention that remains important in contemporary representation. Observing the grief of spectators may amplify the horror of the suffering subject, or it may demonstrate an entirely new pain. This may be illuminated by considering the representations of Mary, and the role they performed in producing her own cult. Pictures up to the eleventh century show Mary tragically composed beside the cross. She is the dignified witness of her son's torment, a detached though sorrowing observer. Her role develops, and by the thirteenth century depictions come to show her as increasingly distressed, typically swooning at the sight of her son's fate. Indeed, watching Mary watching her son's Passion becomes an important prompt to compassion in itself. Such an intention led, in turn, from the end of the thirteenth century, to an entirely new pictorial image, the *pietà*. In this, the grieving mother bears the body of her dead son across her lap.

Such a scene, which produced some of the most moving images in Western art, does not correspond to any identifiable moment in the Gospels – and had no biblical authority. It provided a quiet, sad, contemplative interlude between the anguish of the Deposition from the cross and the bleakness of the entombment. It was the product of a developing emotional rhetoric, aimed at prolonging and modulating feeling. Spectators were invited to feel for the Virgin's sorrow and to be grateful for her willingness to give up her own son to save humanity. It survived because it produced a new image for the human predicament of loss. Many modern news photographs of women grieving echo images of the Virgin's misery.

Where did artists find the prompts to depict the pain so vividly, and what started them elaborating ways of expressing more diverse pains? It is often assumed that pain takes a single, identifiable form. Yet we are aware that bodily suffering is experienced differently in various societies. We also know that individuals experience pain in different ways, and use alternative and culturally determined metaphors in attempting to describe it. Pain has been not merely explained but also *justified* in various ways; thus judicial torture was still practised in France until the eighteenth century, not as a punishment but as a legitimate way of establishing truth, which was seen as a divinely inspired existential fact. Abolishing torture meant that truth was redefined as a human product – but also that bodies were seen as 'a mechanical device, without meaningful connection to the divine'.[21] Thus depicting pain and anguish is not simply a matter of letting the pain speak for itself, for the meaning of pain mutates.

It is, of course, by no means the case that all Christian art of the twelfth to fourteenth centuries dwells on the anguish of victims. On the contrary, much of it emphasizes that mere physical torment is transcended by divine comfort. Great galleries are full of images of exquisitely depicted torture, borne with a serene indifference by holy martyrs. Many saints do not shriek in agony. Typically such victims look exalted – smug even – and bear their ordeals with a puzzling insouciance. In the Victoria & Albert Museum, for example, there is a great fourteenth-century Spanish altarpiece that intrigued me as a child. In it, St George, having slain a feisty little dragon and consequently converted the princess and the town to Christianity, is captured by Arabs. They cut him in half with a convenient saw, nail him to a plank, pluck bits out of him, and put him in a pot of boiling lead. All to no effect. The saint tosses his golden curls blithely throughout the whole

The pietà was an
invented image which
had no scriptural
authority. It produced
a new image of loss
that has enduring
power. (left) Dead
Christ, Luis de
Morales, sixteenth
century, Bilbao.
(below) Mother
carrying her dead child
in Somalia, 1991.

process, secure in the knowledge (I now understand) of his place in heaven. In the last panel, cutting his head off finally does the trick, and he turns a revealing shade of grey and expires. Similarly, representations of St Sebastian seem to specialize in such indifference to torture (the arrows did not, in the legend, kill him anyway). The message of these pictures is either that their holy subjects' invulnerability to mortal pain marks them out or that, because of their saintliness, their minds are on higher things than mortal pain. Today we still expect some people to express little of the pain they may suffer, particularly public figures.

But pain is varied, and representing this variety of suffering is difficult. In the tenth century a new genre emerged: images that attempted to demonstrate what particular and distinct pains felt like. One example of this new convention is provided by the sets of carved ivories that depict the story of the Forty Martyrs of Sebaste. The martyrs were Armenian soldiers who chose to freeze to death on a lake rather than recant their faith, resisting the temptation of the warm bathhouses set up on the edge of the lake to lure them from their chosen path. In doing so they 'laughed as they took off their clothes, and undismayed by the gusts of wind they entered the lake naked, and sent up prayers to Christ'.[22] Although most depictions of the scene show the saints standing solidly in a row, several famous works (one in Berlin, one in St Petersburg) show their suffering with startling realism. The martyrs are depicted as intensely cold; they shiver, rub their arms, and one young soldier falls over and is comforted in his misery by an older man. It is not merely a depiction of vivid suffering, but is particular to the specific suffering – they are very evidently freezing.

In part the ivories are just virtuoso exercises in realistically depicting the effects of cold. As early as the first century St Bart had provided a vigorous and scientifically observant account of the effects of extreme cold on the human body. 'The body that has been exposed to cold first becomes all livid as the blood freezes. Then it shakes and seethes, and its teeth chatter, the muscles are convulsed. A sharp pain and unspeakable agony follows. The extremities of the body are mutilated, as they are burnt by the frost as by a fire.'[23] It was many centuries before artists developed a visual vocabulary that was as vivid as what had been written down so long before.

They eventually did so not simply because at some point they wanted to 'move' people more than they had done previously. The art historian Henry Maguire has argued that the novel replication of suffering was the consequence of a renewed interest in the injunctions and rules of literary style, that the precepts advocated for good writing and rhetorical effect were

The Forty Martyrs of Sebaste. Images of them are often used to demonstrate the effects of a particular pain – extreme cold.

being taken seriously, and that these account for distinct aspects of the motifs used.[24] The vigour of the representation depended on the combination of close observation, attention to written accounts of the effects of cold, and the injunctions of rhetorical writing about how to influence audiences. The ivories are thus a visual rendering of a narrative innovation, and 'the sermons and hymns of the church influenced the ways in which they [artists] illustrated texts.'[25] For example, one contemporary sermon claimed that 'the true accounts of the gospels, succinct, undecorated, must be fleshed out, elaborated, and made more gripping for lay audiences.' This was a kind of 'selective realism'.[26]

Another explanation of why the ivories depicting the fate of the Forty

Martyrs were so keen to demonstrate particular suffering is that they represented a rediscovery of classical and pagan models. They were another kind of exercise: one of reinvention. Thus the ivories make use of motifs – such as the tender image of the older, bearded man protecting a younger one – which the art historian Kurt Weitzmann has demonstrated were directly derived from classical origins.[27] But why did the craftsmen turn to these models? Was it because they wanted to depict the sufferings of the martyrs more graphically? The origin of the visual elements does not explain why they were reused, and to such dramatic effect. At the same time, the pieces had a different meaning from their classical sources, for the martyrs chose their death: they submitted to it willingly. The hunt was on to render specific suffering more tellingly, but its origins were more various than a single drive towards realism. The causes of more or less realistic accounts of suffering in the modern media are also complex. It is not the case that what we are shown simply reflects events.

The image of the Massacre of the Innocents provides another example of the way in which the reaction to horror changed over time. This event is referred to austerely in one sentence in St Matthew's Gospel, which reports that 'Then Herod, when he saw that he was mocked of the wise men, was exceeding wroth, and sent forth, and slew all the children that were in Bethlehem, and in all the coasts thereof, from two years old and under' (Matthew 2:16). This compelling story, based on a documented massacre, is an archetype of horror that lies behind many other images, and reverberates through the fate of innocents caught up in conflict ever since. The frenzied murder of innocent children – who, unlike the Forty Martyrs, were involuntary victims – occurs repeatedly in Western art as a comment on the recurrent phenomenon of state violence.

Early writers and painters who wanted to elaborate disasters and suffering had a ready-made source of imagery to call on: they could translate to a Christian setting the conventions of massacres in war. The sources for their depictions were, of course, both literary and visual. How the audience could be brought to respond to their efforts was quickly established as an issue. Quintilian (writing in the first century) observed:

Without doubt, he who says simply that the city was destroyed, embraces all the ills that such a misfortune comprises, yet he penetrates the emotion of his audience less because his brevity resembles a dispatch. But if you explain everything that the one word destroyed included, your audience will be shown the flames, the frenzy of the troops . . . the women and children weeping . . . the chained prisoners driven each before his captor, the woman trying to keep her infant and the victors

Martyrdom of St Erasmus, 303, under Diocletian, French, 1480–
90. The saint looks typically serene despite the agony of his torture,
because he is secure about his place in heaven.

fighting for the biggest share of the loot . . . And this peak, as I see it, of excellence,
is very easy to reach.[28]

Quintilian's words would not be out of place in a contemporary newsroom. He was advocating emotional identification and colour. Moreover,
he went further. He argued that when you made the pain of the victim vivid
and living you stood on the side of civilization. But if you failed to involve
the audience you became a collaborator in the crime and colluded in the

damage that was done. Even your allies, he argued, commit acts in war that may be necessary but should not be ignored. More startlingly, he claimed that civilization depends on the attempt to comprehend the pain of the suffering victims – even if the destruction was unavoidable. Quintilian was not at all squeamish about the political necessity for violence on occasions, but he suggested that better political decisions would always be made if they were based on a realistic understanding of the costs.

Medieval saintliness and suffering were, of course, closely linked, and the suffering had to be overt and physical to be recognized. Many thirteenth- and fourteenth-century saints came to live out their own lives as fanatical – and uncomfortable – attempts to experience for themselves some of the pain of Jesus, and thus get closer to him. They also believed that their torment would offer a didactic model to contemporaries.[29] They thought that their colourful manifestations of grief, weeping and self-punishment made the suffering of Jesus and the martyrs 'present', immediate, urgent to those who saw them. Thus the experiences of the early saints and martyrs were reworked in this period in a dramatic attempt to move audiences. The object was to bring the pain of the past into the present, and to break down the barrier that exists between those who observe and those who experience suffering. The project was to facilitate the understanding of the pain of others.[30]

Indeed, by the fourteenth century a new generation of believers was prepared to go to extraordinary lengths to imitate Christ's sufferings. Their strange self-multilations and chastisements, the apparent perversity and the obsessive ingenuity of their pursuit of self-punishment, are almost incomprehensible today, outside the casebooks of abnormal psychology. Self-punishing martyrs were known to weep inordinately for years. They starved themselves. Some supposedly neither consumed nor excreted, or refused to wash and welcomed infections. They scourged themselves, and vigilantly advanced their privations into every corner of their experi- ence. They went on pilgrimages barefooted, and lived in tiny cages in cathedrals. If they were frozen they threw their blankets away, if they were hot they bundled them on – all in pursuit of more fully experienced castigation. There was a competitive element, with would-be saints taking self-inflicted suffering to ever more ecstatically experienced limits. Thus Catherine of Siena starved herself to death, and Bridget of Sweden died of sores induced by deliberate self-neglect. One particularly remorseless saint, Henry Suso, slept bound to a cross and wore a shirt of nails while exposed to the elements. When he noticed that he was scratching the insect bites he received, having 'so joyfully offered myself to be food for the insects', he had his hands tied so that he was no longer able to enjoy such indulgent relief.[31] Great ingenuity was used to produce more exquisite torments, and Suso also developed what Richard Kieckhefer has called a new genre, the 'autohagiography', in which the saint described himself when bound as 'tormented by noxious insects, crying aloud and twisting around in agony as a woman does when run through with a needle'.[32]

Modern commentators have often been appalled by the self-inflicted extremes of suffering of the late medieval saints, and have sought scientific explanations for their behaviour. The nineteenth-century American philosopher and psychologist William James, referring to the case of Henry Suso, commented how bizarrely pathological the saint appears from our point of view.[33] However, the phenomenon also needs to be seen in social, as opposed to merely individual, terms. The novelist Günter Grass has observed that Dorothy of Mantua, a German saint of the period, was 'more fool than clever', tormented by insomnia and migraine, and a 'slovenly housekeeper yet remarkably efficient when it came to organizing processions of flagellants and her own career of saintly suffering'.[34] There was in fact a context in which these 'unquiet souls' need to be understood. Significantly, the self-torturers were often women, or men from the lower social orders, who through their penances were able to claim an authority independent of the Church and its hierarchies. Suffering was seen as an opportunity for personal growth and also for social mobility.

Modern news is part of a long tradition which attempts to represent the pain of others to us. Such a project is difficult, however, because pain is impossible for any fellow human being to share and there are many bars to communicating it. If someone suffers a physical pain, no observer, however compassionate, empathetic and sympathetic he or she may be, can share the experience of that reality. The American therapy-talk 'I feel your pain', implying a capacity for empathy, has entered the canon of contemporary humour precisely because everyone knows it is untrue: pain is personal to the sufferer. 'English,' wrote Virginia Woolf, 'has no words for a shiver or a headache . . . The merest schoolgirl when she falls in love has Shakespeare or Keats to speak her mind for her, but let a sufferer try to describe a pain in his head to a doctor and language at once runs dry.'[35] Although we all know what a 'headache' means, the particular qualities of different pains in the head are inexpressible. Pain is, according to the World Health Organization, 'a physical and an emotional experience'.[36] That is, pain involves both a sensation and also an emotional reaction to that sensation. Indeed, while some pains can be identified, we still have few words for the larger issue of how someone's whole condition – which may be more complex than a pain – alters. A doctor's most pertinent question is still the very simple one 'How do you feel today?'

Most of us in the contemporary world have seen very little – if any – of the variety of suffering involved in terrible illnesses. We are very remote from anguish. 'Illness' is a feeble word to describe a whole range of experiences. Some illness is titanic, with a patient's body involved in a mighty, active struggle that looks like the Greek sculpture of Laocoön – the Trojan priest who prophesied the capture of Troy and who, with his sons, is shown wrestling with two mighty sea serpents. Other illness is a series of sharp assaults on the body and person – like El Greco's depiction of Laocoön (a picture believed to be a commentary on the tortures used by the Spanish Inquisition on the Bishop of Toledo).[37] Other experiences can only be endured – the slow rolling through a body of symptoms. The contemporary vocabulary of disease as a battle is insulting to the range of experiences endured by those who suffer – and often limits the understanding of the bravery, courtesy and bitter realism with which individuals face their fate.

Indeed, too fluent an expression of pain can invite scepticism, even ridicule, while the stoicism with which pain is borne was (and is) seen as a sign of its authenticity. Consequently, one of the objects of an effective communication of pain is that it should obey contemporary conventions. There are social and cultural differences in the expression and acknowledgement of pain. The medical specialism concerned with analgesia developed particularly early in Great Britain, and some historians have argued that this is partly because of British social norms. Thus one writer argues that the English and Scottish pre-eminence in anaesthetics and analgesics developed because 'Valuing reserve very highly meant that there was a real urgency in the quest for the means to maintain reserve.'[38] Another suggested explanation is that Victorian Britain combined scientific curiosity with optimistic confidence that regarded the alleviation of pain as progress. In addition, Protestantism did not see pain as a path to salvation. Changes in how pain is represented thus reflect alterations in the evaluation of pain, rather than its essential nature.

Representing pain also poses many problems. Charles Darwin was deeply perturbed by the dilemmas involved in clarifying what visual symptoms of agony meant. On the one hand he noted that photographs showing a man in pain were frequently misunderstood, and quite different feelings were ascribed to the images. There was no simple, universal visual expression of pain; interpreting the pictures required a text.[39] On the other hand he was equally anxious that what *looked* like the pain expressed in the writhings

El Greco's Laocoön *(believed to be a commentary on the torture of the Bishop of Toledo by the Inquisition). This image is a viscerally accurate portrayal of one aspect of a mortal illness.*

of worms should not be dismissed. Darwin was a worm expert, and carried out exhaustive experiments on the boundaries of their sensitivity. He flashed lights at them, put red-hot pokers near them, and used his children to test their hearing: 'Bernard blew a whistle,' according to two of his biographers, 'Frank played his bassoon, Emma performed on the piano, and Bessy shouted, but no worms were roused.'[40] The creatures apparently did not react when subject to any of these stimuli. But when you cut them in two, Darwin observed, 'they generally writhe about with frightful contortions,' and it *looked* to him as if they were in pain.[41]

How to represent pain may depend on context. Doctors typically perceive pain differently from patients. The professionals are interested in what the pain means, while the patients want the pain removed. In fact medical researchers have often submitted themselves to extraordinary experiments in pursuit of answers to pain. Until the 1960s pain was still often seen medically as an inevitable aspect of the experience of the recovering medical patient. Analgesics were prescribed with a view to the long-term health of the subject. It took a revolution in perception to understand the pain of the terminally ill patient as requiring – and permitting – a quite different response to pain relief, which was to attend to the quality of the patient's remaining life, not their long-term health. It was with the emergence of the hospice movement that this new attitude developed, as part of a larger concern to provide patients with the means to be more in control of their experience (perhaps for the sake of others as well as themselves).[42] It was also a product of research that had become increasingly concerned to locate the experience of pain within particular parts of the brain and with the speed and nature of communication of the sensation.[43]

Communicated pain always poses a problem for observers (even if they dismiss it): what ought bystanders to do for the sufferer? Yet communicating pain is a precondition for its alleviation. 'Anyone who suffers pain tries to stop it as soon as possible by his own action or with the help of others,' observed Robert Melzack, a pioneer in the contemporary medical interest in pain. 'First there is the need to communicate with others and those others may have difficulty in understanding the nature of the suffering.'[44] Indeed, while communicating pain may be necessary for the sufferer, it often produces suspicion. It is this suspicion which is the origin of what has been called the 'doubt' that always surrounds another's pain.

Medieval art sought to overcome this 'doubt' through the accomplished mastery and realism of its representation. Modern media approach the problem through devices which accentuate the reality of the depictions, but also by procedures that rank-order pain and prioritize competing claims for attention. 'This pain,' a newspaper or television bulletin in effect claims, 'matters more to you the audience than this other pain.' At the same time the purveyors of news claim that the processes of news, as well as its reputation and habitual place in the life of the audience, should overcome any doubt that spectators may have about its representation of the pain of others. When a BBC news executive claims simply that 'the trust of the audience is the single most valuable thing we have,'[45] he is talking about the conditions which make the authoritative allocation of causes possible. If great paintings have persuasive artistry to advance their case, then great news has persuasive accuracy, a repertoire of procedures, familiarity with reliable presenters, and audience respect to assist it in performing the same role.

But can we quantify pain, and how can we understand it unless we share a language to describe it that we all acknowledge as legitimate? The attempt to measure pain is clearly part of what the media do. Partly through news values, they establish exchange rates for suffering. Meanwhile, it is assumed that they provide some base for comparison of different pains: that the hierarchy of pain they communicate is just. This is a familiar aspect of how the media give attention to a foreign war or an international disaster. At the same time, they exercise influence when there are clashes of fundamental values within societies. Thus, in general, we believe that everyone who needs a kidney transplant should get one, irrespective of wealth; but we recognize that, because of organ scarcity, some allocation will inevitably occur, and some patients will be unfortunate losers. The problem is to reconcile the principle and the allocation as conditions change. The news all too often articulates competing values, but gives no attention to the necessary choice. The news also involves allocation, as airtime (or audience attention time) is scarce. As a result, the news media highlight some causes of suffering or injustice in ways that are often unfair and arbitrary.

There is a parallel here: in a way, news-gatherers and medical practitioners are both in the business of dealing in suffering, and both have to make similar claims. The shared problem is that in expressing pain it is not just that we do not have words, but rather that it is difficult to pin down what words mean. Melzack attempted to tackle this problem by explaining the experience of pain in terms of metaphors of communication. The originality of his approach lay in the attempt to produce both a measure and an agreed set of standards for describing and evaluating pain. The researchers developed a graded and comprehensive set of words and descriptions which, in conjunction with the McGill Pain Questionnaire, formed a diagnostic tool. This made it possible for patients to describe the unique character of their particular pain in a way that allowed comparisons to be made. However artificially, a set of referents was established which permitted real communication about specific pain, taking the observing clinician nearer to the unique individual pain of the patient.

Conventional medical vocabulary described only whether pain was more or less intense. (Although doctors recognized that specific pains were symptomatic of some diseases, they had no precise vocabulary to codify the differences.) Melzack, however, believed that intensity was only one aspect of the experience of pain. His project was to identify the variety of painful experiences. Patients described pain as pulsing – with a temporal dimension. Or it was described as hot and burning – providing a thermal aspect. Shooting and mobile pains were contrasted with others described as static and grinding, and so on. Melzack's work was pioneering because he believed that more adequate description, or expression, of the detail of the pain would assist both in finding effective, appropriate pain relief and in making diagnosis more reliable. At the same time, it offered a breakthrough in the communication of pain to others.

Arguably, it was not an accident that the problem of communicating pain was the focus of innovative research in the 1960s – a decade in which interest in many kinds of communication intensified. Yet the metaphor of pain as a system of communication was taken further. Even pain within the individual patient was also seen as a form of expression, and its experience was believed to be determined by selective 'gatekeepers' within the person – physical, social and psychological barriers which establish and direct different pain experiences. The theory sought to explain both individual differences in pain thresholds and also the varied cultural experiences of pain. In addition, different emotional relationships to pain influence how it is experienced. Thus Melzack and his colleagues were arguing that pain itself was best understood as something that was edited in various ways.

It remains the case that pain can be tackled only if it is communicated.[46] The social scientist Elizabeth Scarry points out that, 'though there is ordinarily no language for pain, with the desire to eliminate pain, an at least fragmentary means of verbalization is available both to those who are themselves in pain and to those who wish to speak on behalf of the pain others endure.'[47] The media play a crucial role in quantifying and articulating pain – and in doing so they legitimate the pain they communicate.

Anyone responsible for an ill child knows how acute the problem of communicating the relative severity of the pain to medical staff can be – quite apart from the problem of what the pain might mean. A number of studies have shown how doctors and nurses are frequently reluctant to give children adequate analgesic relief, both because they are more anxious about the health consequences of the medication for children and also because they find it harder to evaluate the severity of pain in the case of children. Especially stoic adult patients may also fail to get the comfort they need; they may require an advocate, intimate with the individual's own scales of endurance, and capable of translating them for medical staff. Articulating pain and putting it in a scale that is shared is thus vital for its relief. Many of the developments in journalism can similarly be seen as ways of attempting to communicate to audiences the nature of a distant suffering in the terms of an agreed scale. The conflict between a reporter's judgement of the value of a story of this kind and that of editors, or the weight of news values that prefer a celebrity's minor scandal to genuinely dreadful predicaments that have been witnessed, is one of the most frustrating experiences for journalists. The arbitrariness of news attention is felt forcibly in this area.

It is not merely that the reporting of a particular disaster is inevitably pushed through the ruthless machine of the parochial news values of the nation with the dominant news industries. Nor even that these values may be becoming more international, because of the globalization of news technology that makes it easier to buy glossy news from cheap international providers. It is also because our sense of the order of things requires a historical framework, and a sense of place, and an understanding of comparative seriousness. All these are increasingly distant from news production. At the same time, we rely on journalism to give us a sense of shared perspective on the seriousness of competing pains that call for our attention. This is why medieval pictures and modern news both concentrate on the suffering of individuals. It is of course far easier to display as dramatic the consequences of disasters rather than their causes. In sum, there are barriers to depicting distinct and specific pains – yet without a sense of each pain's peculiarity it cannot be addressed.

One mechanism for calculating and communicating suffering has involved the increasing willingness for the news to depict the impact of suffering on bodies. Although different societies tolerate – or welcome – distinctly varied degrees of explicitness in representing suffering in this way, nevertheless even the most reticent have favoured increasingly explicit imagery. Thus modern media representations of suffering share more than purposes with their medieval predecessors. They also share a curious interest in displaying the impact of particular kinds of suffering on their victims. A feature of many of the paintings of the late medieval period is an interest in injured or dismembered bodies. Typically, Christ, descended from the cross, points at his own wounds. Thomas, the disciple who doubted the reality of the resurrected Saviour, is frequently shown inserting a cautious finger into the wound in Christ's side to convince himself of its corporeal existence. Saints and martyrs who suffer extreme forms of execution are sometimes shown in their subdivided pieces – St Agatha's severed breasts are presented in one Florentine image like a couple of blancmanges. Picturing the saints' fragmentation and Christ's wounds were (among other things) attempts to convey the outer limits of endurance of the holy martyrs to spectators. News may perform a similar function, providing illustrations of the extremes of human experience which satisfy audiences' curiosity.

Saints separated from their heads, limbs and organs are made whole again on the Day of Judgement, so all is well. Yet this too is a theme with which we are familiar. The disintegrated hero is an important part of contemporary popular culture, as is his miraculous reintegration. There is a vast industry devoted to the 'realism' of special effects which attempt to simulate reality. Our attitudes towards bodily fragmentation are complex. We take it for granted that the surgical removal of malignant parts of our bodies may be redemptive, and even losing bits of yourself for cosmetic reasons is increasingly accepted. Until recently, 'real' bodily dismemberment was seen as especially sensitive and was often removed from media news stories – or was alluded to rather than displayed. However, conventions have been rapidly altering, so that the consequences of beheadings in Iraq filmed for propaganda purposes (and indeed performed for display), to bring pressure on Western opinion, are shown, although the moment of death is excluded from television news.

Bodily fragmentation is the object of considerable regulation and discussion among journalists and broadcasters. Coverage of the Vietnam War of the 1960s and '70s broke with many of the older conventions and displayed the impact of the war on the injured from the start; this in turn has led to what one journalist called the 'long shadow' of Vietnam.[48] Such pictures, although more frequent, still provoke anxiety. Talking about dismemberment, writing about it, describing it are acceptable. Showing news or documentary images of it, on the other hand, has so far often been unacceptable. When four British hostages were beheaded in Chechnya in 1999, Russian television showed the heads lined up beside the road, but no one in the West – not even on any American channel – showed this easily available footage. When Special Forces landed in Afghanistan in 2001 the Taliban claimed to have killed several Americans, and as proof they displayed a boot – complete with foot – not shown in the West. There remain systematic cultural differences in the willingness to contemplate dismemberment. When an international television news conference after 11 September discussed the events of that day, it became clear that Catholic European and South American broadcasters had shown far more explicit footage of the disaster than their northern counterparts. Some speculated that different religious heritages had influenced attitudes towards news images.[49] Whatever the reason, in news broadcasting, images are frequently edited just before evidence of bodily fragmentation appears.

The medieval impulse to articulate subtle and terrible aspects of the human predicament through the representation of suffering resulted in an astonishing artistic legacy. The aim was to mobilize sentiment and perhaps action. This preoccupation with suffering also broke the isolation of pain and invited a more communal sympathy and sharing. It directed attention towards suffering. Pain was paradoxically valued, and those in pain were redeemed, at least for a moment, from their own solitary experience because their suffering elevated them. Similarly, a willingness to contemplate the suffering of the world in the news depends in part on a perhaps unjustified, but nevertheless potent, sense of the virtue gained – and exhibited – in such knowledge.

In an introduction to an exhibition called 'The Image of Christ', the then director of the National Gallery, Neil MacGregor, observed that

in the hands of the great artists, the different moments and aspects of saints' lives become archetypes of the human experience. The Virgin nursing her son conveys the feelings every mother has for her child. They are love. Christ crucified is innocence and goodness beset by violence. In the sufferings of Christ we encounter the pain of the world ... These are pictures that explore truths not just for Christians but for everybody.[50]

A related capacity to generalize comes into play that distinguishes between two kinds of human-interest story. One kind may provide access to comprehending a more general problem. The other kind focuses attention not on the new event in the outside world but on the weary and familiar cliché: its purpose is to repeat the cosily expected. The purpose of one is to expand understanding; the purpose of the other is to distract attention from potentially disturbing novelty.

Many distinguished works of Christian art representing suffering were endowed with immense authority because the beliefs they were expressing were so pivotal to the material and spiritual power in the society that they functioned in. They were commissioned and displayed by the powerful, and were invectives in disputes over the interpretation of the divine. They were always also political – at least in the sense that politics is about groups with interests in the outcomes of understanding.

News occupies a similar place in our modern secular societies. Indeed, insofar as democracy is the religion of our time – one outside whose confines few can think – then news plays a critical part. It intercedes and interprets on behalf of interests, but it also expresses commitments.

Clearly, contemporary images of suffering can be mobilized in order to argue for compassion, to bring action, to alter and transform. In our secular age, however, the focus for the intercession is not the divine being. We have a new sacred subject, equally vulnerable to heated doctrinal disputes. It is the public – the public in the heaven of stable, rich, 'compassionate' democracies (especially the United States). These democracies are compassionate in the sense that they are able to act with transformative charity to feed, water, clothe, bring peace, intervene or fight for those who suffer

– not that they necessarily do act thus. It is the media that intercede, and, while the public is addressed, it is public opinion as a pressure on political life that is the object of intercession. What was divine is now secular – and, on closer examination, uncomfortably partisan.

Indeed, the language of medieval imagery works perfectly well to discuss the media's use of suffering. The media condense, articulate and clarify the wants of the needy: they give pain a shape. They also distribute importance, placing suffering in a hierarchy. It is their interpretive role that makes the contemporary media simultaneously so powerful and so arbitrary. The aim of the creation of images of the suffering of the Christian saints was in part to give the faithful a greater understanding and comprehension of the suffering of the martyrs, or the nature of Christ. But they were also intended to draw the hearts of the viewers and listeners to God, and simultaneously to draw God to special and favourable consideration of their needs.

In many ways, of course, the Christian inheritance of valuing pain may have contributed to an indifference to alleviating it. And there is evidence that even when solutions to pains are well known and effective, for instance in the palliative treatment of cancer patients, they are often not used. The World Health Organization has argued that 'routine evaluation of pain helps to make pain "visible" so that it is not ignored,' but that this still needs to be built into regular medical assessments in many parts of the world.[51] Similarly, the WHO maintains that 'palliative' care which involves treating the compound of 'total' pain, comforting, and addressing patients' anxieties as well as their physical suffering, is still rare. Meanwhile the media elaboration of minor pain may blunt our capacity to comprehend the awesome stoicism of those who suffer great pain.

What was created in great medieval art was not a simple reflection of the reality of suffering. Although some works represent enduring comments on human pain, even these were a product of a long-drawn-out process that changed the imagery as well as the aims of the depictions of suffering. Suffering was enlisted for new ends. We watch and read about suffering that is often quite as extreme as that in earlier Christian representations, but whose effects are not as intensely felt. We live in a world where pain is unavoidable. On the one hand we expect palliatives to be efficient, and the relief of some kinds of pain is taken very seriously. On the other hand, there is very limited public understanding of the everyday pain of those in a hospital ward near you, let alone in distant places. Indeed, just as in the earlier period there were substantial historical shifts in the willingness to consider others' suffering, the present relationship between reflection on pain and remedial action is neither simple nor direct. These issues are now

Children flee after the napalming of their village in South Vietnam, 8 June 1972, one of the powerful political images that shaped, legitimated and articulated suffering.

principally explored in the press and broadcasting and within the confines of the conventions of the Internet. They themselves become the subject of the news. Indeed, news conventions may owe more than is recognized to a tradition of displaying pain and a long-distant evangelical purpose.

Communicating pain and shaping its meaning are still very powerful political tools, and news constantly throws up images and stories of suffering which can be exploited. Just like great Christian art, the media compete with each other to articulate the suffering of others in ways that will arrest audience attention. The interpretation of such narratives can be the site of a fierce conflict of interests. Pain has to be represented in order to be addressed, but the conventions and politics of what it means are not static. On the one hand difficult political realities often get condensed by the news media into compelling narratives of suffering. On the other, the politics of different groups of victims – and competitive suffering – have played a significant part in many recent conflicts. Sometimes, because of a lack of local understanding (as in Rwanda), the media catastrophically identifies the victims wrongly. From the famous picture of a napalmed child in Vietnam, to atrocities in the Balkans, to the picture of a little Palestinian boy shot by the Israelis while sheltering in his father's arms in 2000, to wounded children in Iraq, images of pain have become powerful weapons.

Television has played a role in this as a kind of megaphone for suffering. Real-time news also focuses attention on the immediate physical impact of disasters, while mobile phones take us to the personal experience of individuals caught up in catastrophes, and generate yet another new, powerful, set of images of calamity. While surveillance cameras provide oddly impersonal, accidental footage, that from mobile phones has a novel intimacy, reporting to us from unfolding events. The news legitimates pains and arranges them in hierarchies. It articulates and shapes fears. Audiences view distant news suffering collectively, yet are often apparently indifferent for many reasons. One is that the news rarely gives the end of the story, but rushes on to the next absorbing tragic (or amusing) spectacle. One tragedy replaces another in a succession of misery. In addition, the differences between crises are often obscured by the ubiquity of the common repertoire of images of pain. But communicating suffering can be tremendously effective and produce life-saving action. One of the stranger products of contemporary news is a great political shift – to the politics of pain. As all suffering innocents know, redemption may be granted by having their plight displayed and their story told.

6

Wars and Sentimental Education

Sensibility is often claimed as the dominant mood of the age. Expressing emotions, it is now suggested, is honourable, healthy and a touchstone of authenticity. Performances are suspect, but real tears are highly valued as evidence of genuine feeling – particularly in broadcasting. This is the case even though tears inevitably turn attention away from the causes of the tears to the condition of the afflicted observer. Sentiment is now seen as less calculating than reason, and more reliable. Audiences believe they can judge the character of participants in public life on the basis of their behaviour under the spotlight of the media.[1] Thus, as more political realities are transformed into emotional narratives, audiences form their opinions of public events through their perceptions of the 'genuine' emotions of participants. News – surrounded by soap operas, drama, game shows and reality programmes – plays an important part in this process, although it is just one format competing for attention. While there are hugely significant differences in the values that drive various media organizations – so that the BBC, for example, when commissioning and putting out programmes, asks very different questions from those of a commercially and politically partisan station in America – nevertheless, genres of programmes are increasingly ubiquitous. And the competitive environment in which broadcasters do battle conditions how they all behave. Which leads us to the question: are the internationally owned media, with their local versions of worldwide programme formats, remaking the world's emotional responses?

The global technologies of communications and the marketing of goods internationally have led to shared forms of media content – that is to say, we all watch the same kinds of programme. This in turn may have produced a shared repertoire of emotional stories and reactions. We may all be moved by the same feelings, in the same way, all over the world. This is not to deny that there are different and even opposed interpretations of political realities, or that people interpret the same events in varying ways; nevertheless, the pattern of expected and approved feeling is increasingly dominated

133

by media-sanctioned formats. People prefer local content that refers to their own lives, but now it is often delivered as little more than a modified version of a more international form. While the common features of the human condition are experienced in dramatically different circumstances, our reactions to the accidents of fate may have become more predictable. If so, the media have undoubtedly played a part – educating the planet into narratives of response that are increasingly general. The emotional styles of what one critic has called 'soap opera time'[2] have seeped into everyone's lives. British reserve, Italian expressiveness, Arab shrewdness, Indian politeness, Russian fatalism, Scandinavian depressiveness, French elegance, Chinese inscrutability cease to apply in a world that shares an appetite for, and identifies with the cast of, *ER* or *Friends*; in which *Baywatch* is shown in 73 per cent of all nations; and in which young men in the Mahgrib, Liverpool and Bangkok listen to the same music and follow the same footballers.

There is also the more perturbing possibility: that we misinterpret apparently similar reactions to events, which may disguise more radical differences. Our capacity to appreciate the ways in which societies differ from each other has arguably been eroded over the last thirty years. We may be less in touch with the reality of the contemporary world than we need to be, and the media are one cause of this.

If so much can be said about entertainment values, could it also be that recent wars have been formatted by the media? This question has two aspects. One is the emotional styling that thrilling but not terribly threatening conflicts (for spectators) have been subject to, as news-vendors struggle to catch the public eye. Wars offer rich opportunities for colourful engagement. The other is that conflicts have to be justified increasingly by a global rhetoric. Of course, some kind of international media dialogue about wars is simply unavoidable, as pictures from one side are relayed to the other. Even in the aftermath of 11 September, when American policy-makers were given a free hand by domestic public opinion, and the catastrophe provided them with a unique diplomatic opportunity to intervene in world affairs (which they largely squandered), dissent at home at first found it hard to articulate any opposition through the media. But this domestic unanimity did not translate into a persuasive case for American actions abroad, where a large section of world public opinion became increasingly hostile to them. An international bazaar of images, emotional appeals and argument swirled around the world, affecting markets and arousing shock and interest – and a tingle of anxiety in comfortably removed places. The news also aroused compassion – but a compassion that was often the prompt for fury.

Successful television programme formats are now global. Are international emotions being re-engineered by these ubiquitous shows? Bodyguards separating fighting guests on The Jerry Springer Show, *April 1998.*

The role of the media in the shaping of feelings about conflicts has been accentuated because many recent wars have been nearer to matters of choice than to matters of necessity. The media have consequently played a greater part in their conduct. Whether wars should be declared, on what conditions they should be pursued, what levels and kinds of engagement are supported, what casualty levels on allied (and enemy) sides are accepted, and how conflicts are brought to a satisfactory conclusion are all matters that involve choosing between options. Confusingly, many recent conflicts have refused to obey the rules. During the decade that followed the Cold War, the constraints on behaviour imposed by the danger of potentially uncontrollable international conflict ceased to operate. During the Cold War any engagement had to be carefully weighed, as it might provoke catastrophic retaliation. But after its end that was no longer the case. When a new international uncertainty arose, as the unconventional attacks of terrorism apparently posed a new threat which was more difficult to estimate, responses became less calculated. Meanwhile the Western media and public had become used to wars that were small, involving few casualties on the Western side and embarked on, rather luxuriously, as one of the vanities of policy options.

In addition, the attempt to regulate international conflict has led to an increasingly common language for legitimizing aggression – one which the media have picked up and elaborated. Arguments about national self-interest have been replaced by a global language of compassion and democracy. This has been true even when – as in the war in Iraq in 2003 – the USA has chosen to ignore international regulation, claiming to be doing so in accordance with its own superior understanding and dedication to ideals that, in its eyes, international bodies inadequately espoused. Indeed, the rhetoric of the Iraq war may have damaged the capacity to argue for it rationally. This global language has been an aspect of international conflict ever since the foundation of the League of Nations in 1919. Such bodies initiated a political process which justified some conflicts and created the 'illegality' of others. Such diplomatic rhetoric is long-established: what is new is the role of the media in giving global currency to the language of Western humanitarianism. This common set of arguments also reflects a reality of modern wars – that they address international public opinion, whether it wants to listen or not.

One way in which public sentiment has been educated is through the development of the 'human-rights' society and the wide range of organizations which campaign around such issues. However, this development was not simply the result of a more 'compassionate' view of international relations. Rather than an expression of the triumph of decency, it was at first a matter of expediency. Thus the historian Mark Mazower has argued persuasively that the concept of human rights was inserted into international agreements after the Second World War less because of a new-found surge in idealism than because the pre-war aim of protecting minorities (a key policy objective of the League of Nations) had been effectively abandoned. Such an aim was no longer desired – and, more importantly, it was no longer practical. The war had displaced minorities and broken up multi-minority nations, while the post-war settlement saw a massive relocation of other groups – for example German minorities – back within national boundaries. Human rights, Mazower suggests, were inserted into international agreements as a vague, but well-sounding, alternative to the protection of minority rights.[3] Only subsequently has the idea been developed into something more robust, through the growth of international law and the proliferation of pressure groups monitoring abuses – as well as through the erratic, but occasionally focused, attention of the media.

Some critics, seeing the increased role of the media in defining conflicts, have exaggerated and mistaken this role. Thus it has been implausibly suggested that wars are increasingly 'virtual' – in the sense that how they are perceived is more important than what happens in them. Such arguments raged over the Gulf War, and were raised again over the wars in Kosovo and Afghanistan.[4] Yet, although the media are implicated in every aspect of contemporary war, and a media-arbitrated public acceptance of wars is necessary, the outcomes of wars are not determined by perceptions. Conflicts still have real consequences, not fantasy ones. Even if some of the risks of some battlefields are diminished, the domestic political risks of going to war are still unpredictable. Thus while Margaret Thatcher's reputation and electoral fortunes were transformed positively by the Falklands War, and the war in Afghanistan in 2001 improved the position of the US president, and then became comfortably (for the governments involved) invisible (through a process of 'burying' a conflict which is quite different from ignoring it, as has been the case for over thirty years with the war in Sudan), the war in Iraq has had a more mixed domestic outcome. Despite President Bush's re-election, it divided American public opinion fiercely.[5] Wars are not virtual: nevertheless, recognition of the complexity of managing a disparate world public means that controlling the interpretation of events, which has always been part of any war effort, has become increasingly important. What used to be thought of as 'domestic' public opinion in any conflict has become international. Although many conflicts have a humanitarian aspect, how this is presented, and how effective it is in mobilizing support, is increasingly determined by media-defined rhetorics of just wars.

The feelings generated by and reflected in the news do not, however, exist in isolation. The stirring of feelings is big business. Television, films and video games all depend on selling emotion. While international affairs impinge on the market for the products of the media industries, they also provide trading opportunities. Thus, in the case of computer games the commercial goal has been the production of systems that combine the 'emotional and narrative engagement of the movies with the direct personal involvement – and feelings – of taking part in competitive sport'.[6] Indeed, the startling relation of computer games to reality was underlined by the attack on the World Trade Center, which was instantly recognizable to the initiated – especially the parents of adolescents – as a game brought to life. In addition, much of the media trades in the emotional narratives of soap operas, game shows and sad stories about animals. These formats are remarkably international in appeal, with only minor regional variations. While the British like 'reality' programmes that show sick pets in reassuringly cared-for environments,[7] dog- and cat-eating Chinese and Koreans prefer shows about sick children in similarly caring circumstances. However, some formats seem to be sweeping the world. Thus Afghanistan has its own version of the *Archers*, for this half-century-old agriculturally based radio soap has proved an elastic international success in twenty-three nations. Indeed, the true mark of the success of a contemporary soap or game show is its cultural universality: the world television industry is now dominated by the hunt for formats (*Big Brother*, *Who Wants to be a Millionaire?*) that can easily slot into a variety of different national systems. Soap operas cross continents, attracting devoted fans wherever they go. While some soap operas, locally made and attuned to their immediate society, can pick up and enhance the public debate about contemporary issues (even issues in the news), many made for international markets have become decreasingly realistic and increasingly melodramatic.[8] The news is made to be seen by an audience which is attuned to the emotional melodrama of soaps. Is the coverage of foreign conflicts so very different in its approach? Perhaps we have come to expect wars to be formatted as entertainment.

What are the ingredients? One is that events should be brief and action-packed. It is not only sound bites that have got shorter – so have wars. In the case of Iraq, it has been argued that the Coalition believed that it had little more than a fortnight to 'conquer' the country before the public and the media would become restless.[9] There is also the requirement that the tide should all move in one direction – towards a resolution, with very few sub-plots – and an assumption that resolution is possible: that the game can be won, that the hero can prevail, that individual character and moral ascendancy are sufficient to produce a solution. Finally there is the expectation that feelings may be involved, but that they will be used for benign purposes.

However, the news has also produced its own unique dramatic emotional forms – and they are awesome. Some events, for a variety of reasons, become world news events. Crashing through television schedules, commanding attention everywhere, they are attended to at home and at work, in communion with screens and speakers. Assassinations, natural disasters, terrorist attacks, royal weddings and royal deaths are all candidates for these collective efflorescences. Such public events are the most highly prized media happenings, often blurring the divide between the sacred and the profane and establishing a new civic religion that is international in its dimensions, though barely recognized. As Daniel Dayan and Elihu Katz argue in *Media Events: The Live Broadcasting of History*, 'When television networks mount a great event they do not mobilize their entertainment

division or drama department, they turn rather to the department of news
. . . for broadcasting officials [news] is in charge of reality.'[10] Ostensibly the
narrative resources of news are less rich than those of drama, yet many of
the same processes are involved: heightening tension, injecting conflict,
exploring the movement of the story, and so on, all conducted on the
unpredictable material of history. These huge events provide the opportunity for compulsive sharing of sentiments, shaping our sensibilities.

*News formats, like much else in television, are instantly recognizable and look
very similar all over the world. However, the all-important news processes and
values of different organizations remain radically different. News is a great
orchestrator of emotions.*

Thus it is a feature of such events that they shift public attitudes. Usually
the impact of the media is long-term, incremental, diffuse and more effective
in reinforcing beliefs than in changing them. Yet great media moments can
bring about sudden and dramatic movements in public understanding and
expectations. They are moments when media accounts of events have a
dramatically enhanced role. It may be that they mark epochs (or that they
come to be used to do so). Thus the attacks of 11 September, whose causes
and consequences were ordered and explained by broadcast news with
remarkable speed and authority – even as potential anarchy developed –
marked some kind of end and some kind of beginning, and the world which
witnessed them understood the effect to be momentous. However, it may

also be that such events crystallize transformations in mood that are already developing, or rapidly produce mutations. At times the media can accelerate moods. Thus political change had been gathering speed throughout the Eastern Bloc before 1989, but the sight of cars full of migrants streaming freely out of East Germany produced a sudden and unexpected momentum. 'Within hours when everyone could see nothing was being done to stop the people leaving – then the previously unthinkable became today's possibility,' noted the historian Robert Darnton, commenting on the pictures that heralded the end of the Communist regime all over the region. 'It was like dynamite to watch.'[11] Moreover, such spectacles taught audiences about political structures and provided vivid tableaux of power in a society. 'You could see power draining away,' commented an East German, 'like water down a drain with every car that you saw, with your own eyes on television, moving out.'[12] The sudden, shared vision of possibility altered people's lives, brought down a regime, and changed the world. It was composed out of a classic media process: a loop showing the audience its own behaviour.

Thus the media are able to mould emotional responses for many different purposes. News is just one of a whole variety of materials that provide the opportunity to wield feelings. But the feelings that news attends to are particularly close to the feelings that politics seeks to mobilize. It has been argued that allegiance through sentiment and identification has become more important in democracies than it used to be – helping to fill the gap created by the collapse of ideological dogmas and the changing nature of political parties' relations to the groups they represent. Many parties in secure democracies are less narrowly tied to the interests of specific groups than they used to be – partly because some of the big building blocks of democratic party allegiance (class, region, work) have altered and in some cases disappeared, and so politicians have felt it necessary to build other kinds of basis for support, but also because electoral politics has increasingly favoured some groups over the interests of others. Thus, for example, historically in most mature democracies the majority was poverty-stricken, and hence favoured ameliorative policies. By contrast, as the American economist J. K. Galbraith observed, towards the end of the twentieth century, the majority of people in such societies are now better off and are less in favour of redistribution.[13] This has made arguing for social justice more difficult. As the interests of the groups that parties represent have become more diverse, the importance of presentation in the political process – and thus the role of the media – has grown. People used to vote almost ritually. They do so still, but they now more often ask themselves whether they like politicians rather than whether they like their policies. Wars, which are essentially political, have in this way become very vulnerable to emotional interpretation and argument.

The internationalization of the media has meant that there is an export trade in the images of conflict, just as there is in arms to fuel it, but how this influences wars has yet to be properly assessed. Nevertheless, there has evidently been a propaganda 'trickle-down' effect. Thus in recent years governments as little associated with humanitarian qualms as those of Russia, Indonesia and Pakistan have claimed to be conducting 'precision' or 'surgical' bombing campaigns. Using rhetoric borrowed from NATO and America, they have attempted to describe action in what they have seen to be the dominant vocabulary of international contemporary opinion. In fact only the USA and NATO have had the kind of sophisticated weapons that can discriminate between targets – and even these often miss, or hit badly chosen objectives. It is a truism, but still important, that even high-tech weapons are only as good as the political acumen which sets their targets.

However, there are genuine differences between different governments' attitudes towards casualties and different publics' views of acceptable casualty levels. Depending on the war and the countries involved, the media often ignore casualties or play down their importance in a situation in which vivid pictures of the dead and wounded are part of the everyday vocabulary of the news. But the view of casualties also depends on context. For example, while the NATO operation in Serbia sometimes bombed the wrong targets, and had imprecise objectives (despite its advanced equipment), its main constraint was the political precariousness of the coalition that supported it – which in turn was answerable to all of the domestic opinions that it represented, each of which was anxious about civilian casualties. These were powerful limitations in a war in which nevertheless many Serbs (who were in danger of being bombed) felt that the short-term cost of casualties was the necessary price for getting rid of an oppressive regime. Moreover, as one defence correspondent has pointed out, very few reporters had any expert understanding of the nature of military equipment and its capacities. 'Too many journalists had no idea of what was happening in Serbia. NATO had some really sophisticated kit, but to judge what they are doing you need to understand it.'[14] The difference between genuine caution and callous cynicism matters in any judgement of conduct in conflict, yet it often gets blurred. This all takes place against the steady transfer of risk from soldiers to civilian populations, who by the end of the twentieth century had become overwhelmingly the principal casualties of conflict.[15]

Thus the involvement of highly developed media systems has changed the way in which conflicts can be defended in the national–global arena.

According to some analysts, the new internationalization of the spectatorship of wars has also produced the possibility of a novel regulation of conflict. Thus the suggestion has been made that the media, by making of us all witnesses, help foster a contemporary hostility to war in general that goes beyond mere repugnance at one's own side taking casualties. People are upset by what they see, and this emotion can be regarded as a positive force in world affairs. Mary Kaldor, for example, argues that the 'global-witness' phenomenon might lead to a system of humanitarian intervention which would be based on international institutions building on 'islands of civility' in war-torn societies, involving 'cosmopolitan law enforcement that would underpin a cosmopolitan regime'.[16] According to this view, the globalized media are essential to such a potential world order. Such a possibility, however, presupposes even-handedness. In practice much of the media inevitably takes sides, seeking to back the 'virtuous' good against the 'culpable' bad. It goes without saying that reality is seldom so simple. Usually the choices that have to be made are political – between the least unacceptable regime when none may be entirely attractive, or for the one with the greatest likelihood of building a relatively legitimate state. These processes take decades, and are given little or no attention by the media, who have largely abandoned incremental, sustained reporting of foreign places.[17] The political realism that is necessary to bring conflicts to a close, end terrorism or sustain a fragile political system is not produced by media obsession with attention-catching suffering.

There are other consequences of the ways in which conflicts are reported. Wars are often caused by political and intelligence failures. Sometimes these failures are single events, as in the mishandling of Argentina before the Falklands War; sometimes they are the result of long-standing misapprehensions and ignorance. The media play a role in these miscalculations – frequently by accepting too passively the political priorities of home governments: the run-up to the war in Iraq was marked by as much a failure of intelligence, local knowledge and informants by the media as by governments. In addition, the conduct of conflict changes the balance of politics within states. In particular, the conduct of war centralizes power dramatically. In Britain or America, this takes the form of concentrating business in the centre. 'War is a very No. 10 affair,' according to the late Sir Frank Cooper, former Permanent Secretary at the Ministry of Defence. 'It is a very White House affair. It is quite difficult, because everyone else in government gets out of the loop.'[18] This can be misleading.

Authorities often attempt to control the publicity given to images of body remains, because such pictures can powerfully sway public opinion during a conflict.

The news media need a steady supply of thrilling uncertainty – and many stories exaggerate risk. Of course there may be military advantage in doing so, and wars have great uncertainties associated with them. Nevertheless, short-term outcomes may have been less insecure in many recent conflicts than they were presented as being at the time. Occasionally the illusion of danger may be fostered to legitimize attacks, when the outcome of engagements is in fact relatively predictable (even if the outcome of the conflict as a whole may be uncertain). Alternatively, the failure (or success) of individual engagements may be given exaggerated importance by 'embedded' journalists. This in itself is a mark of the extent to which wars are played through the lens of the media into the theatre of international opinion – or at least the opinion of those nations deemed part of the community that matters in this respect. On any rational assessment it was always likely that NATO could defeat Serbia, the Americans 'defeat' the Taliban in Afghanistan, and Russia, up to a point, at least brutally contain Chechnya. On the other hand, these were not conflicts without risk. Indeed, we may now have been lulled by quick 'victories' into underestimating risks. As one observer points out, 'One day there may be a war again that can't be won so easily – and that really tests armies and publics.'[19] Yet increasingly the mobilization of worldwide domestic public opinion about international events has developed a degree of autonomy from the conduct of wars itself. Hence domestic support for wars and international views of those wars, both as expressed and as elicited by the media, have become part of the strategic management of conflict.

Considerations of media impact now play a part in tactical decisions that lie at the very heart of conflicts. Whether to deploy certain troops, what advances to make (or not make), and so on, may all now also be decided with an eye to the media – or, in other words, with an eye to how media audiences will come to understand what happens. Soldiers have come to take media considerations very seriously. During the Kosovo campaign, Mark Latey, the BBC defence correspondent, pointed out that military tactics and strategy were framed not in response to media criticism, but rather by calculating future media reactions. The attempt to second-guess media response was built into the most sensitive military campaign thinking. The journalist's point was about not the dominance of 'virtual' conflict, but rather the way in which the media are now at the heart of tactical and strategic thinking, and operate as a guiding factor. The military has to consider media-trained public sentiment all the time. Targets are set, levels of weaponry are chosen, routes are selected, bombs are detonated, and, most critically, armaments are developed all in the light of how their effects will play on the media stage.[20]

The way in which modern wars are also, in this respect, a kind of ceremonial theatre is demonstrated by the curious emergence of the strategic value of victimhood in contemporary hostilities involving democracies. This is the product of a healthy anxiety about casualties, for victims are the most important commodity in the politics of modern wars – and it is not only Islamic terrorists who appreciate their value. Wars have often been presented as just responses to illegitimate attacks. A novel feature of modern wars, however, is that the way in which they are judged by international public opinion has at times to be sustained by fresh losses rather than victories. Losses may not be desired, but they can, paradoxically, have great political value in the media-led international-opinion battle. This has to be qualified, however: the losses must be moderate, and the effect depends on context. Thus, for example, the British sinking of the Argentinian ship the *General Belgrano* in the Falklands conflict was balanced 'luckily – though that is a strange thing to say', as Sir Frank Cooper put it[21] – by the Argentinian sinking of HMS *Antelope*. Equally, the brutal Serbian attack on civilians in the marketplace in Sarajevo was so successful in mobilizing public opinion against the Serbs that they began to say that it had been a Bosnian ploy – and so on.

The emergence of the politics of victimhood is an aspect of the way in which contemporary conflicts are matters of preference rather than inescapable necessity. It is this that makes the media's accounts of wars so critical, and also makes the need for informed public debate more vital to their conduct – yet also more problematic, because the stakes are so high. Despite the very real threats of the Cold War, international tensions never developed into war. However, during this period, as one defence correspondent put it, 'It was Armageddon or nothing – and even the most hard-bitten of news editors could see that Armageddon would be bad for circulation.'[22] During the Cold War, and especially after Vietnam, wars involving the West went out of fashion. In any case, military conflicts had to battle for media attention. Wars are expensive to cover – often nearly bankrupting newsrooms – and audiences expect them to be over quickly, rapidly losing interest if they are not. Advertisers do not like them either – a gloomy or a reverentially patriotic audience does not purchase things. During the invasion of Iraq, American television audiences quadrupled, but advertising revenue fell by a third.[23] Meanwhile, since the end of the Cold War, news editors have found a plethora of minor conflicts hard to judge. Some observers, like Michael Ignatieff and William Shawcross, see the new 'humanitarian' war as an opportunity to intervene on the side of those societies which demonstrate 'civility',[24] but unfortunately the real political problem of choosing the least unpleasant regime has not gone away. Indeed, the recent 'war' against terrorism, although described as a war of 'national' or perhaps 'cultural' survival, posed many problems typical of the confusing conflicts of the post-Cold War era. The debate was concerned with what kinds of attack or defence would be instrumental – or efficient – and was perhaps damaged by its failure to recognize the importance of the world audience.

In the representation of wars on television, there is also the problem of the proximity of fiction, fantasy and reality. Many noted how the images of attack in the first Gulf War looked disconcertingly like those in video games. Some observed that stirring tales of 'saving Jessica', the young American soldier rescued from a hospital during the Iraq war, seemed disconcertingly similar to a movie. In addition, wars on television have a generic similarity not only with popular culture, but also with each other. One explanation of the shocking European failure to intervene in the conflict in the former Yugoslavia was that a war firmly within Europe and fought less than 100 miles away from several European capitals looked, on

The Rambo Loop. An NPA secret camp, 31 March 1987, the Philippines. A real soldier in the picture wears a 'Rambo' cap, identifying himself with the fictional movie fighter.

screen, as remote as if it were in another continent. Remoteness has always been a reason for not going to war. In this case the remoteness was virtual, not physical. The journalist and historian Timothy Garton Ash labelled another version of this problem 'The Rambo Loop'. He suggested that when 'young male fighters charged across our screens, with black headbands and slung around with ammunition belts, they modelled themselves on Rambo'. However, he added, 'they also look to the viewer like Rambo – that is, fiction.'[25] Reality mimics familiar media virtual reality – and is then taken for unreal. It is not merely that combatants and spectators find this show exciting: they both confuse reality and fantasy.

Against this background, military experts have suggested that great armies with sophisticated technologies and vast bureaucratic support lines are becoming increasingly obsolete. They are far too costly and sensitive actually to use. According to the historian Martin Van Creveld, wars are becoming less a matter of conflict between formally established armies, and hardly ever a matter of battles.[26] He suggests that military organization has become bloated and increasingly inappropriate for tackling the enemies it has to confront. The American 'shock and awe' tactic of fast and over-whelming military action in Iraq was supposed to be a response to such an analysis. But, as it turned out, it was based on a stark failure to comprehend local political conditions. Van Creveld also argues that wars are increasingly becoming long-drawn-out guerrilla conflicts – in which civilian populations become the main targets of terror attacks. In such situations, where the results of combat are often ambiguous, the role of the media in defining the meaning of actions for the distant publics is large. Even the definition of what is a war is now largely media-led. Many of the world's protracted conflicts that fit Van Creveld's model are not described as wars at all. The anthropologist Tim Allen has argued that the most accurate definition of a war is not that there is a conflict – for there are many of these – but that there is one labelled as a war by the media.[27] Typically, the short campaigns which launch conflicts are seen as wars (as in Chechnya), but different terminology is used to describe the subsequent military occupation, mopping-up and resistance. Thus we need a more realistic language to describe the political and military mandates and to assess their relative success and failure – and to orchestrate public sentiment.

In these situations the media's resistance to, or compliance with, governing interpretations of what has happened becomes more sensitive. The ability of media coverage to shape public perceptions poses problems for journalists and media organizations alike. At the same time it is also central to the emergence of political solutions. Take the issue of knee-capping revenge punishments in the protracted conflict in Northern Ireland. The numbers of these outrages actually rose for the first three years of the 'peace process': there were more in the year following the Good Friday Agreement than in the year before it. Yet incidents following the agreement were reported less, and were interpreted as residual problems – on the way to resolution – rather than evidence of the process itself breaking down. The media were key in providing a definition of continuing and even rising violence of a particular kind such that it was situated in a context that suggested that things were getting better. Of course they did so out of a close reading of the delicate reality on the ground: this was a conflict carefully, methodically, knowledgeably reported by expert local journalists. However, as one politician pointed out, 'It is difficult. You have to take the media with you – even when everything is so frail, and you need to know how close things are to breaking down. But the media definition of shootings as bad, but not fatal to the process, kept the whole thing moving.'[28] Indeed, such media judgements were part of the magic that translated a new will to have peace into a painfully constructed, continuingly vulnerable reality. This was an important and reasonable exercise of journalistic responsibility by people close enough to the stark politics of the region to be able to interpret reality with balance and acumen. It mattered too much for news values to dominate coverage. It was in this respect unusual.

We seem to be moving into a new era of imperial protectorates, involving peacekeeping forces and the imposition of 'democratic', or more hopefully and realistically 'representative', forms of government on other societies. This process involves the imposing powers selecting and maintaining political winners. As in the democratic success in Ukraine in 2005, it may involve long-term investment in 'soft' civil-society organizations, including the media. Such situations are often inadequately reported, and yet sustaining them requires political will, good intelligence – and compromise. The media are vital to how such regimes survive – and indeed to the adequacy of the military mandate. Thus the political analyst Paul Hirst pointed out that Bosnia and Kosovo (and Afghanistan) require substantial garrisons, and asked, 'How many more ongoing commitments will the military and the public accept?' He argued that there is a further problem: that however difficult it may be to develop a doctrine of 'tolerable' international standards of conduct, ones 'that come in a box marked "made in America" will not be well received . . . yet only the United States is capable of effective peace enforcement in most cases'.[29] These protectorates may in fact fail. Yet the media language for describing what one journalist called 'grey but vital political choices' is feeble.[30] Of course, the public likes – at times – to feel benevolently moved about the condition of the innocent and suffering. This self-reflecting complacency may have positive effects. Yet innocent victims are not always available and – although effective in stirring feeling – when they are they may over time confuse the public.

There are other issues: how far reporting of wars commands audience attention, and how far the other forces that shape journalism – advertising revenues, commercial interests, and public understanding – have altered the way in which conflicts are covered. 'The public appetite for emotionally tinged trivia is insatiable,' suggests Max Hastings, who adds that news items of 'staggering unimportance' boost circulations and audience figures, while important issues sometimes hardly lead to any increase at all. Thus wars are difficult to report, yet may not attract audiences. Even more expensive and less attractive are stories about the complicated nuances of maintaining peacekeeping forces in unstable places. In part this trivialization reflects a kind of reality, Hastings argues. The lack of interest in stories that matter reflects the public estimate of national involvement in affairs. 'When we were important', Hastings remarks, speaking of the British public, 'we took things seriously. We used to count in the world, and so we expected to do things about it.' Now, 'absolutely correctly, the public's lips curl at the suggestion we will do anything about anything much.'[31] The same could not be said of the American public, who certainly do have power to wield. Nevertheless, in America, despite a less vulgar press and a far more culturally impoverished broadcast news than in Britain, the public displays a similar fickle attention. Against this background, the reporting of wars has sought the elusive public interest through a greater emphasis on emotion.

In such a light the new humanitarianism has become a novel basis for legitimating conflicts – sometimes correctly, at other times unfortunately reflecting little more than the translation of older realities into an acceptable contemporary language. It has also made humanitarian issues a key part of every war: smart bombs hunt down regimes which are distinguished from their civilian populations, for whom food and assistance are to be provided. But this in turn affects how wars are reported – frequently in terms of humanitarian consequences – which may make the political impact of conflict, the transfers of power involved, and the harsh realities difficult to communicate to audiences.

There is another problem: the news, and especially television news, is inimical to epics. Broadcasting does have the ability to communicate intimate suffering. It is much less able to communicate the relative size of a disaster. Indeed, there are many news values that discourage journalists from doing so. Thus 'eyewitness' accounts are vital but can be misleading about scale, while the essential 'on-the-ground' expert knowledge of local reality has simply disappeared from much reporting: over the last thirty years, foreign-based correspondents have almost been abolished. In 1974 twenty British newspapers had correspondents in Africa. In 2004 four did.[32]

In addition, the consequences of wars on battlefields often seem the same – the familiar scenario of 'war' – even though in reality they are much more varied than audiences perhaps understand or than the media imply. Some wars and some battles within them produce large numbers of casualties; others produce very few. Which category any particular conflict will fall into is hard to predict: the outcome obviously depends, in part, on the speed of resolution. The scale is not only hard to predict but also hard to estimate and, perhaps most crucially, hard to communicate. Indeed, the modern electronic media are at times even worse at registering differences in scale than the old. Even comparatively small, unimportant wars yield a crop of much-prized action footage – what one journalist calls cynically 'bang-bang pictures'.[33] Mostly, of course, the similarity of news formats and the pressure on time obscure difficult issues of the relative justice and effectiveness of some interventions and the relative failure and hypocrisy of others – even though these are what the public needs to be able to estimate most of all. We need some hard, innovative thinking about how to display and explain the different importance and consequences of different engagements. If entry into conflict and the levels of force used now typically involve choice – and the media tend to make all conflicts seem very similar – how does the public discriminate accurately between different engagements?

In particular, the media impose on conflicts the same ideas and narratives of fault, blame, cause and effect that they use in peacetime. The news – relentlessly mobile, ruthlessly impelled to portray the world as having changed each day – moves on. In any case, the audience is hard to sell news to: it wants fidgeting novelty with an easy resolution, and finds sustained, complex stories unpalatable – perhaps because it is not given the tools to understand them properly. But there is also a media problem here, as the news story has to move on so fast. When the original story about the 1984 famine in Ethiopia broke, a series of flukes meant that it was given time on the midday, early-evening and late-evening news. By the next day virtually the whole British public had seen it.[34] Would any story command such attention now? Nevertheless, better, more responsible news is not necessarily more successful commercially. Audiences are conditioned to expect wars to be just another (admittedly rather exciting, sometimes a little scary) category of news. There is great pressure to make wars short, and have a neat and celebratory victory. This is all the product of the role of the media in conflicts of choice. How these values will adapt to a new unfolding and unpredictable reality is not clear. For the fight against terrorism is unavoidable, protracted, and likely to be close at hand. The enemy, following classic military precept, is choosing to attack societies where they have weak defences. The role that news-makers will play in such a complex world is also uncertain – but vital. Comforting, familiar, even exciting preordained emotional narratives may sell news, but are of little use in a potentially threatening world. Reporting what editors and audiences want may endanger us all.

7

Do We All Feel the Same?

Do those who have suffered respond to the suffering of others with greater compassion because of what they themselves have endured? Does media representation of pain produce an 'empathetic' response? Is feeling for others the mark of an 'improved' society? Direct proximity to pain can certainly have a salutary effect. It is sometimes observed, for example, that refugees from oppression receive a better welcome in poverty-stricken neighbouring states, where people understand their plight, than in rich countries where hunger and fear are abstractions. It has been argued that the media can have a civilizing effect: that images of conflict heighten awareness and increase a desire for peace. Indeed, it is scarcely a coincidence that – as Amartya Sen has famously pointed out – famines almost never occur in societies where there is a free press.[1] One notable test of these views has been the post-Cold War Russian attitude towards domestic suffering and civil conflict. The former Soviet Union has certainly had a radically different experience of suffering from that of most Western countries in recent generations. Have post-Communist media freedoms nevertheless brought it closer to the West in its attitude towards military conflict and its human consequences?

For three-quarters of a century, the Soviet Union, with Russia at its heart, was considered to be monolithically oppressive. Russia, seen for decades as politically sophisticated and alarmingly dangerous, helped shape a world order that, since the collapse of Communism, has simply dissolved. Russia remains alien, but to what extent has the collapse of Communism changed Russian society? Have the Russians become more similar to us in how they respond to wars? This is not an issue about Russian psychology; rather, it is one about the nature of the political system in which the media play a part.

Soviet society was based on a Utopian plan to remodel institutions and personalities, using propaganda and violence. It was headed by a brutal regime with a cold disregard for the welfare of its citizens. A huge bureaucratically controlled system combined relentless scrutiny of individuals with capricious barbarity and uncertainty. Much suffering was hidden. This was not a simple process in which oppressive experiences were buried: it was far more disabling. People were persuaded to embrace their own humiliation. Passive collaboration was for most people not merely the best but the only strategy for survival. 'The people,' wrote the sociologist Pitirim Sorokin in 1937, 'are bewitched by grand illusions. All around, ferocity and slaughter reign supreme, but they do not desist in repeating that the brotherhood of man is being realized . . . All around morality crumbles away, licensed crime, sadism and cruelty are everywhere. The masses call it moral regeneration.'[2]

The First World War, the Revolution, the Civil War, collectivization, the Terror, the famines of 1923, 1937 and 1947, the Second World War, the Gulag camps, and environmental degradation on a massive scale all form a backdrop to contemporary Russian understanding and experience. Every family has its own personal experience of devastation, and of survival against the odds. Suffering in Russian society also has a long literary pedigree. 'When war broke out,' says one character in Pasternak's *Dr Zhivago*, 'its ordinary danger and menace of death were a blessing compared with the inhuman power of the lie, a relief because it broke the spell of the dead letter.'[3] Educated Russians have a style of recounting their personal and national lives which is elliptical and ironic, involving an oblique but constant preoccupation with the central problem of endurance.

Meanwhile the Soviet state also depended on extolling some kinds of 'suffering'. Arbitrary terror was never mentioned, while the endurance of the masses in the face of publicly acknowledged privation was used as a tool of propaganda. The authorities used genuine sacrifices – acts of bravery that the public rightly understood to have been inspiring and valuable – for propaganda as well. The Russian journalist and novelist Vasily Grossman wrote (in one of his many banned works) that war had become 'the splinter in the brain of modern Russian personhood'.[4] It was, he suggested, the painful irritant that made the public accept Soviet savagery. Thus acts of heroic endurance during the 'Great Patriotic War' of 1941–5 were known to have helped save the nation, and the world, from fascism. The tangle of self-justifications did not stop in the 1990s, when suffering from the past began to be re-examined in public. It also opened up new feuds – between the different kinds of victim.

In a society with such a history, the recounting of suffering has often taken the form of a litany involving a moral community of shared pain. 'We the workers', 'We the mothers', 'We the veterans' called on the public to share their experiences. Affliction in Russia, it has been claimed, plays a distinct role so that – as in medieval martyrology – the greater the sacrifice,

The Soviet state exploited acts of genuine heroism, creating a complex attitude towards the politics of suffering. 'Noble Sniper' Zaitsev (on the left), from the Siberian 284th Regiment, during the siege of Stalingrad was used as a tool of propaganda.

the greater the status.[5] Thus the historian Orlando Figes argues that the theme of suffering 'has a special place in Russian writing – it has long been seen as a form of spiritual redemption'.[6] Indeed, glasnost and perestroika, tangible advances that they were, could nevertheless also be seen as another opportunity in the long Russian tradition of 'telling the terrible tale'. Not everyone was taken in. One shrewd Russian observer adds a note of caution, namely that 'suffering in Russia has always been manipulated for political ends. In a way, it doesn't play much here.'[7] Nevertheless, whatever the great changes in Russian society, there are striking similarities in the ways in which Russians have described their condition to themselves over time. Wholesale social disruption, personal loss and suffering have been accepted as necessary preconditions of prosperity in the future.

Nor is Russian pain simply an aspect of a grim past nobly born. Rather it has a terrible new contemporary life. The collapse of the state since the end of Communism has meant that drug, alcohol and crime problems are now combined with economic failure on a scale that it is difficult for Westerners to imagine. Although the new conditions have created opportunities for an entrepreneurial minority, the majority have so far seen little improvement in economic conditions. Male life expectancy has fallen to its lowest level since the aftermath of the Second World War; child mortality has risen, and maternal deaths in childbirth have quadrupled since the beginning of the 1990s. In 2001 GDP was half what it had been in 1990. The situation began to ease only as oil prices increased. Indeed, from the late 1990s the Russian state began to regain its tyrannical hold over Russian institutions. Contemporary attitudes have to be seen against this background. As the British journalist John Lloyd, a passionate-compassionate observer of New Russia points out, 'the diabolic legacy of Soviet history which is the malign companion to all attempts at reform was the belief that suspicion and fear were a necessary part of the social system and a widespread sense that self-betterment comes through betrayal.'[8] Despite the huge changes that the collapse of Communism brought, the Soviet legacy was a system in which 'the only possible message of social life was that it was a game with a loser and winner – and that the winner took all – holding the losers at bay.'[9]

It is said by modern Russians (as one of a raft of similar jokes) that the real problem in Russia was that the whole population believed what they saw on television. So when they 'did' capitalism, they did it just like the monster of depravity and exploitation that the Communist media had always shown it to be. The looting of the surviving economy by the new Russian political-economic elites in the early post-Communist period bewildered foreign investors, who were used to the discipline imposed on capitalism by the restraints of democratic obligation and basic liberalism. This led to the convergence of what passes for politics and economics in the new Russia, and the emergence of a 'kleptocracy'. Successive blows to national pride have also battered the Russian public. 'We used to think, "I'm poor, but at least we are great" – even if we hated the means to greatness,' observed one decent new Russian entrepreneur (who was doing adequately out of the new order).[10] Contemporary Muscovites are hardened fighters in the daily Darwinian struggle for existence, in which the ground rules of success continue to alter at a disconcerting pace. At the same time the new Russia has had some freedoms that it previously did not enjoy, although as President Putin consolidated his power over Russia many of the old abuses returned – not least in relation to the mass media. Nevertheless, Russians have continued to vote for a democratic future, while paying a high price for the privilege. Such experiences might also be expected profoundly to alter the way in which the public relates to the accounts of the misery of others. Anna Politkovskaya, a campaigning journalist, who has survived two attacks on her life, commented in 2004, 'Everyone is convinced that the Soviet Union has returned, and that it no longer matters what we think.'[11]

There are key starting points. Communism was undermined if not destroyed by an unsuccessful war in Afghanistan, while the inauguration of 'New Russia' (if that is the correct term) was accompanied by two cruel wars in Chechnya, combined with and followed by an oppressive occupation. The first war (in 1994–6) was reported to home audiences emotionally and engagedly by young journalists who were evidently shocked by the tragedy unfolding around them. Partly as a result, the Russian public reacted against the continued prosecution of the conflict, which ended in a defeat for the Russian army. The episode was seen by Russian liberal opinion at the time as a breakthrough for journalism and the beginning of Westernized normality. The second war (1999–2000) was reported under much more controlled conditions, with an emphasis on Russian success. It was partly as a result that Vladimir Putin, the leading hawk in the Yeltsin administration, gained election as president and began to consolidate a new authoritarianism. The impression of Russian victory, however, masked the reality. The subsequent occupation failed to stop (and may have helped stimulate) a series of terrorist attacks in Chechnya and in Moscow. It may have helped destabilize the entire Caucasus.[12] Comparisons and contrasts between the two wars and how they were treated in the press raise a number of questions. In particular, did the media handling of the first war reflect a new emotionalism sweeping in from Western journalism? Was the Russian public – unusually, in view of its schooling in state violence – moved by what it saw? Were the second war and the occupation a reversion to an Old Russia or Soviet norm? Did Russian feelings about war shift as dramatically as some have maintained? Or is it misleading to talk about public feelings at all, separated from public perceptions of self-interest? Indeed, do the media, in the end, depend on other institutions rather more than is often believed? Perhaps you cannot have democratic institutions without the media, but the media cannot create them on their own.

Arguments about the conduct of the conflicts were inevitably related to disagreements about the direction of Russian society. Nevertheless, the way in which the outside world has dealt with evidence about what has been happening in Chechnya has not been straightforward. Western governments have been prepared to put up with Russian aggression at home – in the old-fashioned, pragmatic way that is often said to have broken down recently. It was not just that world opinion could have little real impact on a remote region well inside Russia's traditional orbit. Chechnya was low

Anna Politkovskaya, campaigning Russian journalist and Chechen expert, commenting on the conduct of the hostage crisis during the Moscow theatre siege, 2 February 2003.

in the scale of international priorities for Western governments and citizens alike. Russia was seen as an ally in the new world order, and there was a predisposition to give its rulers the benefit of the doubt. Chechen rebellion had at first been seen as a proto-independence movement against Russian tyranny, but once Chechnya had been depicted as a source of 'international terrorism' the Russians were left to act more or less as they wished. Indeed, Western governments, observed Politkovskaya, greeted Putin's consolidation of power 'with choruses of encouragement'.[13] Western media attention was fitful; audience interest wavered. Although the humanitarian organizations – Amnesty International, Human Rights Watch, War and Peace Reporting, representing a new community of watchdogs against civil-rights abuses – maintained an impressive scrutiny of Russian behaviour (and Chechen response), Western journalists struggled to gain attention for the complex troubles of a faraway country. Nevertheless, international opinion was not entirely passive. The West could not, and did not seek to, intervene. However, the ways in which the wars were reported and perceived had some influence on the fluid image of the legitimacy of post-Communist Russia.

The assessment of the condition of Russia at any moment partly depends on judgement about the direction of the conceivable end-state of Russian politics and society. According to Francis Fukuyama in his 1992 book *The End of History*, 'mankind will come to seem like a long wagon train strung down the road. While some nations will arrive in town others will have taken wrong turnings, or be attacked by Indians, or wounded, or forced to bivouac for the night.' The great majority of the 'wagons' or nations, however, will make the slow journey into town, and most will eventually arrive there, 'despite being painted in different colours, looking increasingly similar'.[14] According to the famous Fukuyama prophecy, Western liberal democracy was encroaching on the whole globe, with values like freedom of expression rapidly becoming universal. Today, Fukuyama seems at best half right. At any rate, the transition to Western democratic practices and liberal economies seems far less inexorable and more troubled. Moreover, Fukuyama failed to notice the ways in which apparently stable democracies were themselves evolving fast, with notions of representative democracy giving way to a more volatile and plebiscitary stage – one in which the media play a new role. Furthermore, this was happening when notions of representative government were a more realistic aspiration than simple democracy for many conflict-torn societies. The wagon train was trundling towards a moving destination.

Some classic interpretations of the Russian predicament fit events into a prejudged mould. One approach, for example, asserts that Russian history is characterized by such deep continuities that change is very shallow and the country is condemned to reinvent primordial verities. Of course, such ideas are hard to avoid when institutions have a history as inimical to independence as those of Russia – and where the media have been stifled for so long. Thus, in a minor but revealing example, the Russian expert Mary McAuley has pointed out that jobbing journalists in the provinces seamlessly transferred to the new local monopoly owner the obsequious manner that they had previously used to describe his predecessor, the local party boss.[15]

The idea of Russian otherness has also often been taken to extremes which have led to movements towards greater civility being ignored.[16] Such a view of absolute Russian difference had its corollary in accounts of the Russian media such as that of Frank Ellis, who presents them as permanently and enduringly fraudulent (a view which is often accompanied by a romantic regard for the long-suffering Russian public).[17] Extreme versions of this interpretation are ideological and fatalistic, but there are more subtle views as well. Some critics, like the historian and journalist Anatol

Lieven, suggest that the problem is the passivity of the Russian public.[18] Others blame a fatal unwillingness to take responsibility.[19] Yet assessing the dimensions of genuine change in Russia is difficult, because the comparison with the traditions and habits of the past is always illuminating, and it is easy just to see continuities and deceptions rather than genuine development. Thus Russian journalism has a rich repertoire of evasion to draw on, while large parts of the Russian public display a partly useful – though corrosive – scepticism. In the latter days of the old regime, an alternative and equally bizarre view was held by apologists in the West: namely that the Soviet system offered freedoms (from market competition and owners) not available in capitalist societies. One notable writer on the Russian media even commented as late as 1988 that, 'While in the USSR the right of reply for individuals and organizations wronged by the media is guaranteed', such a situation did not exist in Britain.[20]

Meanwhile, for decades from the 1920s to the 1970s a common view in the West, not just on the left, was that the Soviet system was a politically objectionable but economically – or at least militarily – effective alternative to capitalism. According to this interpretation, the human-rights abuses that abounded in the Soviet Union had social consequences but did not undermine the ruthless efficiency of 'the engine of society'.[21] As one former diplomat has observed, 'The view was that Russia was nasty – but that it worked.'[22] The media were thus to be interpreted for what they inadvertently gave away, not for the messages they intended to communicate.[23] While this view misjudged the severity of the Soviet domestic crisis in the 1980s, it did at least imagine Russia as a society which could develop rationally. Such a view led to the post-Communist interpretation (most forcefully expressed by the economists who had a part in attempting to manage the reform process) that Russia could painfully progress towards some kind of normality. The economist Richard Layard, for example, argued that the transformation of the economy needed time and encouragement.[24] Indeed, such a positive view produced what Catherine Merridale has called 'the years of hope. The Soviet Union system was falling apart, but the possibilities inherent in its collapse seemed promising.'[25]

Some observers of the Russian media, such as the American academic Ellen Mickiewicz, stuck resolutely to the evolutionary view, taking Russian journalists at their own word, examining their development towards greater 'democracy'. Writing in 1997, after the first war in Chechnya, but before the second, Mickiewicz commented that 'the conflict in Chechnya in 1994 had one startling, unintended effect: it finally spelled the end of the Soviet media system.' She added that 'The Russian government were stuck in the previous age and had the illusion of information control. This was no longer possible.'[26] Such arguments implied a simple progress – passing from an ill-chosen system to a new, enlightened, one. Unfortunately, change is not always so simple. Others, however, have a more complicated view. Anatol Lieven argues that Russia is more likely to turn into an unstable (but not necessarily totalitarian) state – perhaps a 'comprador' society, or client state, comparable to many in Latin America.

It is easy to misjudge developments in Russian institutions and condemn them as imperfect (when measured against those in mature democracies), thereby ignoring a more complex reality. John Lloyd, for example, has pointed out that by the 1980s – that is, in the last phase of Communism, but before the collapse – a quite powerful independent media tradition had developed.[27] At least some journalists made decisions and explored stories within confines that were different from those in the West but part of a recognizable journalism. Many of the choices they made were within the familiar repertoire of reporting and were available for knowing readers to decode – as when stories were put in a paper in order to say more than their overt contents, offering accurate information or critical opinion concealed in politically neutral accounts. Indeed, an intellectual revolution had begun to take place in some of the media, as well as in other institutions, long before the overthrow of Communism, and to this extent the optimistic Sovietologists had been right. The presentation of a cut-off point in press oppression with the ending of Communism is too simple. Freedoms existed, control remains – only today the biggest threat to press freedom is the commercial interests that are entwined with the state. In the new Russia, journalists still live in fear – but now they are more likely to be murdered by Mafia hitmen than imprisoned. Several of the most critical of them have been blown up, many receive threats, and some have sought exile.

Yet the most important aspect of Russian journalism is still how lost and provisional it is, as it struggles to find a voice – and how vital the process of searching for that voice remains. This is, of course, something it shares with news-making in many other insecure political systems. Thus the Russian media and journalists are caught between state-dominated traditions of journalism and models which float in from the USA and Europe, which are not their own but which seem to them right – or at least dominant. It is the transactions that journalists make that reveal this. As Lloyd points out, many Russian journalists are corrupt in the sense that 'they sell the space they control in their papers and TV to politicians and business people – but they make deals with their masters which allow them to put un-corrupt news onto the air in exchange.' In this way Russian journalism is like its equivalent in many unpleasant political regimes, namely compromised. But it should not be lightly dismissed on these grounds. As Lloyd adds, 'a real, local account of Russian journalism reveals a mix of almost naïve idealism with low cunning – in the same person.'[28]

'Russian methods,' according to the historian of eastern Europe Hugh Seton-Watson, describing conditions in the nineteenth century, 'won Russia more bitter enemies than reliable subjects.'[29] The post-Communist Chechen wars suggest that little has changed. Chechnya is Muslim, mountainous, comparatively small (about the size of Wales), and currently a land of Hobbesian anarchy. In the absence of the rule of law, the strong destroy the weak. In the nineteenth century the region marked the edge of the Russian Empire, with a dominant clan structure in which there was loyalty to the extended family but little sense of nationality. Repeated wars with Russia in 1810, 1819, 1840 and 1914 had a unifying effect, and an independence movement emerged. Chechens blended Sufism with local religious traditions to provide a tolerant, flexible and unique Muslim tradition. Recurrent wars with Russia in the twentieth century changed that as well, producing a more intolerant belief system – and a savage nihilism. A strong social structure which helped successive generations survive attacks has been refeudalized by robber barons. Chechnya, like Russia itself, has been remade by brutal conflict.

Images of the Chechen Wild West – what the historian Orlando Figes has called 'an exotic and undisciplined counter-culture in the Russian imagination'[30] – have played an important part in Russian history. The poets Pushkin and Lermontov were exiled to Chechnya, and set many of their most famous works there; Lermontov's *Izmail Bey* was a bitter condemnation of the Russian Empire based on military campaigns in Chechnya.[31] 'In Russia, you know,' comments a character in 'The Woodfelling', a short story by Tolstoy about war in Chechnya, 'people visualize it as such a magnificent place, with eternal virgin ice, raging torrents, daggers, felt coats, and Circassian maidens, but basically there is nothing very cheerful about it.'[32] Tolstoy's tale tells of an early-nineteenth-century 'defoliation' campaign in which the Russians cut down all the trees around Grozny in an attempt to deprive the rebels of a terrain that they have exploited so effectively. In the story, the Russian soldiers – who have all fought over the same land before and lost comrades in the same places in earlier campaigns – are picked off by a hidden enemy surrounding them in the mist and dank woods. The Caucasus, claims one officer in the tale, 'deceived me. I feel myself declining here morally every day . . . the main reason is that I don't consider myself fit to serve here: to put it in a nutshell I'm not brave enough.'[33]

The capital of the region, Grozny (now reduced to rubble by Russian artillery), was built as a Russian fort whose purpose was to control the plains of Chechnya. Chechens developed a reputation for being determined fighters, and the region was often seen as dominated by a fierce but honourable society. Little Chechen boys are still brought up to recite the saga of the seven (now, no doubt, increased to eight) attempts by the Russian oppressors to eradicate their people. The resistance of the Chechens throughout the Soviet period – which resulted in a willingness to encourage any enemy of Russia (including, Stalin found it convenient to claim, the Germans during the Second World War) – culminated in the mass deportation of almost the entire population to Siberia in 1946. Over a quarter of the population perished. Nevertheless, the Chechens' identity survived and was even reinforced. The proud loyalty of family groups, the sturdy habits of resistance and the bravery of the people had produced a society with an immense social strength. In one of his great works on the Stalinist camps, *The Gulag Archipelago*, Solzhenitsyn wrote, 'Only one nation refused to accept the psychology of subjection. Not individuals, not insurgents but a nation as a whole, the Chechens. No Chechen ever tried to be of service or please the authorities. Their attitude towards them was proud and even hostile; they only respected rebels.'[34] In 1963, during the Khrushchev thaw, the Chechen people finally got back on the trains and returned home. Many of the key players in the first Chechen war had been born in exile.

The importance of Chechnya increased in the twentieth century because of the key role it played in the geopolitics of oil. The region had major oil reserves, and the most important oil pipeline (carrying nearly half of Russia's oil exports in 1988) ran through it. In addition, Communist planning strengthened its strategic role by locating the entire Soviet production of air fuel there. The politics of oil underlay the crisis which was often discussed in the late 1990s as if it were merely an issue of nationalism both in the Russian media and in the West.[35] Because of the Chechens' history of independence movements, their revolts were described in terms of the new wave of ethnic and nationalist conflicts that were somehow bubbling up again. The reality was far more complex, and certainly less inevitable, than nearly all the reporting made it seem.

For several hundred years Russia has combined fear of Chechen wild ways with ruthless attempts to control them. However, in the post-Communist period Chechnya became restive, sensing opportunities in a novel political situation. As usual, Russian policy simply accentuated this problem: it imposed an economic blockade. Cut off from central budgets and with no banking system – but equipped with a long, porous, frontier and a natural bent for banditry – Chechnya developed a huge black-market arms and narcotics trade.[36] In fact, as one journalist pointed out, the Chechens 'already controlled large slices of the black market in Russia, since they were, long before the Chechen war, the most ruthless and skilled of the various post-Soviet crime gangs'.[37] Another added that the first war would have been sorted out more effectively by arresting a dozen Mafia bosses in Moscow than by shooting anyone in Chechnya.[38]

Not all crime in Russia was committed by Chechens. However, the subject nation soon came to be treated, as one observer noted, 'like the new Jews'.[39] Right-wing Russian nationalists portrayed all Chechens as vermin. 'The Russian media in the nineties treated all crime as black, and all blacks as Chechens,' observed one Russian. 'Every day the newspapers and television had new stories of crime. Partly because there was more crime – Russia had before been very safe – but also because it broke a taboo to talk about it. We were told all the new crime was Chechen.'[40] Brutal racial attacks on supposed Chechens, even on children, were rarely prosecuted.

However, the media-enhanced image of Chechen lawlessness, together with the ramshackle Chechen government, led the Russian authorities to underestimate Chechnya's capacity to resist. One observer pointed out that 'Repeated Russian media images of Chechen criminality suggested that it was not a place that could organize itself. Well, that was a big mistake – it could organize itself very well!'[41] Entrepreneurial disorder was the very basis of the Chechen resistance. One analyst calculated that in 1993, in the run-up to the first war, the amount of artillery circulating in Chechnya was equal to four times the amount stored by the British army – and most of it had simply been sold to the Chechens by Russian soldiers. Grozny became one large, open arms market.[42] By August 1994, wrote another critic, 'Chechnya had turned into a Shakespearean kingdom, and armed groups roamed the country at will.'[43]

The first Chechen war, which lasted from December 1994 to August 1996, demonstrated to a startled world the extraordinary incompetence of the Russian army, a force that had terrified the international community for half a century. The war had been launched to appease the Russian military and to secure the re-election of Boris Yeltsin as president by demonstrating Yeltsin's decisiveness. 'Stalin sorted out Chechnya in two weeks,' said one politician. 'What are we frightened of – the West?'[44] It was also launched because of television pictures. 'I think the plan of war arose,' commented a former presidential aide, 'after the dramatic showing on TV of the way Chechens captured and humiliated Russian soldiers and officers. We tried to direct the President's attention at the pictures, and once he really looked the decision was taken by Yeltsin.'[45] One expert commented, 'Moscow invaded Chechnya out of pique.'[46] The war was intended to project a positive image of decisive presidential action.

This aspect of the first war was highlighted by the fact that it was launched against a leadership in Chechnya which, however inadequate at negotiation, was on the verge of seeking a settlement with Russia.[47] 'I went down there,' said one Russian expert, 'and we could have sorted it. There were people to talk to, things to agree. It could have been done.'[48] The war simply pushed control of Chechnya into the hands of the despotic and terrorist regime of Dzhokar Dudayev (himself an ex-general in the Russian air force and one of those who had been exiled to Siberia with his family as a baby).

This first war was easy to report – if you were brave enough. It was a 'drive-in' war. As Thomas De Waal points out, access to the front was not controlled, and the media were not censored.[49] It was as if the authorities did not understand how far the old Soviet system of control was coming apart. There was at first little consideration of what impact reporting the reality of war might have. In this and in other respects the first war in Chechnya seemed to echo Vietnam. Just as Vietnam had often been reported by young people with little previous journalistic experience who merely turned up to it, so was the war in Chechnya. By contrast, Russia's own Vietnam, the war in Afghanistan, had been reported under conditions of tightly controlled accredited access. Much of the reporting of Chechnya, commented one experienced journalist, was 'really a kind of media revenge – or atonement – for what we had not managed in Afghanistan'.[50] Russian reporters were also working out of a new and reinvigorated 'samizdat' documentary film tradition. Thus a suppressed video of the use of tanks against the peaceful civilian defenders of the Lithuanian parliament in 1994 was widely circulated and well known to the public, and had played an important part in informing indignant public opinion.[51]

Vietnam was a model which young Russian journalists had much in mind. 'Basically we had seen a lot of films when we were growing up, and we just knew that true reporting of a war was like they did it in Vietnam,' commented one.[52] The journalists knew that American media coverage of Vietnam was credited with alerting American opinion to the futility of the conflict. At the same time, contemporary American war journalism had moved on to the new emotionalism of CNN, which the Russians began to see because of media reform and which they much admired.[53] 'We thought you could be a real person on the news for the first time. This was very heady stuff – perhaps you could become a star and a hero and tell the truth altogether,'[54] commented one. Another journalist added that it was 'a moment, it felt like a fracture – if we could get the war right then we might make Russia right.'[55]

Early official pictures had shown inspiring images of tanks rumbling along determinedly. But the conflict soon became a classic guerrilla war, in which the enemy did not lose but simply dissolved away and regrouped, and the Russian army was lured into traps and outmanoeuvred. For the Russians in command, the war was against Chechens in general, and women and children were considered to be as likely to harbour the enemy as to be innocent. 'Discussion of human rights was at first seen as disguised pro-Chechen propaganda, a kind of treachery,' observed John Lloyd.[56] On the Chechen side a fierce battle-hardened community was again doing what it felt it had done before – fighting for survival. If civilians got in the way, they were as dispensable as the enemy. It was a ruthless, barbaric affair.

The key media battles were political, and fought in Moscow – but they were intensified by what pictures from the front began to show. Public hunger for reality became irresistible. The media battle was about the right to show critical views of the war, and this was finally won decisively by NTV (the only independent TV station, owned by one of the great new oligarchs, later shut). The government threatened to withdraw the station's licence and stop its access to the transmitters, and right-wing politicians railed against its lack of patriotism. The boss of the main state channel was sacked. The Glasnost Defence Foundation recorded numerous threats to journalists and restrictions of their rights.[57] But NTV and some key journalists played a heroically shrewd part, and the public's awed eagerness to know what was happening was their strongest card. In crises, new institutional authority can be forged swiftly. Thus, by the third week of the first war 95 per cent of all Russians claimed to be watching NTV, and by the end of the war 87 per cent trusted it most.[58] For a while a virtuous circle between reporting, political acumen and public interest pushed the possibilities of news, and reporters responded with imaginative enthusiasm.

Pictures of petrified Russian soldiers blundering around Grozny, shelling petrified pensioners most of whom were Russians who had lived all their working lives in Chechnya and who consequently had nowhere else to go, shocked the Russian viewing public. In particular, the contradiction between politicians' words and the television pictures was decisive (just as in Vietnam). When the defence minister said that the eighteen-year-old soldiers 'died with a smile on their faces', the bodies on screen showed something different.[59] When Yeltsin claimed that the bombardment of

Grozny had stopped, Russians could see bombs still falling. When the army claimed 'full control' of the city, Russians could see their soldiers' fear of snipers. The Russian army had no experience of working under the restraints normally limiting the behaviour of Western armies. For the first time, concluded one report, it was 'shown in a totally different light, turning in front of the eyes of the Russian public from a defender into a punitive weapon'.[60] Casualties mounted fast.

The first breakthrough was the speed of the news. As one critic put it, 'Chernobyl took days to creep out, but suddenly with Chechnya we watched every day things happening.'[61] Like most gains, this was not a permanent advance – but it set a new benchmark, as absorbing real-time news took over the screens. The second breakthrough was stylistic. Even within the constraints of Communism, Russia had a tradition of serious war reporting to call on, dating back to Vasily Grossman's fine reporting during the Second World War. It was a tradition that had emphasized experience over analysis (as less politically dangerous). A new generation of reporters, many of them women, also used what was for Russians a startling new way of addressing their audiences: personal, direct and emotional. For the first time, distraught and unkempt journalists reported apocalyptically straight to camera, against a backdrop of scenes of Boschian devastation. They expressed and directed a new public mood of disgust.

There was another novelty about the reporting, namely the graphic images of horror and bloodshed that Russian television began to present to its audiences. Previously the media had been almost as prudish about the representation of violence as about that of sex. The Chechen war broke through this taboo – in a society that was simultaneously developing a taste for extremely violent fictional material. Russian television lingered over bloody remains, wounded soldiers, lost limbs, the impact of bombs and shrapnel, bereaved civilians, and beheaded victims. Showing the most graphic footage was seen (or legitimated) as a kind of unarguable visual equivalent of 'modern' Western freedom of expression.

Official incompetence was played out in a novel state ceremony – in front of an appalled public audience. Thus, when Chechen rebels took a whole hospital hostage in 1996 the Russian authorities' clumsy attempt to storm the building (which killed many innocent victims unnecessarily) was watched as it happened. This incident eerily prefigured the disastrous storming of the Moscow theatre in 2002, which was intended to free hostages held by Chechen suicide bombers, but which managed to kill several hundred theatregoers, and the catastrophic storming of the school in Beslan in 2004, when at least 400 children were killed. 'It is as if no one can really think

A woman weeps over a slain relative in Grozny, 1995. Russians were, at first, appalled by the grim images they were exposed to – for the first time in real time, as events occurred.

here,' observed one commentator.[62] The new reporting left its audiences unclear what the war was about. It was not that Russian people did not expect their leaders to be callous: rather that they did not expect to see this demonstrated so publicly.[63]

The reporting was not perfect. One later independent report, produced by the Glasnost Defence Foundation, pointed out that the media traded in 'gross simplifications'. Chechen success was ascribed to the fact that Chechens were 'born fighters', while Russian soldiers were shown as 'simpletons'. It was as if, the report commented, they were all '18–20-year-old kids, virtually torn away from their mother's breast and sent to massacre'.[64] 'There is a difference', one commentator observed, 'between the report of a number of casualties and a picture of charred corpses, left to be gnawed by roving wild dogs. That is what television showed us for the first time.' Sufficiently repeated, he concluded, such images 'lead to symbolism and mythology – not reports'.[65] The considerable attention paid to casualties, another report declared, was very shocking at first. But the audience 'soon became accustomed to viewing the charred remains of their compatriots during the family supper'.[66] 'Values became less easy to define,' observed one journalist. There was, he added, 'an uneasy ambivalence. It became almost impossible to formulate one's own personal moral attitude towards the conflict. It was uncomfortable.'[67] One member of a focus group declared, 'Let the Chechens do what they please. Either that or kill them all.'[68]

Russian public opinion turned against the war: poll evidence demonstrated how hostile the public was by 1996. Yet, despite all the media elaboration of the failure of the war, all the wilder emotions on display, and the humiliation visited on the Russian army, it was paradoxically a defeat with little apparent impact. The war was launched to save Yeltsin, but its *failure* did not stop him being re-elected. 'The media who so criticized the war – it is funny to say – just turned round and supported the President,' observed one critic. 'There was, of course, nowhere else for them to go,' he added, because the critics of the war were those who were democratically inclined, and the opposition to Yeltsin was even less liberal than the incumbent president.[69] Consequently even heady new feelings had to submit to the discipline of the politics of the moment. The media had created a new political climate, but they had not been able to create new political institutions. They had behaved like an opposition – but they did not constitute one.

In a way that was little understood in the West, the war in Chechnya was in itself also not so much a step towards democratic self-determination (the forces that took over in Chechnya were certainly not democratic) as the beginning of another ethnic and faith-based calamity. On the eve of the break-up of the Soviet Union in the late 1980s, Russians felt comparatively little resentment towards their ethnic minorities. However, the withering away of Russians' view of themselves as 'supra-ethnic' altered the picture, and a new hostility towards all minorities flamed up. Soon Chechens (together with Gypsies) topped the most-disliked list.[70] According to public-opinion polls, young Russians were more hostile to other ethnic groups than older ones. This provided an opportunity for ultra-nationalist politics to emerge in Russia. Another problem, however, was the escalating hostility to the large groups of ethnic Russians in the former republics – and their fate in Chechnya was tragic. But by the second Chechen war this was less of a problem – they were nearly all dead.

The second war was different, and the media handled it differently. Instead of being seen as a Russian Vietnam, it was experienced by Russians through the prism of Stalingrad. Compared with the first war, the politics were far more complicated. It was started in the aftermath of the panic in Moscow caused by three terrible bomb explosions in civilian housing areas in 1999. One academic commented, 'Everyone started to send their children out to the dachas in the country; for a while, everywhere felt dangerous.'[71]

The fear was acute in a society where most people still felt paranoid about surveillance. The raids were blamed on Chechen terrorists, although nothing was ever proved. One of the few pieces of propaganda that had gone unquestioned by the Russian public, wrote one commentator, was 'that the Chechen terrorists were coming to get them, personally, in their own homes'.[72] NTV claimed in 2002 to have proof that the bombs were part of a state conspiracy to provide legitimacy for another war. Thomas De Waal argued that they could even have been the work of one Chechen faction in conspiracy with the Russian state.[73] Most people were at least willing to entertain such possibilities. No one was sure. In the first war the Russian media had been impelled towards a novel explicitness, and this had been a real pressure in favour of Russian withdrawal: the images agitated on the side of a clear policy alternative. In the second war and the subsequent occupation, by contrast, stories of human-rights abuses and atrocities were oddly lacking in narrative and policy direction.

However, the second war was also launched against a background of anarchy in Chechnya. After 1996, the province had been permitted a kind of de-facto independence – it had been left alone. But the Chechen authorities, such as they were, had not been able to grasp the opportunity. Anatol Lieven saw the first campaign in Chechnya as the end of Russian imperial power, and described a code of honour among Chechens that had underlain the ruthless violence of the fighters. Contemplating the second, he suggested that Chechen society had degenerated and the code had disappeared.[74] Although Chechens had united to fight the Russians, when the imperial power left they fought each other and fierce clan conflict broke out. They kidnapped, murdered and tortured each other as enthusiastically as they did Russians and foreigners. Chechen gangs mounted piratical kidnapping raids into nearby territories – treating hostages as slaves, keeping them like animals in basements, when they did not simply murder them. Reporters showed as much of this side of the war as they could. However, Chechnya had become a very dangerous territory for first-hand reporting. Several journalists who had risked their lives to support the Chechen cause in the first war were among those taken hostage. Between 1996 and 1999 twenty-seven Russian journalists disappeared in Chechnya and were assumed dead.[75]

Thus one explanation of the difference between the ways in which the Russian public reacted to the two wars is that the wars were themselves different: they were not merely serial episodes of a single drama. Chechnya, brutalized by the first war, had descended several more steps into an intolerable and aggressive nuisance. However politically motivated the war was, it could also be seen as more legitimate in Russia. However ineffective, it could be justified. Indeed, the most critical component of Russian public support for the second war was that this time the Russian people understood why there was fighting.

Another explanation for how differently the war was seen was that few journalists were prepared to take the personal risk of going to Chechnya. Had the Chechens had more of a government and less of a competing set of warlords, they might have recognized that international reporting was a weapon they could more easily use to their advantage than the Russians; but they were too fratricidal, and insufficiently political. In addition, the Russian authorities themselves behaved differently. They stopped those journalists who did visit the disputed territory from getting near to the front, and for the first time the Russian state attempted to 'manage' both the foreign and the domestic media. An information office was set up, modelled closely on how the Russians saw the NATO information oper-ation working during the war in Kosovo in 1996. A key political adviser, who had masterminded Yeltsin's press campaigns, was put in charge of it.[76] Bottled up in a squalid nearby border town, a BBC correspondent wrote of the 'snake-like local Russian commander always finding another reason why nothing can happen, no one can go anywhere'.[77] Excluding journalists from war zones could be called a trick that the Russians relearned. This time they justified what they did in terms of the most sophisticated Western practice.

The war degenerated into a ferociously brutal occupation, with all males over twelve years old deemed to be potential fighters and rounded up by the Russian military into notorious 'filtration' camps, from which many never returned. The ghostliest thing about Chechnya, wrote one journalist in 2004, was the absence of men.[78] An indiscriminate slaughter of civilians was accompanied by an appalling failure to provide any care for the hun-dreds of thousands of Chechen civilians who fled the violence. The policy was not only repressive on a new scale, however: it was also ineffective. In particular, it failed to stop a savage Chechen revenge in the form of a series of suicide-bomb raids in Moscow – mainly inflicted on innocent civilians at leisure. Nevertheless, Russians both elected Putin as president and put up with the war. What had happened?

Fright and hurt do not produce liberal sensitivities. Russian public opinion under attack gave the government a licence 'to sort out the mess'. Thus the Russian government began its own exploitation of atrocities in a propa-ganda war for international public opinion. The military compiled a gruesome thirty-minute atrocity video showing the terrible things the Chechens did, and Russian generals were eager to show it to any foreign government officials and journalists they could find.[79] The intention was plain. Russia, the film suggested, was going to war to stop illegitimate violence. Its actions were to be justified by the universal media convention that some wars are 'humanitarian'. What had started out as a new freedom of expression ended up being used in a macabre auction of the use of horror to legitimate action, just as some contemporary terrorists produce recruiting videos depicting the suffering of innocent civilians in harrowing detail. The idea was to whip up feelings and justify terror: a repressive regime and its terrorist opponents were both aware of the mobilizing power of visual displays of violence and their potential influence on public opinion.

Yet the media also slowly began to respond in this far more difficult and threatening atmosphere. This time it was not so much by producing images – although some reporters persisted in showing the horrors that both the Russian army and the Chechen warring criminal factions perpetrated.[80] Rather, journalists attempted to establish reliable casualty figures. Journalism is by no means the only way of guaranteeing trustworthy knowledge, but because it is public it can be an especially fruitful method. A whole strand of reporting became devoted to an obsessive hunt for accuracy. 'Acceptable' levels of casualties vary considerably from country to country, and between conflicts – and some conflicts are so urgent that the alternative to accepting casualties is defeat – but whatever the level it will reflect public sentiment. Policing acceptable mortality is a key media task in any conflict.

In the case of Russia, acceptable – or at any rate accepted – casualty levels have historically been high. This has been true even without wars. Thus between 1910 and 1914 child mortality in Moscow was 600 per 1,000 – a figure comparable to that of medieval Europe during the Black Death. War losses have routinely been counted in millions. It has been estimated that between 1914 and 1953 a total of 50 million Russians died through war, famine or political murder. Nevertheless, there is nothing inevitable about the acceptance of such figures. Both Germany and Japan lost proportions of their populations that compare in scale to the Soviet mortality figures in the Second World War. In consequence they have been careful to avoid involvement in conflicts. They have also developed an American-style squeamishness about even very small casualty figures. Not so Russia.

However, the Russian state has also had a long history of ingenuity in hiding the scale of losses. Uniquely, Russia did not commemorate its millions of dead soldiers from the First World War in the celebration of the 'sacred dead' which was the characteristic response to the killing of that war in other countries.[81] In 1937, when a census revealed the scale of population loss caused by Stalin's purges and by famine, the document was suppressed – and all the census-takers were shot for good measure. Millions of people killed in the purges and the camps were never officially declared dead. Many of their relatives obliterated the faces of those arrested from their photograph albums as a safety measure. Although things eased a little after Stalin's death in 1953, there were also subsequent periods of greater repression. Against this background the 'habit of denial' came easily.

Nevertheless, Russians also developed some strategies for estimating real losses. What marked the wars and the occupation in Chechnya was the extent to which what had previously been a subterranean discussion became public. Journalists used considerable imagination in their attempts to try to establish real figures. They interviewed mortuary assistants about the number of bodies they were processing, or talked to town clerks about backlogs of paperwork. They considered troop movements, where conscripts were called up from and logistics of supply in the attempt to estimate casualty rates.[82] Journalists questioned regional schoolteachers about conscripts from their schools, and they scrutinized official figures sceptically. This was the small change of journalism in a country still undermined not by anything as simple as secrecy, but rather by a sense that all information may represent or offend an interest. It was a small start in the patient task of representing reality – journalism's most honourable work.

A consensus that includes the Carnegie Foundation, Western reporters and several Russian reports suggests that the first war killed about 40,000 inhabitants of Chechnya, many of whom were ethnic Russians, and something like 20,000 Russian soldiers.[83] No conflict involving the West since Vietnam has come anywhere near such a high level of military and civilian casualties. Figures for the second Chechen war are more difficult even to begin to estimate, because Chechen cities and larger villages were so comprehensively damaged. More steadily devastating still have been the mortality figures for the continuing occupation. With the infrastructure destroyed, the health of the surviving civilian population suffered and diseases like tuberculosis once again became rampant. Nevertheless, in the context of the Russian experience of wars the Russian casualties were not felt to be especially excessive. 'Sixty thousand for us,' as one journalist put it, with a bleak laugh – 'that is not so bad.'[84]

One factor in the emergence of secure, relatively reliable knowledge about wars is a growing appreciation that the public would prefer to know the truth, rather than be lied to. And truth has also come to be seen, grudgingly, as a public need. Governments can carry public opinion with them only by securing public trust, which rests on relatively dependable information. This point has to be qualified, however, as even the public desire for accuracy is not absolute. Sometimes anxious populations are happier not knowing the truth, and react negatively, or in disbelief, if they are told it. It is arguable, for example, that the British public during the Second World War had little desire to know any more about the Dunkirk evacuation of troops from France than the Churchillian account of how the army was saved by a flotilla of tiny boats; this was more comforting than the statistics of defeat. Even colouring the news can sometimes be acceptable to the public. Thus the deliberate misleading of the press about the progress of the invasion of the Falklands in 1982 is not normally seen as an attack on democratic rights, and no one would want to compromise the success of a military operation by demanding published details of engagements.[85] Such complex relationships between public and state, however, require a sophisticated democratic framework – and this has still to be built in Russia.

Another argument about the reporting of wars is part of a more general assertion that accuracy in the media has a commercial basis. Truth and secure practices for legitimizing knowledge, it is argued, are firmly linked to economic interest. Accuracy, according to this view, is desirable not because it is preferable morally, but because it has a commercial exchange value. Thus, for example, the Qatar-based satellite station al-Jazeera broke with all the local Middle Eastern traditions of compromised, corrupt and partisan reporting. It was probably one of the most hopeful political developments in the region as well. Yet the station's pathbreaking independence ultimately depended on the economic liberty its original founding investment provided, and on its commercial success.

Discussion of markets, advertising and audience share has, in the contemporary Russian context, to be put in perspective. Most television stations and most newspapers are controlled by political interests, whose real object is the looting of Russia's natural resources and services. Viewing figures and market research are unreliable – and television and advertising are favoured ways of laundering money. Nevertheless, some counting is more independent than it used to be. 'It is strange to say, but some firms are beginning to need to know their customers, truly,' commented one pollster.[86] Advertising in Russia is weak, because not many people have much money to spend (although there is a new, small but lucrative market for the super-rich). This desperate economic situation affects elusive media 'freedoms' in a number of ways. For example, until 1989 and the collapse of Communism, it was very difficult to get clean videotapes in Russia. Such taken-for-granted items in the West permitted a degree of licence to record, disseminate, and choose content. Consequently, in Russia the supply of tapes was closely controlled. After 1989 it was easy enough to get such treasures, provided you were rich enough. Nevertheless, despite the threats and problems, a more segmented periodical press is tentatively beginning to emerge, addressing a limited section of the population. A new generation of journalists takes a new view of Russia's place in the world.

There is some evidence – surprising, in view of Western perceptions – that before the collapse of Communism the public actually trusted the Russian media more than they trusted many other aspects of official life. This could be interpreted as demonstrating the gullibility of the public, but perhaps it also represented a realistic and cautious assessment of what they were offered. Audiences everywhere bring a wealth of other knowledge to their interpretation of what the media offer them, and in particular they bring a history of media consumption. Russian audiences were sometimes too accepting, sometimes too cynical, weary and bewildered. But the media sometimes told them what they needed to know. In the case of Russia, 'trust' in the media encompassed a knowing acceptance of what the media were able to say – a kind of reliability pact between the media and their audiences. During the second Chechen war and afterwards a new, hesitant realism found public expression in the media, but was continually threatened by re-emerging state power. Journalists in Russia get killed by Mafia hit men – but only because they have continued to tell truths.

Soldiers watch television too. It is often said that generals customarily refight the last war. It might be at least as accurate now to say that in broad terms they refight the last war they saw on television.

Indeed, if nations have their own narratives of wars, there is now a shared international repertoire of conflicts as well. The problem in Russia was again the lack of reliable social and historical understanding. The military is still a hugely powerful part of Russian society. Military expenditure commands an unparalleled 41 per cent of Russian GDP. Controlling the army and expenditure on it are central problems for the impoverished Russian state. One interpretation of both wars in Chechnya is that they were little more than attempts by different wings of the military to command resources. The condition of the Russian army had become catastrophic, and the wonder was that it had not staged a revolt or a coup. In the 1990s this once-feared force lost soldiers, money, power and prestige, and was revealed as 'hungry, barefoot and under-financed'.[87] Members of the military were also treated appallingly, from the brutalized and battered conscripts, to the homeless air-force officers, and the abandoned sailors left to die when their submarine sank. Perhaps not surprisingly, the army began exploiting the golden prospects of plunder.

Against this background, the military authorities promised Yeltsin a swift victory in the first Chechen war. Despite defeat, they promised Putin the same in the second. Taking their cue from the NATO campaign in the former Yugoslavia (and of course the long history of aerial bombardment in wars), they also claimed – quaintly, given their history in Chechnya – that this time they were going to use 'precision' bombing. 'There was much talk of our high-tech new helicopters,' one analyst said, 'but what nobody mentioned was that we only had one of them that worked!'[88] Many of the descriptions of what would happen – 'speedy incursions', 'targeted hammerblows' – were simply borrowed from the US and NATO campaigns. But the situation went beyond the cynical dressing-up of Russian actions in Western clothes. 'It was worse,' observed one critic: 'they really thought they could do it like the Allies. "Let's have a short quick successful war – just like we watch on TV!" '[89]

Thus the impact of TV images on specific elites can be at least as important a global phenomenon as the more commonly considered impact on general audiences. (This is not confined to the Russians, however – a scholarly book on the American secret service has recently pointed out that the FBI launched a campaign to recruit more female agents after the success of the movie *The Silence of the Lambs*, with its heroine agent.)[90] Part of the problem was that Russian generals (as well as the Russian public) had based their views of recent wars on coverage which had often been distorted for propaganda purposes. It has been pointed out, for example, that Russian television-watchers (including generals) had seen British tanks and rockets apparently suppressing communities in Northern Ireland for more than three decades – except that the images were fraudulent and had been taken from military exercises and promotions for international armament sales. Of course the conflict in Northern Ireland did look very different depending on whether the cameras were on the soldiers' side, as they mostly were on British television, or on that of republicans and other protesters, as they were to a large extent in Scandinavian broadcasting. Nevertheless, the conflict in Northern Ireland did not lead to wholesale destruction of cities. Rather, British soldiers became adept at handling tense conditions on the ground with a minimum use of force – an experience they took to other complex situations with great effect. Russian generals had other sources of more accurate information about the conduct of foreign wars. Yet, as one outsider put it, 'There was a blurring, and the usual Russian cynicism that reduces everything to the same calculus.'[91]

The key misconception derived from the consumption of foreign media images was that you could have short, fierce, successful campaigns just because you wanted them: not because you had the capacity to execute them. The conclusions that were drawn from Western military engagements in the late twentieth century, as refracted through the distorting eye of Russian TV, were misleading. The lack of 'reality' which a weak media system produces apparently affected the military as well.

It was not only the generals who had been watching a television impression of the West at war. It was also, albeit in a different mood, aspirant journalists. For several decades before the fall of Communism, the foreign press had been in effect the real opposition in Russia. Merridale points out the high status accorded to anything foreign. 'In Russia, nothing that is not "ours",' she observed, 'from our immediate family, is really "safe" to buy or eat or use, unless it is definitely foreign.'[92] As Alan Romer of the Carnegie Foundation in Moscow put it, 'Everything, after the collapse of Communism, was directed at the West. The best thing – the only thing that mattered – was Western approval. If the West liked it, it was approved of.'[93] This was especially true in journalism – or at least in ambitious journalism – where the model and style of foreign reporting were seen as superior – and uncomplicated. Many, of course, have argued that the steady flow of Western images of affluence and economic well-being was critical in undermining Marxist regimes. Since the collapse of Communism, some Western media came to dominate the country – Western films, for example, almost extinguished the Russian film industry. It was only the weakness of the Russian economy that stopped the influx of Western media becoming even more dramatic.

For Russian journalists, denouncing the government's actions in the first Chechen war was endorsed by the sense that the Western news style was legitimate currency. In the more complicated conditions of the second war and the double horror of the occupation of Chechnya and the Chechen terrorist campaign in Moscow, some journalists attempted to establish accurate depictions of reality. But the media always depend on a wider political climate (as well as helping to shape it). They could not make a new Russia alone – even though they were a vital component of such a possibility. Thus the reporting of the disastrous siege in the Moscow theatre in 2002 was attentive and critical, but failed to make the authorities think through their actions any more carefully. This was a modern tragedy – victims were equipped with mobile phones, and on this occasion cameras.

As a result there was an unprecedented and chillingly personal record of the catastrophe – bungled at every point by the authorities – as it unfolded.

In fact Western reporting of the wars itself faced difficulties. In order to make sense to news-consuming publics in the affluent and often indifferent domestic populations, the wars had to be fitted into the well-worn clichés about Russia. The first was that of the Orwellian bureaucratic state, poised to throw all its military might against a small, independent and spirited nation. The second was that Russia never changes. The first war had been seen as the war that reporters stopped. In the second, Russian obstructionism, Russian brutality and Russian military success, combined with apparent Russian public approval (together with the unlikelihood of any meaningful reaction from outside Russia), made the story more complex. What was difficult to register was the sense that the Russians might also, in their approval of this war, have been exercising some (no doubt qualified) independence of judgement as well. The Russian public preferred action of any kind to inertia, and the prospect of more terrorist bombs in Moscow. None of this provided a justification. But for the West the easiest story to tell was the familiar old one of the innocent victim and the guilty perpetrator.

One of the most frustrating aspects of Russia is the extent to which everything feels – to an outsider at least – as if in order to understand it you have to refer to something else. It is a society in which impartial or objective knowledge of public affairs does not exist. An elusive, exhausting fog, the result of so many years in which knowledge was dangerous, still hangs over many aspects of the Russian reality. All transactions of meaning are exchanges, but in Russia what anything 'means' is political, in the sense that it will be resolved by determining in whose interest it is. The sense that there is a relationship between every event and someone's plan somewhere remains dominant. Writing of the pre-perestroika Soviet Union, the historian Geoffrey Hosking commented on the ubiquity of what he called the 'standard authoritative monological text' – or right political line – that dominated much of the Russian media's description of events.[94] Frankness was unthinkable. There is still a kind of 'dissociation' – a habitual space between words and actions. Catherine Merridale reports one Russian as saying, 'In our society we have made this into something ridiculous. It is not an exception to the rule, it is the rule.'[95]

This meant that – despite the legacy of an education system that before the collapse of Communism had produced generations of well-trained scientists, and an empire which produced a cadre of educated professionals –

the public condition and the public good were tainted topics. Literature had been semi-sacred in the Soviet Union because 'writing had to be politics, economics, social science, history.'[96] It was the onerous weight of the necessary compromise, comments the journalist Arkady Ostrovorsky, that left the Russian arts irrelevant and feeble after the collapse of Communism.[97] The media were in a better position than Russian literary culture to reinvent themselves: Russian journalism is a young profession. Nevertheless, the media were compromised as well, and endlessly available to be interfered with. Meanwhile the new elite of comprador bankers were not fertile ground for the growth of groups dedicated to the public good. As Yegor Gaidar, formerly an acting prime minister, commented, 'the goals of the new Russian policy-makers are of a purely private nature – strengthening the state for the purposes of quick enrichment.'[98]

The great Russian critic Mikhail Bakhtin, writing at the height of the Stalinist repression in 1937, used literary criticism to make acute observations about the effects of state despotism on culture. Bakhtin described how in the sixteenth century the overwhelming excesses of Rabelais's literary masterpieces *Pantagruel* and *Gargantua* made a joke of the deadly weight of official culture. Stifling officialdom had forced popular culture to present a parody of the usual, a world turned inside out: 'it was a reaction against the tyranny of . . . solemn interpretation of reality.'[99] Similarly the Russian media under Soviet control had been ritualistically solemn. Russian humour – like that of most of Eastern Europe – was based on this hollowness. There was a hunger for the authentically serious. Thus the conflict in Chechnya offered an opportunity to break away from the futile stage-managed earnestness of the past, and into a harsh gravity. At first, said a journalist, reporting was 'what journalism was supposed to be – telling the people about serious things, not comforting things. Actually it was also interesting.'[100] The tone of address was critical to a public who appeared to want responsibility. The reporting of the first Chechen war showed that the 'shadow' culture of the Soviet system had shifted. But, as the second war and the subsequent occupation were to show, it changed only painfully slowly in the face of unpleasant and intractable realities in Chechnya as well as the inefficient brutality of the Russian authorities. Solutions look less simple now than they did in the late 1990s. And, before solutions can begin to emerge, reality has first to be confronted.

One aspect of this revolt into seriousness was the part played by subjectivity: the reporting of feelings and experiences. Everywhere in the world, it has been suggested, objective, impersonal news is being replaced by subjective, involved journalism. A number of arguments and reasons have been advanced to account for this shift. One has been the feminization of audiences. Women readers and viewers, it is suggested, want a more intimate reporting style. Others have pointed to economic pressures in which the 'columnist' and the associated confessional style of subjective reporting have emerged because they cost less than the complex structures required to sustain foreign reporting. In addition, it has been argued that in the West this kind of writing is less difficult for advertisers to place copy near. Yet another argument has been concerned with the emergence of what might be called a philosophical individualism: a 'postmodern' insecurity about overarching verities and an emphasis on 'individual' experience – a prioritizing of 'feeling' over reason. Indeed, the movement towards feeling and personality is not restricted to journalism. It is a far broader phenomenon, with parallels in the visual arts and literature as well. The emergence of the female war reporter is another associated phenomenon – a feature of both Western journalism and its Russian counterpart. According to the Freedom Forum, during the first war in Chechnya nearly half of the accredited reporters were women.[101] The appearance of women represented some kind of shift in sensibility. One observer commented, 'Their feelings were more interesting to watch.'[102] Some of the bravest, most determined journalists were women. Thus Anna Politskovskaya continued to indict the repressive horror of the new Russia under Putin by telling individual stories of individual victims. 'Quite simply,' she wrote, 'I am a 45-year-old Muscovite who observed the Soviet Union at its most disgraceful. I really don't want to find myself back there again.'[103] But articulating injustice is only one aspect of producing the political will and the political solutions to remedy it. Establishing habits that genuinely seek to portray reality (even if they fail) cannot be replaced by feeling.

The vociferous critics of the concept – or possibility – of 'media impartiality' as an ideology in the comfortable West ought to consider the frighteningly destructive impact on the Russian social system of extreme cynicism about the independence of any knowledge. The role of the media in Russia demonstrates the legitimacy of the attempt to establish objective understanding. It is a fundamental social precondition for many other political advances. In this respect, values at work in the media underlie many other aspects of social action in societies.

The problem in contemporary Russia is how society can understand itself – and how it can do anything without realistic acknowledgement of its condition. Indeed, the insecurity of much knowledge in Russia also illuminates a threat that all societies face. Of course, many societies indulge in self-deception, but most democracies nevertheless contain mechanisms –

A novel state ceremony played out on television: the inability of the Russian state to protect its citizens. A video-grab image of the Chechen militants holding over a thousand hostage in a school in Beslan, 4 September 2004.

from the market, to dissenting opinion, to campaigning interest groups – that are a source of reality-checking. In the post-Communist situation in Russia there still seemed to be few reliable centres of information, and not many trustworthy instruments to find out with.

There is, in addition, the problem of the capacity of the media to create a space in which it is possible to have discussion about the national interest. 'There was no way to have that discussion before. I don't know whether there is one emerging,' observed one Russian analyst sadly.[104] The problem in the media is a reflection (and a reinforcer) of a wider social problem that Russia's history has imposed. Russia is a place where conversations are difficult. Merridale points out that when she brought victims of Stalinist repression, war veterans or orphans together to talk about their experiences, they very rarely talked *to* each other. Instead, they all produced monologues directed at her, and failed to look each other in the eye.[105] Nevertheless, there are a few grounds for a degree of optimism. 'In the past,' one researcher suggested, 'you all had to agree with everybody you knew – you gave up people you disagreed with about anything at all. But our children can disagree with their friends. It is rather wonderful.'[106] The beginning of a conversation about the national interest may, of course, depend on the existence of groups concerned with that subject.

The philosopher of totalitarian societies Hannah Arendt once argued that 'ideology treated the course of events as though it followed the same law as the logical exposition of ideas.'[107] A sense of what might be called 'narrative closure', in which events can always be fitted into a pre-known pattern, is a peculiarly damaging phenomenon. Such a crude imposition of an ordered pattern on reality is still peculiarly exaggerated in Russia, but it is a process to which the media nearly everywhere are prone. It is not that startling change has not happened in Russia: its citizens had, in the last decade of the twentieth century, to put up with more overturning of their previous understanding than almost any other nation. 'Now,' as one journalist observed, 'we are certainly learning about how to have bad news!'[108] Yet Russians prefer to explain everything by a comprehensible conspiracy, and experience is still not considered a legitimate basis of explanation. The philosophical task that the news media have to perform is precisely to manage the meeting of thought and causality – moulding it to the empirical realities of a society.

Does the Russian reporting of the Chechen wars and occupation show that the Russians have been brutalized by their cruel past? Is their reaction to the wars in Chechnya just another chapter in a violent story of Russian exceptionalism? Merridale points out that one of the clichés that Russians themselves reach for is that 'no one is quite sure exactly how it works, but most people agree that there is some kind of connection between Russia's culture and its history of high mortality.'[109] Observers from materially and morally more comfortable circumstances may find it easy to conclude that the Russian public has different sensibilities from those in the tender-hearted and democratic West. It is perhaps far harder for us to accept that all the people who lived and died in Russia in the twentieth and twenty-first centuries were just as vulnerable to suffering as any other people. It is not that the Russian public failed to react to images of the wars in Chechnya in many of the same ways as their comfortable counterparts – rather that images and feelings about wars and violence are not abstract things but are situated in specific circumstances. What the Russians need is a sense of how politics can be done – how you negotiate with previous enemies to resolve problems – not more images of suffering. Media freedoms are very revealing of more general conditions – and highly sensitive. The twenty-first century has seen attacks on journalists, harassment, imprisonment and murder returning in Russia. There have been increased restrictions on reporting, more sophisticated official lies, government manipulation of the revenues of television and the press, the arrest of media owners: the whole panoply of mechanisms designed to intimidate gatherers of accurate or challenging knowledge. Yet this is not an indication of the quality of Russian 'sensibility'

– rather that that sensibility is itself tempered by other political calculations and realities. Russian responses to violence did not grow out of some national eccentricity, but from a particular combination of events, institutions and circumstances. As do ours.

The issue is not whether we have superior sensitivity to that of the poor, brutalized Russians. The failings of Russian politics are not a consequence of the nature of the Russian character (although we ought to be cautious about the institutions that form and educate character – including, of course, the media). The Russians have feelings as deep as ours, but the Russians live in a different place. At the same time, our real problem is not how similar we all are, but how little the dominant Western media, for all their complexity and sophistication, permit us to see and hear the very different voices and views of those in other places and with other values and attitudes. And how very little we are interested in hearing. This matters because it is realistic interpretations of events that we ought to deal with – not our fantasies of how the Russians should feel or how we would like to think of them feeling, or how we sentimentally believe we would feel in similar circumstances. Indeed, the lesson we might like to consider from Russia is how crippling a lack of knowledge can be – and how ignorant of other places we ourselves are in danger of becoming.

8

Bad Death is Good News

Bitter, violent, unjust death can be a highly prized and valuable news story. Different countries and cultures have varying conventions about the broadcasting of pictures of dead bodies and the moment of death itself (which is rarely shown in the West). Meanwhile the attempt to use increasingly gruesome images, and indeed the performance of executions designed and filmed for display, have altered conventions. What would have been unacceptable a decade ago is often now shown. Nevertheless, attitudes that were apparently freshly minted by the most recent news event are often rooted in older traditions, but with their meaning subtly altered by their new purposes. But the meanings of a news death and disagreements about how it should be displayed are increasingly fiercely contested precisely because the public understanding of the event can have direct effects on policies. The news death is thus highly political – it is always an argument.

It has been argued that death in modern societies is a surreptitious affair: hidden, medicalized, relegated to anonymous spaces – an embarrassment. As the pioneering French historian Philippe Ariès put it in the 1960s, 'The medical profession took over the role of the community by isolating death in the scientific laboratory and the hospital, from which emotion would be banished.'[1] Few, it has been said, conduct their own demise or share a common understanding of the ceremonies attending the 'good' death – the kind where an individual, surrounded by family and supported by a structure of belief and well-understood practices, has some kind of authority over how he dies. Others have argued that in an increasingly secularized society the widely held beliefs about death (that it ought always to be delayed, and is an accident) do little to assist people to accompany those who will soon die. Despite the changes that the hospice movement and Ariès's own work have brought about in how death is approached by individuals and their families, as well as by medical staff, more people than ever die in hospital, where many of the protocols are designed to help doctors and families fend death off rather than conduct it. Few people attend the death of those they know or love.

Yet death is news. News has produced a system for describing and dealing with death that is so widely accepted that it is barely recognized. As one journalist has observed, 'News is driven by killing. We tell bad stories.'[2] Another, talking of the reporting of the 1984 famine in Ethiopia twenty years later, said, 'If the story of the famine was as good as it seemed . . .' then ironically corrected himself: 'Well, that meant bad.'[3] When we consider how different societies relate to the spectacle of suffering there is one indisputable fact: death – and especially hard, undeserved, brutal and often unexpected, that is 'bad', death – is a key feature of news. The subject of death and dying is a source of public fascination and hence is central to the news agenda. For unimportant people suffering unexceptional deaths, dying is private and, in the developed world, clinical. For the famous, on the other hand, or for ordinary people suffering a dramatic demise, death is not only news. Death in these circumstances has become the site of powerful, universal media ceremonies. Telling the story of the unexpected, unjust or simply violent death that fits the demands of the dominant news values secures the proper passage of the victim from life to death. It rebuilds social meaning around the loss. People used to worry about the souls of the dead; now they worry about their stories.

People who shy away from accompanying the deaths of those they are close to routinely watch and read about the deaths of strangers. Contemporary men and women, unfamiliar with death close to home, nevertheless consume news about mortality that takes place elsewhere as a daily staple. The reality of modern 'bad' news death is a complex system of practices, rituals and taboos that are frequently refined and in some cases created by the mass media. Many of these have been recently adapted, often unwittingly, from older traditions. They are the less evident because they are so familiar and accepted. Unlike many of the private rituals that surround modern death, they are not narrowly determined by class, belief or local practices, because they are directed at socially inclusive audiences. Because they are recognized all over the world, they are an important part of the increasingly international scope of news. People in very different societies, with different attitudes and different private rituals, share the universal conventions of the media death. Many try to use its power for their own advantage.

The news death satisfies audiences' fear of mortality, and their thrilled enchantment with extinction. It is a fundamental aspect of journalism: as one reporter put it, news is 'concerned with the dark side of things'[4] –

referring both to the bad things that happen and to the public interest in
them. Another, in order to move a discussion on, usefully commented,
'Journalists turn up after people start dying. One, that is what journalists
do. Two, it is deplorable.'[5] Deaths that have the greatest news value are of
the premature, unexpected, violent kind. Typically they are linked to a
developing story that is already securing coverage and audience attention.
At the same time, the violent or unpredictable nature of a death does
not guarantee it a place in the news. Some kinds of bad death are too
commonplace, or too disturbing, for public attention.

There are many violent and unnecessary deaths that receive no attention.
Only a few become news. However, as news items they have been prolifer-
ating – and the trend began before the 'war on terrorism'. Thus violent
death is an increasingly important part of national news in the United

*'Just another gangland death in Newark', 2001. The appetite for 'reality' death
is so considerable that local media now manage to produce for their areas rates
of mortality stories very similar to those of national media.*

Kingdom. The main national broadcast news-providers in the United
States – ABC, CBS and CNN – have also shown increases during the
last decade. More revealingly, local news reports have shown particularly
large increases in the reporting of violent deaths: levels of homicidal, accidental and otherwise bizarre deaths reported in small localities are now
similar to those in the national media. Even in countries like Sweden and

Finland, where there are strict controls over the level of violence permitted in fictional programming, there have been increases in the portrayal of a wide variety of news about mortalities.[6] In general, the picture is of countries that are relatively safe to live in consuming nearly as high levels of 'true' deaths in the media as countries that are in reality much more dangerous and violent. Such assessments are difficult to quantify. Yet what is significant is the shift: the appetite for 'reality death' – or at any rate the readiness of the news media to feed it – seems to be on the increase, and not least in those countries where actual experience of premature mortality is declining.

Indeed, the waxing demand for 'reality' has reduced the importance of immediacy. Although a 'news' death that has just occurred is harder currency than a death in the past, a real-life news death does not have to be a contemporary event. Unable to supply a sufficient flow of recent mortalities, programme-makers are increasingly abandoning the meagre present in favour of the fertile past. War has not vanished from American and European lives; however, the relatively small toll of Western casualties has encouraged a resort to earlier conflicts. Thus the Second World War goes on claiming lives regularly on our screens. Newly revealed archive film (carefully filed but suppressed) from the Second World War and the Stalinist purges has become a staple of post-Communist Russian broadcasting, while the Japanese watch television films of the destruction of Nagasaki and Hiroshima on average five times a year.

There may be many reasons for the worldwide televised re-examination of the violent past. What is clear, however, is that it often contrasts with conventional attitudes in the immediate aftermath of the events that have been resurrected. It is notable, for example, that information and documentary material about the wartime atrocities committed against Central European civilians was relatively hard to come by in Europe in the years immediately following the Nuremberg trials. Interest has only gradually increased as actual memories have faded: it was not until the 1980s that the American media began to overcome a taboo surrounding the Holocaust, and television turned its attention to it. A small number of tentative programmes grew to a steady stream, and then – by the mid-1990s – a flood: the public desire for ever more horrifying detail became more apparent. Thus there were nearly ten times as many stories about the Holocaust in 1997 as in 1953.[7] Of course, the Holocaust was a quite unique event, offering very specific historical lessons. Nevertheless, while some conflicts have remained too contentious to deal with – Vietnam and the protracted conflicts in Latin America have resulted in relatively few documentaries –

other, long-distant, conflicts are still repeatedly re-examined. It is possible to see this reiteration of death in the past cynically, as the mining of a rich seam, while coming to satisfactory moral conclusions (which reflect well on audiences) about past conflicts is easier than dealing with the complex compromises of contemporary wars. Yet the way in which different countries tackle violence in their own history reveals much about their relationship to contemporary reality. Thus Ian Buruma, comparing Germany and Japan, has pointed out that Japanese history books, news and broadcasting all present contemporary Japanese audiences with very inadequate and partial accounts of Japanese history, in which the Japanese are always shown as the victims of aggression. 'Only the Japanese are killed – yet they were inhuman slaughterers,'[8] he argues. This contrasts with Germans' heart-searching about their own history.

Bad news deaths, of course, are contemporary as well as historic. Whether they are distant or close, they are surrounded by ritual. Death in the news is about shock: a sudden event, whether recent or past; a life or a history stopped in its tracks. Nevertheless, it is managed by the media organizations in routinized ways. The procedures that establish the status of a death and the ways in which it is related to audiences are governed by conventions that are no less elaborate because they are unconscious or unrecognized by the consuming public. In fact news editors' pressured decisions about where to cut images are often some of the hardest calculations that they make. The news death may be taking over from the fictional one, but it owes a lot to it – especially when the underlying aim is to provide entertainment.

Conventions provide order and offer comfort, softening the frisson without removing it. They also help to frame personal experience. The American historian Paul Fussell, in his influential and fertile book *The Great War in Modern Memory*,[9] argued that the experience of combat and loss of life in the First World War had been described, and even felt, through the prism of emotions established in literature that was popular before the war. It was not high culture or even good books that had the most impact, but rather commonly read – often critically disregarded – popular verses, novels and newspapers. The ways of describing experience and the values implicit in this popular poetry and fiction rippled through a generation of soldiers, including some combatants who went on to become political and social reformers. The values became so ubiquitous that men who had never read a poem interpreted their experiences through a dominant, taken-for-granted set of literary assumptions and appropriate language. Later writers have observed the interplay between cultural forms and life and death on the battlefield. Thus another critic, Samuel Hynes, examining the memoirs of soldiers, and the historian Joanna Bourke, investigating evidence from soldiers' letters home, argue that the way in which individuals describe events and articulate feelings is often moulded by literary and cultural forms of which the individuals themselves are unaware.[10] The news is surely an even more dominant form: shaping personal experience and moulding political reality.

Contemplating the carnage of the First World War, Sigmund Freud observed, 'It is, indeed, impossible to imagine our own death; and whenever we attempt to do so we can perceive that we are in fact still present as spectators.'[11] Today we observe faraway places where death has occurred, and other places where death will occur, more often and with more detailed intimacy than was ever previously possible. As mass-media consumers we look at the dead too – and sometimes, in carefully controlled ways, watch the moments before and immediately after death itself – as part of the routines of the broadcast schedules. We are now voyeuristic spectators of the bitter death of strangers in ways and on a scale that was never previously feasible or imaginable.

As spectators, we take certain things for granted. We expect the death to be communicated to us by a reporter who is personally in control of the business of conveying the report. In the case of television, the convention is that the journalist faces us, back turned to the scene described. Such a practice is assumed to be natural, yet it has a history. The figure of the reporter facing viewers was developed in the early silent newsreels, when the presence of the figure provided a guarantee of the provenance of what was seen – otherwise audiences had no way of knowing whether what they saw was a real place in a story or just library film from somewhere else.[12] However, in the mid-1920s the visible figure was discarded, and at first subtitles and then the detached and Olympian voice-over were substituted. Then even the voice of the reporter disappeared and actors read journalists' scripts. The extended disappearance of the person of the journalist can be put down to the dominance of radio over all media conventions, so that even filmed news-reporting adopted its habits. But the reporter also disappeared because the personality represented by a recognizable individual was then felt to detract from the authority of the report – reporters were experienced as a 'fussy distraction to the eye and ear'.[13] In Britain, Robin Day broke with the convention and appeared on screen for the first time in his reports on the Suez crisis.[14] But it was not until the 1960s that the reporter began to appear routinely on screens. Ever since, he (or now, very frequently, she) has become a vital element in the recounting of the tragedy of others to us.[15] Journalists guarantee the veracity of events, and they provide the link between the world of the comfortable and familiar and that of the victim. More recently – only over the last decade – victims have been invited more frequently to speak for themselves. This is also a development of considerable emotional power.[16]

However, the role of the reporter remains highly formulaic. Thus we have come to expect the reporter of death to be sombre and calm and to move little when on camera. As one television journalist puts it, 'being still is important because then the viewers can concentrate on what is happening behind you . . . But if it is a shot of something bad then the stillness is part of underlining what matters.'[17] Such an emotionally detached posture – as if the reporter were a pillar or statue, or possibly a high priest – has evolved over recent decades, with little conscious thinking behind it; but it reflects some ancient instincts. There are even medieval parallels. Paul Binski, describing death in the Middle Ages, argues that 'the calm, emotionless visual symbolism of medieval funeral statuary was only disturbed by the more exceptional – and equally formalized – feminized expression of extreme grief made by the Virgin Mary, or Mary Magdalene.'[18]

Avoiding the overt expression of grief has become another televisual news convention, reflecting a key premiss of 'responsible' news-making: that emotion – for example during a report of civilian casualties – would constitute a distracting personal bias, obscuring the reality of events and getting in the way of objectivity. There is also another worry: that an emotional report turns attention away from the event and on to the reporter. In practice, of course, the situation is not so simple: the audience makes contradictory demands. The reporter is expected to be moved (he or she is human and decent), but not to show it (he or she is also doing a job). Thus the best reporters – the kind the BBC uses for particularly chilling or momentous events – indicate in the subtlest and most understated way the gravity of the occasion, while simultaneously exhibiting a maximum of appropriate self-control. Such a performance, of course, has deep cultural roots. There have always been social positions and groups of whom it has been felt to be inappropriate that they should demonstrate grief. Monarchs, for example, are traditionally not expected to betray their feelings. As the anthropologist Edward Evans-Pritchard, describing funeral practices, once observed, there is a 'specific role in the proceedings assigned to the unmoved'. The unmoved highlight the grief of the moved, and 'may symbolize more effectively the enduring loss'.[19] Composure, or even the failed attempt at it, often amplifies emotions.

Indeed, inordinate grief is socially threatening if unsuitably expressed. In the Old Testament, David's consuming sorrow at the necessary death of his treacherous son is all the more powerfully disturbing because it is so exceptional in a man and so disastrous in a king. 'And the king was much moved, and went up to the chamber over the gate, and wept: and as he went, thus he said, O my son Absalom, my son, my son Absalom! would God I had died for thee.' David's visible grief was so extreme (and so excessively expressed) that it was irresponsible. His army, who had won an important victory, seeing his reaction 'gat them by stealth that day into the city, as people being ashamed steal away when they flee in battle' (2 Samuel 18:33, 19:3). Grief is fissile and uncontrollable. It assaults those who feel it. To feel grief is to be engaged in a struggle with a rapacious and powerful dragon. But the issue was not the overwhelming nature of David's grief, but that his indulgent expression of it damaged those who had saved the city, and to whom as king he owed a duty. As a consequence, his wallowing in the fluent expression of grief destroyed even more of his social world.

Journalists ought not to express 'grief', both because they do not (and have no right to) feel it as the bereaved do, and also because – whatever their actual feelings – the public see them as ambassadorial, and, like ambassadors, they face both ways: both to us and away from us. They symbolize an official or national assumption of courage or, in classical terms, virtue.

There is a paradox here. Few professions are more self-consciously informal than journalism, yet few are, in practice, more rule-bound. Thus journalists and photographers gathering around a dead body in a newsworthy riot or war behave like well-rehearsed dancers as they compete and cooperate for the best angles. Many observers have noted that, in practice, journalistic rituals have a rigidity which seems to conflict sharply with a professional code that exalts change, novelty and originality.

What function do such rituals serve? When they are part of the display of news made to the public, they communicate and affirm beliefs by providing a framework of predictability. Although both participants and spectators may be unconscious of them, these rituals have nevertheless become so much part of contemporary life that those concerned act their role in them with ease. Rituals above all serve to stabilize moments of crisis: they may do this as much for participants as for observers. Thus the rules governing news production, the definition of a good news picture, the nature and treatment of contacts and confidences, the filing of a report – 'just getting on with what you have to do gives you the next clear thing to do'[20] – perform exactly such a stabilizing role for the journalists themselves. Any frustration is at their inability to perform their duty.

Journalists not only perform rituals for themselves: they also establish rituals in which we all share. Indeed, reporting conventions have come to bear the weight of many of the complex aspects of belief and habit that surround death. At the beginning of the twentieth century the anthropologist Arnold Van Gennep argued that death rituals, like other 'rites of passage', accompany and effect a change in the person involved, as 'during them the dead pass from one cosmic or social world to another.'[21] There are, Van Gennep suggested, three different kinds of rite, observable in most societies, namely separation rites, on the one hand removing the dead person from 'the body of the living', and on the other separating their souls, or what Van Gennep called 'the human essence', from their bodies; transition rites, marking the passage of the 'human essence', from one state to another; and finally incorporation rites, in which the 'human essence' of the individual is lastingly located beyond life. The object of the rituals was to bring to conclusion 'the twofold task of incorporating physical remains among those of the earlier dead, and of aiding the soul in its journey to and inclusion in the community of the dead'.[22] During most of this process the eventual fate of the soul is in question, while the responsibilities of the living to the dead are urgent and onerous. It was, argued Van Gennep, the duty of the living to secure the transition of the dead person's soul from one condition to the next, and without their efforts the resolution was unlikely to take place.

Beliefs about the nature of death, the existence of an afterlife, the practices and the requirement of a proper burial – for the benefit both of the social group and of the individuals concerned – are fundamental to all societies, including our own. Within the secular, competitive, partly commercial, partly informative habits of contemporary news-reporting, practices have evolved that conform to at least some of the purposes of those performed religiously in the past. Such practices have become globally recognized, to the point at which they have become a universal language – for example, the very recent convention, hugely encouraged if not actually invented by television, that members of the public should mark a tragic death by placing flowers at the scene of the disaster or the home of the deceased. Such practices reflect beliefs – and in the world-dominating West, however secularized, beliefs with an aspect that is derived from religion and that perform the functions of religion.

How much do today's secular journalists and news organizations bring to the work of reporting death from earlier, less secular, habits and beliefs? Arguably, contemporary journalism and the news occupy some of the same space in our collective lives that the rituals of religion used to do. Moreover, the conventions of journalism are international. Even if the purposes of news are still very different in different parts of the world, the forms are remarkably similar.

In the case of the early Christian Church, practices had to be invented that responded to the needs of the societies in which they first appeared, and these had to provide a lingua franca for a faith which transcended national and social boundaries. Indeed, inventing burial rites was a central part of the empire-building of the new faith. The job of what Frederick Paxton has called the 'impresarios of ritual' was to Christianize death and to weld together the gestures and symbols derived from the past and the novel elements of the new beliefs, combining clerical and lay members of the Church in a satisfying ceremony.[23] At the same time, the early Christians also needed such ceremonies to express their own, radical, views about the nature of death. While contemporary Romans prayed to the dead and worshipped them, Christians prayed *for* them, which involved a radical reappraisal of the status of the departed. Yet St Augustine observed very early on that burial services were above all for the living.[24] They were evangelical, remaking the Christian beliefs of the living as well as dealing with the communal loss.

The ways in which stories about death are managed in news organizations both express and shape contemporary beliefs about the meaning of death. They are accepted so widely only because they are understood by audiences, and quite simply seem appropriate and proper to them. This is a mark of their immense authority. The rites of journalism express beliefs. The fundamental idea communicated in the rituals of journalism is that news attention may reveal the meaning of a death, its particular role in a particular news story – in itself a story sharing similarities and differences with other stories. Any dead body may tell a story, but only those bodies and those stories that fit into news values are likely in practice to get the opportunity. However, journalists and journalism understand that they not only reveal meaning ('tell the story that the body means', 'catch the picture that captures the story', 'get the telling quote'), but, beyond that, they may create meanings and make something of a death. Contemporary journalism expresses a set of beliefs (which it shares with audiences) about the proper transition from life to death of an individual essence which earlier generations were more confident in calling 'the soul'. Thus for journalism the 'life after death' exists in the telling of the story of a particular death as part of the argument of a wider news narrative.

Historically, from the very earliest times, the unburied corpse was 'limber'. It was as yet unintegrated in the rituals of death; and in nearly all societies, in all periods, it has been an object of considerable fear. The limber corpse was frightening because it was a death not yet resocialized. The object of funerary proceedings was to tame the startling unknownness of death and to bring the fact of the death back within the secure social bounds of the meaning to the community. Thus funerals serve to integrate the dead into the new community of the dead, to reinforce the social bonds of the diminished society, and to compensate the bereaved for the loss. They serve to resocialize the dead and to secure the cohesion of those who mourn in a rebuilt social network.

The limber corpse was not alive, but nor was it securely dead. Many traditional rituals helped to establish that no mistake had been made and to confirm that the death was indeed 'true'. To a large extent modern medical practice has taken over this function and made the identification of the process, if not the moment, of death technical – and sometimes less certain and even open to dispute. After all, a man in a coma, on a ventilator, after a brain haemorrhage is certainly alive, but the length and nature of that life are determined by medical judgements and ultimately human decisions. Journalism, by contrast, determines in a very primitive way the significance of the deaths it recounts. In news there is a calculated, necessary disregard for the dead, combined with something similar to the fear of the limber corpse. Souls are understood as not yet being at rest. The contemporary limber corpse is one whose story – in terms of news – has not yet been told.[25]

However, only some deaths are serious candidates for news, and by far the most important of these is the public violent death – the one that no one would want, the 'bad' death that is unexpected and shocking, that is worthy of making news. Death has to fit news values to attract media attention, although not all potentially newsworthy deaths make it. Thus, in the words of Bernard Kouchner, founder of Médecins Sans Frontières, 'Men are dying at this moment in Burma, and Tibet, and Sri Lanka and no one cares because they are not known, and they are not seen to die.'[26] Kouchner was talking about what could be called the bad, violent or negligent death produced by conflict or famine – but in this case unreported, and consequently unresolved, mortalities. There is a systematic arbitrariness about news values that makes the attention of the news distorting. It appears magical in its capacity to transform fortunes.

Bad death is the meat and drink of media activity. One reporter of the conflict in El Salvador observed that his colleagues would change from passivity to animation if bad death was in the air. 'Suddenly the shout, "Un muerto! Un muerto!" (a corpse) rang out in the halls of the hotel . . . the members of the press corps poured into the hall smiling and laughing, hoping this one would be news.' He wrote, 'Like disciplined firemen they jammed into the elevators, ran through the lobby, jumped into their vehicles and were off.'[27]

'Bad', unexpected and violent death has its own history. After the First World War, concern about violent unnecessary death focused with particular emphasis on military casualties. Today, soldiers remain central to conventional ways of portraying death. Indeed, the media's relationship to the announcement and account of military death has altered military practices. Thus at the beginning of the war in Afghanistan, in 2001, a retired civil servant who had played a key government role in wars since the 1950s remarked that 'The one thing soldiers care most about – it is very close to their hearts – is looking after their own casualties, not letting the media announce anything first. They want to get to the families – they want to be in charge of the news over this more than almost anything else.' As twenty-four-hour news has become more available, so army thinking has responded. Previously, families would not be woken in the night to be told of the death of a soldier, to avoid panic and upsetting the children. But now 'the race is always on to get there before they see it on television.'[28] Many of the ideas around the newsworthy violent death were moulded by dealing with the casualties of war. Yet since the Second World War the ratio of civilian deaths to military deaths has swung dramatically – to the point at which, in many recent conflicts, being an active combatant has been a relatively safer option within a war zone than being a civilian.

It is central to the journalistic treatment of violent or sudden mortality that news pronounces judgement over the death. It is often the words that accompany images – though sometimes the narrative sequences in which the images are presented – that are expected to provide particular meanings for us. What we make emotionally and intellectually of the portrayal of death depends not on the horror of the imagery itself, but on how the death is shown and identified. Sometimes the images become part of such a familiar narrative that an accompanying storyline becomes redundant – as, for example, in the final stages of the Vietnam War. In such cases the meaning is implicit. In other conflicts there is less to differentiate pictures of the dead on one side from those on the other. An image of a corpse is not self-explanatory, but requires interpretation. Such interpretations may have considerable consequences. 'Dead bodies,' comments the anthropologist Mark Pedelty, 'have served the metaphorical purpose of sustaining the first-world view of third-world society as conflicted, tortured, and perhaps

1 January 2005: tsunami victims laid out in Takua Pa in Thailand. One response might be that such images dehumanize the dead. But another is that the presence of news-makers means that a civilizing process has begun.

barbaric.'[29] A body on its own without explanation may be that of an innocent victim, a dead combatant, a dead ally or a dead enemy.

The verbal framework in which a journalist frames such pictures is schematic and implicitly regulated. David Stannard argues in *The Puritan Way of Death* that in the late seventeenth century the increasing isolation of the Puritan community of New England amid the hostile values of the burgeoning commercial culture of America led to the development of increasingly flamboyant funeral rituals. Among these was the jeremiad, 'a monumental lamentation for an idealized past which bewailed the un-soundness, rottenness, and hypocrisy of the present' and contained a vision of a better future.[30] Contemporary broadcast reports of death sometimes have a similar rhetoric. It is also arguable that tragedy in contemporary news is shaped partly as a response to comparable pressures – that slick modern conventions reflect the uneasy mix of values in a broadcasting environment determined by an anxious need to attract audiences and hold their attention.

The framework in which the particular account of the death or deaths is situated refers to transcendent values, whether journalists are aware of this or not. The processes of journalism, the ways in which the facts are assembled and checked, involve important values which exist as an ideal beyond any individual – even though their salience varies dramatically between different kinds of journalism and different kinds of media. Thus 'truth' is elusive, and much journalism is indifferent to the struggle to achieve it (much news lies) – yet all journalism is legitimated by the ideal. Otherwise it is propaganda or fiction that is published. News is a historically fashioned literary practice that focuses on a single event: it is the first – and sometimes the defining – draft of history, and increasingly the first source for political judgements and analysis. It is, of course, often mistaken: journalists misunderstand or deliberately distrust what they see – and in any case what they see is only partial, and the causes of the story are not observable, and so on. Eyewitness reports only ever provide evidence of one part of the jigsaw of events, and editorial offices exist to provide depth.

In addition, any event has to be fitted into a larger time frame – this is what adds meaning to an event. It is the larger time frame which provides the structure of the story. At the same time, news is not good at providing historical context. Indeed, such are the pressures on journalism that more of it is based on rumour about what will happen tomorrow than on reporting what happened yesterday (which used to be its primary task). As the journalist Nick Gowing has pointed out, because of the speed of the news cycle rumours are now in danger of getting as much coverage as genuine stories, and are consequently authenticated.[31] Modern journalism, writes Timothy Garton Ash, is 'all about speculation (what will happen), featurism and futurism'.[32] These are all attempts to shape stories – but very different from the perturbing, unformulated nature of history.

Scrupulously correct facts are sometimes fitted into misleadingly conventional narratives (as well as on occasions straightforwardly wrong ones). In the case of violent bad death, they are often fitted into the schematic history of a jeremiad. The jeremiad is a form of story embodying stylized values concerning loss and death into which specific events are slotted. News reports of bad death are thus a genre with a well-understood set of values and tropes. Such accounts often obscure real history in favour of moral exhortation. The jeremiad does not deal with the particular economic, political or social history of the conflict or events that lead to an individual death. Rather, it is a more all-purpose history of 'before the war', 'when life was normal', 'everyday life'. One report from Bosnia, for example, began, 'Last year this was a poor village but a good place to live. Last week it was a frightened village. Yesterday death came.'[33] Another said, 'Sarajevo used to be fun but now there is death.'[34] Yet another, from Zaire, concluded, 'Yesterday was the time for politics, now humans have to be given priority. Unseen, unheard a disaster is unfolding. Tomorrow the international community will be held responsible.'[35] Such generalized reviews of 'history', the time before what is now happening, are easily combinable with strict factual discipline. An article in *The Times* about the protracted war in Somalia (nearly a decade after the conflict had started) opened, 'Recently this was one of the poorest places on earth, but life was normal.'[36] Whatever the experience, urban, sophisticated, multicultural Sarajevo and rural impoverished Somalia contain in these accounts the same past – a seamless time 'before the war'. Astonishingly, news of the worst that can happen to people is given the literary shape of a pastoral.

The next aspect of the jeremiad, condemnation of the corruption of the present, is also prominent in the conventions of the modern news report – and central to its purpose. For the preacher at the Puritan funeral, the death being commemorated was above all a prompt to the living to contemplate mortality and reconsider their ways. Like Jeremiah, the preacher would exhort and warn. In a similar way, journalists locate bad death in a framework of innocence and guilt, reflecting the relationship between the watching world's political stance and the observed world's violence. In this way the first thing established is the moral – that is to say politically defined – 'meaning' of the corpse or corpses. The audience needs to know whether it is on the side of the corpse or not. But the rottenness of the present time in which the report is located is an almost mandatory feature of news reporting from scenes of death. And it is from this corruption that what Stannard identified as the next part of the jeremiad derives. From the corruption of the present, he argues, jeremiads claim that 'seeds of hope to come' will spring.[37] In itself, reporting thus argues that action has begun to alleviate the situation, for the construction of a report and the success of an item in finding its place in the schedule of the news in themselves constitute an appeal. By being made aware of what has occurred the audience may be made to feel superior ('that does not happen here'), anxious ('that may happen here') or involved, even if only passively ('somebody ought to stop that happening'). The very existence of the report, however, is about the possibility of change. Indeed, the spectator is invoked to represent hope. Very few broadcast reports, however grim, imply that the situation they are describing is beyond amelioration. Journalists are assigned tasks of witnessing and revelation on our behalf.

Hope is manifest in the reporting itself. Sometimes this can be genuinely positive: reporting can be redemptive – for there is a real power that the journalist can at times consciously exercise. During the Kosovo conflict, the BBC reporter David Loyn spoke on the news every night for over a

David Loyn, a BBC reporter in Iraq. When a journalist faces the camera it is a convention we all understand. However, the authority and impact of any report are also dependent on the practices of the news organization that journalists report for.

week about the fate of Kosovan villagers driven from their homes on to the hills in the months before the war began. He was describing abject misery, but the meaning was clear: something could or ought to be done. His reports were part of a pressure that delivered relief. On the other hand, sometimes reporting (perhaps in response to pressures on time and news agendas) becomes a baroque but empty rhetorical jeremiad.

The rites of journalism are about establishing, for the audience – the watching, reading, distant mourners – the meaning of particular deaths in the narratives of news. This is normally more than the neutral, 'objective', factual matter it appears to be. The idea that one can and should separate facts from values, and that the facts should be independently verifiable, remains an important part of journalism – indeed, it is the basis of the authority of the news. A version of it is especially powerful in the United States.[38] Some contemporary critics have repeatedly argued that it continues to distort reporting. 'The effect of objectivity,' writes Daniel Hallin, in a reassessment of the conventional role of the media in reporting the war in Vietnam, 'was not to free the news of political influence, but to open wide the channels through which official information flowed, often to keep issues off the political agenda by disguising major decisions as apparently routine and incremental.'[39] Objectivity, Hallin argues, can almost automatically advance established political positions, and suppress more oppositional ones. Similarly, the anthropologist Mark Pedelty has shown how in El Salvador the convention of 'objectivity' effectively disguised the key role of the American government in the conflict. Thus one reporter commented that she could not avoid using the United States embassy as a source, because it was so important in El Salvador, but 'she certainly did not frame the US functionaries as "running the war" when writing news . . . In fact she did not frame them at all. Their identities remained safely hidden behind misleading attribution, while their ideas framed the presentation of news subjects.'[40]

The critics of the idea of objectivity often claim that it is unrealizable, and that all journalists bring values and assumptions to their work that frame how they report stories. More than that, it has also been claimed that it is misleading and makes invisible the ideas that the audience needs to know in order to place the story in a proper context. Yet impartiality and objectivity are indispensable tools; rather than criticize the concept, it is more fruitful to consider the structures that support better or worse practice. The critics of so-called objectivity are particularly vehement because objectivity is not merely a political but also a moral claim. Asserting that the knowledge produced is authoritative – as journalists do – is not merely a claim to exercise a power to define events for others to make up their minds about. It is also a claim to an overarching legitimacy – beyond the reach of any particular political system. Journalists do not ask to be accepted as decision-makers, but they nevertheless claim a legitimacy for what they do that has a priority over the decisions of politicians. Even the scandalmongering, tabloid end of journalism tries to slip under the skirts of this moral claim – and disputes about legitimate representation of public interests that so dominate the relationship between politicians and journalists are a product of a conflict about who exercises the most justifiable authority. News's claim to power in this way has a firm theoretical moral basis – however inadequate the practice.

Indeed, as Michael Schudson has argued, journalists and lawyers both began developing the idea of 'objectivity' as a key component of professionalizing their occupations at the same time. For both important groups, a key task during the twentieth century was 'to pin down objectivity, to establish reliable tests and rules and standards of knowledge. In both professions, there have been attempts to locate an Archimedean point from which pronouncements about the world would be trustworthy.'[41]

Journalism often (inadvertently) reduces the different places it reports from – complex industrial societies and destitute rural ones – to the same 'ruined pastoral' scenes so familiar from news of war, conflict and disaster.

Schudson's argument places the emergence of objectivity in a particular historical framework, and makes the point that it is not the only ideology that journalists have operated with in the past. He also suggests that we ought to be sensitive to alterations in its uses in contemporary journalism. 'Objectivity' is by now a much-abused category. 'All of us,' one journalist has observed, 'carry baggages of prejudices and instinct. We are all emotionally influenced by what we see.'[42] Another commented, 'You can't write about anything without some kind of emotional charge.'[43] But the personal freight that journalists bring as individuals should not be confused (as it has been by many media critics) with the different level of prejudice that Hallin is identifying. One editor puts the insider's, concrete, interpretation of what should happen: 'Journalists are not there to tell the whole truth – they can't possibly see it. That's what editors are there for – to sort out the mess and get the big picture right.'[44] But editorial judgement is under pressure from the speeding-up of the news cycle, while editors in charge are, of course, more directly exposed to the pressures of circulation, the intentions of owners and the structures of the organization than are journalists. Indeed, commercial pressures have recently overvalued a kind of spurious eyewitnessing, preferring to tell the news from reporters in the field even if they have been confined to a very limited part of their exotic locations. The problem is not so much the inadequacy of the ideal of objectivity as how to determine limitations in how it is applied. One such limitation is the wrapping-up of unformulated events into neat stories. Such moulding of reality makes it easier for audiences to comprehend, but it also has dangers. Societies that are incapable of recognizing the true condition of their circumstances are enfeebled. Objectivity – or some value like it – is thus indispensable, and this is not a moral but rather a practical issue.

However, there is another value which journalists and lawyers share, which also affects how they interpret events: namely, a strange assumption that there are right answers to problems. Just as the courts are based on the idea that – after due consideration of precedent, common law and statute – a legal solution is available, so journalists behave as if an objective truth exists, but that it has to be searched for. This guiding principle is the basis of the implicit claim that journalism embodies values that go beyond any particular political movement or system. So, in turn, the 'meaning' of a particular death is situated both within specific political and social contexts, but also within a set of wider values that claim a kind of moral supremacy.

Journalists are outsiders to wars, famines and disasters. It is not merely that their visits to scenes of conflict and misery are usually temporary, and therefore superficial: they may also spend a good deal of that part of their time waiting for the next news opportunity to erupt. They are often in an odd limbo world of waiting. Nor is it just that, while they may be on one side in any conflict, other values in their professional lives drive them to question what they see. Journalists, good and bad, are also travellers between moral worlds. They go from where you must not kill people to where you have to. This distance may, of course, put them in a privileged position to tell the story of the wars that they observe. The best place from which to tell the story of a war is close to the action but at some distance from the values.

At the same time, reporters bring stories of death back to societies where the experience of death has altered dramatically. In the West, people live longer than in the past. Between 1901 and 1995 the death rate for young adults (between the ages of sixteen and twenty-four) in Europe fell by between 70 and 90 per cent. People lead healthier lives, and since the Second World War famine has largely disappeared from Europe. Routine death has different causes. Hence, for all the major investors in news, the distance between what audiences see in the news and what they expect of their own lives has widened. People in the watching societies expect to have comparatively secure and pain-free lives. In many ways this is as true of someone watching the aftermath of a domestic train disaster (when they are safely home) as of a comfortable observer of a disaster in another country. Journalists, however, visit both the watching society and the disaster area and carry messages between them, and so have to be articulate in the conventions of both dimensions. Nevertheless, the way in which they present death nearly always obeys the conventions of the observing society – wherever that is.

Sometimes corpses can be seen and shown in the news; sometimes they cannot. In television coverage and the still pictures of the press, the conventions that determine which pictures are worthy of being shown, or are fit to be displayed, are important features of the news organizations. The conventions are constructed out of commercial criteria – the cost of acquiring and showing the images; the competitive costs of other news items; their value to the photographer and the news organization – mores and written guidelines about what are felt to be acceptable images. Aesthetic values influence choices. But the choices are also political: different corpses mean different things, and are presumed to have distinct influences on outcomes. Corpses are evidence for arguments. Thus a journalist expelled by the Serbs from Kosovo wrote of meeting female Albanian refugees who told the familiar story of being separated from their menfolk who were then murdered by the Serbs. Unable to confirm that the men were dead, the journalist wrote, 'I cannot prove that Sadie and Refi Zachun were shot dead by Serbian forces inside their own home. I have no footage, I never saw the bodies with my own eyes.'[45] But, she went on, the bloodstained clothes of the grieving women convinced her (and should convince us) of their words. Even absent corpses can be compelling evidence.

Corpses, as distinct from the mere fact of death or murder, have produced their own set of ceremonies in journalism. In the war in Iraq the American government believed that public opinion was so sensitive to the sight of the returning bodies of dead soldiers that censorship was tightly imposed on pictures of the coffins. There are two separate but related traditions: the 'body-bag' corpse, which belongs to 'our' side in a combat, and the human remains of foreigners, whether enemy or innocent victim. 'Body bags' have become such an important part of contemporary culture and thinking that they are routinely described as having an impact on American foreign policy, and have certainly played a role in the emergence of the idea of the 'casualty-free' offensive. Body bags are precisely designed to hide corpses decently, yet they produce a powerful imagery. 'Body bags' are corpses in transition – 'made ready for transport'.

There is, everywhere, an uneasy ambiguity about the way in which the society of the living relates to corpses – hovering between the poles of terror and of solicitude. Anthropologists and historians detail many societies in which the dead body is an object of dread. Comfort comes only with a secure sense of the efficacy of the steady working-through and propriety of the rituals involved in dealing with the dead body: that the body will be properly reclaimed for social order. Indeed, the potency of the 'body bag' has become so great that casualties are increasingly returned in coffins, with full military ceremonial. The possibility of such ceremonies, however, depends on there being very few casualties. No pictures of corpses were broadcast after 11 September, and in America and the United Kingdom there were no pictures of people choosing to jump from the towers – although there were pictures of people hurtling to their deaths. This film was never shown live, except inadvertently – only ever as recorded and edited footage. Broadcasting does not show the moment of death. It was as if the moment between the live event and the film record represented the proper weight of respect. There was also fierce (both voluntary and officially imposed) control of the images of the dead and wounded – as if conventions of privacy and non-visibility were important. In short, this terrible public event was treated by the media as if it were a private loss.

9

Media Memorials

Today we often view corpses. In a modern news-made ceremony, we view body bags or corpses laid out in identification lines, assembled in wars in the Middle East, Africa, Iraq and before that Kosovo. Increasingly we witness bodies before even this minimal human ordering has occurred. Such sights and the accompanying stories provide a secular version of the rendering of last rites. The presence of the press is now one part of sending the dead on the final journey. The dead retain elements of the profane carrion they might have remained, but there is a sense that, however horrible the death, a civilizing process is in train. They will be dealt with in a way that is fitting – by the media.

The televised or photographed images of such events, or the written descriptions of print journalism, are new versions of the ancient tradition of 'viewing the corpse', a custom that was still widely practised in most of western Europe and the United States well into the twentieth century. The First World War disturbed the tradition – partly because so many of the bodies of the dead were never found or had been rendered unidentifiable. In addition, early in the First World War the Allies made the decision to bury the casualties where they fell. Hence viewing the corpse became less common because it was less easy to arrange. In civilian life the practice of viewing the corpse went back many centuries, but nevertheless it was a practice which changed. Viewing had the function of communicating condolence to the mourners and expressing final respects to the deceased. Historically, it was less about securing the future life of the soul than about breaking the pollution barrier surrounding the deceased – whose dead but as yet unsocialized body was perceived as a threat. Viewing and touching the dead were thought to help to heal grief, and indeed to help the community 'come to terms with death in general'.[1] This ritual was closely associated with the 'waking' of the deceased. The historian Ruth Richardson has shown how viewing the corpse passed first from a solemn to an exuberant affair, from the beginning to the end of the eighteenth century, and how its function was adapted in the process.[2] In a print in his famous series *The Harlot's Progress* (1731), Hogarth shows just such a viewing turned satirically into an irreverent social event. The Hogarth print marks another slow shift in sensibility, away from high-spirited excess to respect. The transition away from a public viewing to a private and hidden event developed later, in the nineteenth century. The reformer Florence Peacock wrote in 1895 that it was 'a common and most reprehensible practice to make a kind of show of the dead. Not only are the relations and those who love the departed suffered to see the body and watch by it . . . but anyone that likes may come and stare out of vulgar curiosity.'[3] The practice rapidly declined. By the 1930s critics argued that the dead should be protected from 'unnecessary display', and by the 1950s the habit was becoming uncommon. Now, despite an increase since the 1980s of the practice of family members visiting the dead,[4] the bodies of those who die in hospital or hospices are rarely taken home.

In recent years, customs have again been changing in ways that seem to reveal evolving beliefs about the nature of death. First, there has been a renewed concern with the fate of the bodily remains. The military practice of returning the bodies of casualties home has tended to replace the earlier tradition of foreign burial. This depends on the nature of the conflict rather than any simple notion of practicality. If you are fighting a war on foreign soil the return of bodies is usual, but if you are fighting a war in a distant but politically related place then bodies are buried abroad. Thus casualties in the Falklands War were buried on the islands themselves – appropriately in a conflict which was about asserting British sovereignty, although soldiers killed in Northern Ireland – part of the British polity – were returned to the mainland. The bodies of British soldiers who were killed in Iraq were returned home. In part, of course, the return of bodies requires access to them and, in practice, a limited number of casualties – it is nevertheless an issue where policy reflects the politics of any particular conflict.

Yet, significance may be attached to the growing stress – in an increasingly secular society – on 'bringing the body back home'. In the United States, the returning of bodies, whole or in bits, is regarded as particularly important. Considerable expense is devoted to the accurate forensic identification of body fragments. In this growth of what might be termed the symbolism of the macabre, one key factor has been media scrutiny – altering what feels seemly by changing a private act into a public event.

Meanwhile, the last generation has seen the reinvention of the collective viewing of the effects of 'bad' death. Here again the media have reshaped old practices to meet new needs. The collective viewing of representations

The return of the coffin of Lance Corporal Steven Jones to RAF Lyneham, 8 February 2005. Different conflicts lead to different policies regarding the interring of war casualties. But media scrutiny (and attempts at times to control it or evade it) has become one factor influencing policy.

of death in battle is not new, and its functions are complex. A commonplace of fiction, films and photographs, battlefield morality is nevertheless scrupulously removed from broadcast news. Indeed, the evolution of how such deaths have been portrayed is revealing. Thus the art historian Alan Borg points out that the earliest representation of the instant of human death itself was by the virtuoso sculptors of the Greek temple of Pergamon in the second century BC. The temple shows the heroic defeat and death of the vanquished Gauls with compassionate immediacy. Such depictions were an innovation: hitherto, only the death of mythic heroes had been shown. Borg argues that depicting death in conflict as a painful loss was possible only because those who were shown in this way were defeated enemies. It took far longer for conventions to emerge which allowed audiences to consider the glorious death of those on the spectator's side on the battlefield. Even so, such pictures depicted the death of heroes whose death heralds a triumph, the battle won.[5] Thus the point of such a later picture was that the victory ameliorated the tragedy of the loss, while the death provided a measure of the cost of the victory. This breakthrough in time produced a series of great iconic images from Benjamin West's *The Death of General Wolfe on the Heights of Abraham* (1770) to Daniel Maclise's *The Death*

The Death of General Wolfe on the Heights of Abraham, 1759, *engraved by Augustin Legrand, from the painting by Benjamin West. This showed generals (who were soon to move out of danger far behind lines of combat) fatally wounded.*

of Nelson (1863–5). In this developing tradition, John Trumbull produced a whole series of pictures depicting the last moments of the great heroes of the American War of Independence – pictures which played a great part in the American national myth.[6]

Even these pictures, by referring to familiar images of the deposition of Christ, while using the shapes of flags and artillery to refer to the cross, summoned up previous associations of triumph over death. At the same time their novelty lay in the capacity to illuminate the worthwhile bad death. They also came from a moment when generals – soon to recede far behind the lines of combat – were still in physical danger. They were succeeded in the nineteenth century by powerful images of collective rather than individual sacrifice, such as Lady Butler's picture of the charge of the Scots Greys at Waterloo, *Scotland for Ever!* (1881), or W. B. Wollen's *The Last Stand at Gundamuck* (1898), both of which were painted long after the events depicted.

By the twentieth century, battlefield scenes and ceremonials were able to fuse the imagery of the death of a hero with that of Everyman, and the collective memorials made heroes out of the ordinary casualties of war. Indeed, the notion of the tomb of the unknown warrior, passionately non-denominational, scrupulously anonymous, stands as a hugely effective

A detail from The Death of Nelson, 1805, *fresco by Daniel Maclise, the Houses of Parliament, 1863–5, a popular series which depicts the hero's death.*

– and affecting – memorial for a representative death, and one intended to be viewed collectively. It is this tradition that has been developed by the modern media.

Thus images of both individual and collective death were produced for many to view. The purposes of the memorials varied, as did their nature. Some, showing active, realistic models of soldiers, sailors, firemen going about their business, present living people eager for action. Others poignantly show their subjects as if they are just returning home, or else show the dead standing quietly and sadly as if contemplating their own end. These different styles of memorial have different purposes for the living and a different relationship to the dead. All provide opportunities for the collective viewing of images of the dead – of specific generals, but also of individual Highlanders in kilts, artillerymen with guns, firemen with hoses, who stand for the many killed. First World War memorials introduce a new, officially sanctioned, emotion. While some celebrate the deaths they memorialize, others often present a bleak statement or recognition of loss with little attempt at consolation – let alone celebration. In this respect they are the visual equivalent of the poetry of the First World War – anti-heroic, starkly realistic about the consequences of the conflict. A powerful example of this new mood is the most official monument of all, Lutyens's simple, emphatically pan-religious, Cenotaph in Whitehall. It is a sombre, massive and in its time novel model for a new, resolutely non-triumphant, barely victorious embodiment of the tragic slaughter of that war. An abstract,

Royal Artillery Memorial, Hyde Park Corner, by Charles Sargeant Jagger. First World War memorials commemorate the death of ordinary people. They embody a new public emotion, a bleak, non-triumphant, statement of loss. But the image also refers to the Crucifixion.

contemporary memorial, it established a new language for memorializing the dead – one that did not compete with the capacity of the new media of photography and films to reproduce particular likenesses of specific individuals.

Funeral ceremonies stabilize social order and rebuild social cohesion after the loss of a component individual. They do more than provide an orderly structure for the grieving relations at a moment of personal crisis. They knit together the social space left after a death. They are performances which, if beautiful and true, both mark the loss and elevate it for all those who attend. Much of the late-twentieth-century analysis of death customs was prompted by the view that modern practices, increasingly shorn of ritual and ceremony and socially unmarked, were inferior and ineffective for either purpose. Geoffrey Gorer's pioneering work *Death, Grief and Mourning in Contemporary Britain*, which discusses the apparent decline of death rituals and compares contemporary practices unfavourably with an earlier, richer, period, suggests that 'our treatment of grief and mourning has made bereavement very difficult to be lived through'.[7] The French-

The Cenotaph, Whitehall. Sir Edward Lutyens's austere monument to loss is pan-religious. It re-imagined public memorials (and collective grief) in a way that did not compete with the newly emergent media of film and photography.

inspired view that contemporary death ritual – or rather the lack of it – reduced the dignity and autonomy of the mortally ill and then hindered the resolution of grieving, came to dominate writing about funerals and death practices. To some extent this 'pessimistic' analysis has to be seen within the wider context of social science of the 1950s and '60s, in which modern society was portrayed as stripping the working class of valuable culture. Thus Gorer's book needs to be placed alongside Richard Hoggart's *The Uses of Literacy*. Such a view of the emaciation of meaningful ceremony was to dominate writing about funerals and death practices for many decades.

The work of Herman Feifel, Philippe Ariès, Robert Lifton and Steven Strack elaborates a similar approach.[8] Not everyone shares it, however. The historian David Cannadine argues that the modern historiography of nineteenth-century mourning is romanticized and inaccurate – ignoring, in particular, the huge commercial exploitation of Victorian mourning. Cannadine's own view is that, contrary to what he calls the 'conventional' view of the history of death, 'the best time to die and grieve in modern Britain is probably now,'[9] and that 'ostentatious mourning in the nineteenth century was probably more a display of status than a successful way of assuaging grief: does that mean there is any historical justification for the widespread view that, because such rituals have now become much attenuated, grief today is *therefore* harder to bear?'[10]

Beneath such corrective scepticism, however, there is a less argued and more profound hostility to the effectiveness of ritual and ceremony. Thus Cannadine suggests that grief is often unassuageable, dominating the lives of survivors for ever, and ceremonies are empty and simply unable to offer solace. Herbert Asquith's eloquent sentences on the death of his son Raymond in 1916 summed such feelings up: 'Whatever pride I had in the past, and whatever hope I had for the future – by much the largest part of both was invested in him. Now all that is gone.'[11] Some losses, argues Cannadine, are beyond repair, which is true. In Lawrence Binyon's poem 'To the Fallen' (which has itself become an established part of the rituals of military death), the lines 'At the going down of the sun and in the morning / We will remember them' are according to this view more a description of the persistent sense of loss than an exhortation.[12] Ritual, by this puritan argument, adds nothing. However, the definition here of 'ritual' is very narrow. For Cannadine, ritual and ceremony are something fixed, static and, almost by definition, empty. They are what happened in the past, and are conservative. But this is because he is perhaps looking for rituals in the wrong place. For rituals that are effective are often hardly recognized: they seem natural, inevitable responses at the time, for ritual evolves and changes, and often adapts to new public needs and circumstances.

Indeed, as we have seen, not only are there strong if somewhat surprising continuities in the contemporary media management of death, these practices have also been developed to handle the new 'news death'. It could be argued, for example, that death is more visibly apparent in our culture (if not in our personal experience) than before, and the death that is apparent is real and indisputable death, as opposed to mythic or fictional mortality. Rituals exist, but have altered in both form and function. Just as their form has altered, so too, it might be suggested, have aspects of their purpose. Today the aim of the news rituals is less to console than to inform, to perturb or even to confer security on those who watch.

Elite and royal funerals in the past have come to be seen as complex political events concerned with the consolidation and transfer of power. Huge investments were made in royal funerals because they were such powerful propaganda, and because they took place at vulnerable moments in the history of hereditary institutions. The week between the unexpected death and the funeral of Diana, Princess of Wales, seemed to show that the

Jamal al-Durrah protects his twelve-year-old son, Mohammed, as they shelter from a barrage of crossfire in Gaza City, 30 September 2000; he was shortly after wounded and his son killed. All deaths given attention by the media are political, and like the deaths of great rulers in the past the deaths of ordinary people can now have immense effects. Consequently there are bitter battles to control their interpretation.

demise of a prominent personality is still – indeed, more than ever – able to mobilize a volatile mixture of political and emotional disturbance, and, moreover, that the resulting moment can be stabilized by sensitive rituals. However, it is not only the deaths of the prominent that can carry public and political weight. Humble deaths can carry political messages as well. Deaths given media attention through news coverage are, almost by definition, politically relevant. They frequently represent conflicts of interpretation, the consequences of which are about the transfer of power. A child killed by Allied bombing in Iraq, a young man killed in a train crash, a brutally murdered hostage, a cancer patient apparently denied treatment – are all contested events. The battle for their interpretation is fierce, with pictures, words and authorities struggling hard to gain control over them, because what the deaths are said to represent has immense political consequences. The modern news death, the bad and violent death, thus shares common purpose with the pomp and political ceremony of the funerals of the great in the past.

If historical and sociological writing have generally been more concerned with the experience of the private, undisclosed death, then what we have called the 'bad' death is partly the inheritor of another, less personal and more communal, tradition. This 'public' tradition in itself can be approached in two separate ways. The first, as we have seen, is through power relations embodied in the ceremonies surrounding the deaths of rulers and other members of the elite. Thus the bad (violent, unexpected, undesirable, but also newsworthy and potentially attention-commanding) news death is for a fragmentary moment a death with meaning and impact that nearly always involves a conflict over the mobilization of power, and consequently of political attention.

The role of death ceremonies in consolidating power is usually addressed through the history and anthropology of the deaths of social leaders. In the contemporary theatre of media-portrayed bad deaths, the 'power' that is mobilized is public opinion in the watching society: hence recent wars have been conducted in such a way as to avoid altogether any images of death or dying on the winning (that is, our) side.

Yet, for the media and their audiences, death in war – particularly of civilian non-combatants – also refers to another tradition: of seeing civilian death as the signal of imminent social collapse. Rival arguments have elaborated such a view of collective death and politically avoidable doom. Thus a vivid perception of the threat of total annihilation re-emerged as details of the Holocaust and the use of the atom bomb on Japan at the end of the Second World War began to emerge. As the American social scientist Robert J. Lifton put it, 'With Hiroshima something more is involved – a dimension of totality, a sense of ultimate annihilation.'[13] It is not only that the history of deaths in wars serves as a backdrop to foreign policy, and that this in turn influences how the media represent the wars: it is also that it forms part of the 'argument' in which any particular media representation of death in war operates. Some collective deaths represent political arguments; others represent the overarching sense of an ending. And there is a disturbing possibility that in the restlessness of the news there is a frenzied pursuit of stories that exaggerate some risks (at the expense of underestimating others) until their time in the headlines has passed, and media preoccupations move on.

How then should we consider the press's power to mobilize public opinion in relation to death? Who controls it, and what are the purposes and effects of using it? The first point to make is that reports of deaths are political, and competing groups often attempt to use the meaning that a death is endowed with in their own interests. The interpretation of some news deaths is hard fought because the view which dominates will influence public attitudes. Are casualty figures acceptable? Is this particular, emblematic, death representative of some larger malaise? Is this assassination a sign of the terrifying power of terrorist groups or evidence of their inhumanity, not their strength? The battle for controlling meaning is complex; it is also an area where media power can challenge the status quo.

Nevertheless, many of the writers who have looked at the political functions of funeral practices (and the suggestion is that the media now perform directly related work) have seen such practices as inherently conservative, reiterating, re-expressing and confirming continuities of power. Clifford Geertz, writing about the royal funeral ceremonies of Balinese islanders in the middle of the twentieth century, points out that they involved intense competition among individuals to assemble and mount ceremonial, but that the competition nevertheless served to reinforce the social hierarchy.[14] It sounds in many ways like the news, which moulds ever-changing events into reliable and familiar formats. A journalist remarked that 'News is a very internalized operation. It is very competitive – you compete with colleagues.'[15] Geertz goes on to argue that the elaborate ceremonies attending the fabulous theatre of a royal cremation were not 'an echo of a politics taking place somewhere else', but 'an intensification of a politics taking place everywhere else'.[16] This is helpful, for the news certainly also produces its own political realities, however complex its relationship may be to other political events. The historian Jonathan Goldberg, developing the theme of the relationship between political power and ceremony suggested by Peter Burke, Roy Strong and others, particularly in looking at funeral practices, has argued that in late-sixteenth- and seventeenth-century Europe 'power was manifested in spectacle.'[17] Certainly, as Shakespeare demonstrated, some at least at the time had a reflective distance on the way in which ceremonies persuaded other people:

> And what art thou, thou idol ceremony?
> What kind of god art thou, that suffer'st more
> Of moral griefs than do thy worshippers?
>
> .   .   .   .
>
> O ceremony, show me but thy worth.
>
> .   .   .   .
>
> Art thou aught else but place, degree, and form,
> Creating awe and fear in other men?[18]

It is precisely Shakespeare's sense of death as an argument, of ceremony as a mobilization of power, that journalists understand. But so, sometimes, do audiences. Spectators of death rites expect to be edified, but some are suspicious that what they consume is intended to manipulate them. It is at this point that the slowly won (though easy to lose) trust that the audience places in the media in which the story is displayed makes the difference. However, the political fear, as in the response to hostage-taking in Iraq, is that the public mood is swayed by terrible sights, just as the kidnappers plan.

What role do the audience play in the rituals of news death? The performance of news is carried out in the name of the audience. It is 'for' them. But how do they participate in it? If ceremonies work, they are never merely imposed on spectators: they are involving – the product of shared concerns. Nevertheless, some news in some places at some times is not really aimed at the wide public audience, but at a very specific audience of policy-makers or politicians – or even, as research has shown, other journalists.[19] Increasingly, news is directed at demographically attractive audiences – as defined by advertisers. News may also be intended for consumption by its own sources: for example the military or the political elites. Meanwhile, journalists trade with their informants as well as with the public. For journalists and editors, the audience – that is, the public one – can become an abstraction. By comparison, sources are more immediate. In addition, even though a news item may be information that it is important for the public to know, one purpose of it is the same as that of all other kinds of journalism – namely to maintain or increase numbers of readers, viewers and listeners.

What is the role of audiences themselves in the screen rituals of death? Attending a funeral, taking part in a ceremony surrounding death, even as a passive spectator, can be experienced as a spiritually (and socially) uplifting event, offering involvement in a communally healing transaction. It may be that 'attendance' at a news death has some of the same characteristics. The funerals of victims of violent death are – or can be – important political events, yet the people they commemorate are only rarely public figures. The bread-and-butter news death is that of a previously anonymous victim – which raises the question of how ordinary people relate to deaths of people like themselves who are made fleetingly famous by the media.

A conventional view of the use of public ritual in general is that the spectators are merely passive recipients of messages delivered by their rulers, in the interests of the powerful. Rituals are seen as 'mystifications', ways of disguising reality in order to permit the ruling elite – or at least other people with power and purposes undisclosed to the audience – to manipulate the lower classes in their own interest.[20]

As we have seen, news deaths are – whatever else – by definition both political and commercial events, or are made so by the decision to include them in the news. They may be exploited to yield the elusive 'shock' value that is at such a premium in entertainment. They may manipulate audiences for purposes of which the audiences are unaware. However, the audience is not merely passive. In order for media rituals to work, they must operate within conventions that are accepted by the audience as appropriate. The question of taste in the media is never more applicable than in the case of the bad news death.

News death (like news suffering) has increasingly become a commodity,

The 1984 Brighton bombing. The IRA attack on the Grand Hotel killed two members of the government and came very close to killing the Prime Minister, Mrs Thatcher, and her husband. News (like funeral rituals) had to move swiftly to stabilize a crisis. It was the first time since the Second World War that news organizations realized that, had more of the government been killed, they would, in practice, have been responsible for maintaining order in a political vacuum.

to be sold to audiences or advertisers. It has a value in attracting audiences, but it also exists within a political framework. Indeed, as we have seen, *only* deaths with political meaning have value. Or, to put it the other way round, any death that is reported or described in the media thereby acquires a meaning which it previously lacked. The 'meaning' is something around which audiences can organize their political views, fitting them into a world-view which they are continually reconstructing. (This is also one reason why good journalists become so concerned about news values.) Thus, while ceremonies are instruments of power, they depend on the compliance of audiences as well.

There is also another issue. What do audiences in their historical and social context bring to, and get out of, the screened ceremonies? Rituals are not necessarily merely vehicles for propaganda, even if the conscious purpose of providing them is to hold the attention of the audience. Rather, there has to be some shared values between those who make the news,

The funeral of Diana, Princess of Wales: mourners in Hyde Park during the service, 1997. The (hotly disputed in the studio) inclusion of the public mourners in the televised Abbey service helped defuse an unpleasantly volatile political moment.

those who present it and the audience of ceremonial occasions. Thus the BBC's televising of the funeral of Princess Diana was planned and scripted as a broadcast from within Westminster Abbey, concentrating solely on the service. But the producer, sitting in an outside-broadcasting-unit studio, realized that the funeral ceremonies were also taking place in the crowds of spectators lining the funeral route and in Hyde Park and that the reaction of these spectators was a sensitive part of the politics of the ritual. There was a dispute about how shots during the ceremony itself should be composed. 'I realized, as a newsman,' said the producer Ron Neil, 'that the story was going on in the Park as well as in the Abbey, and in the end we cut between the two. But it was a close-run thing.'[21] It nearly led to an on-air row, as the presenters inside the Abbey wanted to keep to the planned order of the script. This newsman's incorporation into the event of the public, which was in turn communicated to an even wider television audience, seemed to help calm the emotionalism and punitiveness of the previous week. The choreography and the visual codes of the ceremony as it was screened helped to create a new kind of sympathy as the public mourning was involved in the official ceremony.

The funeral of Princess Diana was not, of course, the first occasion on which a royal demise provided a kind of political theatre. Although mostly concerned with securing the succession of rulers, previous nineteenth- and twentieth-century rituals were also opportunities for what has been called 'collective effervescence' – the need to uphold and reaffirm at regular intervals the collective sentiments that make up a society's personality and give rise to its unity. In this way, political theatre is a routine part of mending, and displaying the nature of, the social fabric. There is a process of reaffirmation. In such a case, news becomes one of the most potent ways of agreeing, in public, what we care about.

The quiet, urgent, summoning of foreign death to our screen and pages confirms the difference between audiences and the scenes they learn about, and perhaps also their superiority and detachment. It confirms the social order of the receiving society, in contrast to the social disorder of the reported societies. However weary, dirty, bloodstained, muddy, sweaty the observed society may be, reporters strive to appear clean, tidy and orderly. Thus the television journalist Martin Bell (not a man to make light of his situation) records that his trademark white suit was preserved in the most difficult situations, in a conscious and calculated bid to raise his moral authority.[22] In addition, there is an assumption of explanatory coherence in news-telling – that the news has a story to tell. This stands in stark contrast to the incoherent, uncut experiences that are the events themselves. In addition, the tone, style and personality – the psychology – of societies are composed or confirmed by how societies have these stories of death and destruction told to them. Thus reporting carries an implicit image of the magisterial authority of the viewing society.

The fact that the ceremonies of news-reporting serve to stabilize and reassure audiences – in short, that they have a conservative tendency or function – does not mean that they cannot also be destabilizing and even disruptive. The news ceremonial can be transformed into a means for disposing of the old and legitimizing the new. However, through its unintended disorder, it can also mark a social or political breakdown.

It is important here that there is a strong, almost missionary, imperative in news broadcasting: that the show should go on, without rude interruption. Thus a dominant anxiety in newsrooms is to get the process of putting news out, as one American observer suggests, 'right, logical, straight, looking good and going smoothly'.[23] Intense work goes on behind the scenes to produce 'a clean show' (that is, something well done and professional). This is not easy, and testifies to the rational and concentrated power of news organizations to understand and order reality. One experienced British journalist, Brian Hanrahan, highly commended for his steady reporting of the Falklands War, describes how the events of 11 September reduced him to tongue-tied inarticulacy for the first hour as the events broke. 'I could not speak,' he recalls; 'I could not get the words out. At first I could not get things clear. It was chaos.'[24] In fact, when he did appear, two hours later, his commentary on the disaster represented to the viewing public one of the first moments of control and the mastery of the events by reason. During the afternoon of the same day, other news programmes began to explore the wider consequences of what was known; by the evening news at nine o'clock the BBC had produced an account of events that was a brilliant exposition of what had happened and what was known. The ceremonial must be intact, and bringing it off can be fraught, yet it represents both for the news organization and the audience a vital sense of professional control.

Getting it wrong, however, sends out distinctive signals – as with any other kind of botched ritual. The messages are not necessarily negative: they can even, accidentally, enhance the purpose of a broadcast. Thus an occasion like the wounding of the BBC reporter Martin Bell on camera in 1992 was an unintended addition to the script, but it heightened and did not detract from the intended message about anarchy and danger. On the other hand, the 'spoiling' of a report by the intrusion either of inappropriate material or of jarring comments (or, indeed, of technical breakdown) gives the story an undesired twist. Usually, however, everyone – producer, reporter, interviewee – will cooperate to make sure that the possibility of a ceremonial breakdown does not occur.

Another potential snare discussed by journalists is the deceitful ceremony. Expensive foreign correspondents, dispatched to remote stories, may know little of how the situation around them is developing. Journalists and editors identify this as a daily pressure. As one put it, 'Ego-tripping personalities assume an air of knowledge while they solemnly say to camera what the office back home has just told them.'[25] Audiences sense that this is false and do not trust what is said, and this in turn undermines the authority of more reliable reporting. In this case the spoilt ceremony threatens the legitimacy of the genuine ritual. Other journalists complain that ever-higher production values have interfered with the real purpose of the ritual – to explore reality. According to one freelance reporter, 'News is far too finished these days. Production values are driving out the real stories. It means that freelance stuff from tight places often doesn't make it to screen. The stories may be better, but they look too rough.'[26] He adds that this is making the economic situation of freelancers ever more perilous: 'Basically, we are always at the bottom of the food chain.' However, freelancers – more mobile and more willing to take risks; unfamiliar faces, and consequently freer agents – often produce the more difficult, testing and innovative stories. 'We keep the currency honest,' he adds. The currency that all good journalists worry about is the accurate reflection of reality – not merely a display of a performance of it.

The power of the conventions and the almost universally shared desire to abide by them can be profound; and so can the breakdown of the same conventions. Take, for example, the extraordinary expectation and assumption – shared worldwide – of the proper way to speak to camera. For a start, practically everyone wants to do it, regardless of the circumstances – refusing to be interviewed occurs only in the most extreme conditions of anger or fear. But not only do people speak if asked: they conform to what they have come instinctively to understand is expected of them. There is a rational element: the fact that people in stressful situations turn aside from their private tragedy to tell a camera or a journalist about it may be an accurate recognition of the capacity of the attention of journalism to do something for them. But there is also a ritualized one. The pattern is so familiar that we all take it for granted, in every country: coverage of bad death requires a witness to, or a victim of, the event, who is invited to address the viewing public about what he or she has seen – to say, in his or her own words, what has happened, or, in the case of a victim, what he or she is feeling. Usually, in this familiar scene, the words paint a picture; but the picture may be enhanced if the ritual is unexpectedly 'spoilt' by an unspoken action or gesture. Thus, following the Omagh bombing in August 1998, a woman whose son had been badly injured started to answer questions about what she had seen – 'terrible crying . . . a baby . . .':[27] a normal part of the pattern. She then turned away from the intrusive camera, overwhelmed by her feelings. The impact of the interview was created not by her conformity to the ritual in the most appalling circumstances, but by her disconcerting inability to conform. The incapacity to express what she had seen served to underline its power over her.

Thus if audiences expect to be reassured by smoothness, they also expect the occasional frisson of being perturbed and even quite painfully shocked – in short, they want order, but order occasionally shaken by chaos which in turn draws comforting attention to the normality of order. They understand the conventions of what they expect to see quite as well as those who orchestrate what is seen – and like to put their own interpretation on departures from them. Broadcasting (and newspaper) authorities justify the intrusion of shock on the grounds that the world is a shocking place, and a degree of shock may lead to a desire for reform and remedial action. Yet the impact may be ambiguous. Just as rituals confirm beliefs and reinforce values, prompting conservative trust rather than radical reappraisal, so departures from rituals ('shocking' departures from schedules and routine) may have the perverse effect of making audiences feel more secure in relation to the vulnerable, superior in relation to the oppressed, even empowered by the feeling that the shocking disturbance is nevertheless contained and cushioned within a generally well-ordered medium.

There is the couch-potato syndrome: feeling cosily different from, and therefore better than, the events and suffering that take place on the other side of the secure glass curtain that constitutes the television screen. Actual physical death (as opposed to the real screen death of news) has become remote. In a modern, medicalized society, millions live for decades with only occasional proximity to it. In Freud's words, we try 'to hush [death] up ... Our habit is to lay stress on the fortuitous causation of death – accident, disease, infection, advanced age; in this way we betray an effort to reduce death from a necessity to a chance event.'[28] With the actual sensation of death kept at arm's length, the true-life horror on the screen occupies a no man's land between fiction and experience.

Television shows death all around, to a degree that has made the sight of the dead and dying much more familiar than it was a generation ago. The electronic media tend to make mortality – whether accidental (air crashes) or deliberate (murder) – appear an arbitrary visitor, attending other – often distant – people. It is important that the risk of such events happening to the viewer is nearly always statistically tiny. War deaths are in a slightly different category, because they raise the stakes – providing a stark warning of the fragility of contemporary affluent society, and raising fear thresholds. In war, producers and reporters alike are acutely aware of a debasement of the currency of horror and of the need to compete in a gruesome marketplace. Thus in the Vietnam, Falklands, Kosovo, Afghan and Iraqi conflicts, the levels of the 'acceptable' – to the needing-to-be-informed adult public – have inched forward.

What is it today to shock or be shocked? Shocking images are ever more sought after, and not just in news or entertainment. So far from being resisted, shock value has become a lauded aim, a desired effect, across the whole range of the contemporary arts, from fine art and literature to the movies. What painter or writer is not delighted to have his or her work described as truly shocking? What dealer does not automatically put up the price of a work that has achieved a *succès de scandale*? In this competition for the capacity to arrest consumers' attention newspapers and television producers are certainly not alone. Indeed, the capacity of news and real events to produce a reaction in the audience has to be seen within the wider range of products which also attempt to 'shock' audiences.

In visual art, the attempt to shock is far from new. Art has often sought to jolt conventions and to draw attention to unpalatable realities. Shock tactics may all be arguments, ways of commanding attention against the competing din of events and information seeking audiences' time.[29] Thus 'shocking' news items, which seek to grab the public's gaze away from rival items offered by competitors, have an uphill struggle as an increasingly sensation-hungry audience seeks to have its comfortable equilibrium shaken, its conventional expectations ruffled, in any way it can – in order the more happily to enjoy, and take satisfaction in, its immunity from actual, direct experience of the things that disturb it. In sum, shocking has become a safe convention.

What are the symbols of the contemporary reporting of death? Ruined buildings, anguished children, dead bodies strewn randomly and in various stages of decomposition, or lined up for identification in rows, evidence of mass graves, distraught relatives – the images are familiar. Yet what the public sees on television or in the newspapers is often, in reality, a theatre-set, and a highly ordered one at that – however genuine the deaths that are shown and the smells of putrefaction that are described.

There is a conventionalized (partly because easy to display) landscape of war – either urban and involving bodies against a backdrop of ruined buildings, or rural, against a background of trees and fields. In both cases, symbolism is provided by destruction – human and inanimate – rather than by the visible disruption of services such as electricity, gas, water and sewerage, which are often the earliest and most damaging casualties of war. Only occasionally are wars illustrated by the continuation of life through them.

War propaganda, on the other hand, does the opposite: bodies, especially if they are on your own side, are considered disconcerting, and bad for morale. In the Second World War the Nazis showed the destruction of German cities to the German public. This was believed to brace morale by rousing indignation. But they carefully avoided showing the personal tragedies that took place within the cities. The British arrived at an even stranger set of images, which could be summed up as 'Dunkirk spirit' or 'whistling through the Blitz'. So far from being about death and decay, war was transformed into an opportunity for ordinary people to display communal virtues – generosity, thrift, doggedness, good humour, triumph over adversity. A milkman picking his way through rubble to deliver bottles or bowler-hatted readers perusing volumes in a bookshop or library whose shelves were still standing in the middle of a bomb site conveyed the appropriate image.

Modern reporting – ostensibly (and indiscriminately) opposed to the horror of war, and seeking to illustrate its monstrousness – has turned such an approach on its head. Instead of avoiding the evil effects of war as distasteful, it seeks them out as salutary, in a supposed attempt to shock an almost unshockable audience into doing something about it. In both cases, however, items are selected, stages are set – there is no possibility of a neutral or objective reality: only interpretation. Another way of identifying what is going on is to see that news, like art, seeks to shock – but only within very tight conventions of what is acceptably shocking. The concept 'to shock' or 'to be shocked' is an interesting one, and highly conventionalized. Tracey Emin's bed is not shocking – people taking it seriously is. But there are taboo behaviours which are simply not engaged in, or – if they are – there is such universal condemnation that no one does so again.

What is the point of view from which we inspect death? Much of the meaning of images depends on whether the scene is viewed from the point of view of those doing the killing or, on the other hand, of those being killed. Many soldiers who fight wars do so by watching screens, in much the same way that millions of people watch their television or computer screens. One commentator has suggested that, in modern war coverage, satellite and computer-generated images of air strikes provide armchair generals with the eerie opportunity of watching – as it takes place – the infliction of death and suffering from the perspective of the weapon itself. It has even been suggested that 'the defense strategy geared to nuclear weapons will give way to one based upon ubiquitous orbital vision of every territory . . . eyeshot will generally get the better of gunshot.'[30] 'I'd put it like this,' an American defence secretary recently observed. 'Once you can see the target you can expect to destroy it.'[31]

In Vietnam and Serbia and Iraq the enemy managed to dissolve into the civilian population for much of the time: it was hard to 'see' them. It has been argued that modern post-Cold War conflicts are increasingly characterized by the way in which combatants and civilians have become indistinguishable – although this has been recognized as a feature of contemporary conflict since Guernica in 1937. In addition, the convention of the aerial image of battle long pre-dates the invention of photography: maps of battles have since the earliest known examples displayed the scene of the battle as if from the sky. Nevertheless, there is an old convention concerning the delivery of death, which still dominates how it is pictured for us. It is seen from the point of view of the person doing the shooting (and is registered by the effect of the shot). Moreover, the convention of the weapon's-eye view (although not new, as some writers have argued)[32] is also familiar to those who watch action movies or play computer games.

Of course it is these seductive images of hits and near-misses that amplify the notion of the surgical, airborne, precision war. Such a concept requires moral weapons: ones that can discriminate between the worthy and the unworthy, avoiding the former while targeting the latter. In fact some modern weaponry *is* capable of pinpointing targets, and explosive power can be accurately calibrated for different levels of precise destruction. Videos are usually fixed only to the wings of aircraft carrying 'smart' bombs. Nevertheless, it is still the human agency that determines targets – and preoccupation with technology should not obscure the human judgement that this involves. Thus, retrospectively, the bombing of the Serbian television station in Belgrade in 1999 may have crossed a critical barrier, legitimating the targeting of journalists (which has been a feature of subsequent conflicts).

It was a significant feature of the war in Kosovo that computer-generated images of destruction that had been such a feature of the Gulf War ceased to be part of officially released television footage. This was not because they were no longer available, but because they were not felt to be the right kind of image to provide in an allegedly 'humanitarian' war.

As we have noted, from the start of mass journalism in the 1860s until recent decades, wounding and blood were seldom on public display. Images of wounds were scrupulously collected for teaching medical staff, but they were never released and were kept studiedly anonymous – as representations of an injury, not of the person who bore it. In the last generation, however, there has been a significant shift. The historian of photography Caroline Brothers has identified two ways of representing death in the media that have gradually made it more acceptable. 'The aestheticization of death', she argues, has been one means of 'deflecting its impact and sheltering the public from scenes considered too gruesome'. In the past, dead bodies (when shown) were portrayed in heroic postures, while appropriate accessories accompanied them. In images of the Spanish Civil War in the 1930s, wounds were alluded to by dressings, while actual representations of death were carefully composed and arranged for the camera. Thus the famous image of the moment of death of a republican soldier was in fact composed (or faked), not merely taken. The other ameliorative convention was pathos. Attentive medical staff, charming nurses, even sumptuous temporary hospitals, were shown in images that consequently associated injuries and death with places of sympathy and recreation, and indeed imposed on wartime wounds the extraordinary connotations of pleasure.[33] Death was shown, but in the poignant company of close comrades, attending to last wants, writing last letters.

The Spanish Civil War was fought in an atmosphere of fierce propaganda, with visual imagery as a powerful political tool. Yet even then there were striking differences in the willingness of different international societies to view images of death or suffering – with the British public notably more squeamish than the French.[34] Public squeamishness, however, often reflected political and bureaucratic attitudes, which in turn found expression in censorship and in broadcasting guidelines. National differences still remain significant. The chairman of an international television conference after the attacks of 11 September pointed out that there had been 'a real difference between the kind of pictures that were shown on northern-European TV and the much greater detail of the carnage that was shown in the south'. He added, 'I think you have to conclude that religion made a difference. The Catholic south was more comfortable with death on screen.'[35]

Nevertheless, in recent years there has been a change. In the past, arguments between editorial offices and journalists about how far a particular story could push the conventions would take place after the story had been received in newsrooms. The rows now take place before it is shot. The speed of technology and the tightening of deadlines have shifted power towards the journalists in the field. 'Some of the really tense exchanges now happen on the phone before a reporter files,' comments one editor. 'There is not that much we can do about a story once it is in.'[36] But such considerations are in turn politically manipulated. In the war in Kosovo there was an official relaxation of the rules that govern what is permissible, because shocking atrocities were the reason for the military intervention. Clearly, much depends on the purposes of the journalism: sometimes it must not be permitted to disturb; at other times the more disturbing the better.

Yet the meaning of images and their uses mutate. Pictures or footage acquired for one kind of purpose – to make a record, to be used as propaganda, even to be used as publicity to intimidate those depicted – may later serve another argument more powerfully. Thus television reportage of key government meetings in Serbia, employed to intimidate politicians, reveals, when shown in a later British documentary, the threat that participants felt themselves to be under.[37]

The point of view of the reporting journalism is so powerful that it can have major political consequences. During the early part of the recent troubles in Northern Ireland, Scandinavian commentators would observe that as their audiences often saw riots from behind the lines of the protesters, while British audiences always saw the same incidents from behind police lines, the two publics understood what was going on very differently. They understood different people to be the aggressors, and different groups to be the victims. Of course, neither view was wholly accurate, and neither view was particularly helpful in producing political solutions to a complex historical situation. But 'point of view' was a powerful mobilizer of sympathies – sometimes inappropriately. The angle of a shot can produce anger, identification or empathy.

In the media handling of death, there is an unspoken rule that corpses should be encountered only in company – that is, the viewer should not be left alone with them. Like other media practices, this rule is deeply embedded, yet reinvented and adapted to suit new circumstances. The convention is paralleled by medical practice, which requires three or more students to be present when a body is uncovered in a laboratory for dissection.[38] Rules about the handling of bodies in mortuaries also require two or more people to be present when a body is to be touched. Many of these practices have a long history and a powerful hold on the public imagination. In the nineteenth century, grave robbers stealing bodies for medical dissection supposedly worked in pairs or gangs, and in lurid police magazines the testimony of convicted robbers was often full of the horror of being left alone with corpses. Broadcasting conventions may reflect the same superstitions. When a body is in the frame, you the viewer will not be left alone: a broadcaster will typically accompany you. But there will also have been a battery of other unseen adjustments before the cadaver reaches your screen: what is shown may be the product of many intermediary viewings and filterings. Discussions are held frame by frame about what is permissible, and self-censorship will remove material that is judged to have broken the contemporary invisible but powerful line of acceptability. Such discussions attempt to balance public taste and mores with the importance of the story and the relevance of what is shown to other stories in currency at the time. But the aim is always to go to the very edge of what is currently acceptable. However, values are continually shifting – as are the commercial imperatives that drive news organizations, along with the political conditions in which any story may flourish or perish.

Viewing is also often collective, and audiences share conceptions about what should be shown. The processes of editing and meeting audience expectations produce a distancing from what is observed. Indeed, the public is now so accustomed to death viewed on a screen that they choose its predictable conventions rather than unmediated reality. Thus, relatives required to identify corpses (of those killed in accidents, for example) increasingly choose to do so by watching a video of the body. 'This is less upsetting and more efficient, both for relatives, and indeed for officials,' an inquiry into the practice commented, 'and the public is more comfortable and familiar with such a display than a direct viewing of the corpse.'[39]

The conventions of the broadcast death may also have helped contribute to the notion of the casualty-less war. The return home of body bags, apart from its political significance, has the virtue of separating death from physical destruction. But the media also provide conventions which discriminate between the deaths of those close to us and other, more distant, casualties. There is a whole political vocabulary of burial displayed in the media. Thus body bags are for winners: losers lie in the earth. In recent wars, 'our' side gets killed in finite numbers, and the dead are treated as individuals: the dead on the other side, or the side we are protecting, are generally civilian, anonymous and numerous, and frequently the victims of massacres. Although less affecting to the sensibilities of Western audiences, their portrayal is attended by conventions as well. To denote quantity, they are typically filmed in rows. Often (as with body bags) they are in transit. Indeed, the long framing shot of the collection of bodies has become a news staple.

Then there are the once-buried but recently dug-up dead. These transitional bodies are nearly always removed from the soil for the purpose of playing a part in a political argument. On the grounds that corpses speak louder than words, this practice is often directed at the media, with cameras and news journalists in mind: a media-made ritual. Reporting of recent wars in the Balkans frequently involved ceremonial exhumations. So familiar has the process become that it has produced cinematic allusions in many movies. The exhumations typically have a double purpose: to demonstrate the atrocity of a furtive large-scale killing and to demonstrate the outrage of deaths not accorded the dignity of funeral rites. Media coverage of the exhumations conveys both messages. Such messages can be powerful ones. The dead can mobilize action. As one NATO press official commented, 'Milošović could kill thousands of people, burn down half of Kosovo, create a quarter of a million refugees and get away with it. But one not-so-mass grave is found and it turned out we had to bomb him.' He went on to describe the impact of one exhumation just before the war started. 'I can testify to the galvanizing effect of that one incident,' he commented.

Albanian villagers in Prekaz exhume the victims of an attack to give them a proper burial, 11 March 1998. Such events have become a news staple, part of a familiar media-influenced politics of war.

'Suddenly editors, who while the Serbian offensive was well under way had labelled Kosovo boring, couldn't get enough.'[40]

Thus, death in the news – apparently a simple, verifiable fact – is in reality a many-faceted phenomenon, open to a thousand interpretations and presentations. But above all – like 'real' death in the mundane domestic existences of everyone – rites, ceremonies, superstitions and taboos, the functions of which are far from straightforward, surround it. Does the bad, violent death that fills the typical Western news bulletin exist to provide a contrast with the good, peaceful death we would all hope for? Is part of its purpose to make our own future deaths seem sweeter? Perhaps, like spectators at executions, we are interested in how others deal with the terrible chances of life. Or is it that we prefer to see death as a mistake, a disaster, and an avoidable news calamity? Certainly, the cool command of journalism subdues and socializes death for spectators. This is not a criticism but an observation. It does it by integrating the dead in an explanation, and sometimes in an argument. Just as modern forensic pathologists using DNA technologies can identify individual corpses in mass graves and 'give the dead their names back' (and perhaps help secure the prosecution of those that did the killing), so the news performs a similar function. But the news

A policeman carries the body of a dead child from the disaster in Aberfan, when a waste tip from a local coal mine engulfed the village school – an image (captured by a local photographer) whose moving dignity helped reveal the nature of the community in which the calamity had occurred.

also stabilizes a crisis, creates a memorial, recivilizes the dead, and involves the audience in a comforting ritual.

In the past, Ariès argued, the good death was the conscious management by the sentient subject of the passage from life to death. The dying person and his or her sympathetic attendants moved ideally through a performance whose gestures were understood and approved of by everyone. There are few commonly agreed practices that can be relied on in such situations now. Those who will soon die and those who are close to them may create their own ceremonies. These may be as intense and precious as any historical ritual. Nevertheless, such private creations contrast sharply with our publicly agreed conventions around the 'bad' deaths that make engrossing news.

Certainly much that appears technical, contemporary and functional is in part derived from the media's need to produce satisfying ceremonies at moments of social crisis. But the bad deaths of the news are also – and this is the hardest aspect fully to comprehend – *designed to be enjoyed*. Comparisons across epochs must be treated with caution, especially when political and social values are so widely different. Nevertheless, in this respect at least there are parallels to be drawn between press and especially television coverage of the 'good bad death' and historic rituals involving the audience's enjoyment of ritualized killing.

10

Moved to Tears

News generates feelings. It elucidates and shapes our sensibilities. It can be passionately eloquent. Under the guise of giving us information, it mobilizes emotion. Recently many critics have complained that the news has become sensationalized, orchestrating collective passions at the expense of establishing reality. But, while it is easy to disapprove of this, trying to explain what it might mean is more complicated and less attended to. We need to be more curious and to question the easy rhetoric that 'the whole of public discourse is vulgarized,' for there are helpful distinctions we can make about how the news sculpts how we feel about events. And this sculpting of public mood is potentially so powerful that we ought not to accept clichés about what is happening.

There is a paradox. On the one hand, much journalism seeks to engage feeling, and succeeds in part by doing so; on the other, 'higher' journalism prides itself on its dispassionate observation. At the beginning of the Coalition war in Afghanistan in 2001, the head of one major public-service news organization pledged in the conclusion of a private seminar, 'We will seek to tell the public everything.' He added solemnly, 'All without any hint of feeling.'[1] The dual promise encapsulated a code: it spoke to the duty of news gatekeepers to respect audiences sufficiently to allow them to make their own judgements based on the evidence, while at the same time resolving to keep the emotional powder-keg dry – so that the weight of events could register proportionately. Professional news-makers are masters of emotional colouring.

Nevertheless, the stories that news-makers construct are often shaped by a limited range of established narratives into which diverse real events are fitted. One aspect involves moulding difficult news stories into a language that reinvents familiar clichés but stays close enough to them to make such news more accessible to audiences – this is part of the purpose of scrupulous and inventive journalism. News ought not to fall into the exhausted formulas which fail to engage people, but nevertheless it has to make connections to take audiences with it. At the same time, journalism too concerned to attract can denude mobile historical reality of its uncertainty, reducing it to easily appreciable formulas.

Journalists talk about the real world as if it were a quarry; the skill needed is the ability to fit random facts into a recognizable story. John Steinbeck once said of the great news photographer Robert Capra, 'He knew what to look for and what to do with it when he found it. The news was always there but he saw it because he observed with a curious, alert eye. His skill was in identifying material when he saw it. He knew for instance that you cannot photograph war because it is largely an emotion.'[2] Journalists characterize a good news story as one 'with legs', one that 'can stand up' and 'grab' its audiences. However important the material to be reported, the reporter's first fear is of being boring. The best news is 'hot', which also means that it is commanding. It crashes through routine order and 'demands' attention. It is fashioned in the newsroom in order to be 'sharp' and 'punchy' – to create an impact: so far from being emotionally neutral, it is designed to stir, arouse and manipulate. Thus the veteran reporter Murray Sayle claimed that there were only two stories worth writing: one was 'we name the guilty man,' and the other was 'arrow points to the defective part.'[3] All stories anticipate some kind of reaction in the recipient – otherwise there is no point in them.

Of course, news is also a description and a record. It establishes categories of fact, providing sequence and chronology. These are fundamental aspects of the reporting process. The authority of news has been enhanced by its relationship with history – but also with legal evidence. Both historical and legal forms of account have developed professional distance from emotion. Such associations have until recently dignified news. The idea of witnesses' accounts of events is ancient. Nevertheless, the idea of legal 'eyewitness' evidence to courts and that of 'eyewitness' reports in the press emerged at the same time, and they are intimately linked. More than that, as Michael Schudson put it, 'journalists began talking self-consciously about "objectivity" only at the time (the 1920s) when intellectual life more broadly and changing journalistic practices specifically made reflective journalists aware of how subjective journalistic judgement ordinarily is. Legal realism arose in the same cultural atmosphere and made a similar kind of shift in legal thinking.'[4] However, the contemporary climate of opinion has altered, and 'objectivity' has been under attack for several decades both philosophically and in news organizations. Thus, while theorists have argued that it is unobtainable, newspapers – always partisan – have sought to distinguish themselves by setting agendas rather than reporting what has happened. In turn, broadcasters have increasingly adopted the more partisan approaches of the press. In the United States in particular 'impartiality' is a far less important value for broadcasters than it used to be, with terrible costs for public knowledge of events and their causes. But the reliable accounts of the world that are necessary for informed choices depend on some value like it.

The values of a journalist are largely determined by the expectations of the organization he or she works for. The vital independent-mindedness of good journalism has to be supported by institutions that respect journalists' judgement. Choosing to explain events rather than seeking to exploit the maximum emotional charge from them by heating feelings is an aspect of one set of values. Thus when John Simpson, the BBC foreign editor, was attacked (and his translator killed) by American fighters in an incident of 'friendly fire' in Iraq in 2003, his response was calm and stoical – as was that of his cameraman, who went on filming. Of course Simpson pretty obviously had a scoop. But how he handled it was at least in part because Simpson worked for a public-service broadcaster and was under less editorial pressure to heat up what was in any case a compelling news item. And his phlegmatic response also came from his understanding the mayhem of war. He brought his experience to bear on interpreting a frightening and tragic event. 'It is,' he said, 'one of those things that happen. Mistakes happen in wars.'[5] Simpson made sense of what he had experienced by reference to a far wider frame than many journalists could have brought to such an incident – and the report (accompanied by the cameraman's blood being wiped from the camera lens) was no less affecting for being cool. If in law the courts and legal reason are supposed to put together the more nearly complete truth, in the news it is editorial judgement that should do so, and this is also a matter of structures, culture, pressures – and the quality of judgement of individuals.

News stories are about well-tried narratives. They are also about witnessing, in the sense of 'bearing witness'. News can be seen as testifying, and may involve accepting the burden and responsibilities of what has been recorded. Readers and viewers also become witnesses to a form of telling the story for moral edification and restitution, even if they do not act on it. In the case of journalists, 'bearing witness' in this more complicated sense involves responsibility to the record of the event – not that the journalists have to be morally 'good', but that the reporting should be seen to serve a higher purpose.

Yet the creation of emotional genres, the conventional styling and the direction of feelings – especially where major 'catastrophic' stories are involved – are not merely the shifty underside of the cool process of determining events: they are fundamental to news-making. This is true whether the news is sordid sensation-seeking or principled investigation. You cannot – however attractive and simple the proposition – distinguish well-made from badly made news simply on the basis that the inferior kind is concerned vulgarly to raise emotions. It is rather that the emotions that are summoned up and their purposes are different, and that this has profound political consequences.

The capacity of news to engage and to whip up feelings is an aspect of media power that has been particularly feared as a threat to liberty. Thus in 1859 John Stuart Mill identified the overpowering influence of popular sentiment, then as now conveyed through the press, as the greatest danger in a democracy. Mill pointed out that most people find real toleration of disagreeable minority views upsetting. 'Protection against the tyranny of the magistrate is not enough,' he wrote in *On Liberty*: there was also an equally important need for protection against the tyranny of prevailing fashion, 'against the tendency of society to impose by other means than civil penalties its own ideas and practices as rules of conduct on those who dissent from them'.[6]

Such news-fomented mob rule is a familiar aspect of the media in action. Thus the 2002 press campaign which made public the names and addresses (and faces) of convicted paedophiles (all of whom were under police and social-services observation) did not 'create' the aggressive feelings in the public, but it enflamed pre-existing emotions and gave them legitimacy. As a consequence, several paedophiles were physically assaulted, several went into hiding, with the result that the authorities could no longer monitor their behaviour, and in one instance the illiterate public targeted a paediatrician, confusing the title with that of 'paedophile'. In pursuit of a sellable story, newspapers deliberately stirred up emotion in a way that was essentially similar to the whipping up of nationalist or racist sentiments in less secure political systems. The way the local media created the conditions for war in Bosnia, or incited conflict in Kosovo and genocide in Rwanda, was by exciting public hatred for a minority. Such media-fomented hatred and fear can easily take hold in societies in which other institutions are weak – the police, the law, the political systems were all feeble in these societies. Nevertheless, despite the greater security of our mature democratic systems, the way in which the press can nurse public outrage is similar.[7] This ought to warn us to give great care to the independence of a whole variety of institutions – from broadcast news, to the police, the judiciary, the universities, and the compilers of crime and health statistics. Whipped-up outrage

Protest against convicted paedophiles allegedly living in the Paulsgrove area of Portsmouth, 11 August 2000. The media are especially effective at whipping up feelings, irresponsibly, when the campaigns are based on genuine anxieties.

may be satisfying for audiences and yield rewards for the media, but it is not always reasonable or just. Indeed, the attempt to protect democratic systems from such a perversion of feeling is part of the institutionalization of the news in public-service broadcasting.

The emotional forms produced by the news are similar to those of drama, because they are also directed at the shared experience of the audience. People watch and read the news collectively: even if they are in separate places, reading or switching on at separate times, the news relates to a concept of 'the public' as an entity. Twenty-four-hour news, online news services, the web sites of interest groups all fragment audience experience, but they still depend on some notion of a public: however personalized news consumption becomes, it is not a secret.[8] Audiences want to know what is happening, but they also want to know what it is that other people know.

We tend to think of feelings as hot and perturbed, but cool rationality is also an emotional form – even if not a very fashionable one at the moment. Thus when journalists admitted having 'misunderstood' or 'misread' the extent of the conflict in Macedonia – which they had believed early in 2001 to be about to ignite as had the conflict in Kosovo – they spoke about 'defusing' or 'readjusting' public interpretation of what was happening.[9] They were talking about managing feelings – both in the public and in policy-making elites. The dilemma with which they grappled was that a lower emotional temperature might be a hopeful sign in Macedonia, but it was not very valuable news – and journalists tend to be brought home by cynical newsrooms when aggressive feelings recede. 'Small civil war in the Balkans. Not many enraged. Things possibly getting better. Political reasonableness just tentatively holding' did not make for a gripping headline.

Generally speaking, the emotional response of any individual to the routine stories of the news is of a very low order. As one commentator laconically observed, 'A dropped milk bottle, for example, is more upsetting (to the average person) than a plane crash.'[10] Nevertheless, news is a powerful orchestrator of sentiment in two ways: it relates to collective feelings, and it develops them over time. Through its narratives, the news media build opinion, and keep it simmering between crises.

Part of the problem of the media's relationship to feeling is that emotions do not have to have a legitimate basis to be felt. This is especially important because news always claims to be concerned with justice, but feelings are not necessarily just. Newspapers speculate, in particular, in that most reptilian of feelings – righteous indignation. Emotion is in one sense always 'real'. Feelings, observed Descartes, are 'so close and interior to our own soul that it is impossible that they should be held without their being in reality just as they are felt'.[11] Arguably, it is this intimate interiority that makes emotion so fundamental to our sense of ourselves.[12] After all, 'I' feel angry, but I do not feel that my identity is involved in the same way when my body has a temperature.[13] It is this that occasionally takes news into the construction not only of our public lives, but also of our own private biographies as well.

Unfortunately, the misconstruction of reality can produce quite as powerful an emotion as accurate knowledge. If you are waiting for a child to come home from school and the child is later than the reasonable delays you can easily account for, then you may become agitated. Your feelings are 'real' because you feel them, even if they are not rationally justified, and even if you know this to be the case. Actually, when the child arrives after being held up by a problem on the Tube, the recognition of the mistaken view of reality you had experienced produces its own powerful response. In the case of a severely delayed child your response might well be a kind of euphoria. This corrective emotional moment is interesting. It is often missing from the narrative of news misconstruction. That the National Health Service is doing better than expected, that crime has declined, that the much-discussed 'heavy snow' that was supposed to

Evacuee children returning to their parents in 1945. Such moments of euphoria are often ignored by the media, for whom the story must always move on.

impede action in Afghanistan did not materialize, that there are twice as many nurses in the UK in 2005 as there were in 1985 were not celebrated in the news. This may be understandable – in news-reporting the story always 'moves on' – but in some circumstances the ignoring or glossing over of failed speculation may have dreadful effects.

In addition, 'real' emotion – the kind that brings a lump to your throat, a tear to your eye, or a benevolent tranquillity to your coffee – may also be regularly manufactured. Which comes first, the instrument or the feeling? When I sing the words of Blake's 'Jerusalem' I struggle not to weep. Is this because we sang it at my wedding and thought of it as a kind of manifesto for our marriage, because the words are beautiful and Utopian, because it speaks of hope for my nation, because it poignantly evokes the countryside, because of the obligation it expresses to strive for a better world – or because we all fail to live up to the strenuous demands it makes on us? Or is it just that I have often wept at it before and it reminds me of all the times that I have wept in the past? Or perhaps it's simply that I am weepy (which I am). 'Jerusalem' is a great and beautiful poem. So, if at first sight we dismiss emotions that are called up and created as 'false' or 'sensational', nevertheless we value very highly some of the instruments of feeling that create them.

News shares with drama, poetry, novels, film, painting and music the capacity to engineer audiences' feelings, and, like these forms if they are successful, well-made news shares with great art the capacity to do so creatively. The reporting of the Ethiopian famine in 1984 can be criticized in many ways now. We can seek to explain the coincidences that made it effective (there were only four channels, so that by the second day of the story almost everyone in the country had seen it, and in those far-off days pop stars watched television news). We can point to a moment in collective morality when many people were anxious about the assumptions of the propriety of greed that seemed to underpin Thatcherism. We can dispute its effects (that, for example, it led to food aid being substituted for more valuable development aid). But, nevertheless, a carefully crafted piece of reporting, visually arresting, beautifully written, gathered and directed a public mood empathetically, just like much great art, and then led to individual action and people attempting to take some kind of responsibility for the plight of others, just like good politics.[14]

The media are busy machines attempting to raise feelings across a range of material. Nearly all media products – dramas, soaps, quizzes, documentaries, sports – seek to stimulate emotion. Some of these are subtle and carefully crafted; others are exploitative. News, however, has historically been disciplined by the reality it engineers, and has at times exercised greater caution than these. But, in a harsh economic climate in which the privileges of journalism as a democratic necessity are being eroded by pressures of competition which mean there are few opportunities even to discuss the public good, news also has to compete more intensely with these other media forms that find it easier to shape feelings for political or commercial advantage.

A novel may arouse sentiment in readers by constructing characters who engage us in their stories by focusing our attention particularly on the movement of their feelings. We are fascinated by emotional fluidity. News, documentaries and 'live' news offer us a spectacular display of emotional change. Because their raw material has the authority of having actually occurred, the potential for emotional manipulation is particularly wide. News can sanitize events and thus make other people's tragedies palatable. Alternatively, it can dwell on horror – but this in itself is no more a guarantee of truth than cutting and editing. Simply showing more is not, as is often argued, more truthful in itself, as the veracity of a report depends on the processes which guarantee its accuracy and the context into which it is put. The displaying of horror can have many purposes.

Thus news deals in mobile feelings, unfolding reaction. Indeed, the speeding of the news cycle has stoked up emotional mobility as well – but at a cost. The sober routines of fact-checking are increasingly difficult to maintain. As one journalist has remarked, 'I couldn't do a piece until I'd made at least one telephone call to make sure that it was true – even if that meant we lost our edge in being the first in putting it out.'[15] However, he worked for a public-service broadcaster. Yet one aspect of verifying reports is that this also adjusts the demand that the news makes on people's feelings: a rumour reported hurriedly as a fact not only distorts understanding – it also has an impact on how audiences feel. Accuracy, in responsible journalism, sets fair emotional prices.

The worry is that genuinely held emotion, really experienced, may have been falsely conjured up. Many felt strongly when Princess Diana died, and some wondered where the lumps in their throats had come from. They were disturbed by the experience of what felt like an irrational personal feeling. Even more perturbing was the sight of so many others gripped by the same emotion. This was especially the case when the collective feeling turned to what Ben Pimlott called 'floral fascism'.[16] Not only did the media-enflamed emotion demand a response from the public: it also twisted the approved feeling from a mood of sentimental grieving to an aggressive and punishing one as well. The events around the Princess's death demonstrated some of the dangerous aspects of the media's relationship to collective emotions. In the words of Seneca, 'the emotions possess us, we do not own them.'[17] News coverage often (but not always) amplifies emotion. Thus, the milling crowd in the Mall were repeatedly asked by broadcasters what they felt, and their responses were beamed back at other audience members. Through the media, people watched the impact of their feelings on others, and then adjusted their response again. They did not, on the whole, want to stand out against the crowd. It was perturbing to see.

Playing with the light-hearted engagement of the audience is the basis of the new symbiosis between the Internet, telephones, voting and broadcasting. This has been seen as encouraging a move towards a more plebiscitary kind of democracy (although the major argument against such a form is the grip that public emotion can have on public affairs). Thus in an increasing number of programmes the audience is offered a moment of participation – by voting by telephone or email for a winner or a loser, or for or against some proposition. Millions respond. Politicians eye such electoral enthusiasm enviously.

Floral fascism.

Of course, audiences are pretty sophisticated. Often they understand that their feelings are being exploited – and they enjoy what goes on anyway. Much humour depends on making use of the gap between what you know you are supposed to feel and what you would feel if what you were seeing was actual. Indeed, the rigid conventions in news broadcasting have been a rich source of satire – because audiences are so familiar with them. Yet, despite the competence that audiences demonstrate, we still sometimes worry about the calling-up of emotions, and are suspicious of the way in which they are experienced.

How can we say both that audiences are apparently happy with some ways in which their feelings are mobilized, and which they ought not to accept, and simultaneously that there are things that they do not want to consume that they ought? Both are uncomfortable positions: it is far easier to claim that the public can vote with its feet and therefore, by definition, gets what it wants. The truth, however, is that people can be coaxed into emotions and partisanship by the way in which the news is presented, and encouraged to support causes which they would oppose if they realized the manipulation that was going on behind the scenes.

The idea of 'informed consent' (and the corresponding idea that there are feelings we would not agree to – indeed would prefer not to experience – if we knew their purposes more fully) is helpful. It alerts us to a way of discriminating between legitimate and improper moulding of feelings by the media – and allows us to impose standards. Recently, institutions like the health service – seeking to negotiate settlements between the interests of authorities and those of patients – have developed codes of conduct which emphasize rights in this way. As a consequence, 'informed consent' has become a key criterion. Yet, if such ideas are to be applied to the ways in which the news media summon up feelings, it is particularly relevant to consider the cases of those subjects whose capacity to give a meaningful consent can be doubted. For consent to be meaningful it *has* to be informed.

Of course, there are groups of people whose informed consent may be difficult to assess. For example, there has been a recent debate about children's consent to medical treatment. The British Medical Association guide to good practice argued that it was a difficult area, because the relevant ideas 'were fraught with uncertainty': the notions of best interests, benefit and harm, even the definition of 'child', were so diverse. It went on to point out that 'Acquiescence when the person does not know what the intervention entails, or that there is an option of refusing, is not "consent".'[18] Decisions, it concluded, depend on adequate information and the ability to assess it. 'The constant argument,' according to Priscilla Alderson, whose research has done much to advance the application of the principle of informed consent, 'is that it is a token of respect for the rights of autonomous people, in this case patients.'[19] Such a view perhaps obscures reality: that the professional expertise of doctors provides the only adequately informed basis for decisions. Yet, against the grain of developments in other areas, the rights of citizen news-consumers are protected by increasingly frail mechanisms.

Indeed, in the case of the media, plausible versions of audience 'consent' can act as a very effective ideological smokescreen. Media owners have always maintained that there exists what we might call the 'assumed consent' of purchasers and audiences. Consent, it has often been suggested, is implicit in market choice. But the market in information *about* the media is very imperfect, while for matters that are distant from our daily experience we have few alternative means of information. In addition, standards of journalism are hardly policed as are those of medicine or the law. Our consent to the raising of our sympathy – or hackles – may thus often be ill-informed. We have to ask: for what purposes are emotions elicited, and in whose interests?

Of course, other media forms attempt to stir feelings. 'Everything, from a news item to a soap serial episode, follows the same law,' claims the highest-selling manual on writing for television in America. 'You have to have one main plot, one main protagonist, one central conflict, one central emotion and one climax.'[20] Another journalism manual observes, 'The first problem for any writing is engaging the audience's emotion – it is a matter of words, script, editing and action.'[21] Much of the writing about how to 'do' news, and indeed journalists' own accounts of themselves, is concerned with the all-important recognition of what constitutes a story. 'Journalists have something the audience wants: information,' argues one textbook account. 'They want it because it is new, important and relevant to them,' it continues, but it warns that 'however much they need it they will only receive it if it is presented in a way that is both interesting and entertaining. You have to aim to hit an emotional button.'[22] Recently, news has become more personalized and opinion-led in pursuit of the elusive interest of audiences and perhaps in anxious emulation of the cheery stoking of feelings that is so much easier in other forms of entertainment.

The comparison of news and tragic drama helps differentiate between the calling-up of feelings for purposes that audiences would approve of (if they understood what was being done to them) and for those that they might reject. News, like tragedy, deals with accidents of fate. Tragic drama coaxes us into feeling some kinship with others with whom, at first sight, we have little or nothing in common.

Classically, in tragedy we identify with characters *despite* their behaviour. In *Medea* – one of the most difficult plays to understand and relate to – the heroine's murder of her children is hard to comprehend; Jason, her husband, describes her as 'a carrier of doom, a lioness far fiercer than any monster'.[23] Medea's acts are horrifying, and the play repeatedly ratchets up the tension in the audience by allowing us to hope against hope that she will not commit the last act of revenge on her husband by murdering her sons, 'my babes, whose bodies, whose bearing are all so beautiful'.[24] The tragedy never excuses Medea, yet it reconciles us to her. We long for her to save herself, and we are awed by the rage that runs through her. Despite her crime, we feel for her – but this does not involve us in any concession to the crime itself. Thus great tragedy achieves an objectivity of vision and

Women grieve for a neighbour's child, killed in the school siege in Beslan. News and the stories and images it comments on can be, at times, genuinely tragic, and enlarge rather than narrow human sympathy.

takes audiences on emotional journeys which enlarge their understanding of human complexity.

News can be tragic in just this way, and when it is it also helps audiences understand the world more fully, and consequently leads to better attempts to solve problems – or even a sober recognition of how intractable some problems are. Yet much news concentrates on blame alone – as if all events have a single promoter. How can a public brought up on a diet of blame distinguish between those who are genuinely culpable and hapless scapegoats? How can they get to grips with the slow processes of reason? Often it has been 'current events' – slightly more distanced from the rigid time frame of news immediacy – that has explored the reason for things happening. Yet everywhere current-events broadcasting and the more reflective exploration of news are under threat, driven to the edges of the schedules, and so drawing smaller audiences. This is because of increasing competition with more channels, and the reduction of regulation which used to secure a guaranteed place for such programming on democratic grounds.[25] Meanwhile, news has been driven by the demands for more up-to-the minute reporting, and so is focused on acts and events divorced from frameworks of explanation that provide news with a tragic dimension.

Audiences both respond to headlines and story lines and know that these are crafted to call up familiar emotions. The proper tariff of feelings called up in response to an event is continually traded between journalists, news organizations and audiences. Thus hyperbole – or setting the feeling rate too high – may be a difficulty as well. But the problem is that people like to feel predictably. It is not that they are opposed to being moved, or shocked: on the contrary, they often enjoy it – so long as it takes place within a secure structure. The enjoyment of the harvest of expected feelings can be very satisfying. It is novel, contradictory feelings that audiences often reject. Yet the state of international events and domestic developments is often disquieting, obscure and uncomfortable.

It is also the case that the 'reality' claims of news, documentaries and news analysis have been challenged by a whole new range of programme formats, from pet and vet shows to quizzes, games and various 'ordeal' series. These also show genuine events – often in real time – and have thus eroded the singular authority of news to be representing the 'factual'. Such shows, which display 'real' feelings, and which undoubtedly call up 'real' feelings in the audience, may have begun to claim some of the authority of 'news' – but, being less serious, less bound by fact, they are freer to produce more conventionally satisfying melodramatic forms, with tidier resolutions.

The discovery that the news seeks to organize feeling, routinely and discreetly, may cause concern. Perhaps the emotions displayed are too bureaucratically constructed, too frequently consumed? News thrives on audience anxiety – perhaps it manufactures threats? Perhaps there is a gap between the object of emotion and the emotional response demanded? Alternatively, the audience may be wary, fatigued or apathetic and hopeless about the emotion demanded of it. 'Performed emotions' have, in any case, always invited suspicion. Thespis, the first actor, was called a liar by the Greek philosopher and politician Solon, because his job was to pretend to be someone else. The inability to 'act a part' has often been seen as a touchstone of sincerity. As the historian Jonas Barish has observed, while poetry, sculpture and the epic have always been seen as good and worthwhile forms, a profound scepticism has been reserved for 'theatrical' behaviour and the theatre. Barish argues that the origin of this distrust lies in the suspicion that the 'aim of theatrical representation is not to discover the truth ... but to delight'.[26] Henry Crawford in *Mansfield Park* is a famous example of a character whose convincing command of the personality of others in acting is mirrored by a lack of command of his own. His charming malleability is a sign of moral laxity. Suspicion of 'spin' and 'presentation' and 'public relations' is based on a similar hostility to performance.

There has often been opposition to representation, as the anthropologist

Jack Goody has argued. Sometimes the antagonism has come from those in power who are suspicious of the seduction of the audience's attention: thus Goody argues that 'the life-like immediacy of the theatre puts it into unwelcome competition with the everyday realm and with doctrines expounded in schools and churches.'[27] But the suspicion can also bubble up from the public, fearful of deception and pleasure. This helps to explain the recurrent prohibition of performances at puritanical moments in all cultures throughout history.

Another factor in the re-evaluation of performance is technology – television exposes intimacy, showing audiences how people look and behave in unguarded moments. As these exposures come to bear such weight, they are defensively rehearsed – and then performed. We hardly live in puritanical times, yet there is a great contemporary misgiving about performance, and at times a savage hunger for what lies beyond it.

News and current events may not be theatrical, but they are certainly performances. Yet evidence that they are nevertheless enacted displays is threatening. This may be one of the many reasons why journalists are often so hostile to discussion of how they make the news. (Other reasons are a sense of threatened skills and an uneasy perception of the difficulty of defending professional standards.) Of course, as the historian Robert Darnton has observed, all groups with vested interests (not just professionals) are similarly, and understandably, hostile. 'History professors and heart surgeons and doctors of all kinds', he points out, are also uncomfortable with observation by outsiders.[28] This is partly because they feel that they know why and how they do what they do better than any mere observer.[29] But journalists in particular may have much to lose in the exploration of the way in which they 'perform' the news, because the more that what they present is seen as 'staged', the more open to doubt and disbelief it becomes. This can most obviously be seen in the periodic crises about allegedly 'fixed' documentaries, where stories are constructed without the audience being informed. There is a real sense in which the audience's trust is a fixed stock that is hard to re-establish once lost. Establishing the line between legitimate performances and illegitimate falsifying enactments looks more complex to an outsider than it is to film-makers, who understand very well where the line can be drawn. However, standards change over time. Thus the path-breaking documentary series *The Century of War* (1968) established novel standards of visual authenticity in which footage was scrutinized not just for its suitability but also for its provenance.[30] But the scrupulous regard for evidence has costs. These are difficult and expensive standards to maintain.

In fact, not all the pressures towards narrative completion are bad. There is evidence that the public wishes to understand more of what has happened to the victims of famines, wars and disasters after the crisis is over, and to see the 'end' of the story when normal life has returned. Such reporting would help correct the prevailing view of the abnormality of the developing world, and provide a corrective vision of everyday ordinariness.[31] But the pressure to make what one journalist called 'nice little cosy or thrilling stories'[32] that are cheaper, quicker to produce and more readily understood than the more challenging complex event is not helpful. Journalism, as it competes with more fictionalized 'reality' forms of entertainment, may become more subject to the kinds of suspicion that attend 'theatricality'. Making up trivial news may not matter, but news under pressure may seek to please by giving audiences what it believes they want to hear.

News comes – say journalists – from the 'dark underside'. 'People just don't understand,' commented one veteran reporter. 'News is only news because it's doom.'[33] It is often an unhappy form – partly for the reason, extensively discussed in this book, that audiences relish disasters. But by contrast with novels, for example, which often display the contradictory and sometimes shameful emotions that people experience but would find it difficult to acknowledge, news often tidies emotions up. It thus provides audiences with reassuring simplicities in which bad feelings are what bad people have, while good feelings are the prerogative of the good – like a soap opera.

Nevertheless, the news often declaims in the language of one emotion but appeals to another. Thus calling on compassion for victims is often a disguise for self-righteous fury against the perpetrators – which excites audiences without helping those in need. In his analysis of the way in which broadcast adverts work, Schudson points out that 'advertisements can be taken as a kind of ironic game.' He suggests that that is how they are most persuasive: 'like other forms of irony, advertising says what it does not wholly mean, but nobody is obliged to believe its statements literally, hence it creates an illusion of detachment and mental superiority – even when one is obeying its exhortation.'[34] Such communications, he suggests, do not mean what they say, and their power is enhanced by the ambiguity. Unlike good novels, they try to perform a sleight of hand. Thus much news attacks public figures for lying (thereby demonstrating a still vigorous public concern for the truth). Yet very few news organizations – notable exceptions are the BBC, the news agencies, and some of the quality papers – ask themselves any questions about the truth of what they themselves report.

The ambiguities inherent in communication may, when audiences are considered, go even deeper. The German film-maker Wim Wenders, analysing the impact of a controversial film about Hitler in the 1980s, pointed to the contradictions that the pursuit of 'truth' can give rise to. 'You cannot,' he argued, 'show an abundance of something that you want to distance yourself from at the same time.'[35] Righteous indignation is a staple of the tabloid press that exploits this double standard. But even the most serious reporting may also be double-edged in its impact: providing the public with something that they find horrible but which they also relish.

Not just tabloids but the reporting of violence and atrocity in general often operates in precisely this way. One experienced reporter points out how this ambiguity works, namely by seeking to 'sell wars and then milking them for more coverage by decrying them'. There are several aspects to such news, he claimed. 'The individual's reputation is made not by reporting the truth or analysing the factors that go into war, but rather by feeding the appetite for feeling.' Reporters and audiences 'get a buzz out of wars, and then they get a buzz out of slagging them off'.[36] This particular kind of reporting requires an emphasis on feeling and 'morality', and always emphasizes the 'futility' of wars. Journalists, he argues, feel superior in such commentating. Such reporting endlessly imposes on very different wars a repetitive cycle of moral simplicity, and drains contemporary conflicts of the particularities that would alert the public to the real predicament. The brevity of television clips, and the repetitive cycle of constant news in which stories 'break' but are never explored in depth, may also be a factor here. This exacerbates a situation in which our attachments to conflicts are more complex, political and distant than in the past.

One aspect of this raising of feeling is the conventionalized exaggeration of anxiety – for pleasure. Indeed, much news is a kind of disguised Gothic form. Such writing originated in the nineteenth century, thrilling and delighting readers by implicating them in the private delirium of the experience of others. But it also emphasized awareness, involved both guilt and fear, and offered the spectacle of the terror of other people. Indeed, a key feature of Gothic sensibility, that emotions produce outward forms that correspond to inner states (typically that the landscape reflects feelings), has a direct descendant in televised news. The repertoire of outward signs of distress involves a stylized choreography of clichés (similar to the excesses of romantic literature).[37] Inner-city landscapes, deserts, glum or miserable inhabitants are all familiar visual themes. The darkness of news reflects part of the reality of what it has to cover but is also an aesthetic choice. We like fearfully predictable black news.

*

Emotions are sought because the Holy Grail of news is the attention of the audience. This is the commodity that keeps the presses rolling and the screens filled. While other kinds of media content can be exploited ruthlessly for the most successful way of securing attention, news has a problem. It is (up to a point) dependent on the fortuity of events. Journalists are unremitting in their capacity to make news-like stories out of unpromising material, injecting the most routine of events with surprise and conflict. Nevertheless, there is no substitute for the real thing.

'Attention' depends on culture, and culture on tradition and history. In the mid and late twentieth century, the dominant culture switched from the printed page and the radio to cinema, television and computer screens. Computer screens have become particularly seductive. Modern thrillers frequently have sequences involving the scrutiny of computer screens, which are often portrayed as providing clues and solutions to problems in the plot. Meanwhile, shows of contemporary art are typically accompanied by video presentations, often of the artists discussing their work, or experts explaining it. Audiences invariably spend longer watching the screens than looking at the objects of the displays.

But paying attention has drawbacks. A characteristic of the evolving media is that each generation regards with bewilderment and fear the innovations available to its successors. Thus in the 1950s broadcasters were worried about the siren attractions of the BBC's Light Programme, which 'makes too many adolescents passive listeners'.[38] Today we are worried about computer games. Children suffering from 'attention disorders' who cannot concentrate properly and are 'mobile, jumpy, always moving, and distracted'[39] are frequently identified as those who supposedly pay too much attention to television and computer games. Disorders of attention in childhood are associated with failure in schoolwork, and a variety of personality problems. Many of the classic works analysing the impact of the media have been concerned with the problem of what the American researcher David Riesman once called 'degenerative attention'.[40] Riesman suggested in the 1950s that absorption in the new electronic media was fundamentally altering personality types, producing dysfunctional citizens. Similarly, Hannah Arendt's image of 'the dazed, tranquillized behaviour of the television viewer',[41] who manages to cancel out the rest of his or her environment, seems to some (especially parents) to retain its applicability.[42] The concern with attention is an anxiety about the capacity of the media to reshape the inner subjective experience of the audience.

The attention we bring to news is the result of a historically constructed state. It has its origins in the theatre, public life and techniques of psychological control, as well as in the technologies that emerged to focus attention in specific ways – the camera and the cinema. Its growth, it has been suggested, can be traced through the visual experiments of the Impressionists and the early attempts of illusionists and photographers to capture aspects of reality and to filter them through developing machineries of viewing. In fact it was not only sight that had to be taught; so too did listening. 'Listening' in the 1920s was seen as a version of scientifically induced amateur experimentation, some of which had to do with the skills required to construct the new 'listening apparatus'. During the same decade scientists began to measure reaction time, which was seen as providing some identifiable yardstick of the effect of attention.

However, much of this work has ignored the simple fact that 'attention' is also produced by events. Nearly all of the mass media have been transformed by a relationship to crises. The news needs public fear. Thus in Britain the 1926 General Strike produced a hunger for news that transformed radio into a mass form. 'The sensation of the General Strike,' Beatrice Webb noted in her diary, 'centres around the headphones of the wireless set.' People, she added, 'gathered in rapt attention' to listen.[43] More recently the fortunes of CNN were altered by the first Gulf War, and those of the Arab satellite station al-Jazeera by the war in Iraq. Such crises delivered the innovative news stations the attention of the audiences they needed.

In all of these cases, hypnotic attention was the product of the new technology, but also of the nature of the events which the news described. At the same time, the public's fascination with a new medium has often seemed potentially subversive to uneasy authorities. Thus the passionate, private 'rapture of reading' was identified as threatening wherever literacy began to spread from elites to broader publics. The capacity of reading to dissolve the reader's sense of the distinction between his or her own inner world and the outer world was viewed with distrust. While we are anxious about the contemporary attention given to computer games (which have replaced television as the main focus of anxiety), we are also concerned that audiences no longer give news the attention it needs. Yet we are perturbed by the mesmerized absorption in, for example, the replaying of the images of the collapse of the twin towers of the World Trade Center.

There is a long history of distrust of the purposes of private attention. Fiction has often aroused suspicion. In sixteenth-century Spain, novels were regarded with deep ecclesiastical distrust since they seemed to threaten the Church, because, according to one study, 'works of devotion were pushed from pride of place and imaginative literature began to impinge on areas of emotion which the church wished to reserve for religious feeling.'[44] It was not just novels but the forms of attention given to them which were often seen as dangerous. Later, in England, novel-reading women servants were regarded as potentially ill-disciplined and insubordinate. Indeed, the theme of the duped, besotted, unreasonable and misled reader became a theme of novels themselves. Don Quixote and Madame Bovary are both rendered incapable of distinguishing between reality and fantasy by their indulgent absorption in novels. The power of fiction to persuade and over-come its readers was seen as a pathology of attention. In the early nineteenth century an ancestor of the Labour Chancellor of the Exchequer Hugh Dalton flung his novel across the room in an attempt to give up his perni-cious vice.[45] Indeed, the looser notions developed to account for spectators' absorption in theatre and its powers to engage – such as the notion of the 'suspension of disbelief' – seemed inadequate in the face of the new fascination. The theatrical convention suggested a willed and rational effort, whereas the immersion in fiction (and now in screens) appeared all too ominously effortless. Thus a recurrent anxiety about the media is that the consumer cannot disengage from them. The problem has been one of how to emerge from the attention – not how to give it.

Recently, broadcasting has generated another cycle of political gloom. The American political scientist Robert Putnam, in an analysis of the forces which are reshaping democratic society, argues that the 'social capital' of voluntarism is declining alarmingly. From a careful examination of data, and in what turns out to be a brilliant metaphor, he maintains that, although people are bowling more, everywhere in America bowling leagues are collapsing. People are literally 'bowling alone'. His study shows that the key variable in this decline is not any of the obvious factors which others assumed have accounted for social change – working women, greater geo-graphical mobility, longer working hours – but age group. The key variable that distinguishes the experience and habits of different generations is television. People born after television became widespread watch television and no longer do things together.[46] They bowl against themselves – not in leagues. Similar research in the UK has shown that it used to be the case that people were typically uninterested in politics when they were young, but that they turned to political involvement and community action as they grew older. But since the 1970s that has ceased to be the case.[47] Again a key factor is thought to be the increase in private forms of entertainment. This kind of argument again implies a disorder of attention, but in a sense a social disorder rather than a private, psychological, one. But it is a disorder that must be closely related to developments in the news and the kinds of interest that people have in it.

Is there anything distinct about the kinds of attention that news requires? The desire for news is often experienced as a need. Has anything important happened? Or anything unimportant which everyone will be talking and thinking about? All news seeks to enter our consciousness with a bang. Sigmund Freud, on holiday, wrote back to his family in 1907 about his experiences in a Roman piazza:

From time to time terrible yells are heard in the otherwise quiet and rather distinguished crowd: this noise is caused by a number of newspaper boys who, breathless like an ancient herald of war, hurl themselves into the piazza with the evening editions, in the mistaken idea that with the news they are putting an end to an almost unbearable tension. When they have an accident to offer, with dead or wounded, they really feel kings of the situation: I know these papers, they are cheap, but I must say there is never anything in them that could possibly interest an intelligent foreigner.[48]

In some cases, of course, the tension that Freud describes as ended by the news boys is real enough. In 1939 Beatrice Webb wrote in her diary about hearing the Second World War declared as if getting the news at long last was cathartic: 'Listened at eleven this morning to Chamberlain's admirably expressed declaration to the House of Commons of war with Germany. In his sorrowful admission of the failure of his policy of appeasement and sombre but self-controlled denunciation of Hitler, he was at once appealing and impressive.' She records the way in which the final, collectively heard moment was shared: 'We paid that painful attention to the moment that makes it lodge in one's life. Now that we have the clear news that we are at war – I feel detached and calm; the strain has ceased.'[49]

Another aspect of the attention paid to news is the willingness to be changed by what is absorbed. Attention is prized because it implies a fuller opening of the audience to the possibilities of the content. Yet, in the case of news, the opportunities to consume it have increased and more and more of it is angled at ever smaller communities of interests in an attempt to attract an elusive public. Thus even broadsheet papers have become more narrowly focused on the interests and habits of readers, while broadcasters also ask that programmes provide what audiences prefer, and everywhere the attempt to target specific audiences (especially economically valuable ones) has become more intense. Yet this specialization has not delivered to news greater authority or larger audiences. It is, of course, important that news reinvents itself. Yet news and democratic political forms are closely related, and they both seem to be experiencing difficulties that may also be related. The classic explanation of the attention that audiences bring to

Pedestrians watching the news, 11 September 2001. The commodity that the media actually trade in is audience attention. (And their democratic function depends on their success in attracting and engaging audiences in this way.) However, some events get the concentration they deserve from audiences irrespective of the media.

news is that they need to survey the world and to watch out for their own interests. It is assumed that audiences understand well enough what matters to them. Yet even in this apparently rational mode they consume news because it alerts them to fears and threats, opportunities and challenges. Thus even the most informed of news consumption has a tinge of feeling to it.[50]

'Emotion' itself has always been seen as 'agitating', just as the best news grabs attention because it is disturbing. The original Greek word meant 'something which happens to a person', while the Latin verb *movere* is the root of 'movement' as well as of 'emotion'. Essential to nearly all ideas of emotion is the sense of the journey between inner feelings and outward circumstances. In Aristotle's famous description, emotions overcome us and we experience them as the uncontrollable flight of running down a hill: we may start out in control, but we soon lose it.[51] News is predicated on a sense of change and movement. News hurries. 'Do not use passive verbs,' enjoins a CNN style sheet. 'You are aiming for narrative movement, pace and speed.'[52] The 'mobilizing', 'active' impact of the media is central to their democratic role. Indeed, newscasters everywhere read from copy written entirely in capitals, in itself a kind of demand. The language of news aspires to urgency. 'Do not write a story starting "Yesterday",' admonishes another instruction manual, but 'seek to concentrate time into the here and now.'[53] Style manuals advocate the breaking-up of even the current day to make the time more pressing. '"Late morning" sounds more precise and more immediate than "this morning",' another manual suggests.[54] The process of news-gathering is also replete with words and metaphors which indicate force, movement, running and change. One of the key ones is the idea that news – like the ocean or a cup – breaks.

The idea that news will speed, stir and race is part of the notion that news has the capacity to engage. Yet reporters complain that time is more of a problem today than it used to be. Deadlines come more frequently; reporters have less chance to pause for thought or consult other sources, check facts, venture outside their offices. Complaints of the speeding-up of processes are, of course, a common feature of the history of industrialization. But journalists argue that there has been a particular acceleration in their work recently. 'The news cycle is so much faster now,' commented one, 'and important stories die just as fast as the trivial ones.'[55] The desire for immediacy means that the news is more susceptible to unverifiable rumour – and many groups now seek to exploit this opportunity in their own interest.

The sense of news as a mobile force in society, pushing through constraints, is expressed in many official documents. Thus, according to the UN Charter, 'Freedom of Information is a fundamental Human Right and is a touchstone of all the freedoms to which the United Nations is consecrated. That freedom implies the right to gather, transmit, and publish news anywhere and everywhere without fetters.'[56] The idea of information as active is also what those who do not like the idea complain about. 'In developing countries we cannot have a free-wheeling press. It might be too deceptive and people would get too excited,' claims the Indonesian government, defending censorship.[57] Indeed, censorship is often described (by its opponents) as the opposite of movement: as 'restrictive', 'binding' and 'stultifying'.[58] News is thus everywhere seen as something rather like emotion – news agitates. Thus, while news disturbs the previous calm, emotions are also seen as disruptive, particularly of cognitive processes. Feelings 'boil up' and may continue to exist despite rational knowledge. Emotions are also often discussed as if they are not the responsibility of the people who express them. Rather it is as if people are besieged by feelings. It is as if the reasoning part of the people had not positively endorsed the felt emotion, but had failed to intervene to check it.

Turning an unpromising event into an attention-catching titbit of news is always a matter of shaping it emotionally, and the feelings that a story will arouse (as opposed to those a mere report might elicit) are often close to judgements. In order to turn a trivial event into a story, a reporter will find a 'conflict' angle, often disguising his or her own contribution. Take the journalist's question 'Do you feel any moral conflict?' 'No,' replies the interviewee – who has to say something. The report may then read, 'X claims he feels no moral conflict' – not exactly a misquote, but the journalist is active and the respondent trapped. It makes a 'story' by inviting a judgement.

Modern news emerged in an age more comfortable with feelings of shame and guilt. Reported news is increasingly predicated on narrative patterns that imply that all stories have beginnings – and ends. Yet many issues that the news deals with are insoluble or may take decades to ameliorate. In such cases, having your emotions stirred so unresolvedly may not be pleasant. Difficult news may make people feel ashamed or guilty or simply uncertain about what to think – and they can choose to avoid such feelings.

Some journalists have sought to deal with the 'crisis of public attention' by heightening feelings and personalizing reporting. News may attach us to valuable causes for justice through engaging our emotional involvement. Many campaigners and journalists claim that this is a justification for more explicit news coverage of the terrible things that happen to people. As such they are part of a more general argument that positively values passion.

We live in an anti-stoic age. It is common to compare our own, more emotionally articulate, time with the inhibitions of the past. As the anthropologist Catherine Lutz argues, 'emotions are still undervalued (as antithetical to market values) but they are more commonly overvalued (as a source of personal identity and the really-real).'[59] Contemporary consideration of the revamping of the news within organizations tends to emphasize how it needs to become more 'direct', 'more affective', 'less boring', 'less depressing', and that it should 'lighten up'. It needs to be 'more fluid', explained one news executive. News should be fun, yet touching – up to a point. But are the evolving of emotions, the presentation of them and the calling-up of them in eager audiences useful? And is it emotions or the form that they are given that matter? We have had, at times, very different views of emotions.

Some of those most cautious about the evolution of collective emotions have nevertheless also been acutely aware of their benign personal effect.

John Stuart Mill describes in his autobiography his own Pauline conversion to emotion. He had come to a halt in his life, and suffered a terrible depression. He felt he 'worked without hope, like drawing water in a sieve'. He found nothing that comforted him – until he began to reread Wordsworth's poetry. What made the poems 'a medicine for my state of mind', he maintains, was that 'these expressed, not mere outward beauty, but states of feeling, and of thought coloured by feeling.' The poetry, he claims, 'educated' his feelings.[60] It was not, Mill argues, the object of the poems that had the healing impact. Wordsworth's poems were about the beauty of nature and the countryside – which, however lovely, had not helped or liberated the philosopher's mood. It was the impact of a cultured enlargement of sympathy that Mill perceives as having transformed his life. He feels for things that had previously not touched him. Elsewhere, Mill is acutely suspicious of the authoritarian domination of commonly held public feelings. Would he have objected if the entire society had felt compellingly moved by daffodils (in homage to Wordsworth)? Or would this have been a good thing? Whatever the answer on conformity of feeling, Mill clearly believed that the re-engineering of sensibility could be triumphantly positive. The news certainly educates sensibilities: in the short term it affects what is felt about individual incidents, and – much more powerfully – in the long term it teaches us to care and to ignore. But does it enlarge our sympathy in the way that Mill saw as key?

From the other side of the creative divide from Mill, that of trying to influence readers, D. H. Lawrence later wrote, 'It is the way our sympathy flows that really determines our lives.' An appreciation of the feelings of others, which he called 'sympathy', was, he argued, key. 'Properly handled it can inform and lead into new places the flow of our sympathetic concerns, and it can lead our sympathetic recoil at things gone dead.'[61] Lawrence identified a key problem that writers tackle, namely the exploration of abhorrence. He suggests that in order to judge people and their actions, you have to understand how they feel about them – although you do not have to agree with how they feel. 'Recoil' is in this way as dependent on 'sympathy' as is agreement. Beatrice Webb, a formidable judge of character, wrote in her diary that 'without sympathy there is an irreparable barrier to real knowledge of the inner workings which guide the outer actions of human beings. Sympathy is the only instrument for the dissection of character.'[62] In this way, the notion of 'sympathy' is to be distinguished, as Adam Smith distinguished it, from 'benevolence', which is a positive and kindly view. Sympathy, to Smith, was 'no more than common understanding of feeling'.[63]

The notion of 'mutual sympathy' – encouraging people to understand each other – is one basis of good news-reporting. Through the description of outward circumstances and events, the best news has enabled audiences to appreciate how other people feel the allegiances they do. Thus, while all news needs to raise its audiences' feelings, sensationalist news agitates the feelings of audiences only for its own purposes – it is not concerned to educate sympathies in this key sense. This means that the judgements it arrives at are an inadequate basis for thinking about remedies.

News based on the understanding of others (as well as resentment on one's own behalf) underpins all passion for justice. Inescapably, news stories are always attempted judgements. This makes news sound very grand (which at times it can be), but news is above all a commodity: the idea that news is a machine of moral enthusiasm and moral indignation would require saints to man the galleys, and good journalists are not saintly. More importantly, nor are the organizations they work for necessarily well intentioned. Nevertheless, it is the role of news as a judge and sometimes the jury on events that is always closely related to its capacity to move us.

This has to be seen in a context in which the classical ambition of removing passion from influence over public life has recently been turned on its head. Today, the public manifestation of feeling is rapaciously hunted out by the media, and the failure to display emotion is interpreted not as austere and admirable self-control, but rather as a damning absence. The very idea of inexpressibility – which has traditionally accentuated feeling – is under threat. The role of the news ought to be to bring sombre, chilling realism to bear on the fantasies produced by feelings. But feelings are now often considered to have greater integrity than facts.

One influence on the new attitude towards expressed emotion has been feminism. The contemporary re-evaluation of emotion has been seen as a corrective to earlier hostility – which was a component of misogynist discrimination. The philosopher Martha Nussbaum comments that a distrust of feeling has been 'familiar in western and non-western tradition alike'. It has been used, she argues, 'for thousands of years in various ways to exclude women from full membership of the human community'. Emotions, Nussbaum argues, are not 'brutish, irrational forces', but rather 'intelligent and discriminating elements of personality'.[64] She also suggests that emotions form valuable parts of rational judgement, and that as such they have a role in our public as well as our private lives, pushing 'thought around', and so 'they bring to bear on rational calculation a useful extra dimension.' But, in particular, she argues that emotions are directed at absences in our lives. They 'picture human lives as somewhat needy and incomplete'.[65] For Nussbaum, emotions 'educate' knowledge.

News is certainly one important way in which we imagine the needs of others. News has always been in part directed at the unfolding tableaux of fate and accident, the unwilled, undeserved, unexpected befallings of other people. Some are seen to be lucky and others shockingly unfortunate, but the theme of the accidental chance of life is one enduring feature of news. A high proportion of the 'others' one contemplates are indeed 'needy'. News also alerts us to threats to our safety. News thus brings both our needs and those of other people to our attention.

Emotions are also increasingly legitimized because they are seen as 'natural'. All that used be held against them now works on their side. Catherine Lutz argues that 'as both an analytic and an everyday concept in the West, emotion – like the female – has typically been viewed as something natural rather than cultural, irrational rather than rational, chaotic rather than ordered, subjective rather than universal, physical rather than mental, unintended and uncontrollable.'[66] According to Lutz, to experience emotion is to acknowledge dependency and to register neediness. She goes on to claim, like Nussbaum, that this explains why women are more 'emotional' than men – 'because they are more tied to the biological processes that produce neediness and dependencies and thus lead to emotion'.[67] In this way the distribution of power in society does not so much repress emotion in men as produce it in women, whose greater sensitivity is just the product of the fears they feel which are a consequence of their close involvement with others who are dependent on them.

The new evaluation of emotion also prizes the turbulence of emotion (nearly as much as older critics distrusted the same quality). As we have seen, the agitating qualities of news are highly valued commercially, as well as being a key part of the social role of news. Yet, in this kind of analysis of emotion, turbulence is equated with change, and change with something not unlike progress. Nussbaum thus comments that emotion had previously been distrusted because it is destabilizing. Indeed, emotions may breach the most conventional and powerful of social ties – even those to children or parents (thus Medea kills her children under the influence of her thwarted love). And emotions also embody various kinds of instability – not only because people experience them as having such an unstable internal structure, but also because they 'may attach importance to unstable external things'.[68] News can make us feel for the insecure and the threatened – and there is a cost involved in taking on knowledge of (let alone responsibility for) such uncertain categories.

Has what has happened in the media reflected (though also possibly helped shape) a wider movement, repositioning the evaluation of the emotions and changing their contours in our lives? In some respects, the case presented by philosophers like Nussbaum, although eloquent, itself seems to be less an example of clear thinking and more a justification of a shift already on its way. It has also been frequently observed that we have seen the emergence of a whole new set of 'emotional identities': not just in therapies or treatments, but also, for example, in the law, where litigation and compensation for damaged feelings as well as physical hurt are now increasingly common.

But there are some problems both with the intellectual defence of emotions (however corrective it has been) and with some of the practical consequences of this new climate of approval. Both have led to a curiously one-sided argument: one in which 'emotion' has been uncritically prized. The discussion has been perversely narrow. It is striking that in many respects thinkers like Nussbaum talk about the 'value' of emotion in much the same way as chat shows and quizzes. The only emotions discussed are good and morally worthy ones which reflect well on the holders. 'Bad' emotions are considered only in the context of the purgative value of expressing them.

Unfortunately, emotions are not all nice, and it is many of the nastier ones that news trades in. Expressing feelings does not only purge them. It also often raises them. Indeed, the misunderstanding is deeper. Thus many of those who write about the re-evaluation of feeling identify 'neediness' as the key to emotional engagement. Emotions, it is said, work on the ties that people have to children, parents and loved ones, by representing 'holes' in the fabric of the self – the places where an individual's happiness and sense of identity are vulnerable to the needs of others. But these are 'good' needs. They relate to care, affection, duty and respect.

Yet 'needs', 'absences', 'holes in the self' can also be the source of malign dependencies. Jealousy and envy are arguably also based on neediness, but they rarely produce care. Nor does others' vulnerability always provoke solicitude. So why should witnessing the needs of others in the news produce care and sympathy? Vulnerability can equally well produce rejection, fury, anger and despair – and the desire to display power – in bystanders, so it may also produce these feelings in audiences.

Another worry is that arguments 'in favour' of emotional expression fail to distinguish between individuals holding emotions and societies subject to emotion. While it is hard to imagine being a whole person without emotions (indeed, it is not merely a term of abuse, but in its more extreme form a medically recognized infirmity to be 'unfeeling'), it is also true that the collective emotional life of societies is fraught with danger.

It is the power of the media to make individuals feel collective emotions that is rightly a source of democratic anxiety. It would, of course, be nice if societies became more compassionate through some increase in emotional capital. However, it is less nice if they become more jealous, more distrustful, more angry. Moreover, the positive evaluation of feelings also, rather glibly, asserts that 'fear' and 'anxiety' and 'loss' (which are frequently described as female emotional attributes and consequences of female obligations to care for others) are benign emotions. Fear for one's own child can be the basis of empathy with the tragic inability of others to protect their children. It has frequently been used to mobilize audiences. A little girl in Vietnam, running towards the camera; a murdered baby in the Oklahoma bombing; a child shot while sheltering in his father's arms; a dreadfully maimed small boy in Iraq – these have been images that have tremendous capacity to stir feeling. Their power depends on universal empathy with pain, and with the defenceless. However, the feelings they have provoked also include rage and vengefulness as well as compassion and shame. Even fear is not simply a 'good' emotion – as Nussbaum seems to suggest. It is often the fear of other 'ethnic' or cultural groups that is the basis of hatred – not caring. And perfectly reasonable fears can lead to dangerous views.

Indeed, the whole argument is fallacious. 'Approving' or 'disapproving' of emotions is quite irrelevant. What matters is what emotions, about what factors, expressed to whom, elicited for what purpose, with what effects. Eliciting emotions is not in itself 'bad': it all depends on what use is to be made of them. To say that we found a film, a book, a poem or a news item moving is always a compliment. Nevertheless, the positive re-evaluation of emotional forms has paid little attention to the questions raised by the social manipulation of feeling.

But there is an even more fundamental problem, because what is talked about as emotion disguises what is really meant – understanding. When George Eliot suggested that 'there is no human being who having passions and thoughts does not think in consequence of his passions,' she was describing feeling as a reasonable summation of rational experience.[69] Readers value the sympathy and feeling of Dickens's heroine Sissy Jupe, in *Hard Times*, not simply because she is an attractive person (though of course she is), but because these qualities make her rational appreciation of the causes of things more adequate. Her human judgement is better (not merely nicer) than the blind empiricism of the narrowly utilitarian villain of the novel, Gradgrind. The ties to others that Nussbaum values are based on the experience and knowledge of caring for others. But what use are our feelings in developing more truthful appreciation of things when we know little about them? They may still be useful – seeing the condition of distant sufferers may be important. But it is surely not just the same as the feelings we have about things we also know about.

In periods of classical emotional restraint, 'emotions' are distrusted because they lead to false judgements about things not fully known. 'News' ideally seeks to provide us with the information necessary for better judgement, but it certainly deals with subjects that may threaten the individual: indeed, these two features are the basis of its democratic function. Yet 'neediness' and 'fear' are disconcertingly plastic. The media may mould public apprehension for other purposes – to sell things; to please and titillate – and by concentrating on some needs they may disguise the importance of others. But there is another paradox. If the contemporary theorists of feeling are right, greater emotional interest should reflect greater 'neediness'. If we are all experiencing emotions more intensely, this should be because we are more aware of and sensitive to needs. Yet if the change in sensibilities is located in the recent past (some put it in the 1960s, some locate it in feminism, but there is wide agreement that it has occurred), have we in Western news-consuming societies become more 'needy' in this period?

In fact the evidence is that the majority of citizens in the comfortable societies have become far less 'needy'. We may be more emotionally articulate, but this has not in practice had much influence on our actions. Over the last thirty years the gap between those best and those worst off – either globally or within nations – has become greater. Some countries have become absolutely poorer during the period in which richer countries and richer people have become more concerned with emotional expression. In the same period the gap between the better off and the poorest *within* many Western nations has also increased. On the whole, the news agendas of the media are shaped by the interests of wealthier groups, who both consume the media more frequently and are more lucrative audiences (which attract advertising) and hence are favoured by advertisers. These same groups are increasingly favoured by democratic political systems – in many of which the poor have become a minority. The problem is one not so much of feeling but of the relationship between sensibility and action.

Yet it is possible to distinguish between the kinds of emotional change that news may bring about that are helpful and those changes that narrow feelings and incite alarm and hate. The notion of enlargement suggested by the literary critic Barbara Hardy may help. Hardy argues that poetry can be judged by whether there is in it a 'movement to a larger world, a deployment of knowledge, a reasoning, a sense of human justice that keeps it from being sick and private . . . resisting closure'.[70] News is not poetry, but the standard is helpful. Much news reinforces agreeable prejudices. It is not about the world but is self-reflective – about itself. It may have political and commercial agendas it does not articulate. It may also provoke malicious, demeaning feelings. By contrast, enlargement means that the way in which an event is used moves from the particular to the more general; it goes beyond itself, and takes its audiences with it. Sylvia Plath, whose work was often criticized for self-obsessed despair, wrote, 'I think one should be able to control and manipulate experiences – even the most terrifying – like madness, being tortured – this kind of experience, with an informed intelligent mind, I think that personal experiences shouldn't be a kind of shut box and mirror – looking narcissistically at experience – I believe it should be generally relevant.'[71] She was seeing writing as a way of generalizing an experience in a way that enlarges sympathy.

This is helpful – because it provides a way of judging how the news modulates emotion. This idea gets us beyond simply condemning sensationalism, and permits us to distinguish between raising emotions usefully and damagingly. As we have seen, emotions – even ones we have come to think of sympathetically, like fear – are neither good nor bad in themselves. It all depends on context. The news always deals in the particular and the immediate. That is what news is. It also has to make sense of what is happening by putting it into a context. Yet one of the pathologies of news is that a vivid, robust, absolute difference of place, event, history and circumstance is lost by the very conventionalizing nature of the form. Lazy, bad, misleading journalism evades its obligation to the particularity of events by misdescribing unique particularities as conventions (that all military coups are right wing; that all politicians are venal; that those in distant places are victims and never agents; that violence is all there is to wars) and by cynically but profitably exacting an emotional tariff. This fitting of many-sided reality into conventions may generalize – but at the cost of damaging an event's particularity. Bad journalism confirms prejudices, reaffirms conventions and narrows sympathy. Good journalism extends the scope of sympathy, is true to the particularity of events, and uses emotions justly to assist understanding.

11

Global Compassion

Much news is about arousing our interest in things, people, places and events that are distant from us. Often it deals in situations that are not merely physically, but also qualitatively, remote from our everyday experience. This has become increasingly true of news violence: the gap between daily life and daily observation through the media has widened. We are safer than we used to be, but we watch more graphic horror, from which we are comfortably separated. Electronic communication is an insulating window on a distant world. But it is also believed by some to be creating an intimacy that will lead to a new sense of global responsibility. Are the two views reconcilable?

How does reading or watching terrible news relate to the direct experience of trauma? There is a prima-facie case for believing that personal experience of real violence in one area of life is likely to have an impact on the consumption of violence in others. Involvement in a real conflict appears to make the public more sensitive to the images of its effects. One photographic historian has claimed that in the twentieth century the censorship of distressing images of the direct physical impact of war on soldiers – even enemy soldiers – was always greater during wars than after them.[1] In part this was because of military taboos about respect for the dead and official anxiety about demoralizing the domestic public. However, other evidence shows that this reticence was also a feature of public response itself. 'People simply do not want to see more of the horror of bombing,' commented one Mass-Observation report during the Second World War. 'They say that they are too close to it every night to need to see it, it is not decent. It is not a matter of lying, they can tell well enough when reports are misleading, it is just wearying and unnecessary.' Nor had they any interest in seeing dead Germans. They were 'pretty pleased when Jerry copped it, but that was all, no-one wanted to see any of it'.[2] As the Second World War progressed, censors and audiences became accustomed to more explicit images, and by the end of that conflict expectations had shifted somewhat.

Dead Nazi officer in the snow, towards the end of the Second World War, 1944. As wars progress, censors – and the public – are prepared to consider increasingly explicit images. However, recently the display of corpses for political purposes and as part of the news has increased dramatically.

Nevertheless, when real slaughter takes place, some people who are most familiar with it do not care to see it reproduced. This presents a more nuanced picture of the realism of audiences. It reveals a sense of propriety governing the display and consumption of images that we need to acknowledge. There is the damage done by the events and the damage done by casual spectatorship.

However, conventions vary between different societies, at different times.[3] Recent wars show how far public mores have altered. During the conflicts in Afghanistan and Iraq, British newspapers (though not television screens) were full of pictures of dead enemy fighters – some even shockingly with their arms tied behind them. Sometimes the display of images was the product of horrified pity – showing (as in Vietnam) the effects of our actions on others, counting the costs of conflict. On other occasions, in other places, the sights of dead enemy fighters have been paraded as trophies, evidence of success. Sometimes, of course, the same picture can carry both messages simultaneously. Indeed, the use by Arab networks of pictures of dead Allied soldiers in this way in 2003 played a part in producing such a misleading account of the Iraq war, so that, for example, Syrian television simply went off air for four days after the Allied forces took Baghdad – because its news coverage had been so distorted (showing a false story of Coalition defeat) that there was no way of explaining what had happened.

Common sense suggests that the public emotional response to events depends on how directly and personally the audience feels implicated in what has occurred, but that impact is not necessarily straightforward. Aleksandr Solzhenitsyn once put it well, when considering how knowledge of Stalin's Terror had affected the world beyond the Gulag. 'There are several different scales of values in the world, if not many,' he commented. 'There is a scale for events near at hand and a scale for events at a distance; there is a scale for old societies and a scale for young ones; a scale for happy events and a scale for unfortunate ones. Generally, the divisions of the scales fail to coincide, they dazzle and hurt our eyes, and so that we do not feel the pain we wave aside all alien scales.'[4]

How do the media generate such 'scales'? One answer is news values which code international events into the local contexts of the audiences they sell to – and these are influenced as much by commerce, what audiences and advertisers appreciate, standards of journalism, and the economic climate as they are by any impartial assessment of importance. As the number of foreign bureaux that the media maintain has sharply fallen, foreign reporting is now usually done by visiting journalists, interested only in stories high on the domestic news agenda where they come from. Thus the news values of the country being reported on have lost out to those of the reporting nations. Another mechanism is the careful pitching of images and stories 'just where they will excite most interest, and just beneath where they would really shock'.[5] The aim is to produce content 'just' this side of what is bearable. When the World Trade Center was destroyed there were live, on-air accounts by shocked witnesses of people jumping from windows. Yet the pictures were all cut at the point where people jumped. The day after the tragedy, only one British paper (the *Star*) printed a picture of people falling. Two days later all the newspapers carried the same pictures. The 'just bearable' criterion was still in operation – it was simply that the parameters had moved a little. Indeed, most of the great iconic images of pain and disaster, war and atrocity, are almost without exception bearable rather than unbearable – very precisely situated, within the conventions of the time. Sometimes restriction can even add

The Void of War, *Paul Nash, 1918. As any image of the corpses that littered the battlefield was forbidden, both Nash brothers produced desolate landscapes.*

weight to representation. Thus the press failure to reveal the nature of the First World War was partly a product of censorship and partly ideological. Yet strict censorship also produced a response. John Nash, acting as an official war artist, was expressly forbidden to depict the bodies strewn in no man's land. However, the restriction in this case led him to imbue the shattered landscape itself with all of the intensity of the battle. 'I am not sure,' he wrote later, 'that I would have wanted to be more graphic . . . I think the work makes its point.'[6] In this case the images were bearable, but this did not stop them making their case with lasting impact. The art managed to find a means of expressing the reality that the press had simply ignored – but it was not through explicit horror.

Conventions may shift, but the interpretation of images of violence is also related to what groups of people are accustomed to, and this varies widely across communities. Thus, for example, it has been suggested that Turkish communities in Britain, familiar with the restrained conventions of British broadcasting, are at first distressed (and then distrustful) of Turkish satellite news accounts of troubles in Turkey which they now consume alongside British television. The Turkish media emphasize violence and heighten the colour of their reporting. The communities in Britain, used to the cooler context of British conventions, were at first alarmed by what appeared to them wholesale social collapse pictured on the satellite news, but when they anxiously checked with relatives they found that 'things simply are not that bad when we phone or go home.'[7] These audiences experienced a clash of scales – or rather, in this case, a clash of conventions.

It has long been recognized that our compassion for others is directly based on our own individual – though socialized – sense of ourselves. 'As we can have no immediate experience of what others may feel,' Adam Smith pointed out in *The Theory of Moral Sentiments*, 'we can form no idea of the measure in which they are affected, but by inspecting what we ourselves would feel in the like situation. Though our brother is on the rack, as long as we ourselves are at our ease, our senses will never inform us what he suffers . . . It is the impression of our own senses only, not those of his, which our imaginations copy.'[8] Yet, in making the news of disasters, catastrophes and disease (as well as of trivial events), it is precisely this gap which the media has to bridge, and with it the doubt that accompanies our apprehension of the experience of each other. At the same time, Smith offers a clue to how the news, if it is to work on our sympathies, has to make itself not only relevant to our lives, but also imaginable. It needs to work on its audience's understanding of how things occur.

In this way the conventions of the news establish, within a well-understood framework, different scales of relevance of events for audiences, and in doing so they pitch stories with appropriate shades of emotional colour. As William James once put it, 'Common sense says we lose our fortune, are sorry and weep, we meet a bear, are frightened and run. The hypothesis here says that this sequence is incorrect . . . and that a more rational statement is that we feel sorry because we cry, angry because we strike, afraid because we tremble.'[9] Media conventions are professionally honed to invoke reactions in audiences: they are designed to induce the outward effects first – the feelings may follow. So getting the right balance of the two different qualities that good news-making requires – arousing involvement and clear information – is difficult.[10] It is all too easy for the exciting emotion to overcome the cool information.

How discomforting an episode 'feels' is the product of many factors, but the media which present audiences with images of distant pain (even though it may be happening only two streets away) have a variety of instruments to help in pitching a story. Thus, in one psychological study, researchers measured the impact on Western audiences of images of tribal circumcision. The discomfort of watching the images was reduced if the soundtrack explained what was happening from an anthropological and 'expert' perspective, but if the soundtrack concentrated on the practical details of what was happening, without any authoritative framing, the stress levels of volunteer observers shot up. Contextualized by legitimate authority, the impact was lessened. The position of the news media in this is difficult, for on the one hand they are legitimate authorities and on the other they seek impact.

One common way of explaining contemporary changes is to point to the way in which new electronic technologies have nullified distance – which is often seen as not simply a kind of fact but as an admirable moral advance. It is both a cause and an effect of globalization that communication moves

Globally organized 'anti-global' anti-G8 Summit demonstration, 1 June 2003. Such events give us the comforting (but misleadingly oversimplified) sense that communications have made us all 'closer'.

ever faster, and that pictures and text can speed ever more rapidly over increasingly long distances. It is sometimes loosely argued that such greater global visibility is the motor of a developing sense of global responsibility. We certainly see more distant suffering, and it no doubt affects us. Yet there has not been a mutual exchange. As one recent report pointed out, 'the traffic of interest has continued to be one way – with news about the economically dominant world still preoccupying faraway places, while news about the economically distant world plays a far smaller, almost invisible role, in the West.'[11] It is understandable that we believe, as we phone our dear, travelling, teenager on another continent, that we experience ourselves as being 'closer' to him or her than we used to be able to be. Mobile phones are undoubtedly reconfiguring social life, and their use has taken us into a new place: close to the heart of tragedies as they unfold. Now in many disasters people about to die spend their last moments phoning those they love. Similarly, the Internet-based arrangements for international demonstrations bring together protesters from all over the globe in a novel form of organization, while immigrants now use videoconferencing to keep in touch with relations back home, or watch satellite broadcasts from their countries of origin and consequently feel more 'in touch' with how things are developing where they come from. These are all ways in which we instinctively 'feel' closer to others through the impact of new technologies of communication.

But this diminished geographical distance has all too often been translated into a qualitative judgement. The world, it is implied, is 'closer' – and warmer as well. Yet, although electronic communication has altered the effects of distance in many ways, in doing so it has also changed them far more fundamentally than is often assumed. Part of the problem is that the notion of distance that is used still confuses geographical and social space on the one hand and ethical responsibility on the other. Thus it has become a commonplace of British inner-urban living, especially in London, that some of the poorest neighbourhoods in Europe are also the richest, with deprived households living cheek by jowl with highly affluent ones. They are physically close, but exist in different social worlds, go to different shops, eat different foods, send their children to different schools, and encourage them to play in different ways at the opposite ends of the same parks. Physical and social proximity are not directly related. We need to question some of the glib assumptions about the effects of communications 'bringing us closer together'.

The electronic media have certainly altered the significance of presence. We can see the precise moment an American president learns of a catastrophe, and this intimacy influences feelings and policies. As the sociologist Joseph Meyrowitz argued, a sudden shift occurred when Jack Ruby murdered Lee Harvey Oswald on real-time TV on 24 November 1963 and 15 million citizens became legal 'witnesses' to the event. Such 'voyeurism' has since had a long time to re-engineer social relationships. Not only physical presence but social space has altered irrevocably, making earlier taboos unsustainable. Television's 'dissolving' of the walls within homes has meant that children cannot be protected from knowledge of adult behaviour. 'Such restructuring of social arenas,' according to Meyrowitz, 'is at least a partial

Jack Ruby, shooting the accused assassin of President Kennedy, Lee Harvey Oswald, 24 November 1963. The live event turned millions of television watchers into witnesses to murder.

reason for recent trends including the blurring of conceptions of childhood and adulthood and the lowering of political heroes to the level of average citizens.'[12] Thus contemporary anti-deference is not only the product of greater democratic equality but also an inevitable side effect of the media's 'dissolution' of some kinds of distance.[13] Moreover, not all these irresistible effects are positive – they are just different. Such an analysis suggests that the electronic media affect us not so much through their content as by radically altering the arenas of social life.

Contemporary interest in the life that exists behind formal roles is, at least in part, a consequence of such a media-led remapping of social life. We are interested in 'overhearing' speech and behaviour not intended for our consumption, and in 'getting behind' the scenes of performances. The electronic media have thus systematically extended the limits of what is exposed as a performance. This is usually perceived as an advance, but it has had costs as well. Above all it means that politicians find it harder to engage the public in anything like a discussion, and they are given less opportunity to speak on their own terms without being challenged. This in turn has influenced the press.[14]

Electronic closeness also produces new distances – and distortions. Take the familiar and engaging televised depiction of a tennis court. Modern cameras can follow contestants' expressions and register their breathing and minute changes in stance and facial muscles that are too remote to be seen by the actual spectators, thus involving distant viewers in the intimate arena of a game. Indeed, the close camera shot is both a creator and a revealer of personality – and, in the extremity of the game, what is evidently 'true' personality. Yet, a spectator at the 'real' match has a powerful physical impression of the player's command of play, the dimensions of the space and the choreography and architecture of the game denied to the distant viewer of a small screen. Certainly the electronic media modify distance, but they do not merely reduce it (even if that is how it feels). The privileged television spectator has advantages over the present witness, and the televised performance is no less 'authentic' than the physically observed occasion. Nevertheless they are different.

There are also other problems with the notion of a revolutionary increase in social closeness. Arguably, what seems recent and dramatic is actually the continuation of a long process. 'Closeness' and the shrinking of time and space are scarcely novel. The first submarine cable between Britain and France was laid in 1851, and by 1861 all the inhabited continents were connected. In 1884 this cabling of the world permitted the first international agreement on the synchronization of time zones.[15] Nor have we reached a new plateau. Indeed, as one sceptical commentator puts it, 'We just cover the wars we can reach – it's as simple as that. We will go to the conflicts the kit can take us to.'[16] The ease of communication has also posed new problems for journalists, as satellite links are traceable and open up new possibilities for the surveillance and even targeting of journalists. On the one hand, one freelance correspondent argues that a new generation of technology that permitted more mobile transmissions would again 'shift news-making back into the more adventurous hands of freelance and less risk-averse news-makers'.[17] On the other hand, the ease of satellite broadcasting has meant that it is easier to fly journalists to report a foreign story, but these have often replaced local 'stringers', permanently employed in regions and with in-depth local knowledge. Thus, if the media have 'brought the world closer', this is part of a long evolution and, although the significance of recent changes is undeniable, the way the change has altered the meaning of distance is complex. Indeed, public understanding of a 'closer' world needs to be seen in context. It is sobering to note, for

The Queen in tears on Remembrance Day, 7 November 2002. Intimacy may make audiences feel 'closer' to the prominent, but the response can be aggressive hostility.

example, the results of one study that show that 36 per cent of Boston undergraduates could not identify the six adjacent states of New England, 65 per cent could not locate the Seine in France, and 95 per cent could not identify Vietnam on a map, and in a 2004 survey 98 per cent could not find Baghdad on a map.[18] In some respects the world may have shrunk – but global understanding has not grown commensurately.

Indeed, insofar as we are 'closer', this may in some respects be a more neutral (or even unwelcome) process than many have claimed. After all, the public relish of 'scandals' also depends on the idea that the media now provide access to intimate secrets of the great or the famous. A taste for scandalous gossip may be a healthy corrective to the abuse of power, but it can also be misleading – as well as savage. As Robert Darnton points out, in the period before the French Revolution scurrilous stories about the sexual habits of the French royal family gave readers 'a specious sense of familiarity' with the life of the court. Precise physical descriptions, dialogues and excerpts from letters were used by pamphleteers 'to build up an illusion of witnessing the inner life of the court from the perspective of an invisible voyeur'.[19] Such accounts make audiences feel closer to those in power, but they are hardly about producing sympathy: on the contrary, this kind of familiarity feeds aggressive hostility.

Nevertheless, critics have been positive about 'closeness' – partly because of their anxiety about 'distance'. Distancing mechanisms are seen as obstructions to full understanding and empathy. In ordinary parlance, to say that a person is 'distant' is usually pejorative. Yet the media operate many techniques that distance audiences from what they observe. One powerful distancing mechanism is that of comparison: seeking to place events in genres and then measure them against each other. This is, of course, one of the functions we need news to perform for us. Comparative estimates are also a powerful tool for establishing the importance and dimensions of an event. Yet the need to place events in a scale and in order may also mask realities: news may provide a distorted (and sometimes non-existent) understanding of history, and exaggerate the significance of what has happened. Typically the news attracts attention by hyperbole. An occurrence is the 'worst', the 'most major', the biggest, longest, loudest, most costly event of its kind – since the last, and until the next. The exercise always involves comparison – but the scales of comparison are often dramatic (how sad, how awful, how moving) rather than historical ones.

'Comparison' may involve a turning away from the particularity of a happening towards technical issues in relation to its performance which then break down an event into component parts.[20] Take the live enactment of a real death in a bullfight before a novice audience. The killing of the first bull is disconcerting (or at least I found it so). Nevertheless, the death is unique. The second bull already provides a space for comparison, and this is a more comfortable place because attention is directed not at any individual bull and its demise, but rather at the comparative behaviour of two bulls. Experienced bullring aficionados automatically compare and contrast the actual present dying beast with the very many they have seen before. They will compare the skills of the matadors and discuss the technical aspects of performance against a great set of similar events. The media's habitual way of dealing with comparison between events is to place them in sets in a similar way. Thus 'ethnic tensions erupt again into slaughter'[21] was a dominant set (which looked like an explanation but was not) that many of the events of the post-Cold War unruly world were fitted into. 'Insurgent terrorist attack' is now a similar convention which disguises more than it reveals by fitting many different events and groups into a convenient and familiar category.

Thus comparison can reduce the peculiarity of events. The power of the news to diminish the impact of an event by placing it in a sequence, not of history, but of technically similar events, is thrown into relief by the especial power of unique tragedies such as the Holocaust. Contemporary accounts of the organized slaughter of millions of people on the basis of their race did not emphasize the event's uniqueness. On the contrary, most press stories attempted to locate what was known about what was happening within other familiar accounts of the time – about deportation, life in ghettos, or the conditions in occupied countries. The true particularity of the events was recognized and described only later.[22]

The issue of comparison is particularly complex for modern news-makers, as contemporary audiences bring such a profusion of possible comparisons to watching any particular catastrophe. It is not only that real famines, real terrorist attacks, real disasters are relatively familiar, but images of wars and disasters are the common stuff of entertainment. Indeed, not only Hollywood movies, but increasingly video games, provide a Western media audience with endless comparative material. The boundary between reality and fiction in images is porous, and the templates for technical comparison and distancing are numerous. Historical events are often assigned to unfruitful conventional categories, and what is unique about them gets lost. Of course, tragedies do share many features, and we need to understand their more general causes, yet the problem is that what is unique about them – and part of the unfolding uncertainty of history – sometimes gets obscured rather than clarified by comparison.

Another aspect of distancing is numerical comparison. News judgements assign importance to events on the basis of their magnitude. These decisions are modified by geography and time and in comparison with the numbers associated with other contemporary events. However, it is also the case that the news often deals in 'mythic' – or perhaps 'iconic' – numbers. These may (or may not) have a relationship to reality, but they are the numbers of fatalities that will command attention. Such figures are reported by journalists sometimes from eyewitness estimates, sometimes from other sources. Campaigning politicians and organizations use the figures in speeches and reports, which are then reported by other journalists. The figures become the 'commonly known' statistics, and enter the history books – setting a standard by which subsequent events are measured. Accounts of the nineteenth-century Balkan wars, for example, dealt in this kind of 'mythic' number. These wars were brutal, and were reported by journalists determined to mobilize intervention.[23] It is not only that the same figures frequently appeared, but there was a kind of shorthand to them: 10,000 dead meant 'a lot'; 30,000 meant 'a really important event'. Such figures may err not only in the sense that they exaggerate in order to provide a stimulus to action: they may also underestimate and deter it. Thus by 1937 the number of Jews killed by Hitler, it was claimed in unofficial reports, in newspaper accounts and by campaigning organizations, was 700,000. This was a suspicious figure, which seems to have been taken from estimates of atrocities against the Kurds during the First World

War. The figure was repeated in pamphlets and at all the mass protest meetings organized before the outbreak of the Second World War. In 1937 it was probably an overestimate. Yet the same figure was still being reported and used in public argument in 1942, by which time it was an appalling underestimate.[24]

Often we have a limited appreciation of the reality behind numbers. Thus the numbers we find comfortable in media accounts are related to the numbers we understand socially. It is like the sense of triumph and discovery that children find when counting up to a thousand for the first time. The exercise extends the child's sense of the size of things, and incorporates a new, enlarged limit into children's understanding of themselves. Similarly, quantities of money (millions) or astronomical distances (trillions) are presented as generalities that are meant to indicate 'very big' rather than a specific quantity. Large numbers command attention because of what they symbolize as much as for the actual scale they represent.

However, there are other forms of numerical distance at work in the media. Here, as Jonathan Glover pointed out, 'there is always a preference for known lives over even millions of statistical lives.'[25] Glover sees this as an aberration which he disapproves of since it 'involves people responding to image and publicity rather than reality',[26] and as an irrational deviation from the otherwise accepted and legally defined responsibility of giving known and unknown persons equal weight. Thus, for example, prioritizing medical treatment in emergencies – 'triage' – depends on assessing the need, not the person. There is a long, ubiquitous social aversion to the horror of choosing lives to save at the cost of other equally deserving lives. The press and broadcasting have often played an important role in policing this value, and indeed in pushing forward its evolution. In the nineteenth century the law was changed by the campaigning entry of the press into the case of the *Mignonette* – a merchant vessel which had sunk in 1884 in the South Atlantic. The shipwrecked crew, who were adrift on a raft for twenty-four days, had killed and eaten the cabin boy (who they claimed had already drunk sea water and was dying). Cannibalism was not the problem: this was acknowledged as a justifiable resort *in extremis*. Indeed, the sailors did not attempt to hide what they had done when they eventually got back to England. Rather, it was the process by which the victim had been selected that was seen as the issue and which resulted in their being accused of murder and taken to court. The recognized practice in such circumstances was that victims would be chosen fairly, by lot. The 'choice' of the weakest crew member was thus seen as an outrage.[27] The press campaign on this emphasized the illegality of the powerful dominating the weak in this way.

Carolina Chirindza was forced to give birth to her baby in a tree because of the floods in Mozambique, 1 March 2000. Her dramatic rescue gave a face to a disaster and prompted a greater relief effort. (However, there is a dispute about the rationality of the international response to the catastrophe.)

It reflected but also led to a change in public opinion, and subsequently legal views, about the acceptability of any cannibalism. The idea that the individual ought to be protected against either arbitrariness or partiality had long been an important part of judicial thinking. In this case the intervention of the press provoked the law to act, and voiced a new climate of opinion about such issues.

At times the media use 'known' lives with great ingenuity to represent statistical ones. Looking back on a particular report, a journalist commented, 'It lacked the emotional engagement you can get with just one person to focus on. The story needed a face.'[28] The preference for saving the single known victim – the woman giving birth to a baby in a tree; the maimed or sick child (or, in Britain, the trapped dog) – can be defended if it leads to a wider engagement in which the fate of one child focuses attention and delivers care for others. Moreover, our preference for saving known victims reaffirms in a more general way our belief in the sanctity of life. This is the positive, engaging use of the human-interest story – to

Two days after her rescue, Carolina Chirindza proudly shows the world her daughter, Rositha.

reach out and explain events to audiences comprehensively. But sometimes emphasis on the single victim distorts understanding, diverting attention from a tragedy to a comforting story of relief. A novice journalist observed, 'It's just a weird convention. We're told to "put a face" on stories, many of which are distorted by doing so. Many important stories don't have faces.'[29] It may actually have the effect of obscuring what needs to be done, and bewilder beleaguered professionals attempting to alleviate the conditions of a multitude – who find one symbolic victim chosen for attention while all the rest are ignored. It may also comfort us by disguising the choices we make under a mask of benign compassion. Thus we are apparently willing to spend a great deal of money to save one sick child, but very little to stop other children in similar situations falling sick.

Meanwhile, different kinds of 'statistical' victim get different treatment by the media. Thus news prefers unpredictable mortality: wars, natural disasters, unexpected plagues can at times all get plenty of attention. Much less has been given to the many who will die of Aids because policies and health care in Africa, India and China have failed, or to the children in the West who will die because car speeds have not been reduced. Mortality levels attributable to Aids are huge, and more children have been killed on the roads in the UK in the last fifty years than British soldiers killed in combat. In both cases we know that large numbers of people will die – in the future. Car accidents are the single biggest cause of child mortality in Britain, and poor children are far more likely to be killed in them than rich children. 'Why,' asks one recent study, 'are the more exotic problems faced by children, such as satanic abuse, so much more newsworthy, and more likely to attract the attention of researchers and funders? Why do we remove children from "dangerous families" but tolerate "dangerous places"?'[30] Of course, news values are not isolated, and even the law on road accidents assumes that some accidents are inevitable because modern life is unthinkable without cars. Indeed, communities have been destroyed to build roads, and ever since cars were invented the slaughter of children on the roads has been treated as if the issue was as much about how children behave as about the curtailing of drivers. We adjust the value we put on saving lives against our dependence on things we think make our lives more comfortable until there is an acceptable exchange rate. Nevertheless, if such 'statistical' lives could be saved in the future, then they are susceptible to being reduced by better policies, by wiser choices and more comprehensive ideas of the public good. Statistical deaths are – in this sense – not at all inevitable, but in fact always *political* mortalities.

Yet there is another problem: translating willing help into effective assistance depends on understanding what works and what the causes of problems are. This is where the media (and we, the audiences) really fail. In the case of an ill child, or the woman giving birth in a tree surrounded by flood water, what needs to be done is reasonably clear and finite. News stories can indeed draw attention to the need for life-saving structures – and even will them into being. But it is far less easy to understand what has to be done to save 'statistical' lives, for they often require far broader political and social reform. The victims of Aids in Africa can be saved only by political and social change (in Africa, but also in the West) as well as medicine and care – and this idea may seem remote or even incomprehensible. The children slaughtered on the roads of Britain can be saved only by tackling the inequality and poverty that condemn poor children to riskier lives. Glover's objection that image and publicity 'ought' not to be what determines policy ignores a key aspect of public will – understanding.

'Compassion fatigue' is a term that describes the public's perennial and obvious inability to feel equally concerned about the myriad problems and categories of suffering in the world about which we now know and to which the media constantly demand that we attend. Audiences have 'jaded palates'. The modern couch potato is, in this respect, not so very different from the spectator at the Colosseum – except, of course, that the Roman spectator was not expected to feel 'compassion'. Yet, if audiences are realistically to will that action be taken to tackle problems, they need to be able to imagine what a solution might look like – just depicting the misery may be misleading.[31]

One aspect of the impact of events on audiences is believed to be their visibility. Pictures provide the most compelling sense of immediacy, they override words, but do they bring us to the right kind of closeness? Picturing things changes how we consider them. Thus, for example, the status of the living foetus, previously protected from public scrutiny, was altered when its life could be seen. In 1965 the Swedish photographer Lennart Nilsson published a path-breaking series of photographs of the unborn child within the womb.[32] An article containing the pictures in *Life* magazine produced one of the greatest postbags the journal had ever had. One staff writer commented that 'those who saw Lennart Nilsson's marvellous photographs of fetuses . . . wrote in to say that they could never again think of their babies in the same way.'[33] In the context of a debate about when a foetus became a person, the notion of a sharp boundary – at birth – was dispatched by these photographs. But, while the radical changes brought about by conception were illuminated, the idea that the first cells were already a recognizable human was also changed. It made the notion that becoming a person was an abrupt event more questionable. Now, scans have made such images commonplace, and expectant mothers email their friends pictures of their future children (although scans do not have the clarity and beauty of Nilsson's early pictures). Visibility has altered millennia of how mothers have related to their previously felt, but not seen, unborn child.

Nilsson's images were a kind of news. It was as if pregnant women had transparent bellies. Indeed, the novel visibility of the child in the womb had a complex impact on attitudes towards the foetus; but the 'seen' was evidently felt to be more profoundly known, and the pictures changed attitudes for ever. Women bond strongly with the babies they can see as a real person – although women who have stillbirths find this intimacy with the seen and expected child especially painful. In the case of the pictures of foetuses, a MORI poll pointed out that 82 per cent of viewers thought that the pictures showed 'how very complex making a baby turned out to be',[34] and in the longer term the pictures also facilitated embryo research by increasing understanding of the process of development and growth.

But does 'seeing' things make people more compassionate? The truth is that neither visibility nor proximity in itself inevitably produces sympathy – after all, violent crimes are conducted by assailants physically close at hand. Large-scale atrocities, violating internationally accepted codes, are also committed by people who are frequently (although not always) in face-to-face contact with their victims. It may be that those who commit such crimes are exceptional and not representative. However, we all see many images of pain and anguish, and most of them we manage to ignore. The consequences of the new 'publicness' that media images produce are not just an extension of historic 'face-to-face' communications.[35] Perhaps what matters is the authority of the images – especially when it is combined with some means of attachment. After all, mothers could not doubt the reality of what Nilsson's pictures showed them: their attitudes changed because what they saw was convincing, and the pictures showed them something already precious to them, so the attachments they already had were reinforced.

Thus what makes a difference to the impact of media images and narratives on audience's reactions to events is how authoritative and trusted the media are. Indeed, with so many sources of information available, trusted ways of organizing knowledge become more important. As Schudson has argued, even were we all to become our own journalists in the new information-rich world, sending and receiving reports, in time 'a demand would arise not only for indexers and abstracters but for interpreters, reporters, editors. Journalism – of some sort – would be reinvented.'[36] Such an institution, he points out, would have to have some authority – that is to say, people would have to believe it. Much of the trust we accord the media is based on genuine exchange. We take our newspapers with a pinch of salt, yet have trusted broadcasters. This is a reflection of institutional reality – and experience. Yet authority is a powerful commodity – and can be abused.

In the 1960s the social psychologist Stanley Milgram famously conducted a series of experiments in which he tested whether obedience to authority (taken to extremes) was sufficient to overcome what might be assumed to be people's natural compassion. In Milgram's experiments, participants were told they were taking part in tests about learning in an authoritative institution (Yale University) and were asked to punish the 'victims' with increasingly powerful electric shocks whenever they made an error in a learning task presented to them by 'professional' experts wearing white coats. The volunteer participants were not told that the 'victims' were in fact actors, who were party to a deception – and no painful shocks were in practice inflicted. Despite the actor 'victims'' carefully calibrated cries of pain, the volunteers obeyed instructions and went on inflicting punishments they believed to be real.[37] Milgram's frightening conclusion was that, if instructed to do so by people in authority, average Americans were as likely to behave with cruelty as Nazi camp guards had been during the Second World War. In particular, he emphasized that afterwards the participants reported having felt 'at the philosophical level of values that they ought not to go on [hurting the subject] but they were unable to translate this conviction into action'.[38] The methods of the experiments and the conclusions drawn from them have been disputed ever since, but they do address the problem of authority – and especially the authority of the media, which is one key to their impact. The findings were extended by the equally pessimistic Stanford Prison Experiment in the early 1970s. In this test, randomly allocated 'abnormally normal' volunteers were assigned roles as either prisoners or warders. Within three days each group had developed typical behaviour in their assigned roles: 'warders' became tyrannical; 'prisoners' became passive – while the social psychologists running the experiment began to act like prison managers. It took the wife of one of the psychologists who visited the experiment from outside to bring the disturbing charade to an end.[39] Both experiments apparently demonstrate the frailty of face-to-face experience as a prompter of compassion, and both simultaneously show the role of authority in framing responses.

Arguably the media have an authority that is similar to that of the institutions in these experiments – even sceptical audiences accept the frameworks of understanding that the media use to situate stories. But the outcome of the experiments was not completely depressing. Although a majority of Milgram's participants obeyed orders, nearly a third flouted the experimenter's authority to the extent of managing to stop the experiment. Slavish acceptance of authority is not inevitable. In the experiment, the subjects who resisted authority were distinguished by anti-authoritarian incidents in their history, or by social origins that made them less deferential, but they all expressed adherence to a firm value system. Interestingly, the key to compassion seemed to be not visibility on its own, but mutual visibility. Another way of considering this might be that someone you can see – and who you know can see you – is under some circumstances more of an equal agent. In other words, 'compassion' is greatest towards people with whom you can most easily identify. In the context of news, it is not only *how* the news shows us the needy that will affect our attitudes, but also the background: whether we have come to believe that the needy are like us. Indeed, some of the qualities that elicited compassion in Milgram's subjects seem rather close to the qualities that distinguish real-life 'savers'. The resisters in Milgram's experiment showed some affinity with historical individuals who saved Jewish refugees, or protected Tutsis from genocidal slaughter. They had direct personal contact with those whom they 'saved'. Studies of real-life 'resisters' suggest that they also had values that marked them out – whether it was religion or even ideology: a sense that the honour of their nation demanded action, or adherence to a tradition of sympathy and sanctuary.[40] So mutual visibility, an understanding of victims as human agents, and values that endorse compassion seem to be the elements that are needed for active attempts to save others. The media can, at times, meet all these requirements, and their authority can frequently be used for benign ends.

Audiences trust the media because of a shared collective experience of news-consuming during great crises over time. Indeed, we are more dependent on the quality of the authoritative media institutions than we acknowledge. Yet authority may persist whether it is used well or badly. The nature of media organizations and what drives them affects the quality of what we consume as well; thus the notions of the obligations which follow from the right to address the public have in the UK been elaborated in a public-service tradition.[41] This is very different from the 'free-market' approach governing the press – in which it is argued that authority resides only with the readership and readers' preferences – which are themselves seen as natural rather than made. Such commercial and institutional factors may affect whether the mutual surveillance that Milgram hesitantly pointed to as an important potential condition for 'saving' behaviour is or is not present in the media. The key may be news that shows us the reality of how others see us as well as the comforting nostrums of how we like to see them and how we like to think they see us. This has little to do with feeling, and more to do with a commitment to realism.

There is another problem with how the media mobilize sentiment-based compassion. 'Victims' have to be passive angels to call on the sorcery of the media. Innocence is defined in media terms as being acted on – not acting. Indeed, any intention or purpose may raise doubts about the complete merit of a casualty. Nevertheless, the logic of the news implies that victims who are good may have things done to help them – they may be saved. This virtue is powerful: it legitimates action. In a related way, the media prefer aesthetically attractive and appealing victims.

So powerful is the convention of the innocence of victims that it has produced a counter-response. Médecins Sans Frontières, the charity set up by the charismatic Frenchman Bernard Kouchner, argued for a novel approach to aid based on medical ethics, namely that 'The only aspect that requires attention is the need . . . not the worthiness of those who bear it.' Kouchner also argued that the organization should mount media campaigns like a 'guerrilla army raising attention, agitating on behalf of the suffering'.[42] The French sociologist Luc Boltanski argues that this involved a philosophical shift. Instead of wondering whether the victims have done wrong in the past or will be reformed in the future, such a view addresses only the present suffering, indifferent to politics. 'To be concerned with the present,' Boltanski concludes, 'is no small matter. For over the past, ever gone by, and over the future, still non-existent, the present has an overwhelming privilege: that of being real.'[43] Kouchner claims that it is necessary to act on behalf of victims irrespective of the politics of the situation they are in – almost as if they are (like the working class in earlier theories) transcendent. He has even suggested that advocacy of this new principle of assistance can be the agent of a new French international authority based on humanitarian principles – as a bulwark and lever for national pride and authority.

Yet, in practice, even French interventions have not been able to avoid politics. The French have been happy to have rows about parts of the world where their interest is not dominant. They have campaigned about Ethiopia, but not Algeria, Somalia or Chad, and their role in francophone Rwanda was anything but principled – or people-saving. Indeed, the foreign policy of France is no less political and self-interested than that of other nations, despite Kouchner's emphasis on its role as the advocate of human rights. The idea of addressing the suffering rather than evaluating the sufferer is attractive, and indeed rather well adapted to the style of the dominant commercial pressure in the media – concentrating on emotional appeal, and consequently turning all those in need into worthy recipients of compassion. However, the uncomfortable truth is that willed intention to alleviate suffering has on occasions prolonged wars (arguably this happened in Ethiopia in 1984), provided resources for warlords (as it certainly did in Rwanda in 1993 and 1994), and more generally sometimes protected the strong and failed to help the weak (as it did for much of the time in Sudan between 1985 and 2005). Meanwhile, even affecting news coverage has reduced many different situations to a repetitive display of misery that has done little to inform or even interest audiences. What is needed is a way of making clear to audiences that discrimination is possible between successful interventions and damaging ones – and that solutions are possible, but often not simple.

Politics obstinately refuses to go away, however little it is addressed. But it may also be that politics is what transforms our view of passive innocents into one of active agents. And, as we have seen, although the media find worthy innocents easier to deal with, compassion flows more easily to those whom we recognize as being – like us – agents.

The philosopher Oonora O'Neil has suggested that 'seeing misery at a distance may lessen the anguish but can easily produce confusion rather than clarity. At a distance views multiply.'[44] What she means is that causes may be less clear. Yet this replicates the mistaken view that closeness per se produces understanding. Journalists among themselves tend to value 'closeness' very highly, but it is legitimated by purpose. One, describing the moment in which he felt he stopped being a voyeur and became a reporter, remarks how key the transition from observer to recorder felt. After spending months in Sarajevo, sharing life on the civilian front line, he saw young women blown up. His Bosnian friend told him to get his camera. He writes:

In my desire to learn of war I sought the cloak of anonymity in the community. I had ended up not wanting even to carry cameras, let alone use them. Yet it was impossible to integrate totally . . . The words 'get your camera' re-identified me as the outsider I was. And if I could not accept that status, if I could not use my cameras, then I should not be there. I could not stay on and feed off the misery of people just to 'see a war'. I had to use it.[45]

But, again, we need to make some distinctions. What journalists mean by 'closeness' is the attempt to form an unmediated view ideally independent of any of the agencies so devoted to shaping interpretation of what is going on in their own interest. This is at the heart of good journalism that provides independent, impartial, informed, individual observation. But while being 'close' to the front line may tell you things you may need to know, it may not, unfortunately, always mean being 'close' to the important things that are happening.[46]

Indeed, much writing about our relationship to distant suffering is really moralizing. It is concerned with how we 'ought' to feel and deal with things. Even in other respects clear and helpful thinking in this area seems strangely unconcerned with how it is that we arrive at knowledge, succumb to feelings, and turn them into behaviour that influences policy-makers. News is often predicated on policing and protesting a variety of 'oughts' as well. The news media are aggressive (and largely unscrutinized) condemners and exploiters of the failures of others – especially if the public can be expected to display a prurient interest in the revealed misbehaviour. Tabloid newspapers (and tabloid values that get exported to other areas of the media) are almost irrationally devoted to 'getting' people and nailing culprits.[47] In this way, the news is in a constant state of semi-judicial condemnation while the public cheerfully and self-righteously appreciates the misadventures of other people. News can be seen as a machine which pumps out injunctions. And – more than that – news audiences are addressed as if they are morally superior.

Of course, it is also often easier to market individual failings than treacherous structural faults. Journalists typically overvalue explanations of events dependent on personality. In a book linking public cynicism about politics with the systematic corruption of political campaigning in the USA, the American analyst Larry Sabato argues that at regular intervals 'the American press and public have interrupted this degenerative cycle and made the cost of corrupt practices higher than their gain on Election Day. If *corruptus interruptus* can be engineered now, rollback and cleanup can begin.' But it will depend, he argues, on the capacity of the media to fulfil their traditional role and stop 'the unthinkable becoming commonplace'.[48] In order to do this, they will have to scrutinize different aspects of the political process.

Sometimes when a media 'feeding frenzy' is running, a terrifying and misdirectional mood is cultivated, full of swirling condemnation, fed by a new appetite for rumour and a new media willingness to publish unsubstantiated gossip.[49] Counter-arguments, discrediting evidence, justice (let alone comparison or understanding) are dismissed. News in this mode can be destructive. It can be anti-deferential, but without respect for justice. Indeed, news is often at its most dangerous, volatile and incendiary in its condemnatory mode – although this is also the basis of much that we value.

Stating moral imperatives is ridiculously easy; implementing them is extremely hard. It involves making choices between less than ideal alternatives. It often means dealing with less than perfect victims. It may require producing a consensus out of conflicting interests. It is often perplexing to know what to do for the best: quite often we may make things worse – even though we mean to help. Yet it can be done 'well enough' (because it will nearly always be impossible to get exactly right) only if it is based on the best possible, unflinchingly stark, unconventionalized information. We may have obligations to distant others because, in a world with a highly complex division of labour, and living a modern life that relies on the natural resources of faraway places, we depend on them, as O'Neil argues.[50] And it is the news which articulates these obligations to us, and, perhaps more importantly, provides the knowledge we need in order to discharge our obligations as well as we can – if we are minded to. The quality of news is one important determinant of what choices people can support – in the real, grey, shifting world of particular realities, not the refined air of clear and simple injunctions.

At best the news addresses our emotions on behalf of justice. As David Hume observed, the proposition that 'tyranny is wrong' will not produce an effect, let alone practical opposition, until it is felt. 'Reason,' Hume wrote, explaining this, 'is and ought only to be the slave of the passions.'[51] Hume's famous inversion of stoicism suggests that only an emotional revulsion to oppression can lead to resistance. In this way the careful construction of stories and meanings and consequently feelings in the news is indeed part of the media's democratic role. But constructing responses is also dangerous.

In classical times, even tragic drama provoked argument. Plato respected poetry, but excluded poets from his ideal commonwealth because they lied and stirred up emotion. 'If a poet turns up,' the Greek philosopher wrote, 'we will kneel to him as to a sweet, holy and wonderful Deity . . . and having anointed him with myrrh, and crowned him with flowers, we shall send him away to another city.'[52] By contrast, Aristotle argued that tragedy 'discharged emotion' and was consequently desirable.[53] Both recognized that art transformed emotions. Today one explanation of why we enjoy tragedies is that the feelings we experience are hypothetical. We weep at the idea of what might have happened, rather than at an actual disaster. The pleasure of tragedy has thus been linked with its unreality and its controllability.

News may be more like this than we assume – because we are disturbed by what we would feel if we were the poor unfortunates that we observe. Classic tragedy deals with the fate of the great – yet modern news (despite the obsession with celebrity) is concerned with the fate of citizens, normally going about their everyday business. However, the subjects of news are endowed with temporary greatness by their newsworthy circumstances. In this way great news can be a new, demotic, tragic form. Indeed, tragedy is bearable because someone is in control of it – as we are not in control of

A Rwandan boy crying beside his dead father. The two had taken refuge in Zaire.

fate – just as someone is in control of the news, even if not of the events that prompt it. Both news and tragedy give pitiable and terrible events a make-believe grandeur. They release our emotions from practical responsibility and, by making the pain majestic, permit enjoyment of it.[54]

What is our mood when we observe distant suffering (even if only distant in our own town or street)? Are we, as Plato feared, left with feelings that may lead to bad actions? Or, as Aristotle hoped, purged by the medicine of catharsis? To put it in another way, do we leave the news like a football crowd – sometimes charged with feeling? Or like a theatre crowd – quiet and inward? Or are we stirred as if by an orator? At different moments we feel any of these sensations, but the contemporary tragedy of the news rarely seeks to purge us of feelings and often prefers the nurturing of a conventional, commercially useful, sensational response.

Much recent political theory has been concerned with extolling the role of the attractive and necessary feeling of empathy.[55] But it may be possible to distinguish between empathy and compassion. The news can be ingenious in its attempts to elicit common feelings – and it is a more attractive enterprise than the alternative: to reduce those suffering at a distance to the status of a peep show. But feeling empathy is sometimes about making spectators feel good about themselves, with the glow of shared humanity substituted for an arduous comprehension of what is different about other people.

Empathy is necessary, but it does not always assist understanding. News must alert us to the difficult things we would prefer not to have to admit – and give us the grounds for gruelling toleration, not just the cosy belief of similarity. The democratic expectation is that news, unlike tragedy, will move beyond feeling to action – or at least willed pressure and change. Indeed, if audiences are passive and uninterested, sometimes the media have to stand in for them, and agitate on their behalf. But what if news has become something which overwhelmingly seeks to please and comfort – so that what we know of distant strangers gets more remote from the as yet unshaped contemporary reality? Or, even worse, if reality remains unpredictable but we have little appreciation of it. This is a matter not of our concern for others, but of our own survival. Thus *understanding* is the problem – not how we feel for others.

Conclusion:
All the News That's Fit to Enjoy

There is news of violence and there is the news as violence. Violent news is an arena in which actors suffer while passive spectators observe life and death in a bloody battle over meaning. Violent news shows us life as we do not want to have to experience it. No one envies those who suffer. Yet – it has been a theme of this book – we enjoy the pursuit of victims in the media theatre of cruelty.

To a large extent it is an involuntary pleasure. It is indeed an irony, but not an accidental one, that, in a century in which the developed world seeks more than ever to keep any direct experience of physical violence at arm's length, images and representations of violent behaviour have become harder to escape than at any previous time in history. In the contemporary world, only an anchorite or an Amazonian tribesman can avoid a regular barrage of electronic news and accompanying images of disease, injury, death and destruction. Almost every child in the civilized world has seen the immediate aftermath of real-life killing on the screen, before he or she can read.

Do we wish for less? It has been an argument of this study that images of suffering are supplied to us because we want them, for reasons that are only partly to do with a practical or a public-spirited need to be informed. It is argued, furthermore, that – from the games of classical antiquity, through the religious contemplation of torment in the Middle Ages, to the 'breaking-news' ethic that permits live coverage of mass killings in the twenty-first century – conventions of public taste in relation to 'real' violence have been continually in motion, while consistently reflecting the urgency of a human need. Romans watched lions eating Christians; modern audiences witness homicidal explosions and their macabre outcomes. The public justifications are different, but the phenomena are not so far apart. The issue is not about relative degrees of gentleness or sadism, but about the existence of a social universal. Moreover, this book has also argued that the relationship of a voyeuristic viewer to a violent reality is not marginal to the rest of human experience. It is part of the mainstream of collective life.

People who watch, listen to or read news do so with a mix of sensations. They expect to have their prejudices reinforced, to be thrilled or outraged, and to learn. At the same time, they expect news to be uncomfortable. News can tell us – if we want to know – how the world decides that suffering comes to some people and not to others. News occupies the awkward territory in which societies have made choices but often cannot stomach the consequences. Such contradictions are the consequence of beliefs we hold with passion but which cancel each other out. Often news helps us deceive ourselves by disguising difficult choices. 'How is the world ruled and led to war?' asked the Viennese journalist Karl Kraus. 'Diplomats lie to journalists and believe those lies when they see them in print.'[1]

Of course, news can also be unflinchingly precise, showing us the paradox of our conflicting values and in doing so helping us confront the choices we make. But who or what forces are interested in preserving our critical capacity? Sometimes, it seems, hardly any.

Meanwhile, news is a commodity under threat. Impartial news that attempts to put information forward without an interpretative spin is particularly endangered. Newspaper circulations sink – gently in the UK, more quickly in Europe, and faster still in the USA. They may finally collapse catastrophically. Broadcast-news programmes struggle to find audiences, while partisan Internet sites increasingly bombard news-makers and audiences with information that pre-empts traditional media. Advertising buyers desert the news. In America, serious broadcast news has been largely displaced by short bursts of opinion-laden socially acceptable entertainment. Viewers are less and less interested in foreign news – or at any rate they get less. In 1990 the average US consumption of broadcast foreign news was 1,340 minutes a year. By 2003 this had fallen to 815 minutes.[2]

A partial explanation is that newspapers and news channels are minor parts of large entertainment industries, while being expensive and frequently unprofitable. News organizations are typically acquired as useful fig-leaves, designed to deliver political rewards in exchange for commercial favours. A second reason is that the combination of regulation and political and cultural will that had hitherto kept news as a privileged public good in broadcasting has been increasingly undermined. The USA used to have the largest broadcast-news operations in the world; today, although some key American newspapers continue to supply high-quality news, the big broadcast-news providers have been demolished. Commercial broadcast news in the UK has been affected by similar pressures.

As far as violent news is concerned, audiences are characteristically fickle. Sympathy for those involved in disasters is easy to arouse, but equally easily fades away. Audiences like quick fixes. They also have short attention spans, and are apparently reluctant to grapple with any but the simplest issues and arguments. Interest in general political and social news has therefore been waning. In an ever more disorderly world, the need for news may pick up. Treat audiences with more respect and imagination and they could well grasp more complex issues. Anyone watching the empty format of any of the twenty-four-hour news channels – repetitive and shallow – can see that radical thinking needs to be done. But, for the moment, news economics do not stack up. News is in danger. Yet what can we know without it?

There is a long history of regarding the pursuit of reality as a fundamental human right and an expression of political liberty. Attention to how things really appear and the sophisticated competition between different attempts to demonstrate reality to audiences – and the imaginative capacity to create convincing illusions of that reality – have often been seen as heralds of great and radical changes in human values. Democracy is regarded as a superior system of government in part because, through the ballot box, it reflects a greater reality, while totalitarianism or anarchy results from governments based on illusion and ignorance. 'Realism' also has to do with self-definition. The art historian Ernst Gombrich, discussing the ancient Greek 'discovery of nature' in sculpture, suggested that a compulsion towards involving audiences in stories drove expression in a realistic direction. He argued that the impulse of narrative requires that characters become more lifelike and more individual. The story is given dramatic verisimilitude: emotions are given substance by realism.[3]

'Realism' is not the same as accuracy. Realism in journalism, as in art, means seeking to persuade the audience to believe in the reality of the images presented and the story told, and that these convincing devices are based on scrupulous observation and human judgement. The drive to portray reality more tellingly generates its own momentum – like any great cultural innovation. Hence able people borrow and recognize each other's achievements in a fierce competition to improve the illusion. News can be triumphantly imaginative in its attempt to sum up and communicate to audiences what has occurred and what the consequences are likely to be. It is thus the most significant contemporary realist form – and an absolutely vital one.

Conversely, the distortions posed by the ideological framing of events have been seen as an expression of tyranny and oppression. It is also reasonable to assume that societies that know little about themselves and the condition of the world around them have greater difficulty in dealing with what happens to them. But it is the ideological framing that we take for granted that is most lethal – the definition of reality that we unquestioningly accept and act on. All around us a great battle is going on between those who want to describe the world as it is and those who want to sell a picture that will fit an agenda, be popular, not inhibit us from buying things, compete with easier-to-make narratives – or attract attention to the gruesome because there is a taste for it and it can sway political opinion.

News is necessary. It is a truism that the news media are sanctimonious, threatening and destructive. News journalism can be lofty or base, libertarian or tyrannical, idealistic or cynical. News pretends to be neutral, but never is. News is seldom constructive. A Martian picking up television signals from Earth would wonder how human society holds together: contemporary news, feeding a hunger for the sensational, is nearly always attacking and negative. Yet news is not a luxury item in a free society. The alternative to news – with all its imperfections – is ignorance, rumour, panic and chaos.

Perceptions of violent news change. Public reactions also evolve. What contemporary audiences are prepared to watch and what they make of what they see are not the same as they used to be, and they will go on changing. At any point such values feel fundamental and even 'natural', yet they shift with great rapidity. The way in which violent death and political and social collapse are viewed and the way in which witnesses are expected to respond have their own histories.

As well as changing values, there are changing economics and changing symbolism. In Roman times, the delivery of actual violence from rulers to ruled through the circus was political. It was related to a savage escalation of violence and a corruption of political rule, but also to an ethic of fastidious self-control. In the Middle Ages, humanly inflicted violence acquired religious meaning, while the intense struggle to depict suffering produced great art. At the same time, contemplating exemplary suffering was intended to transform spectators. Today, the reporting and presentation of violent acts often occupy a borderline between evangelism and entertainment.

Much contemporary reporting amounts to a kind of atrocity competition, in which the battle for domestic and international opinion takes the form of rival images of violence and suffering. Yet the way in which these are interpreted still frequently depends on how audiences understand their own condition. It is these differences between people that the news needs to explore – for such differences form the basis of our dealings with each other. News often asks us to identify with victims, but this is easy, and often misleading. News frequently consists of packaged messages, advertising a predetermined storyline, designed to conform to a brand image and be popular. But difficult decisions in the real world cannot be reduced to the simplicities of marketing – hence the distance between public expectation and pragmatic political reality grows.

Guilt by association, damning by innuendo, narrative built on rumour are the news journalist's stock in trade. The issue, however, is not one of conspiracies. Sometimes reporting is driven by politics or by the whim of proprietorial interest, or by a combination of the two. But the main contemporary influence is more indirect, deriving from the organizational pressures of a cut-throat industry. Indeed, in the modern media, marketing directors are often more powerful, if less visible, than editors, and the questions at issue have more to do with the social composition of the intended audience (and consequently its market value) than with the quality of the product.

In all news, there is one overriding factor. The news media are desperate for public attention. They therefore devise strategies for increasing audience size and attracting the 'right' kind of viewer, listener, reader or online consumer – constructing, as a result, a diluted and one-sided product. Terrible – and complex – events frequently find a space in the news only by having what makes them unique generalized away. But democratic society requires flourishing news media just as much as the other way round. Because they tell us – albeit in bowdlerized form – things we need to know, and because democracy depends on an at least partially informed public, we need the media to reach out, by almost any means, to audiences whose attention it is difficult to engage.

We have a contemporary formula for successfully purveying news about violence – absent from the wallowing in cruelty of the Roman circus, or the pious appeal for identification of medieval martyrology. With a modern audience, the best way to command attention is simultaneously to flatter sensibilities, engage sympathy or anger, and provide a pleasurable thrill through an impudent – but not too impudent – assault on canons of public taste. There is also a need for a guilty party, preferably one easily identifiable and near at hand. Often journalism acts like a barrister in a legal case – willing to be retained by one side or the other in a dispute. Such an approach is deeply antithetical to political understanding and the difficult compromises of political solutions.

However, while there is journalism that exposes violence, there is also attack journalism. Such reporting has many of the characteristics of physical violence itself, directed by the press against an individual, with prominence given to the thrill of the chase, the stalking down and suffering of the prey. The Roman games could scarcely match a British tabloid closing on a powerless victim. With both real and sublimated violence, the press is adept at engaging the herd instinct of its public. It is here that circus appetites take over, and the crowd shamelessly gorges on victims as culprits who, the press makes clear, deserve no mercy.

Acting as inquisitor is a long-established role of the press. Here it emulates Robespierre. Described by Michelet as the 'eternal denunciator'[4] and by Comte as a 'sanguinary phrase-maker',[5] he constantly exposed others for their alleged treachery. The modern media have become a prosecutor-general, with the power to destroy wielded relentlessly under the cloak of democratic necessity but often motivated by political and commercial interests that are rarely disclosed. Like the French revolutionary, the modern media routinely appeal to the human sympathy of their audience, while sometimes invoking the weapons of terror: the defence of one group or individual translates into the oppression of another. In his petition to the National Convention, Robespierre famously declared, 'For pity, for the love of humanity, become inhuman!'[6] It was a totalitarian slogan that resonated in Orwell's Ministry of Truth, and it fits one particular media ethic today. One reason why the media are so terrifying is that in pursuit of a 'story' they have no interest in the truth. Once a media mob is hunting a victim, little can halt the stampede – except a kill.

In the climate of the French Revolution, sentiment was valued as the touchstone of political legitimacy and hypocrisy was the ultimate crime. According to Hannah Arendt, 'if we enquire historically into the causes likely to transform citizens into *enragés*, it is not injustice that ranks first, but hypocrisy . . . French moralists saw in hypocrisy the vice of all vices.'[7] As one biographer of Robespierre put it, 'His conscience may have been twisted but it was all of one piece,'[8] and some have argued that his radicalism was 'a mask'.[9] Nevertheless, his ability to strike terror into the hearts not just of the privileged, but of the idealistic, arose not because he did not believe in what he was doing, but because he did.

Is there is a Robespierre-like quality to the modern press, which in pursuit mode has no qualms – content to bring down leaders and even governments if that is where the trail leads? If vanity is the besetting sin of politicians, self-righteousness is a frequent flaw in the press. In practice, crusading journalism is often as conformist as the rest, and the fastidious incorruptibility that characterized Robespierre as he bore down on enemies of the Republic is replicated in the modern journalist's self-justification in terms of the rhetoric of the public good.

There is another link to Robespierre: the contemporary media preoccupation with what is now called 'transparency'. Robespierre aimed at the 'open' state, where differences of interest between competing groups would disappear in the face of direct democracy offered through the general assembly. This aim degenerated into an obsessive opposition not just to secrecy, but to privacy of any description. Every aspect of life was to be available for public scrutiny; any attempt to conceal was compelling evidence of guilt – opposition equalled betrayal and treason. In a strikingly similar way, the relentless pursuit of the private (often at the expense of serious consideration of the public) characterizes one mode of contemporary news-reporting. Thus the media not only seek to root out private facts: they also create a political environment in which private character matters more than public policy. According to the sociologist Colin Crouch, electoral competition, under the new media scrutiny, takes the form of a pursuit of individuals with admirable characters. 'The search is futile because a mass election does not produce data on which to base such assessments.' As a result, what happens is that politicians promote images of 'their personal wholesomeness and integrity, while opponents only intensify the search through the records of private lives to find evidence of the opposite'.[10]

The search for the private is one aspect of attack journalism: the personalizing of the impersonal. The arousing of pity, linked to anger directed at perpetrators, is another. There are different kinds of compassion, and the word is much abused. The active compassion of the Good Samaritan is a mark of a civilized society. The reporting of wars and disasters can arouse active compassion through charitable giving and by putting pressure on governments. Serious journalists aid the process by witnessing on our behalf (and sometimes pay a heavy personal price for the dreadful things we delegate them to see, and treat so casually ourselves). Indignation and pity, aroused by effective journalism, can be powerful motivating forces. Pity can be satisfying for those who do the pitying, and retain a power that the objects of their pity have lost. Pity can be creative, or it can be purely sentimental. However, pity is *post hoc* – directed at things that have gone wrong, not at prevention. Often what is aroused is not constructive compassion but an ersatz or righteously indignant moral fervour. Media-aroused sentimentality is no substitute for the sensitive responses of a politically educated public.

We have woven what we witness of news deaths into our own everyday lives. Audiences, journalists and news organizations have created novel rituals around the increasingly familiar images of media mortality. But the ways in which this process is subtly changing – as images get cut and framed in response to an evolving sense of the boundaries of public taste – is always politically charged. The powerful new rituals developed to deal with death and the reconstruction of society in the wake of loss lay great emphasis on the duties of journalism to tell the story of the dead. In an evolution of age-old beliefs, they reinforce, in a highly secular society, a notion that salvation can be attained by suffering.

The search for a 'moral' approach is another aspect. Few would dispute that the media do have a role in political morality, if only in bringing to public attention morally inconvenient facts. The media are part of the scaffolding of law and custom on which society rests and without which (as Montesquieu maintained) 'the nation loses its capacity for responsible political action.'[11] The media are the product of the nation's mores. They are also responsible for patrolling them – something which, indeed, they are seldom reluctant to do. Yet, although news has always had to make a profit, it would be naive to imagine that the guarding of standards is an activity that most media organizations now take as seriously as raising their circulations or ratings.

The issue here is not just about news values. Nor is it about truth and accuracy. Many journalists are scrupulous about sourcing their reports, and rightly defend their professionalism in doing so. However, their relentless and forensic exploration of detailed evidence can be put to work to expose either a genocidal crime or the minor sexual peccadilloes of a public figure. On occasions, it can give circumstantial reality to a completely fabricated story. The issue is rather about the definition of a legitimate story. Increasingly, in the broadsheets as in the tabloids, neatly packaged human interest or noisy attacks against easy targets win the day. This may help explain why audiences are sometimes bewilderingly indifferent to things that matter, and perplexingly obsessed with trivia.

Surely 'all the news the public wants' – equating public interest with what people find interesting – can be presented as a democratic slogan, rather than as a threat? Many people in the news industry, daily engaged in the struggle for stories that will grab readers or viewers, will hotly defend what they do. And rightly. But what about the news which should not have to please in order to justify itself? News that contributes not to enjoyment or diversion, but to citizenship? After all, the principle that the primary duty is to feed a shifting public appetite for sensation could be used to justify the Roman circus or the martyr's pyre just as much as news journalism – and has been.

To defend public-service news-reporting, especially in the psychologically complex area of reporting 'carnage', is to be neither old-fashioned nor simplistic. It has been argued in this book that, contrary to the claims of news organizations and reporters, there is no such thing as 'straight' reporting of horror. There is always an agenda, always partisanship and selection, just as there is always a play to the contradictory emotions of the audience that the report is seeking to engage. The basic truth that people like to be disturbed by the news they instinctively recoil from is central to this study, as it is uncomfortably central to the news industry's economy.

The prurience of the mass audience is fed and watered by the piously condemnatory tone of news coverage. That this is so needn't make us cynics. The scale and power of corporate ownership, the insistent demands of the global marketplace, may easily induce a world-weary fatalism. But they could also encourage rational relativism: namely a belief that, while ultimate truth is a chimera and all reporting is to a degree socially and politically determined, values survive that are worth defending, and in a violent world it is essential that they *are* protected.

This book has examined the malleability of human attitudes to violence and to the presentation of violence both before and after the contemporary news industry was invented. It has sought to question assumptions and legends across two hundred years of modern news-gathering. It has called for news-disseminators to be more reflective about what they do – both why and how they do it. But it is also a call for us all to care for the quality of news. Much that we value depends on it.

A common practice among hospital doctors in Ivy League American teaching hospitals is to hold confidential, off-the-record 'mortality and morbidity' conferences, at which participants discuss mistakes and frankly admit to disasters and errors of judgement visited on their own patients. It is part of the unwritten code that whatever is said or confessed will not be revealed. These exercises in discretion and candour enable the best surgeons and physicians to learn from what has gone wrong and build on what seems to have worked.[12] Perhaps modern political actors – ministers, officials and journalists – could profit from similar sessions to discuss their own missed opportunities and errors. Contemporary democracies need to learn how to have the same kind of frank and bleakly realistic discussion. The news industry, at any rate, would be a beneficiary, for news is in danger of smothering debate rather than nurturing it. Perhaps news should adopt the same principle as the doctors – exploring its limitations when sectarian conflict flares up, or when the unnoticed poor go hungry. Journalism is an extrovert activity: periodic exercises in self-examination might encourage its practitioners to reflect on the shortcomings of well-tried formulas. But it is not just up to journalists to do this. We have to will the structures that can help it happen.

This book is a celebration of news, not an attack on it – a declaration that principled, honest reporting is not an incidental, but an essential, part of a free society. At the same time, it seeks to show news, including news of violence and slaughter, as more than a dispassionate record of events. So far from being cold, news is hot and living – a great artistic backcloth to twenty-first-century life, the substance of which determines the choices we make and how we live our lives.

News is *The Guardian* and *The Sun*. But it is also Goya, George Eliot and George Orwell. News is about observation and imagination, not mechanics. It is, or should be, about recording our perception of the world, not fitting new events into a matrix of the familiar. Above all it should be a stimulus to new thinking, not an anaesthetizing escape from it.

Notes

INTRODUCTION

1. Homer, *The Iliad*, trans. R. Fitzgerald, Oxford, Oxford University Press, 1984, p. 393.
2. M. Schudson, *The Power of News*, Cambridge, Mass., Harvard University Press, 1995, p. 3.
3. See P. Norris, 'Revolution? What Revolution?', in J. S. Nye (ed.), *Governance.com: Democracy in the Information Age*, Washington, DC, Brookings Institution Press, 2003, pp. 59–81.
4. J. Rawls, *A Theory of Justice*, Oxford, Oxford University Press, 1999, p. 514.

CHAPTER 1: BLOOD IN THE HIGH STREET

1. H. Ritvo, *The Animal Estate*, London, Penguin, 1987, p. 30.
2. Ibid., p. 280.
3. Ibid., p. 249.
4. Ibid., p. 117.
5. Ben Pimlott, private communication.
6. T. Arkwright, 'Comet the Bull: Breeding Pure Bloodlines', *Agricultural History Review*, vol. 20, no. 3 (1986), p. 271.
7. P. Bourdieu, *Distinction: A Social Critique of the Judgement of Public Taste*, London, Routledge & Kegan Paul, 1984, p. 15.
8. Quoted in F. Braudel, *Civilization and Capitalism, 15th–18th Century*, London, Collins, 1981, p. 47.
9. F. Le Gros Cork & R. M. Titmuss, *Our Food Problem and its Relation to our National Defences*, Harmondsworth, Penguin, 1939, p. 50.
10. Ibid., p. 123.
11. E. J. Hobsbawm, 'The British Standard of Living 1790–1850', *Economic History Review*, Second Series, no. 10 (1957), pp. 131–45.
12. B. Harrison (ed.), *British Historical Statistics*, vol. 1, Oxford, Oxford University Press, 1964, pp. 15–27.

13. Ministry of Agriculture and Food, *The Urban Working Class Diet*, London, HMSO, 1939.

14. Ibid., p. 123.

15. Ministry of Agriculture and Food, *Domestic Food Consumption and Expenditure: Annual Report of the National Food Survey*, London, HMSO, 1964, p. 24.

16. M. Sahlins, *Culture and Practical Reason*, Chicago, University of Chicago Press, 1977, p. 173.

17. D. Morley, 'Domestic Relations', in J. Lull, *World Families Watch TV*, London, Sage, 1988, p. 23.

18. L. Van Zoonen, *Feminist Media Studies*, London, Sage, 1994, p. 60.

19. R. Sennett, *The Fall of Public Man*, New York, Vintage, 1973, p. 24.

20. Bourdieu, *Distinction*, p. 185.

21. The argument is a version of a familiar – and important – one: that the mass market requires and produces homogenized and bland products that appeal to the lowest common denominator of the largest possible audience's taste. Writers such as Douglas Kellner (*TV and the Crisis of Democracy*, Boulder, Col., Westview, 1990; *The Persian Gulf TV War*, Boulder, Col., Westview, 1992) and the Glasgow University Media Group have put versions of this case.

22. The idea that the media have to get more salacious to attract audiences is also long-running. It has perhaps mostly been applied to the press and to movies rather than to television news – at least until recently.

23. E. H. Whetham, *Beef Cattle and Sheep, 1910–1940: A Description of the Production and Marketing of Beef Cattle and Sheep in Great Britain from the Early Twentieth Century to the Second World War*, Cambridge, University of Cambridge Department of Land Economy, 1976, p. 12.

24. Bourdieu, *Distinction*, p. 1.

25. Ibid.

26. Polly Toynbee, private communication. The effect of the *Daily Mail* is often bewailed and rarely grappled with. In a pre-1997 election seminar for shadow ministers, a senior civil servant pleaded that the incoming government would not let the agenda of each day in every department be determined by having to respond to headlines in the *Daily Mail*. It was a vain hope. See P. Hennessy, R. Hughes & J. A. Seaton, *Ready, Steady, Go! Labour into Office*, London, Fabian Society, 1997.

27. Whetham, *Beef Cattle and Sheep, 1910–1940*, p. 132.

28. *Livestock Age and Slaughtering Statistics*, London, HMSO, 1910–27, 1983.

29. Meat Marketing Board, *Meat Movement Regulations*, London, HMSO, 1967, p. 3.

30. *Pork Rearing*, London, HMSO, 1995, p. 230.

31. R. Perren, *The Meat Trade in Britain 1840–1914*, London, Routledge & Kegan Paul, 1978, p. 46.

32. *Meat Trade News*, vol. 27, no. 3 (2000), p. 26.

33. J. Walsh, *The Meat Machine: The Inside Story of the Meat Business*, London, Columbus, 1986, p. 340.

34. B. Harrison (ed.), *British Historical Statistics*, vol. 5, Oxford, Oxford University Press, 1999, pp. 173–7; *British Consumption Index 2000*, London, HMSO, 2001, pp. 251, 273.

35. Department of Health, *Report on Flavouring Additives*, London, HMSO, 2002, pp. 1–11.

36. See 'Public Preferences and Meat Presentation', in *Meat Marketing Report*, vols. 7–27: 'tender' heads the preferences from 1967 (replacing 'tasty'), but 'brightness' or 'visually appealing' enters only in 1973. By 1993 'fresh and clear bright red' is the most important.

37. M. Gurevitch, 'The Global Newsroom', in P. Dahlgren & C. Sparks (eds.), *Communication and Citizenship: Journalism and the Public Sphere in the New Media Age*, London, Routledge, 1991, pp. 191, 201.

38. 'Guidelines for the presentation of meat in-store', *Meat Trader*, April 2001, p. 12.

39. BBC Written Archive (News Policy), News memo, News and Current Affairs Minutes, R34, 101, 7 June 1976.

40. *The Independent*, house style rules, 2000, p. 7.

41. Content analysis conducted by University of Westminster BA Media Studies Year-3 undergraduates and presented in 2001.

42. *Meat Marketing Review*, no. 3 (1957), p. 12.

43. Ibid., special issue, 'New Opportunities in Meat Presentation', no. 1 (1985), p. 26.

44. *Meat Trader*, vol. 23, no. 18 (May 1965), pp. 21–2.

45. P. Delamar, *The Complete Make-up Artist*, Basingstoke, Macmillan, 1995, p. 122.

46. V. J. R. Kehoe, *The Technique of the Professional Make-up Artist*, London, Focal Press, 1995, pp. 219, 27.

47. Ibid., p. 29.

48. D. Dalla Palma, *Make-up Artist's Handbook for Screen*, New York, Sterling Books, 2004, p. 7.

49. H. Baines, *Make-up for Stage and Screen*, New York, Dainton Books, 2001, p. 123.

50. *The Standardization of Motion Picture Make-up*, Hollywood, Max Factor, 1937.

51. 'Report of the Committee on Modern Make-up for the Movie Industry', *Journal of the Society of Motion Picture Engineers*, vol. 10, no. 4 (1963).

52. Kehoe, *The Technique of the Professional Make-up Artist*, p. 671.

53. D. P. Starr, *Blood: An Epic History of Medicine and Commerce*, London, Little, Brown, 1999, p. xiii.

54. R. M. Titmuss, *The Gift Relationship: From Human Blood to Social Policy*, London, Allen & Unwin, 1970, p. 245.

55. Ibid., p. 27.

56. Starr, *Blood*, p. 67.

57. A. Gawande, *A Surgeon's Notes on an Imperfect Science*, New York, Metropolitan Books, 2002, p. 76.

58. I am indebted to the staff at the University College Hospital Haematology Unit, especially Dr Rao and Dr Kirsty Thompson, for this inevitably crude representation of a sophisticated medical practice and discipline.

59. C. Marvin & D. W. Ingle, *Blood Sacrifice and the Nation: Totem Rituals and the American*, Cambridge, Cambridge University Press, 1999, p. 66.

CHAPTER 2: FILTH

1. A Clerk of the House of Commons, private communication, November 2004.

2. I. Connell, 'Tales of Tellyland', in Dahlgren & Sparks, *Communication and Citizenship*, pp. 29–40.

3. M. Douglas, *Purity and Danger*, London, Routledge & Kegan Paul, 1966, p. 23.

4. Ibid., p. 35.

5. D. Kellner, *Media Culture: Cultural Studies*, London, Routledge, 1997, p. 43.

6. See MORI and BBC evidence for the decline in the respect for journalists from 1980 to 2000, and YouGov and BBC work that shows that, if you separate the kinds of journalist, varying degrees of trust are represented.

7. First reference 1657.

8. Quoted in J. Serpell, *In the Company of Animals: A Study of Human–Animal Relationships*, Cambridge, Cambridge University Press, 1996, p. 168.

9. D. Rixon, *The History of Meat Trading*, Nottingham, Nottingham University Press, 2000, p. 15.

10. J. Goody, *Cooking, Cuisine and Class*, Cambridge, Cambridge University Press, 1982, p. 230.

11. See J. Goody, *Representations and Contradictions: Ambivalence towards Images, Theatre, Fiction and Relics*, Oxford, Blackwell, 1997.

12. Department of Trade and Industry, reports of the *Survey of Retail Outlets in the UK, Annual Review*, London, HMSO, 1983–98.

13. J. Serpell, *Animals and Human Society*, London, Routledge, 1994, p. 207.

14. J. Rifkin, *Beyond Beef: The Rise and Fall of the Cattle Culture*, New York, Dutton, 1993, p. 12.

15. Ibid., p. 33.

16. Industrial Safety Standards Agency, *The Meat Trade in the USA*, Department of Health and Safety, US Federal Government Report, Washington, DC, 2001.

17. D. Stull & M. Broadway, *Anyway You Cut It: Meat Processing in Small Town America*, Lawrence, Kan., University Press of Kansas, 1995.

18. Rifkin, *Beyond Beef*, p. 227.

19. M. Rothschild, *Animals and Man*, Oxford Romanes Lecture, Oxford, Oxford University Press, 1986, p. 16.

20. *Pigshead and Pease Pudding*, Waltham Forest, Waltham Forest Workshop, Oral History Project, 1985, pp. 23–25, 27, 15.

21. This famous passage in a speech was written for Stanley Baldwin by Rudyard Kipling. The speech was given in Queen's Hall, London, in 1931, and was part of what Roy Jenkins called 'One of the most memorable inter-war orations' (R. Jenkins, *Baldwin*, London, Macmillan, 1995, p. 118).

22. G. Lukács, *History and Class Consciousness*, London, Merlin Press, 1971; K. Mannheim, *Essays on the Sociology of Knowledge*, London, Routledge, 1997; E. Shils, *The Calling of Education*, Chicago, University of Chicago Press, 1997; E. Hobsbawm, *Interesting Times: A Twentieth-Century Life*, London, Allen Lane, 2002.

23. Schudson, *The Power of News*, p. 34.

24. L. Brake & A. Jones (eds.), *Investigating Victorian Journalism*, Basingstoke, Macmillan, 1990, p. 172.

25. See R. Lindley, *And Finally: The Last Days of ITN*, London, Politico's, 2005.

26. See M. Foucault, *The Birth of the Clinic*, London, Tavistock, 1973, or his *Discipline and Punish: The Birth of the Prison*, London, Allen Lane, 1977.

27. V. Crapanzano, *Waiting: The Whites of South Africa*, London, Granada, 1985, p. x.

CHAPTER 3: REALITY VIOLENCE FOR FUN: THE ROMAN GAMES

1. Pliny the Elder, *Natural History: A Selection*, trans. and intro. J. F. Healy, London, Penguin, 1971, p. 119.

2. Tertullian, *Tertullian English Selections: Christian and Pagan Witness in the Roman Empire*, ed. R. P. Sider, Washington, DC, Catholic University Press, 2001, p. 112.

3. E. Gibbon, *The Decline and Fall of the Roman Empire*, London, Dent, 1910, vol. 3, p. 235.

4. G. Mazzini, *The Duties of Man and Other Essays*, ed. T. Jones, London, Everyman, 1907, p. 22.

5. St Augustine, *Confessions*, trans. R. S. Pine-Coffin, London, Penguin, 2003, p. 38.

6. W. E. H. Lecky, *A History of European Morals from Augustus to Charlemagne*, vol. 2, London, Longmans, Green & Co., 1911, p. 71.

7. M. Grant, *Gladiators*, London, Penguin, 1971, p. 21.

8. Ibid., p. 111.

9. C. Barton, *The Sorrows of the Ancient Romans: The Gladiator and the Monster*, Princeton, Princeton University Press, 1993, p. 15.

10. Ibid., p. 124.

11. Quoted in W. Magnus, *Entertainment and Violence in Ancient Rome*, Studia Graeca et Latina LVI, Göteborg, University of Göteborg Press, 1992, p. 19.

12. Juvenal, *The Sixteen Satires*, trans. P. Green, London, Penguin, 1998, p. 15.

13. Quoted in P. Plass, *The Game of Death in Ancient Rome: Arena Sport and Political Suicide*, Madison, Wis., University of Wisconsin Press, 1995, p. 116.

14. Tertullian, *Disciplinary and Moral Works*, trans. M. Massey, Cambridge, Cambridge University Press, 1982, p. 123.

15. Grant, *Gladiators*, p. 48.

16. P. Veyne, *Bread and Circuses: Historical Sociology and Political Pluralism*, trans. B. Pearce, London, Allen Lane, 1990, p. 134.

17. Grant, *Gladiators*, p. 40.

18. Martial, *Martial's Epigrams: De spectaculis*, ed. D. R. Shackleton-Bailey, Cambridge, Mass., Harvard University Press, 1993, vol. 1, no. 35, pp. 3–4.

19. Petronius, *Satyricon*, trans. P. G. Walsh, Oxford, Clarendon, 1996, p. 14.

20. Martial, *Martial's Epigrams: De spectaculis*, vol. 1, no. 104, p. 32.

21. Quoted in G. Jennison, *Animals for Show and Pleasure in Ancient Rome*, Manchester, Manchester University Press, 1937, p. 124.

22. Seneca, *Moral and Political Essays*, trans. and ed. J. M. Cooper & J. F. Procope, Cambridge, Cambridge University Press, 1995.

23. Martial, *Martial's Epigrams: De spectaculis*, vol. 2, no. 10, p. 15.

24. Ibid., vol. 1, no. 104, pp. 32–3.

25. Quoted in Jennison, *Animals for Show and Pleasure in Ancient Rome*, p. 63.

26. Quoted in K. Coleman, 'Fatal Charades', *Journal of Roman Studies*, vol. 80 (1990), p. 47.

27. Gibbon, *Decline and Fall*, vol. 1, p. 92.

28. Seneca, *Moral and Political Essays*, p. 140.

29. M. Bieber, *The History of the Greek and Roman Theatre*, Princeton, Princeton University Press, 1961, p. 227.

30. See Coleman, 'Fatal Charades', pp. 46–57.

31. Tertullian, *Apologia*, trans. A. Souter, intro. J. Mayor, Cambridge, Cambridge University Press, 1917, p. 12.

32. Ibid., p. 17.

33. See Coleman, 'Fatal Charades', p. 52.

34. Tacitus, *Dialogue on Oratory*, trans. and ed. R. Mayer, Cambridge, Cambridge University Press, 2001, p. 15.

35. Lecky, *A History of European Morals*, p. 275.

36. See Grant, *Gladiators*, p. 76.

37. Ibid., p. 77.

38. See C. Barton, *Roman Honor: The Fire in the Bones*, Berkeley, University of California Press, 2001, p. 137.

39. Quoted in M. Grant, *Nero*, London, Weidenfeld & Nicolson, 1970, p. 15.

40. Gibbon, *Decline and Fall*, vol. 1, p. 334.

41. Quoted in P. Bratlinger, *Bread and Circuses*, Ithaca, NY, Cornell University Press, 1983, p. 37.

42. Quoted in K. Hopkins, *Death and Renewal*, Cambridge, Cambridge University Press, 1983, p. 78.

43. Veyne, *Bread and Circuses*, p. 127.

44. Ibid., p. 131.

45. R. Auguet, *Cruelty and Civilization: The Roman Games*, London, Routledge, 1994, p. 37.

46. Seneca, *Seneca in English*, ed. D. Share, London, Penguin, 1998, p. 74.

47. Quoted in M. Hornum, *Nemesis: The Roman State, and the Games*, New York, E. J. Brill, 1993, p. 53.

48. See P. Brown, *Society and the Holy*, London, Faber, 1982, *Power and Persuasion in Late Antiquity: Towards a Christian Empire*, Madison, Wis., University of Wisconsin Press, 1992, and *Authority and the Sacred*, Cambridge, Cambridge University Press, 1995; C. Barton, *The Sorrows of the Ancient Romans* and *Roman Honor*.

49. Foucault, *Discipline and Punish*, p. 147.

50. Quoted in G. W. Bowersock, *Martyrdom and Rome*, Cambridge, Cambridge University Press, 1995, p. 111.

51. Gibbon, *Decline and Fall*, vol. 2, p. 33.

52. Quoted in G. W. Bowersock, *Fiction as History: Nero to Julian*, Berkeley, University of California Press, 1994, p. 168.

53. Ibid., p. 172.

54. Bowersock, *Martyrdom and Rome*, p. 109.

55. See C. W. Bynum, *Fragmentation and Redemption: The Resurrection of the Body in Western Christianity 200–1336*, New York, Columbia University Press, 1995, p. 203. See also for general views C. W. Bynum, *Metamorphosis and Identity*, New York, Zone Books, 2001.

56. P. Brown, *The Body and Society: Men, Women and Sexual Renunciation in Early Christianity*, London, Faber, 1988, p. 14.

57. D. S. Potter, *Literary Texts and the Roman Historian*, London, Routledge, 1999, p. 59.

58. See J. D. Peters, 'Witnessing', *Media, Culture and Society*, vol. 23 (November 2004), pp. 137–48. Also J. D. Peters, *Speaking into the Air: A History of the Idea of Communication*, Chicago, University of Chicago Press, 1999. This is some of the most original contemporary work done on the media.

CHAPTER 4: SUFFERING IS GOOD FOR YOU

1. Quoted in E. Larson, *A Flame in Barbed Wire: The Story of Amnesty International*, London, Muller, 1978, p. 16.

2. Quoted in H. Haug, *Humanity for All: The Red Cross and the Red Crescent*, Geneva, Peter Haupt, 1993, p. 5.

3. H. James, 'Amnesty's First 10 Years', *The Observer*, 10 October 1971.

4. On Amnesty International see D. Winner, *Peter Benenson*, London, Exley, 1991; Amnesty International, *Against Oblivion*, London, Fontana, 1978; *Amnesty International Campaign Handbook*, London, Amnesty International, 1998. Other organizations with a similar agenda set up at a similar time include the Child Poverty Action Group, the Consumers' Association and Shelter.

5. Comment by John Lloyd followed up in J. Lloyd, *The Power and the Story: What the Media Have Done to Our Politics*, London, Constable, 2004.

6. Human Rights Watch, *Charter*, Washington, DC, and London, Human Rights Watch, 1986.

7. *Report on Massacres in Afghanistan: A Human Rights Watch and Eyewitness Account*, no. 2, London, Human Rights Watch, 1998.

8. C. Geertz, *The Interpretation of Cultures*, New York, Fontana, 1973, p. 451.

9. C. Geertz, *Local Knowledge: Further Essays in Interpretive Anthropology*, New York, Basic Books, 1983, p. 173.

10. Plato, *The Last Days of Socrates: Euthyphro; The Apology; Crito; Phaedo*, trans. H. Tredennick & J. Tarrant, London, Penguin, 1993, p. 64.

11. See P. Ahrensdorf, *The Death of Socrates*, New York, State University of New York Press, 2003.

12. Plato, *The Last Days of Socrates*, p. 67.

13. Tertullian, *Apologeticus; De spectaculis*, trans. T. R. Glover, London, Heinemann, 1931, p. 45.

14. Tertullian, *The Octavius of Minucius Felix*, trans. G. H. Rendall, London, Heinemann, 1931, 36.8, p. 117.

15. J. Reith, *Broadcast over Britain*, London, Cassell, 1926, p. 13.

16. See J. Perkins, *The Suffering Self: Pain and Narrative Representation in Early Christianity*, London, Routledge, 1994, p. 151.

17. See M. Barasch, *Imago Hominis: Studies in the Language of Art*, Vienna, IRSA, 1991, pp. 90–92.

18. H. Belting, *Likeness and Presence: A History of the Image before the Era of Art*, Chicago, University of Chicago Press, 1994.

19. See for example Glasgow University Media Group, *Bad News*, London, Routledge & Kegan Paul, 1976.

20. Belting, *Likeness and Presence*, p. 213.

21. Alexander Stunc in G. Finaldi, *The Image of Christ*, London, National Gallery, 2000, p. 13.

22. See G. Millet, *Byzantine Art*, trans. H. Jennings, London, Macmillan, 1975, and R. Cormack, *Byzantine Art and Rhetoric*, Oxford, Oxford University Press, 2000.

23. When attempting to explain the meaning of an icon to my (well-behaved) eight-year-old son at an exhibition of Russian icons at the Royal Academy in London, I was taken to task by an irate woman who said that I was not treating the image with the proper respect – as I was talking.

24. J. Herrin, *The Formation of Christendom*, Oxford, Blackwell, 1987, p. 309.

25. J. Herrin, *Women in Purple: Rulers of Medieval Byzantium*, London, Weidenfeld & Nicolson, 2001, p. 252.

26. Herrin, *The Formation of Christendom*, p. 311.

27. J. Herrin & A. Bryer (eds.), *Iconoclasm: Papers Given at the Ninth Spring Symposium of Byzantine Studies, University of Birmingham, March 1975*, Birmingham, University of Birmingham Centre for Byzantine Studies, 1977.

28. N. Spivey, *Understanding Greek Sculpture: Ancient Meanings, Modern Readings*, London, Thames and Hudson, 1996, p. 23.

29. See A. Cameron & J. Herrin (eds.), *Constantinople in the Early Eighth Century: The Parastaseis Syntomo Chronokai*, Leiden: E. J. Brill, 1984, Introduction.

30. See C. Barnard, 'The Theology of Images', in Herrin & Bryer, *Iconoclasm*, p. 7.

31. See C. Schönbon, *God's Human Face: The Christ Icon*, San Francisco, Ignatius, 1994, pp. 10–11.

32. Herrin, *Women in Purple*, p. 175.

33. St Basil, 'St Spiritu Sancti', in *The Writings of St Basil*, ed. T. J. Sprottiswell, Oxford, Oxford University Press, 1927, p. 23.

34. C. Mango, *Studies on Constantinople*, Aldershot, Variorum Reprints, 1993, p. 13.

35. Leontius, quoted in L. Barnard, *The Theory of Images*, Birmingham, University of Birmingham Press, 1975, p. 17; Herrin & Bryer, *Iconoclasm*, p. 52.

36. Herrin & Bryer, *Iconoclasm*, p. 275.

37. H. van Os, *The Art of Devotion in the Late Middle Ages in Europe, 1300–1500*, London, Merrel Holberton, 1994, p. 15.

38. H. Maguire, *Art and Eloquence in Byzantium*, Princeton, Princeton University Press, 1981, p. 9.

39. K. Weitzmann, *Art in the Medieval West and its Contacts with Byzantium*, London, Variorum Reprints, 1982, p. 73.

CHAPTER 5: PAINFUL NEWS

1. See A. Derbes, *Picturing the Passion in Late Medieval Italy: Narrative Painting, Franciscan Ideologies and the Levant*, Cambridge, Cambridge University Press, 1996.

2. R. Cormack, *The Byzantine Eye: Studies in Art and Patronage*, Aldershot, Variorum Reprints, 1989, p. 241.

3. R. W. Southern, *The Making of the Middle Ages*, London, Hutchinson, 1953, p. 58.

4. St Benedict quoted in R. W. Southern, *Robert Grosseteste: The Growth of the English Mind in Medieval Europe*, Oxford, Clarendon, 1986, p. 93.

5. Southern, *The Making of the Middle Ages*, p. 47.

6. Ibid., p. 218.

7. Belting, *Likeness and Presence*, p. 96.

8. Ibid., p. 58.

9. Ibid., p. 10.

10. Quoted in Finaldi, *The Image of Christ*, p. 105.

11. Quoted in R. Goffen, *Spirituality in Conflict: St Francis and Giotto's Bardi Chapel*, University Park, Pa., Penn State University Press, 1988, p. 8.

12. Quoted in Derbes, *Picturing the Passion*, p. 278.

13. See C. W. Bynum, *Holy Feast and Holy Fast*, Berkeley, University of California Press, 1991, on this point.

14. See R. W. Southern, *Saint Anselm: A Portrait in a Landscape*, Cambridge, Cambridge University Press, 1990, p. 5.

15. Ibid., p. 201.

16. Derbes, *Picturing the Passion*, p. 56.

17. O. Steinberg, *The Sexuality of Christ in Renaissance Art and the Modern Oblivion*, New York, Pantheon, 1983, p. 114.

18. Bynum, *Fragmentation and Redemption*, p. 67.

19. Ibid., p. 92.

20. Ibid., p. 98.

21. L. Silverman, *Tortured Subjects: Pain and Truth in France*, Chicago and London, University of Chicago Press, 2001, p. 176.

22. H. Maguire, *Rhetoric, Nature and Magic in Byzantine Art*, Aldershot, Ashgate, 1998, p. 111.

23. H. Maguire, *The Icons of Their Bodies: Saints and Their Images in Byzantium*, Princeton, Princeton University Press, 1996, p. 56.

24. H. Maguire, *Magic and Byzantium*, Cambridge, Cambridge University Press, 2000, p. 15.

25. Ibid., p. 28.

26. Cormack, *The Byzantine Eye*, p. 11.

27. Weitzmann, *Art in the Medieval West*, p. 67.

28. Quintilian, *The Institutio Oratoria*, vol. 3, trans. H. E. Butler, London, Heinemann, 1922, p. 113.

29. See R. Kieckhefer, *Unquiet Souls*, Chicago, University of Chicago Press, 1984.

30. See E. Ross, *The Grief of God: Images of the Suffering of Jesus in Late Medieval England*, Oxford, Oxford University Press, 1997.

31. Kieckhefer, *Unquiet Souls*, p. 172.

32. Quoted in ibid., p. 27.

33. W. James, *The Varieties of Religious Experience: A Study in Human Nature*, New York, Simon & Schuster, 1997, p. 282.

34. G. Grass, *The Flounder*, London, Secker & Warburg, 1978, p. 62.

35. V. Woolf, 'On Being Ill', in *Collected Essays*, vol. 4, London, Chatto & Windus, 1967, p. 164.

36. R. Kaiver, *Looking Forward to Cancer Pain Relief for All: The Secret of Pain*, Oxford, World Health Organization, 1997, p. 21.

37. See X. Bray, *El Greco*, London, National Gallery, 2004, p. 33.

38. P. Farley, *The Conquest of Pain*, Michael Joseph, London, 1998, p. 67.

39. C. Darwin, *The Expression of Emotion in Man and Animals*, London, Harper-Collins, 1998, p. 121.

40. A. Desmond & J. Moore, *Darwin*, London, Michael Joseph, 1991, p. 649.

41. L. Bending, *The Representation of Bodily Pain in Late Nineteenth Century English Culture*, Oxford, Clarendon, 2000, p. 187.

42. See C. Saunders, *Hospice and Palliative Care*, Sevenoaks, Edward Arnold, 1990.

43. R. Rey, *The History of Pain*, Cambridge, Mass., Harvard University Press, 1995.

44. R. Melzack & P. D. Wall, *The Challenge of Pain*, 3rd edn, London, Penguin, 1982, p. 206. For further work on assessing pain see R. Melzack, *Handbook of Pain Assessment*, London, Guiford, 1992.

45. World Service, at BBC seminar on the war against terrorism, October 2001.

46. E. Scarry, *The Body in Pain: The Making and Unmaking of the World*, Oxford, Oxford University Press, 1985, p. 9.

47. Ibid., p. 13.

48. See J. Seaton, 'Is Impartial News an Endangered Species?', in J. Lloyd & J. Seaton (eds.), *What Can be Done? Making Politics and the Media Better*, Oxford, Blackwell, 2005, p. 13.

49. Discussion at Freedom Forum seminar on war reporting, October 2002.

50. N. MacGregor, Introduction to Finaldi, *The Image of Christ*, p. 7.

51. World Health Organization, *Cancer Palliative Care: A Report of the International Conference on Pain Relief*, Oxford, World Health Organization, 2000, p. 20. See also W. Parris, *Cancer Pain Management*, Boston and Oxford, Butterworth, 1997.

CHAPTER 6: WARS AND SENTIMENTAL EDUCATION

1. This has been an international trend seen in many countries, but is especially pronounced in the UK and the USA. See Gallup, *Who Do We Trust and Why?*, London, Gallup, 2003; YouGov, *Public Trust*, London, YouGov, 2003; J. S. Nye,

P. D. Zelikow & D. C. King (eds.), *Why People Don't Trust Government: Visions of Government in the Twenty-first Century*, Cambridge, Mass., Harvard University Press, 1997; J. Lloyd, *The Power and the Story: What the Media Have Done to Our Politics*, London, Constable, 2004.

2. See D. Dayan & E. Katz, *Media Events: The Live Broadcasting of History*, Cambridge, Mass., Harvard University Press, 1992, p. 32.

3. See M. Mazower, *Dark Continent: Europe's Twentieth Century*, London, Allen Lane, 1998, p. 142, and his inaugural lecture, 'The Strange Triumph of Human Rights: Hitler, the UN and the Making of the Post-War World', Birkbeck College, 31 January 2002.

4. See J. Baudrillard, e.g. *Selected Writings of Jean Baudrillard*, ed. M. Postner, Cambridge, Polity, 1998; *The Illusion of the End*, trans. C. Turner, Cambridge, Polity, 1994; *La Guerre du Golfe n'a pas eu lieu*, Paris, Editions Galilée, 1991.

5. For a discussion of some of the background in American nationalism, see A. Lieven, *America Right or Wrong*, London, HarperCollins, 2004.

6. J. Johnson, 'The Future of Computer Games – Welcome to the Feelies!', *The Guardian*, 14 January 2002.

7. A. Hill, *Reality Television*, London, Routledge, 2004.

8. See J. A. Seaton, 'Public, Private and the Media: Where Do We Draw the Line?', *Political Quarterly*, vol. 74, no. 2 (2003), pp. 174–84.

9. BBC seminar on covering the war in Iraq, September 2003.

10. Dayan & Katz, *Media Events*, p. 121.

11. R. Darnton, *Berlin Journal 1989–1990*, New York, Norton, 1991, p. 12.

12. Ibid., p. 76.

13. See J. K. Galbraith, *The Culture of Contentment*, London, Penguin, 1993.

14. Author's interview with Mark Latey, BBC defence correspondent (subsequently NATO press officer).

15. See E. Hobsbawm, *The Age of Extremes: The Short Twentieth Century, 1914–1991*, London, Michael Joseph, 1994.

16. M. Kaldor, *New and Old Wars: Organised Violence in a Global Era*, Cambridge, Polity, 1999, p. 41.

17. See 'Famine, Aid and the Media', a workshop on the twentieth anniversary of the reporting of the 1984 Ethiopian famine, led by J. A. Seaton, S. Franks & A. McNicholas, part of the BBC official history, 12 October 2004.

18. Author's interview with Sir Frank Cooper.

19. Author's interview with Mark Latey.

20. Discussion at seminar on conflict reporting, LSE, July 2004; Reuters programme seminar on Kosovo war, 1999; Birkbeck College seminar on contemporary conflict, 2003.

21. Author's interview with Sir Frank Cooper.

22. Author's interview with Mark Latey.

23. J. Capelstein, *Media Audiences and Advertizing Spend During the War in Iraq*, Media Review Report, New York, 2003.

24. See M. Ignatieff, *The Needs of Strangers*, London, Hogarth, 1994, and *Empire-Lite*, London, Vintage, 2003; W. Shawcross, *Allies: The US, Britain and Europe and the War in Iraq*, London, Atlantic, 2004. See also Kaldor, *New and Old Wars*, p. 102.

25. T. Garton Ash, *History of the Present: Essays and Dispatches from the New Europe*, London, Penguin, 2000, p. 211.

26. M. Van Creveld, *On Future War*, London, Brassey's, 1991, p. 16.

27. T. Allen & J. A. Seaton (eds.), *The Media of Conflict*, London, Zed Books, 1998.

28. Mo Mowlam, when she was Secretary of State for Northern Ireland.

29. P. Q. Hirst, *War and Power in the 21st Century: The State, Military Conflict and the International System*, Cambridge, Polity, 2001, p. 87.

30. Author's interview with Anatol Lieven.

31. Author's interview with Sir Max Hastings.

32. *UK Press Report*, comparative survey: vol. 23, 1974; vol. 53, 2004.

33. K. Adie, *The Kindness of Strangers: The Autobiography*, London, Headline, 2003, p. 124.

34. BBC 'Famine, Aid and the Media' workshop, 12 October 2004.

CHAPTER 7: DO WE ALL FEEL THE SAME?

1. A. Sen & J. Drèze, *Hunger and Public Action*, Oxford, Clarendon, 1989, pp. 76–83.

2. P. Sorokin, *The Crisis of Our Age*, London, One World, 1992, p. 124.

3. B. Pasternak, *Dr Zhivago*, trans. M. Hayward, London, Penguin, 1988, p. 453.

4. V. Grossman, *Life and Fate*, trans. P. Whitney, Evanston, Ill., Northwestern University Press, 1997, p. 15.

5. See N. Ries, *Russian Talk: Culture and Conversation during Perestroika*, Ithaca, NY, Cornell University Press, 1997, p. 21.

6. O. Figes, *Natasha's Dance: A Cultural History of Russia*, London, Allen Lane, 2002, p. 335.

7. Author's interview with Yevgeny Kiselyev.

8. J. Lloyd, *Rebirth of a Nation: An Anatomy of Russia*, London, Michael Joseph, 1998, p. 23.

9. Ibid., p. 75.

10. Author's interview with Natasha Kozyrev, Validata.

11. A. Politkovskaya, *Putin's Russia*, London, Harvill, 2004, p. 271.

12. Ibid., p. 259.

13. A. Politkovskaya, *A Small Corner of Hell: Dispatches from Chechnya*, trans. A. Burry, Chicago, University of Chicago Press, 2003, p. 45.

14. F. Fukuyama, *The End of History and the Last Man*, London, Hamish Hamilton, 1992, p. 338.

15. M. McAuley, *Russia's Politics of Uncertainty*, Cambridge, Cambridge University Press, 1997, p. 67.

16. A. Lieven, *The Baltic Revolution: Estonia, Latvia, Lithuania and the Path to Independence*, New Haven, Yale University Press, 1993, p. 231.

17. F. Ellis, *From Glasnost to the Internet: Russia's New Infosphere*, Basingstoke, Macmillan, 2000, and Ellis's earlier interesting book on an extraordinary Russian journalist and writer, *Vasily Grossman: The Genesis and Evolution of a Russian Heretic*, Oxford, Berg, 1994.

18. Author's interview with Anatol Lieven.

19. Author's interview with Vladimir Mau.

20. B. McNair, *Glasnost, Perestroika and the Soviet Media*, London, Routledge, 1991, p. 202.

21. M. Wyman, *Public Opinion in Post-Communist Russia*, London, Macmillan, 1996, p. 43.

22. Author's interview with Sir Roderick Braithwaite.

23. See B. McNair, *Images of the Enemy: Reporting the New Cold War*, London, Routledge.

24. See R. Layard, 'Russia's Future', *Economic Review*, vol. 52, no. 3 (1998), p. 122.

25. C. Merridale, *Night of Stone: Death and Memory in Russia*, London, Granta, 2000, p. 415. This is a remarkable book.

26. E. Mickiewicz, *Changing Channels: Television and the Struggle for Power in Russia*, New York, Oxford University Press, 1997, p. 56.

27. Author's interview with John Lloyd.

28. Ibid.

29. H. Seton-Watson, *The Russian Empire: 1801–1917*, Oxford, Clarendon, 1988, p. 1.

30. Figes, *Natasha's Dance*, p. 384.

31. A. Pushkin & M. Lermontov, *Narrative Poems*, trans. C. Johnston, London, Bodley Head, 1984, pp. 170–83.

32. L. Tolstoy, 'The Woodfelling: A Cadet's Story', in *How Much Land Does a Man Need? and Other Stories*, London, Penguin, 1993, p. 16.

33. Ibid., p. 23.

34. A. Solzhenitsyn, *The Gulag Archipelago: An Experiment in Literary Investigation*, London, Collins, 1986, p. 77.

35. There is some dispute about how important oil really was. Thomas De Waal argues that it is a Western preoccupation – not something discussed in Chechnya. See T. De Waal & C. Gall, *Chechnya: A Small Successful War*, London, Pan, 1997. On the other hand Anna Politkovskaya's influential book *A Dirty War: A Russian Reporter in Chechnya* (trans. and ed. J. Crowfoot, London, Harvill, 2001) argues that controlling oil and natural resources is what all 'politics' in Russia is concerned with.

36. See S. Handleman, *Comrade Criminal: The Theft of the Second Russian Revolution*, London, Michael Joseph, 1994, p. 86.

37. Author's interview, and see Handleman, *Comrade Criminal*, pp. 30–97.

38. Author's interview.

39. See J. B. Dunlop, *Russia Confronts Chechnya: Roots of a Separatist Conflict*, Cambridge University Press, Cambridge, 1998, pp. 127–9.

40. Author's interview, Validata.

41. Author's interview, Itogi.

42. Handleman, *Comrade Criminal*, p. 89.

43. De Waal & Gall, *Chechnya*, p. 203.

44. Martin Barilsev reported in De Waal & Gall, *Chechnya*, p. 21.

45. Author's interviews, and see J. B. Dunlop, *Russia Confronts Chechnya*, and his *The Rise of Russia and the Fall of the Soviet Empire*, Princeton, Princeton University Press, 1993, for discussion of these views.

46. S. Blank & E. Tilford, *Russia's Invasion of Chechnya: An Assessment*, Carlisle, Mass., US Army College, 1995, p. 11.

47. See Lieven, *The Baltic Revolution*; Lloyd, *Rebirth of a Nation*; De Waal & Gall, *Chechnya*.

48. Author's interview.

49. De Waal & Gall, *Chechnya*, p. 5.

50. Author's interview with Oleg Golembyovsky.

51. See G. N. Vachnadze, *Secrets of Journalism in Russia: Mass Media under Gorbachev and Yeltsin*, Commack, NY, Nova, 1992, p. 389.

52. Author's interview.

53. M. E. Price, *Television, the Public Sphere and National Identity*, Oxford, Clarendon, 1995, p. 4.

54. Author's interview.

55. Author's interview.

56. Author's interview with John Lloyd.

57. *The Chechen War and the Media: The Glasnost Defence Foundation Report*, Moscow, Glasnost Defence Foundation, 1997, p. 7, and see also *Glasnost – How Open?*, Freedom Forum Report, New York, Langham, 1997, p. 12.

58. Visticom Public Opinion Poll Agency, Moscow, reports and interviews, 1996–2001.

59. Mickiewicz, *Changing Channels*, p. 67.

60. European Institute for the Media, 'Report on Russian Broadcasting and the Legal Framework', in *Media Bulletin*, vol. 3, no. 2 (2003), pp. 13–15.

61. Author's interview with Natasha Kozyrev, Validata.

62. Author's interview.

63. J. B. Dunlop, 'Russia in Search of an Identity', in I. Bremner (ed.), *New States, New Politics: Building the Post-Soviet Nations*, Cambridge, Cambridge University Press, 1997, p. 51.

64. *The Chechen War and the Media*, p. 26.

65. P. Khlebnikov, *The Selling of War. Media Coverage and the Chechen War*, Geneva, Creda European Institute for Media, 1996, p. 59; see also his *Godfather of the Kremlin: Boris Berezovsky and the Looting of Russia*, New York, Harcourt, 2000.

66. *Reporting Chechnya*, Russian American Press Information Center, Moscow, 1996, p. 7.

67. Author's interview with Oleg Golembyovsky.

68. Author's interview with Natasha Kozyrev, Validata.

69. Author's interview.

70. Visticom Russian-wide Survey 1993.

71. Author's interview with Bill Thompson.

72. V. Bennett, *Crying Wolf: The Return of War to Chechnya*, London, Picador, 1998, p. 340.

73. Introduction to Politkovskaya, *A Dirty War*, p. 3.

74. Author's interview.

75. On the increasing number of journalists who are casualties of modern wars, see *Journalists Disappear*, Moscow, Glasnost Defence Foundation, 2000, and *Journalists in the Frontline*, Washington, DC, Freedom Forum, 2001. The Rory Peck award for the best freelance work was set up in memory of a journalist killed while on a job. In the past journalists sometimes died accidentally because they were in the wrong place at the wrong time. Now, in conflicts all over the world, journalists are deliberately targeted.

76. See C. W. Blandy, *Chechnya: Dynamics of War*, Cambridge, Conflict Research Centre, 2002, p. 7.

77. Rob Parsons, BBC, 13 December 1999.

78. Politkovskaya, *A Small Corner of Hell*, p. 6.

79. Author's interview with Blue Cunningham.

80. Politkovskaya, *A Dirty War*, is a collection of remarkable journalism that does just this, and a wave of documentary films dealt with these issues. See *Greetings from Grozny*, New York, Channel 13, 1996; N. Kirtaoze, *Chechen Lullaby*, Moscow, Unite Documentaries, 1999.

81. G. Mosse, *Fallen Soldiers: Reshaping the Memory of the World Wars*, Oxford, Oxford University Press, 1990, p. 231.

82. The estimates vary, and expose for the first time official attempts to hide mortality rates.

83. See *Russia and the Chechen Wars*, Moscow, Carnegie Foundation for Peace, 2000, and *Russia/Chechnya Mortality during Sweep Operations*, London, Human Rights Watch, 2002.

84. Author's interview.

85. See V. Adams, *The Media and the Falklands War*, Basingstoke, Macmillan, 1986; L. Freedman, *Britain and the Falklands War*, Oxford, Blackwell, 1988; R.

Harris, *Gotcha! The Media, the Government and the Falklands Crisis*, London, Faber, 1983.

86. Author interview, Validata.
87. S. E. Miller & D. Trenin, *The Russian Military: Power and Politics*, Cambridge, Mass., MIT Press, 2004, p. 23.
88. Author's interview.
89. S. J. Cimbala, *The Russian Military*, London, Frank Cass, 2001, p. 171.
90. See R. J. Aldrich, *The Hidden Hand: Britain, America and Cold War Secret Intelligence*, London, John Murray, 2001, p. 145.
91. Author's interview.
92. Merridale, *Night of Stone*, p. 241.
93. Author's interview.
94. G. Hosking, *Culture and the Media in Russia Today*, Basingstoke, Macmillan, 1989, p. 15.
95. Merridale, *Night of Stone*, p. 365.
96. Author's interview.
97. Arkady Ostrovorsky in Lloyd, *Rebirth of a Nation*, p. 43.
98. In P. K. Baev, *The Russian Army in a Time of Troubles*, London, Sage, 1996, p. 104.
99. L. M. Bakhtin, *The Italian Renaissance and Other Writings*, trans. J. Green, New York, Picador, 1982, p. 12.
100. Author's interview.
101. *Journalists in Danger: Recent Russian Wars*, New York and London, Freedom Forum, 1998, p. 307.
102. Focus group response to women journalists, Validata, 1999.
103. Politkovskaya, *Putin's Russia*, p. 259.
104. Author's interview.
105. Merridale, *Night of Stone*, pp. 267–8.
106. Author's interview with Marsha Volkenstein.
107. H. Arendt, *On Violence*, London, Allen Lane, 1970, p. 54.
108. Author's interview.
109. Merridale, *Night of Stone*, p. 12.

CHAPTER 8: BAD DEATH IS GOOD NEWS

1. P. Ariès, *Images of Man and Death*, Cambridge, Mass., Harvard University Press, 1985, p. 23.
2. Tom Walker, the *Sunday Times*, Freedom Forum seminar on war reporting, 2003.
3. Michael Buerk, at the BBC 'Famine, Aid and the Media' workshop, 12 October 2004.
4. Author's interview with Jason Burke of *The Observer*.
5. Brian Hanrahan, at the Famine, Aid and the Media workshop, 2004.

6. A. Andren & N. Montan, *The Incidence of Film and Television Violence in Scandinavian Nations*, Stockholm, Svenska Institute, 1999.

7. *Reporting the Holocaust: Fifty Years of Press Stories*, New Haven, Shorenstein Center for the Study of Press and Politics, Kennedy School of Government, Harvard University, 1999.

8. I. Buruma, *The Wages of Guilt: Memories of War in Germany and Japan*, London, Vintage, 1995, p. 123.

9. P. Fussell, *The Great War in Modern Memory*, Oxford, Oxford University Press, 1975.

10. S. Hynes, *The Soldier's Tale: Bearing Witness to Modern War*, London, Pimlico, 1998; J. Bourke, *Dismembering the Male: Men's Bodies, Britain and the Great War*, London, Reaktion, 1996, and *An Intimate History of Killing: Face-to-Face Killing in Twentieth-Century Warfare*, London, Granta, 1999.

11. S. Freud, 'Thoughts for the Times on War and Death' (1915), in J. Strachey (trans. and ed.), *The Standard Edition of the Complete Psychological Works of Sigmund Freud*, vol. 14, London, Hogarth Press, 1957, p. 289.

12. Author's interview with Jerry Keuhl; also see J. Turner, *Filming History: The Memoirs of a Newsreel Cameraman*, London, British Universities and Film and Video Council, 2002.

13. BBC Written Archive (News Policy), 'Comparing Newsreel Reporting and Radio News Reading', R34, 12, Paper 3, 1936.

14. R. Day, *Grand Inquisitor: Memoirs of a Broadcaster*, London, Weidenfeld & Nicolson, 1989, p. 43.

15. B. Winston, *Damn Lies and Documentaries*, London, British Film Institute, 2000, looks at the ways in which the authority of what is seen can be maintained, and distinguishes between legitimate and illegitimate practices in the past and the present.

16. Even in the mid-1980s the only victims who spoke to camera had to have English. Now it is acceptable to translate what they say, and this is a great improvement. The next step must surely be more varied sources of news.

17. Kate Adie, City University symposium on war reporting, 2001.

18. P. Binski, *Medieval Death: Ritual and Representation*, London, British Museum, 1996, p. 32.

19. E. Evans-Pritchard, *Nuer Religion*, Oxford, Clarendon, 1956, p. 301.

20. M. Pedelty, *War Stories: The Culture of Foreign Correspondents*, London, Routledge, 1995, p. 142.

21. A. Van Gennep, *Rites of Passage*, trans. M. Vizedon & G. L. Caffee, London, Routledge & Kegan Paul, 1909, p. 231.

22. Ibid.

23. F. Paxton, *Christianizing Death: The Creation of a Ritual Process in Early Medieval Europe*, Ithaca, NY, Cornell University Press, 1990.

24. P. Brown, *St Augustine of Hippo: A Biography*, London, Faber, 1969, pp. 27–32.

25. See J. Glaister, *Medical Jurisprudence and Toxicology*, in collaboration with E. Rentoul, 10th edn, Edinburgh, E. & S. Livingstone, 1957, p. 116.

26. B. Kouchner, *Saving Lives: Médecins Sans Frontières*, London, Macmillan, 1997, p. 31.

27. Pedelty, *War Stories*, p. 34.

28. Author's interview with Sir Frank Cooper.

29. Pedelty, *War Stories*, p. 3.

30. D. E. Stannard, *The Puritan Way of Death: A Study in Religion, Culture and Social Change*, New York, Oxford University Press, 1997, p. 175.

31. Interview with Nick Gowing, and papers presented at seminars at Goldsmith's College, 2002, and developed at LSE, 2004.

32. Ash, *History of the Present*, p. 35.

33. BBC, *Evening News*, 12 October 1992.

34. ITV, *Evening News*, 15 January 1994.

35. Sky News, *Early Evening Report*, 21 September 1999.

36. *The Times*, 12 March 1997.

37. Stannard, *The Puritan Way of Death*, p. 105.

38. See Kellner, *Television and the Crisis of Democracy*, and, more importantly, M. Schudson, *Origins of the Ideal of Objectivity in the Professions: The History of American Journalism and American Law*, New York, Garland, 1990, and his *The Good Citizen, a History of American Civic Life*, Cambridge, Mass., Harvard University Press, 2000.

39. D. C. Hallin, *The 'Uncensored War': The Media and Vietnam*, New York, Oxford University Press, 1986, p. 35.

40. Pedelty, *War Stories*, p. 86.

41. Schudson, *Origins of the Ideal of Objectivity*, p. 121.

42. A. Loyd, *My War Gone By, I Miss It So*, London, Doubleday, 1999, p. 213.

43. Author's interview.

44. Author's interview with Sir Max Hastings.

45. S. Maitland, 'Death in Kosovo', *The Independent*, 15 September 1993.

CHAPTER 9: MEDIA MEMORIALS

1. R. Richardson, *Death, Dissection and the Destitute*, London, Penguin, 1989, p. 26.

2. Ibid., p. 87.

3. F. Peacock, *Tradition and Place*, London, Merton Press, 1895, p. 2.

4. In Camden & Islington NHS Trust, for example, 12 per cent of relatives visited the body of their deceased family member in 1980; in 2004 this had risen to 61 per cent. However, it is also a practice influenced by the kind of death that occurred – and whether families had been present when the person died. (*Families and Bereavement: The Changing Role of the Hospital*, London, University College

Hospital and Camden & Islington National Health Service Trust, 2004, pp. 2–3.)

5. A. Borg, *War Memorials: From Antiquity to the Present*, London, Leo Cooper, 1991, p. 47.

6. H. Cooper (ed.), *John Trumbull: The Hand and Spirit of a Painter*, New Haven, Yale University, 1982.

7. G. E. S. Gorer, *Death, Grief and Mourning in Contemporary Britain*, London, Cresset, 1965, p. 14.

8. See H. Feifel, *New Meanings of Death*, New York, McGraw-Hill, 1977; S. Strack (ed.), *Death and the Search for Meaning*, Northvale, NJ, Aronson, 1997; R. J. Lifton, *The Broken Connection: Death and the Continuity of Life*, New York, Simon & Schuster, 1979, and *The Genocidal Mentality: Nazi Holocaust and the Nuclear Threat*, London, Macmillan, 1991.

9. D. Cannadine, 'Death and Grief in Modern Britain', in J. Whaley (ed.), *Mirror of Mortality: Studies in the Social History of Death*, London, Europa, 1981, pp. 187–242, 189.

10. Ibid., p. 239.

11. Ibid., p. 216.

12. Ibid., p. 217.

13. R. J. Lifton, *Death in Life: Survivors of Hiroshima*, Chapel Hill, NC, University of North Carolina Press, 1991, p. 245.

14. See C. Geertz, *Negara: The Theatre State in Nineteenth-Century Bali*, Princeton: Princeton University Press, 1980, ch. 4 and conclusion, pp. 98–136.

15. Michael Buerk, BBC History Project witness seminar, 2004.

16. Geertz, *Negara*, p. 120.

17. J. Goldberg, *James I and the Politics of English Literature*, Baltimore, Johns Hopkins University Press, 1983, p. 149.

18. W. Shakespeare, *Henry V*, IV.i.222–9.

19. See M. Schudson, *The Sociology of News*, New York, Norton, 2003; H. Tumber, *Media Power, Professionals and Policies*, London, Routledge, 2000; P. Schlesinger, *Reporting Crime*, Oxford, Clarendon, 1994; J. Curran, *Media Power*, London, Routledge, 2002, and (ed.) *Mass Media and Society*, London, Edward Arnold, 2000.

20. See Richardson, *Death, Dissection and the Destitute*.

21. Interview with Ron Neil, Director of Outside Broadcasts, the BBC, 1997.

22. Martin Bell, 'Reporting Wars', *Press and Politics*, vol. 3, no. 2 (2000), p. 20.

23. Phillip Johnson, CNN, at a seminar at the Freedom Forum, 15 October 2002.

24. Brian Hanrahan at a BBC seminar on the World Service, May 2002.

25. David Loyn, the BBC.

26. Rory Peck Trust, London.

27. BBC, *Six O'Clock News*, 28 August 1998.

28. Freud, 'Thoughts for the Times on War and Death', pp. 289–90.

29. B. Pimlott, 'Should the Arts be Popular?', Lloyds TSB Forum, Royal Academy lecture, 2001.

30. Quoted in P. Virilio, *War and the Cinema: The Logistics of Perception*, London, Verso, 1989, p. 135.
31. Donald Rumsfeld quoted in T. Schyler, 'Iraq: Why We Went to War', *New York Review of Books*, 2 October 2004.
32. C. Brothers, *War and Photography: A Cultural History*, London, Routledge, 1997, pp. 20–32, suggests that it was a new phenomenon.
33. Brothers, *War and Photography*, p. 163.
34. B. Crosthwaite, 'Newsreels Show Bias', *World Film News*, vol. 1, no. 7 (1963), p. 1.
35. Author's interview.
36. Mark Damazar, the BBC.
37. See BBC, *The Death of Yugoslavia*, episode 4, 1999.
38. C. Quigley, *The Corpse: A History*, London, McFarland & Co., 1996, p. 37.
39. *Report of the Committee on the Use of Video Recordings in Identification*, Manchester, National Police and Mortuary Practices Board, 1996.
40. Author's interview.

CHAPTER 10: MOVED TO TEARS

1. BBC seminar on the war against terrorism, October 2001.
2. Quoted in R. Whelan, *Robert Capra: The Defiant Photographer*, London, Phaidon, 2001, p. 22.
3. Murray Sayle, quoted in M. Linklater, 'Harry Evans's Good Times', *Prospect*, December 2001, p. 44.
4. Schudson, *Origins of the Ideal of Objectivity*, p. 3.
5. J. Simpson, BBC, *Ten O'Clock News*, 6 April 2003.
6. J. S. Mill, *On Liberty*, Oxford, Oxford University Press, 1975, p. 98.
7. Allen & Seaton, *The Media of Conflict*, p. 57.
8. Peters, *Speaking into the Air*, p. 195.
9. 'Reporting the World', Freedom Forum workshop, 17 October 2001.
10. Ben Pimlott, commenting on a draft of this chapter.
11. Quoted in A. J. P. Kenny, *Action, Emotion and Will*, London, Routledge, 1963, p. 13.
12. See M. C. Nussbaum, *Passion and Perception*, Cambridge, Cambridge University Press, 1993, p. 39.
13. Children when they have fevers do, however, feel as if their whole personality is disturbed. Ill children are often bad before they are sad.
14. See S. Franks, 'Reporting Africa', *British Journalism Review*, April 2005.
15. Torin Douglas, BBC media correspondent.
16. See B. Pimlott, 'The Media and the Monarchy', in J. A. Seaton (ed.), *Politics and the Media: Harlots and Prerogative at the Turn of the Millennium*, Oxford, Blackwell, 1998, p. 110.

17. Seneca, 'De ira, On Anger', in Seneca, *Moral and Political Essays*, trans. and ed. J. M. Cooper & J. F. Procope, Cambridge, Cambridge University Press, 1995, p. 229.

18. *Consent, Rights and Choice in Health Care for Children and Young People*, London, BMJ Books, 2001, p. 15.

19. P. Alderson, *Choosing for Children: Parents' Consent to Surgery*, Oxford, Oxford University Press, 1990, p. 105.

20. R. C. Walters, *Broadcast Writing: Principles and Practice*, 5th edn, New York, McGraw-Hill, 1994, p. 291. Cited in the *Communication Handbook 2001* as the top-selling undergraduate text.

21. W. Junger, *Character, Emotion, Action! Writing for Television*, ed. J. Freidman, New York, Anchor Books, 1996, p. 208.

22. C. Caman, *Creating the News for Electronic Media*, Berkeley, Wadsworth, 1997, p. 271.

23. Euripides, *Medea*, trans. J. Brooks, London, Methuen, 1988, p. 49.

24. Ibid., p. 227.

25. See S. Barnett, *Westminster Tales: The 21st Century Crisis in Political Journalism*, London, Continuum, 2001.

26. J. Barish, *The Anti-Theatrical Prejudice*, Berkeley, University of California Press, 1981, p. 20.

27. Goody, *Representations and Contradictions*, p. 313.

28. R. Darnton, 'Becoming a Journalist: News and News Rooms', *Daedalus*, The Journal of the American Academy of Arts and Sciences, vol. 97, no. 2 (spring 1968), p. 142.

29. Ibid.

30. The film researcher and historian Jerry Keuhl has, for example, contributed many years of establishing and maintaining standards in the use of film sources in this way in a series of ground-breaking documentaries.

31. BBC, *What Audiences Want from Stories*, London, BBC, 2000.

32. Author's interview.

33. Author's interview.

34. M. Schudson, *Advertising: The Uneasy Persuasion, its Dubious Impact on American Society*, New York, Basic Books, 1984, p. 25.

35. W. Wenders, *Emotion Pictures*, London, Faber, 1989, p. 13.

36. Mark Latey, NATO press division.

37. See C. A. Howells, *Love, Mystery and Misery*, London, Athlone Press, 1978, p. 24.

38. BBC Written Archive (Policy Radio), R36, 12/32, 'Light Programme Listening', 1956.

39. S. Sandberg (ed.), *Hyperactivity Disorders in Childhood*, Cambridge, Cambridge University Press, 1996, p. 12.

40. D. Riesman, *The Lonely Crowd: A Study of Changing American Character*, New Haven, Yale University Press, 1951, p. 236.

41. H. Arendt, *Eichmann in Jerusalem*, Harmondsworth, Penguin, 1979, p. 99.

42. J. Crary, *Suspensions of Perception: Attention, Spectacle and Modern Culture*, Cambridge, Mass., MIT Press, 1999, p. 1.

43. B. Webb, *The Diary of Beatrice Webb*, vol. 4: *1924–1943, The Wheel of Life*, ed. N. & J. MacKenzie, London, Virago, 1985, p. 1.

44. B. W. Ife, *Reading and Fiction in the Golden Age of Spain: A Platonist Critique and Some Picaresque Replies*, Cambridge, Cambridge University Press, 1985, p. 32.

45. See B. Pimlott, *Hugh Dalton*, London, Cape, 1985, p. 17.

46. R. Putnam, *Bowling Alone: The Collapse and Revival of American Community*, New York, Simon & Schuster, 2000, p. 44.

47. BBC research on politics and young people, 2002.

48. E. L. Freud (ed.), *The Letters of Sigmund Freud 1873–1939*, trans. T. & J. Stern, London, Hogarth Press, 1961, pp. 236–7, entry for 22 September 1907.

49. Webb, *Diary*, vol. 4, p. 278, entry for 3 September 1939.

50. Van Zoonen, *Feminist Media Studies*, p. 75.

51. Aristotle, *De anima* (*On the Soul*), trans. H. Lawson-Tancred, London, Penguin, 1984, p. 27.

52. CNN style manual, *Writing News*, New York, CNN, 2000.

53. T. White, *How to Write News*, Boston, Mass., Focal, 2002, p. 12.

54. B. Itule & A. Anderson, *News Writing and Reporting for Today's Media*, 5th edn, New York, McGraw-Hill, 2000, p. 140.

55. Author's interview.

56. UN Resolution 59, para 1.

57. Indonesian government spokesman, *UK Press Gazette*, 12 May 1997, p. 2.

58. See *Article 19 Handbook*, London, Article 19, 2001.

59. C. A. Lutz, *Unnatural Emotions: Everyday Sentiments on a Micronesian Atoll and their Challenge to Western Theory*, Chicago, University of Chicago Press, 1988, p. 225.

60. J. S. Mill, *Autobiography and Literary Essays*, ed. J. M. Robson & J. Stillinger, Toronto, University of Toronto Press, 1981, p. 151.

61. D. H. Lawrence, *A Propos of Lady Chatterley's Lover*, London, Phoenix, 1938, p. 171.

62. B. Webb, *The Diary of Beatrice Webb*, vol. 1: *Glitter Around and Darkness Within, 1873–1892*, ed. N. & J. MacKenzie, London, Virago, 1982, p. 210, entry for 22 February 1883.

63. A. Smith, *The Theory of Moral Sentiments*, ed. D. D. Raphael & A. L. Macfie, Oxford, Clarendon, 1976, p. 15.

64. M. C. Nussbaum, 'Emotions, Women and Capabilities', in M. C. Nussbaum & J. Glover (eds.), *Women, Culture and Development*, Oxford, Oxford University Press, 1995, p. 360.

65. M. C. Nussbaum, *Love's Knowledge*, New York, Oxford University Press, 1990, p. 75.

66. C. A. Lutz, 'Engendered Emotion', in C. A. Lutz & L. Abu-Lughod (eds.), *The Language and Politics of Emotion*, Cambridge, Cambridge University Press, 1990, p. 90.

67. Ibid., p. 94.

68. M. C. Nussbaum, *The Fragility of Goodness*, Cambridge, Cambridge University Press, 2001, p. 160.

69. G. Haight (ed.), *Selections from George Eliot's Letters*, New Haven, Yale University Press, 1985, p. 85.

70. B. Hardy, *The Advantage of Lyric: Essays on Feeling in Poetry*, London, Athlone Press, 1977, p. 140.

71. S. Plath, 'The Scope of Writing', *Triquarterly*, no. 7 (fall 1966), p. 71.

CHAPTER 11: GLOBAL COMPASSION

1. See G. Roeder, *The Censored War: American Visual Experience during World War Two*, New Haven, Yale University Press, 1993.

2. T. Harrison & C. Madge, *Britain by Mass-Observation*, London, Cresset, 1986, p. 103.

3. R. Nye, 'The End of the Duel', in P. Spierenburg (ed.), *Men and Violence: Gender, Honor and its Rituals in Modern Europe and America*, Columbus, Ohio, Ohio State University Press, 1998, p. 82.

4. A. Solzhenitsyn, 'One Word of Truth', in *Collected Works*, Sphere Books, London, 1972, p. 2.

5. Author's interview.

6. R. Cork, *A Bitter Truth: Avant-Garde Art and the Great War*, London, Yale University Press, 1994, p. 219.

7. For a discussion of these issues see R. Tsagarousianou, *Cyberdemocracy*, London, Routledge, 1998; K. Robins, *Beyond Imagined Community*, London, Goldsmith's College, 2001; K. Robins & A. Aksoy, 'Thinking across Spaces: Transnational Television from Turkey', *European Journal of Cultural Studies*, vol. 3, no. 3 (2000), pp. 343–65.

8. Smith, *The Theory of Moral Sentiments*, p. 9.

9. W. James, *The Principles of Psychology*, vol. 2, New York, H. Holt & Co., 1890, pp. 449–50.

10. See B. Parkinson & A. Coleman (eds.), *Emotion and Motivation*, London, Longman, 1995, p. 81.

11. Department of Foreign Development, *TV and the Developing World*, London, HMSO, 2001.

12. See J. Meyrowitz, *No Sense of Place: The Impact of Electronic Media on Social Behaviour*, New York, Oxford University Press, 1985, p. 56.

13. J. A. Seaton, 'Public, Private and the Media: Where Do We Draw the Line?', *Political Quarterly*, vol. 74, no. 2 (2003), pp. 174–84.

14. See C. Seymour-Ure, 'Are the Broadsheets Becoming Unhinged?', in Seaton, *Politics and the Media*, pp. 43–55.

15. T. Rantanen, *Foreign News in Imperial Russia: The Relationship between International and Russian News Agencies, 1856–1914*, Helsinki, Suomalainen Tiedeakatemia, 1990, pp. 23–4.

16. Comment at Reuters seminar on the reporting of the conflict in Kosovo, Green College, Oxford, 1997.

17. Interview with Rory Peck.

18. M. Monmonier, *Maps with the News: The Development of American Journalistic Cartography*, Chicago, University of Chicago Press, 1989, p. 16; M. Monmonier, 'Mapping the American World: College Students' Geographical Understanding', in M. Monmonier (ed.), *Maps and Public Understanding*, Chicago, University of Chicago Press, 2005, p. 32.

19. R. Darnton, *The Forbidden Best Sellers of Pre-Revolutionary France*, London, HarperCollins, 1996, p. 241.

20. I owe this insight to Jenny Hartley.

21. *The Sun*, 17 February 1997; the *Daily Mail*, 21 February 1997.

22. See J. A. Seaton, 'The Holocaust', in J. A. Seaton & B. Pimlott (eds.), *The Media in British Politics*, London, Longman, 1987, p. 45.

23. S. Goldsworthy, 'The Balkan Atrocities and the Press', Ph.D. thesis, University of Westminster, in preparation, 2005.

24. Seaton, 'The Holocaust', p. 47.

25. J. Glover, *Causing Death and Saving Lives*, Harmondsworth, Penguin, 1977, p. 211.

26. Ibid., p. 213.

27. See A. W. B. Simpson, *Cannibalism and the Common Law: The Story of the Tragic Last Voyage of the Mignonette and the Strange Legal Proceedings to which It Gave Rise*, Chicago, University of Chicago Press, 1984, p. 55.

28. Author's discussion, David Loyn.

29. Author's discussion, Daniel Pimlott.

30. S. Roberts, S. Smith & C. Bryce, *Children at Risk? Safety as a Social Value*, Buckingham, Open University Press, 1995, p. 8.

31. See S. Moeller, *Compassion Fatigue: How the Media Sell Disease, Famine, War and Death*, London, Routledge, 1999, p. 23.

32. L. Nilsson, 'The Miracle of New Life', *Life* magazine, 23 July 1965, pp. 3–17.

33. Introduction to L. Nilsson, *A Child is Born*, New York, Delacorte Press, 1977, p. 5.

34. MORI poll, 'Attitudes towards Images of the Foetus', 12 June 1966.

35. See J. B. Thompson, *The Media and Modernity*, Cambridge, Polity, 1995.

36. Schudson, *The Power of News*, p. 7.

37. S. Milgram, *Obedience to Authority: An Experimental View*, London, Tavistock, 1974, p. 88.

38. Milgram, quoted in T. Blass (ed.), *Obedience to Authority: Current Perspec-*

tives on the Milgram Paradigm, Mahwah, NJ, Lawrence Erlbaum Associates, 2000, p. 35.

39. P. G. Zimbardo, *The Stanford Prison Experiment*, Stanford, Stanford University Press, 1985, pp. 66–9.

40. See F. Rochat and M. Mogdigliani, 'Captain Greunnengerr', in Blass, *Obedience to Authority*, pp. 15–32.

41. See J. A. Seaton, 'A Fresh Look at Freedom of Speech', in Seaton, *Politics and the Media*, pp. 117–29.

42. B. Kouchner, *Charity Business*, Paris and London, Médecins Sans Frontières, 1999, p. 33.

43. L. Boltanski, *Distant Suffering: Morality, Media and Politics*, Cambridge, Cambridge University Press, 1999, p. 130.

44. O. O'Neil, *Faces of Hunger: An Essay on Poverty, Justice and Development*, London, Allen & Unwin, 1986, p. 13.

45. Loyd, *My War Gone By, I Miss It So*, p. 45.

46. Department of Foreign Development, *TV and the Developing World*.

47. Thus *The Sun* lost circulation every day it put Elton John on its front page as part of an extended vendetta against the singer.

48. L. Sabato & G. Simpson, *Dirty Little Secrets: The Persistence of Corruption in American Politics*, New York, Times Books, 1996, p. 339.

49. See L. Sabato, *Feeding Frenzy*, New York, Free Press, 1991.

50. See O'Neil, *Faces of Hunger*, chs. 4–5.

51. D. Hume, *A Treatise of Human Nature*, ed. L. A. Selby-Bigge, Oxford, Clarendon, 1896, p. 415.

52. Plato, *The Republic*, ed. T. Irwin, London, Everyman, 1993, p. 24.

53. A. D. Nuttall, *Why Does Tragedy Give Pleasure?*, Oxford, Clarendon, 1996, p. 37.

54. Ibid., p. 47.

55. Rawls, *A Theory of Justice*, p. 514.

CONCLUSION

1. Quoted in R. Scott, *War in Iraq*, London, Profile, 2002, p. 1.

2. G. Wills, *Foreign News in America*, Cambridge, Mass., Shorenstein Center for the Study of Press and Politics, Kennedy School of Government, Harvard University, 2003.

3. See E. H. Gombrich, *The Story of Art*, London, Phaidon, 1995, p. 13.

4. Quoted in F. Crouzet, *Historians and the French Revolution: The Case of Maximilien Robespierre*, Swansea, University College of Swansea, 1989, p. 3.

5. N. Hampson, *The Life and Opinions of Maximilien Robespierre*, London, Duckworth, 1976, p. 231.

NOTES

6. See G. Dart, *Rousseau, Robespierre and English Romanticism*, Cambridge, Cambridge University Press, 1999, p. 68.

7. Arendt, *On Violence*, p. 65.

8. J. M. Thompson, *Robespierre* (1935), Oxford, Blackwell, 1988, p. 587.

9. J. Hardmen, *Robespierre*, Longman, London, 1999, p. 27.

10. C. Crouch, *Coping with Post-Democracy*, London, Fabian Society, 2000, p. 21.

11. Montesquieu, *The Collected Essays of Montesquieu*, London, Dent, 1958, p. 76.

12. See Gawande, *A Surgeon's Notes*.

Bibliography

Adams, V., *The Media and the Falklands War*, Basingstoke, Macmillan, 1986

Adie, K., *The Kindness of Strangers: The Autobiography*, London, Headline, 2003

Ahrensdorf, P., *The Death of Socrates*, New York, State University of New York Press, 2003

Alderson, P., *Choosing for Children: Parents' Consent to Surgery*, Oxford, Oxford University Press, 1990

Aldrich, R. J., *The Hidden Hand: Britain, America and Cold War Secret Intelligence*, London, John Murray, 2001

Allen, T., & Seaton, J. A. (eds.), *The Media of Conflict*, London, Zed Books, 1998

Amnesty International, *Against Oblivion*, London, Fontana, 1978

Amnesty International Campaign Handbook, London, Amnesty International, 1998

Andren, A., & Montan, N., *The Incidence of Film and Television Violence in Scandinavian Nations*, Stockholm, Svenska Institute, 1999

Arendt, H., *Eichmann in Jerusalem*, Harmondsworth, Penguin, 1979

—— *On Violence*, London, Allen Lane, 1970

Ariès, P., *The Hour of Our Death*, Harmondsworth, Penguin Books

—— *Images of Man and Death*, Cambridge, Mass., Harvard University Press, 1985

Aristotle, *De anima (On the Soul)*, trans. H. Lawson-Tancred, London, Penguin, 1984

Arkwright, T., 'Comet the Bull: Breeding Pure Bloodlines', *Agricultural History Review*, vol. 20, no. 3 (1986)

Article 19 Handbook, London, Article 19, 2001

Ash, T. Garton, *History of the Present: Essays and Dispatches from the New Europe*, London, Penguin, 2000

Aslund, A., & Layard, R. (eds.), *Changing the Economic System in Russia*, London, Pinter, 1993

Auguet, R., *Cruelty and Civilization: The Roman Games*, London, Routledge, 1994

Augustine, St, *Confessions*, trans. R. S. Pine-Coffin, London, Penguin, 2003

Baev, P. K., *The Russian Army in a Time of Troubles*, London, Sage, 1996

Baines, H., *Make-up for Stage and Screen*, New York, Dainton Books, 2001

Bakhtin, L. M., *The Italian Renaissance and Other Writings*, trans. J. Green, New York, Picador, 1982

Barasch, M., *Imago Hominis: Studies in the Language of Art*, Vienna, IRSA, 1991

Barish, J., *The Anti-Theatrical Prejudice*, Berkeley, University of California Press, 1981

Barnard, L., *The Theory of Images*, Birmingham, University of Birmingham Press, 1975

Barnett, S., *Westminster Tales: The 21st Century Crisis in Political Journalism*, London, Continuum, 2001

Barnouw, E., *The Image Empire: A History of Broadcasting in the United States*, vol. 3: *From 1953*, New York, Oxford University Press, 1970

Barton, C., *Roman Honor: The Fire in the Bones*, Berkeley, University of California Press, 2001

—— *The Sorrows of the Ancient Romans: The Gladiator and the Monster*, Princeton, Princeton University Press, 1993

Basil, St, 'St Spiritu Sancti', in *The Writings of St Basil*, ed. T. J. Sprottiswell, Oxford, Oxford University Press, 1927

Baudrillard, J., *La Guerre du Golfe n'a pas eu lieu*, Paris, Editions Galilée, 1991

—— *The Illusion of the End*, trans. C. Turner, Cambridge, Polity, 1994

—— *Selected Writings of Jean Baudrillard*, ed. M. Postner, Cambridge, Polity, 1998

BBC, *The Death of Yugoslavia*, episode 4, 1999

BBC, *What Audiences Want from Stories*, London, BBC, 2000

BBC seminar on the war against terrorism, October 2001

BBC World Service, *Annual Report*, London, BBC, 1990–2000

BBC Written Archive (News Policy), 'Comparing Newsreel Reporting and Radio News Reading', R34, 12, Paper 3, 1936

BBC Written Archive (News Policy), News memo, News and Current Affairs Minutes, R34, 101, 7 June 1976

BBC Written Archive (Policy Radio), R36, 12/32, 'Light Programme Listening', 1956

Beevor, A., *Stalingrad*, London, Penguin, 1998

Bell, M., *In Harm's Way: Reflections of a War Zone Thug*, London, Penguin, 1995

Belting, H., *Likeness and Presence: A History of the Image Before the Era of Art*, Chicago, University of Chicago Press, 1994

Bending, L., *The Representation of Bodily Pain in Late Nineteenth Century English Culture*, Oxford, Clarendon, 2000

Bennett, V., *Crying Wolf: The Return of War to Chechnya*, London, Picador, 1998

Bieber, M., *The History of the Greek and Roman Theatre*, Princeton, Princeton University Press, 1961

Binski, P., *Medieval Death: Ritual and Representation*, London, British Museum, 1996

Blandy, C. W., *Chechnya: Dynamics of War*, Cambridge, Conflict Research Centre, 2002

Blank, S., & Tilford, E., *Russia's Invasion of Chechnya: An Assessment*, Carlisle, Mass., US Army College, 1995

Blass, T. (ed.), *Obedience to Authority: Current Perspectives on the Milgram Paradigm*, Mahwah, NJ, Lawrence Erlbaum Associates, 2000

Boltanski, L., *Distant Suffering: Morality, Media and Politics*, Cambridge, Cambridge University Press, 1999

Boone, P., Gomulka, S., & Layard, R. (eds.), *Emerging from Communism: Lessons from Russia, China and Eastern Europe*, Cambridge, Mass., MIT Press, 1998

Borg, A., *War Memorials: From Antiquity to the Present*, London, Leo Cooper, 1991

Bourdieu, P., *Distinction: A Social Critique of the Judgement of Taste*, London, Routledge & Kegan Paul, 1984

Bourke, J., *Dismembering the Male: Men's Bodies, Britain and the Great War*, London, Reaktion, 1996

—— *The Field of Cultural Production: Essays on Art and Literature*, Cambridge, Polity, 1993

—— *An Intimate History of Killing: Face-to-Face Killing in Twentieth-Century Warfare*, London, Granta, 1999

Bowersock, G. W., *Fiction as History: Nero to Julian*, Berkeley, University of California Press, 1994

—— *Martyrdom and Rome*, Cambridge, Cambridge University Press, 1995

Boyd-Barret, O., Seymour-Ure, C., & Tunstall, J., *Studies on the Press*, London, HMSO, 1977

Bratlinger, P., *Bread and Circuses*, Ithaca, NY, Cornell University Press, 1983

Braudel, F., *Civilization and Capitalism, 15th–18th Century*, London, Collins, 1981

Bray, X., *El Greco*, London, National Gallery, 2004

British Consumption Index 2000, London, HMSO, 2001

Brothers, C., *War and Photography: A Cultural History*, London, Routledge, 1997

Brown, P., *Authority and the Sacred*, Cambridge, Cambridge University Press, 1995

—— *The Body and Society: Men, Women and Sexual Renunciation in Early Christianity*, London, Faber, 1988

—— *Power and Persuasion in Late Antiquity: Towards a Christian Empire*, Madison, Wis., University of Wisconsin Press, 1992

—— *Society and the Holy*, London, Faber, 1982

—— *St Augustine of Hippo: A Biography*, London, Faber, 1969

Buruma, I., *The Wages of Guilt: Memories of War in Germany and Japan*, London, Vintage, 1995

Bynum, C. W., *Fragmentation and Redemption: The Resurrection of the Body in Western Christianity 200–1336*, New York, Columbia University Press, 1995

—— *Holy Feast and Holy Fast*, Berkeley, University of California Press, 1991

—— *Metamorphosis and Identity*, New York, Zone Books, 2001

Caman, C., *Creating the News for Electronic Media*, Wadsworth, California, 1997

Cameron, A., & Herrin, J. (eds.), *Constantinople in the Early Eighth Century: The Parastaseis Syntomo Chronokai*, Leiden, E. J. Brill, 1984

Cannadine, D., 'Death and Grief in Modern Britain', in J. Whaley (ed.), *Mirror of Mortality: Studies in the Social History of Death*, London, Europa, 1981

Capelstein, J., *Media Audiences and Advertizing Spend During the War in Iraq*, Media Review Report, New York, 2003

Caputo, P., *Means of Escape*, London, Simon & Schuster, 1992

Carroll, N. *Philosophy of Horror, or Paradoxes of the Heart*, New York, Simon & Schuster, 1990

The Chechen War and the Media: The Glasnost Defence Foundation Report, Moscow, Glasnost Defence Foundation, 1997

Cimbala, S. J., *The Russian Military*, London, Frank Cass, 2001

Coleman, K., 'Fatal Charades', *Journal of Roman Studies* 80 (1990)

Connell, I., 'Tales of Tellyland', in P. Dahlgren & C. Sparks (eds.), *Communication and Citizenship: Journalism and the Public Sphere in the New Media Age*, London, Routledge, 1991

Consent, Rights and Choice in Health Care for Children and Young People, London, BMJ Books, 2001

Cooper, H. (ed.), *John Trumbull: The Hand and Spirit of a Painter*, New Haven, Yale University, 1982

Cork, R., *A Bitter Truth: Avant-Garde Art and the Great War*, London, Yale University Press, 1994

Cormack, R., *Byzantine Art and Rhetoric*, Oxford, Oxford University Press, 2000

—— *The Byzantine Eye: Studies in Art and Patronage*, Aldershot, Variorum Reprints, 1989

Crapanzano, V., *Waiting: The Whites of South Africa*, London, Granada, 1985

Crary, J., *Suspensions of Perception: Attention, Spectacle and Modern Culture*, Cambridge, Mass., MIT Press, 1999

—— *Techniques of the Observer: On Vision and Modernity in the Nineteenth Century*, Cambridge, Mass., MIT Press, 1990

Crosthwaite, B., 'Newsreels Show Bias', *World Film News*, vol. 1, no. 7 (1963)

Crouch, C., *Coping with Post-Democracy*, London, Fabian Society, 2000

Crouzet, F., *Historians and the French Revolution: The Case of Maximilien Robespierre*, Swansea, University College of Swansea, 1989

Curran, J., *Media Power*, London, Routledge, 2002

—— *Media Theory*, London, Routledge, 2004

—— (ed.), *Mass Media and Society*, London, Edward Arnold, 2000

Cutler, A., *Images and Ideology in Byzantine Art*, Aldershot, Variorum Reprints, 1992

Dalla Palma, D., *Make-up Artist's Handbook for Screen*, New York, Sterling Books, 2004

Darnton, R., 'Becoming a Journalist: News and News Rooms', *Daedalus*, The Journal of the American Academy of Arts and Sciences, vol. 97, no. 2 (spring 1968)

—— *Berlin Journal 1989–1990*, New York, Norton, 1991

—— *The Business of Enlightenment: Publishing History of the* Encyclopédie, *1775–1800*, Cambridge, Mass., Harvard University Press, 1979

—— *The Forbidden Best Sellers of Pre-Revolutionary France*, London, Harper-Collins, 1996

—— 'Writing News and Telling Stories', *Daedalus*, The Journal of the American Academy of Arts and Sciences, vol. 104, no. 2 (spring 1975)

Dart, G., *Rousseau, Robespierre and English Romanticism*, Cambridge, Cambridge University Press, 1999

Darwin, C., *The Expression of Emotion in Man and Animals*, London, Harper-Collins, 1998

Davenport-Hines, R., *Gothic: 400 Years of Excess, Evil and Ruin*, London, Fourth Estate, 1998

Davies, S., *Popular Opinion in Stalin's Russia: Terror, Propaganda and Dissent*, Cambridge, Cambridge University Press, 1997

Day, R., *Grand Inquisitor: Memoirs of a Broadcaster*, London, Weidenfeld & Nicolson, 1989

Dayan, D., & Katz, E., *Media Events: The Live Broadcasting of History*, Cambridge, Mass., Harvard University Press, 1992

De Waal, T., & Gall, C., *Chechnya: A Small Successful War*, London, Pan, 1997

Delamar, P., *The Complete Make-up Artist*, Basingstoke, Macmillan, 1995

Delaware, G., *The Size and Organization of Fan Clubs*, Cambridge, Mass., MIT Press, 1999

Department of Foreign Development, *TV and the Developing World*, London, HMSO, 2001

Department of Health, *Report on Flavouring Additives*, London, HMSO, 2002

Department for International Development, *Viewing the World*, London, HMSO, 2000

Department of Trade and Industry, reports of the *Survey of Retail Outlets in the UK, Annual Review*, London, HMSO, 1983–98

Derbes, A., *Picturing the Passion in Late Medieval Italy: Narrative Painting,*

Franciscan Ideologies and the Levant, Cambridge, Cambridge University Press, 1996

Desmond, A., & Moore, J., *Darwin*, London, Michael Joseph, 1991

Douglas, M., *Purity and Danger*, London, Routledge & Kegan Paul, 1966

Dunlop, J. B., *The Rise of Russia and the Fall of the Soviet Empire*, Princeton, Princeton University Press, 1993

—— *Russia Confronts Chechnya: Roots of a Separatist Conflict*, Cambridge, Cambridge University Press, 1998

—— 'Russia in Search of an Identity', in I. Bremner (ed.), *New States, New Politics: Building the Post-Soviet Nations*, Cambridge, Cambridge University Press, 1997

Elias, N., *The Civilising Process*, trans. E. Jephcott, Oxford, Blackwell, 1994

Ellis, F., *From Glasnost to the Internet: Russia's New Infosphere*, Basingstoke, Macmillan, 2000

—— *Vasily Grossman: The Genesis and Evolution of a Russian Heretic*, Oxford, Berg, 1994

Euripides, *Medea*, trans. J. Brooks, London, Methuen, 1988

European Institute for the Media, 'Report on Russian Broadcasting and the Legal Framework', in *Media Bulletin*, vol. 3, no. 2 (2003)

Evans-Pritchard, E., *Nuer Religion*, Oxford, Clarendon, 1956

Families and Bereavement: The Changing Role of the Hospital, London, University College Hospital and Camden & Islington National Health Service Trust, 2004

Farley, P., *The Conquest of Pain*, Michael Joseph, London, 1998

Feifel, H., *New Meanings of Death*, New York, McGraw-Hill, 1977

Figes, O., *Natasha's Dance: A Cultural History of Russia*, London, Allen Lane, 2002

Finaldi, G., *The Image of Christ*, London, National Gallery, 2000

Foucault, M., *The Birth of the Clinic*, London, Tavistock, 1973

—— *Discipline and Punish: The Birth of the Prison*, London, Allen Lane, 1977

—— *The History of Sexuality*, vol. 2: *The Use of Pleasure*, London, Penguin, 1985

Franks, S., 'Reporting Africa', *British Journalism Review*, April 2005

Freedman, L., *Britain and the Falklands War*, Oxford, Blackwell, 1988

Freud, E. L. (ed.), *The Letters of Sigmund Freud 1873–1939*, trans. T. & J. Stern, London, Hogarth Press, 1961

Freud, S., 'On Humour', in A. Dickson (ed.), *Sigmund Freud on Art and Literature: Jensen's Gradiva, Leonardo da Vinci and Other Works*, trans. J. Strachey, London, Penguin Books, 1985

—— *Jokes and Their Relation to the Unconscious*, trans. J. Strachey, The Pelican Freud Library, vol. 6, London, Penguin, 1974

—— 'Thoughts for the Times on War and Death' (1915), in J. Strachey (trans.

and ed.), *The Standard Edition of the Complete Psychological Works of Sigmund Freud*, vol. 14, London, Hogarth Press, 1957

Fukuyama, F., *The End of History and the Last Man*, London, Hamish Hamilton, 1992

Fussell, P., *Doing Battle: The Making of a Skeptic*, Boston, Little, Brown, 1996

—— *The Great War in Modern Memory*, Oxford, Oxford University Press, 1975

Galbraith, J. K., *The Culture of Contentment*, London, Penguin, 1993

Gallup, *Who Do We Trust and Why?*, London, Gallup, 2003

Garnham, N., *Emancipation and the Media*, Oxford, Oxford University Press, 2002

Gauntlett, D., & Hill, A., *TV Living: Television, Culture and Everyday Life*, London, Routledge, 1999

Gawande, A., *A Surgeon's Notes on an Imperfect Science*, New York, Metropolitan Books, 2002

Geertz, C., *The Interpretation of Cultures*, New York, Fontana, 1973

—— *Local Knowledge: Further Essays in Interpretive Anthropology*, New York, Basic Books, 1983

—— *Negara: The Theatre State in Nineteenth-Century Bali*, Princeton, Princeton University Press, 1980

Gellhorn, M., *The Face of War*, London, Virago, 1986

Gero, S., *Byzantine Iconoclasm during the Reign of Leo III*, Louvain, Corpus Scriptorum Christianorum Orientalium, 1973

Gibbon, E., *The Decline and Fall of the Roman Empire*, London, Dent, 1910

Gitlin, T., *Inside Prime Time*, London, Routledge, 1994

Glaister, J., *Medical Jurisprudence and Toxicology*, in collaboration with E. Rentoul, 10th edn, Edinburgh, E. & S. Livingstone, 1957

Glasgow University Media Group, *Bad News*, London, Routledge & Kegan Paul, 1976

Glover, J., *Causing Death and Saving Lives*, Harmondsworth, Penguin, 1977

—— *Humanity: A Moral History of the Twentieth Century*, London, Pimlico, 2001

Goffen, R., *Spirituality in Conflict: St Francis and Giotto's Bardi Chapel*, University Park, Pa., Penn State University Press, 1988

Goffman, E., *Asylums: Essays on the Social Situation of Mental Patients and Other Inmates*, Garden City, NY, Doubleday, 1961

—— *The Presentation of Self in Everyday Life*, Edinburgh, University of Edinburgh Social Research Centre, 1956

Goldberg, J., *James I and the Politics of English Literature*, Baltimore, Johns Hopkins University Press, 1983

Goldsworthy, S., 'The Balkan Atrocities and the Press', Ph.D. thesis, University of Westminster, in preparation, 2005

Gombrich, E. H., *The Story of Art*, London, Phaidon, 1995

Goody, J., *Cooking, Cuisine and Class*, Cambridge, Cambridge University Press, 1982

—— *Representations and Contradictions: Ambivalence towards Images, Theatre, Fiction, Relics and Sexuality*, Oxford, Blackwell, 1997

Gorer, G. E. S., *Death, Grief and Mourning in Contemporary Britain*, London, Cresset, 1965

Graber, D., McQuail, D., & Norris, P. (eds.), *The Politics of News: The News of Politics*, Washington, DC, Congregational Quarterly Press, 1998

Grant, M., *Gladiators*, London, Penguin, 1971

—— *Nero*, London, Weidenfeld & Nicolson, 1970

Grass, G., *The Flounder*, London, Secker & Warburg, 1978

Greetings from Grozny, New York, Channel 13, 1996

Grossman, V., *Life and Fate*, trans. P. Whitney, Evanston, Ill., Northwestern University Press, 1997

'Guidelines for the presentation of meat in-store', *Meat Trader*, April 2001

Gurevitch, M., 'The Global Newsroom', in P. Dahlgren & C. Sparks (eds.), *Communication and Citizenship: Journalism and the Public Sphere in the New Media Age*, London, Routledge, 1991

Haight, G. (ed.), *Selections from George Eliot's Letters*, New Haven, Yale University Press, 1985

Hallin, D. C., *The 'Uncensored War': The Media and Vietnam*, New York, Oxford University Press, 1986

Hampson, N., *The Life and Opinions of Maximilien Robespierre*, London, Duckworth, 1976

Handleman, S., *Comrade Criminal: The Theft of the Second Russian Revolution*, London, Michael Joseph, 1994

Hardmen, J., *Robespierre*, Longman, London, 1999

Hardy, B., *The Advantage of Lyric: Essays on Feeling in Poetry*, London, Athlone Press, 1977

Harris, R., *Gotcha! The Media, the Government and the Falklands Crisis*, London, Faber, 1983

Harrison, B. (ed.), *British Historical Statistics*, vols. 1 and 5, Oxford, Oxford University Press, 1964, 1999

Harrison, T., & Madge, C., *Britain by Mass-Observation*, London, Cresset, 1986

Haskell, F., *History and its Images*, New Haven, Yale University Press, 1993

—— *Taste and the Antique*, New Haven, Yale University Press, 1981

Hastings, M., *Going to Wars*, London, Macmillan, 2000

Haug, H., *Humanity for All: The Red Cross and the Red Crescent*, Geneva, Peter Haupt, 1993

Hennessy, P., Hughes, R., & Seaton, J. A., *Ready, Steady, Go! Labour into Office*, London, Fabian Society, 1997

Herrin, J., *The Formation of Christendom*, Oxford, Blackwell, 1987

—— *Women in Purple: Rulers of Medieval Byzantium*, London, Weidenfeld & Nicolson, 2001

Herrin, J., & Bryer, A. (eds.), *Iconoclasm: Papers Given at the Ninth Spring Symposium of Byzantine Studies, University of Birmingham, March 1975*, Birmingham, University of Birmingham Centre for Byzantine Studies, 1977

Hill, A., *Reality Television*, London, Routledge, 2004

Hirst, P. Q., *War and Power in the 21st Century: The State, Military Conflict and the International System*, Cambridge, Polity, 2001

Hobsbawm, E., *The Age of Extremes: The Short Twentieth Century, 1914–1991*, London, Michael Joseph, 1994

—— 'The British Standard of Living 1790–1850', *Economic History Review*, Second Series, no. 10 (1957), pp. 131–45

—— *Interesting Times: A Twentieth-Century Life*, London, Allen Lane, 2002

Hobsbawm, E., & Ranger, T. (eds.), *The Invention of Tradition*, Oxford, Oxford University Press, 1983

Homer, *The Iliad*, trans. R. Fitzgerald, Oxford, Oxford University Press, 1984

Hopkins, K., *Death and Renewal*, Cambridge, Cambridge University Press, 1983

Hosking, G., *Culture and the Media in Russia Today*, Basingstoke, Macmillan, 1989

Howells, C. A., *Love, Mystery and Misery*, London, Athlone Press, 1978

Human Rights Watch, *Charter*, Washington, DC, and London, Human Rights Watch, 1986

Hume, D., *A Treatise of Human Nature*, ed. L. A. Selby-Bigge, Oxford, Clarendon, 1896

Hynes, S., *The Soldier's Tale: Bearing Witness to Modern War*, London, Pimlico, 1998

Ife, B. W., *Reading and Fiction in the Golden Age of Spain: A Platonist Critique and Some Picaresque Replies*, Cambridge, Cambridge University Press, 1985

Ignatieff, M., *Empire-Lite*, London, Vintage, 2003

—— *The Needs of Strangers*, London, Hogarth, 1994

The Independent, house style rules, 2000

Industrial Safety Standards Agency, *The Meat Trade in the USA*, Department of Health and Safety, US Federal Government Report, Washington, DC, 2001

Institute for War and Peace Reporting, *Chechnya: The Bitter Conflict*, Bulletin no. 34, London, Institute for War and Peace Reporting, 1995

Institute for War and Peace Reporting reports at http://www.iwpr.net

Itule, B., & Anderson, A., *News Writing and Reporting for Today's Media*, 5th edn, New York, McGraw-Hill, 2000

James, H., 'Amnesty's First 10 Years', *The Observer*, 10 October 1971

James, W., *The Principles of Psychology*, vol. 2, New York, H. Holt & Co., 1890

—— *The Varieties of Religious Experience: A Study in Human Nature*, New York, Simon & Schuster, 1997

Jenkins, R., *Baldwin*, London, Macmilllan, 1995

Jennison, G., *Animals for Show and Pleasure in Ancient Rome*, Manchester, Manchester University Press, 1937

Johnson, J., 'The Future of Computer Games – Welcome to the Feelies!', *The Guardian*, 14 January 2002

Journalists Disappear, Moscow, Glasnost Defence Foundation, 2000

Journalists in Danger: Recent Russian Wars, New York and London, Freedom Forum, 1998

Journalists in the Frontline, Washington, DC, Freedom Forum, 2001

Junger, W., *Character, Emotion, Action! Writing for Television*, ed. J. Freidman, New York, Anchor Books, 1996

Juvenal, *The Sixteen Satires*, trans. P. Green, London, Penguin, 1998

Kaiver, R., *Looking Forward to Cancer Pain Relief for All: The Secret of Pain*, Oxford, World Health Organization, 1997

Kaldor, M., *New and Old Wars: Organised Violence in a Global Era*, Cambridge, Polity, 1999

Kehoe, V. J. R.,*The Technique of the Professional Make-up Artist*, London, 1995

Kellner, D., *Media Culture: Cultural Studies*, London, Routledge, 1997

Kenny, A. J. P., *Action, Emotion and Will*, London, Routledge, 1963

Kermode, F., *Forms of Attention*, Chicago, University of Chicago Press, 1985

Khlebnikov, P., *Godfather of the Kremlin: Boris Berezovsky and the Looting of Russia*, New York, Harcourt, 2000

—— *The Selling of War. Media Coverage and the Chechen War*, Geneva, Creda European Institute for Media, 1996

Kieckhefer, R., *Unquiet Souls*, Chicago, University of Chicago Press, 1984

Kirtaoze, N., *Chechen Lullaby*, Moscow, Unite Documentaries, 1999

Kouchner, B., *Saving Lives: Médecins Sans Frontières*, London, Macmillan, 1997

Larson, E., *A Flame in Barbed Wire: The Story of Amnesty International*, London, Muller, 1978

Lawrence, D. H., *A Propos of Lady Chatterley's Lover*, London, Phoenix, 1938

Layard, R., 'Russia's Future', *Economic Review*, vol. 52, no. 3 (1998)

Le Gros Cork, F., & Titmuss, R. M., *Our Food Problem and its Relation to our National Defences*, Harmondsworth, Penguin, 1939

Lecky, W. E. H., *A History of European Morals from Augustus to Charlemagne*, London, Longmans, Green & Co., 1911

Lieven, A., *America Right or Wrong*, London, HarperCollins, 2004

—— *The Baltic Revolution: Estonia, Latvia, Lithuania and the Path to Independence*, New Haven, Yale University Press, 1993

Lifton, R. J., *The Broken Connection: Death and the Continuity of Life*, New York, Simon & Schuster, 1979

—— *Death in Life: Survivors of Hiroshima*, Chapel Hill, NC, University of North Carolina Press, 1991

—— *The Genocidal Mentality: Nazi Holocaust and the Nuclear Threat*, London, Macmillan, 1991

Lindley, R., *And Finally: The Last Days of ITN*, London, Politico's, 2005

Linklater, M., 'Harry Evans's Good Times', *Prospect*, December 2001

Livestock Age and Slaughtering Statistics, London, HMSO, 1910–27, 1983

Lloyd, J., *Rebirth of a Nation: An Anatomy of Russia*, London, Michael Joseph, 1998

—— *Re-emerging Russia*, London, Foreign Policy Centre, 2000

—— *The Power and the Story: What the Media Have Done to Our Politics*, London, Constable, 2004

Lloyd, J., & Seaton, J. (eds.), *What Can be Done? Making Politics and the Media Better*, Oxford, Blackwell, 2005

Lorenz, J. V., *News: Reporting and Writing for Print, Broadcast and Public Relations*, Boston, Allyn & Bacon, 1995

Loyd, A., *My War Gone By, I Miss It So*, London, Doubleday, 1999

Lukács, G., *History and Class Consciousness*, London, Merlin Press, 1971

Lutz, C. A., 'Engendered Emotion', in C. A. Lutz & L. Abu-Lughod (eds.), *The Language and Politics of Emotion*, Cambridge, Cambridge University Press, 1990

—— *Unnatural Emotions: Everyday Sentiments on a Micronesian Atoll and their Challenge to Western Theory*, Chicago, University of Chicago Press, 1988

McAuley, M., *Russia's Politics of Uncertainty*, Cambridge, Cambridge University Press, 1997

McCullin, D., *Unreasonable Behaviour: An Autobiography*, with L. Chester, London, Cape, 1990

McNair, B., *Glasnost, Perestroika and the Soviet Media*, London, Routledge, 1991

—— *Images of the Enemy: Reporting the New Cold War*, London, Routledge, 1998

Magnus, W., *Entertainment and Violence in Ancient Rome*, Studia Graeca et Latina LVI, Göteborg, University of Göteborg Press, 1992

Maguire, H., *Art and Eloquence in Byzantium*, Princeton, Princeton University Press, 1981

—— *The Icons of Their Bodies: Saints and Their Images in Byzantium*, Princeton, Princeton University Press, 1996

—— *Magic and Byzantium*, Cambridge, Cambridge University Press, 2000

—— *Rhetoric, Nature and Magic in Byzantine Art*, Aldershot, Ashgate, 1998

Maitland, S., 'Death in Kosovo', *The Independent*, 15 September 1993

Mango, C., *Studies on Constantinople*, Aldershot, Variorum Reprints, 1993

Mannheim, K., *Essays on the Sociology of Knowledge*, London, Routledge, 1997

Manoff, R. K., & Schudson, M. (eds.), *Reading the News*, New York, Pantheon Books, 1987

Martial, *Martial's Epigrams*, ed. P. Howell, London, Athlone Press, 1980

—— *Martial's Epigrams: De spectaculis*, vols. 1 and 2, ed. D. R. Shackleton-Bailey, Cambridge, Mass., Harvard University Press, 1993

Marvin, C., & Ingle, D. W., *Blood Sacrifice and the Nation: Totem Rituals and the American*, Cambridge, Cambridge University Press, 1999

Mazower, M., *Dark Continent: Europe's Twentieth Century*, London, Allen Lane, 1998

—— 'The Strange Triumph of Human Rights: Hitler, the UN and the Making of the Post-War World', inaugural lecture, Birkbeck College, 31 January 2002

Mazzini, G., *The Duties of Man and Other Essays*, ed. T. Jones, London, Dent, 1907

Meat Marketing Board, *Meat Movement Regulations*, London, HMSO, 1967

Meat Marketing Review, no. 3 (1957)

Meat Trade News, vol. 27, no. 3 (2000)

Melzack, R., *Handbook of Pain Assessment*, London, Guiford, 1992

Melzack, R., & Wall, P. D., *The Challenge of Pain*, 3rd edn, London, Penguin, 1982

Merridale, C., *Night of Stone: Death and Memory in Russia*, London, Granta, 2000

Meyrowitz, J., *No Sense of Place: The Impact of Electronic Media on Social Behaviour*, New York, Oxford University Press, 1985

Mickiewicz, E., *Changing Channels: Television and the Struggle for Power in Russia*, New York, Oxford University Press, 1997

Milgram, S., *Obedience to Authority: An Experimental View*, London, Tavistock, 1974

Mill, J. S., *Autobiography and Literary Essays*, ed. J. M. Robson & J. Stillinger, Toronto, University of Toronto Press, 1981

—— *On Liberty*, Oxford, Oxford University Press, 1975

Miller, S. E., & Trenin, D., *The Russian Military: Power and Politics*, Cambridge, Mass., MIT Press, 2004

Millet, G., *Byzantine Art*, trans. H. Jennings, London, Macmillan, 1975

Ministry of Agriculture and Food, *Domestic Food Consumption and Expenditure: Annual Report of the National Food Survey*, London, HMSO, 1964

—— *The Urban Working Class Diet*, London, HMSO, 1949.

Moeller, S., *Compassion Fatigue: How the Media Sell Disease, Famine, War and Death*, London, Routledge, 1999

Monmonier, M., 'Mapping the American World: College Students' Geographical Understanding', in M. Monmonier (ed.), *Maps and Public Understanding*, Chicago, University of Chicago Press, 2005

—— *Maps with the News: The Development of American Journalistic Cartography*, Chicago, University of Chicago Press, 1989

Montesquieu, *The Collected Essays of Montesquieu*, London, Dent, 1958

Morley, D., 'Domestic Relations', in J. Lull, *World Families Watch TV*, London, Sage, 1988

—— *Family Television: Cultural Power and Domestic Leisure*, London, Routledge, 1988

—— *Television, Audiences and Cultural Studies*, London, Routledge, 1992

Mosse, G., *Fallen Soldiers: Reshaping the Memory of the World Wars*, Oxford, Oxford University Press, 1990

Mulgan, G., *Communication and Control*, Oxford, Blackwell, 1991

Nicholson, M., *A Measure of Danger: Memoirs of a British War Correspondent*, London, HarperCollins, 1991

Nilsson, L., *A Child is Born*, New York, Doubleday, 1990

—— 'The Miracle of New Life', *Life* magazine, 23 July 1965

Norris, P., 'Revolution? What Revolution?', in J. S. Nye (ed.), *Governance.com: Democracy in the Information Age*, Washington, DC, Brookings Institution Press, 2003, pp. 59–81

Nussbaum, M. C., 'Emotion and Social Interaction', in C. A. Lutz & L. Abu-Lughod (eds.), *The Language and Politics of Emotion*, Cambridge, Cambridge University Press, 1990

—— 'Emotions, Women and Capabilities', in M. C. Nussbaum & J. Glover (eds.), *Women, Culture and Development*, Oxford, Oxford University Press, 1995

—— *The Fragility of Goodness*, Cambridge, Cambridge University Press, 2001

—— *Love's Knowledge*, New York, Oxford University Press, 1990

—— *Passion and Perception*, Cambridge, Cambridge University Press, 1993

Nuttall, A. D., *Why Does Tragedy Give Pleasure?*, Oxford, Clarendon, 1996

Nye, J. S., *Democracy in the Information Age: Visions of Government in the Twenty-first Century*, Cambridge, Mass., Harvard University Press, 2003

Nye, J. S., Zelikow, P. D., & King, D. C. (eds.), *Why People Don't Trust Government: Visions of Government in the Twenty-first Century*, Cambridge, Mass., Harvard University Press, 1997

Nye, R., 'The End of the Duel', in P. Spierenburg (ed.), *Men and Violence: Gender, Honor and its Rituals in Modern Europe and America*, Columbus, Ohio, Ohio State University Press, 1998

O'Neill, O., *Bounds of Justice*, Cambridge, Cambridge University Press, 2000

—— *Faces of Hunger: An Essay on Poverty, Justice and Development*, London, Allen & Unwin, 1986

Parkinson, B., & Coleman, A. (eds.), *Emotion and Motivation*, London, Longman, 1995

Parris, W., *Cancer Pain Management*, Boston and Oxford, Butterworth, 1997

Pasternak, B., *Dr Zhivago*, trans. M. Hayward, London, Penguin, 1988

Paxton, F., *Christianizing Death: The Creation of a Ritual Process in Early Medieval Europe*, Ithaca, NY, Cornell University Press, 1990

Peacock, F., *Tradition*, London, Merton Press, 1895

Pedelty, M., *War Stories: The Culture of Foreign Correspondents*, London, Routledge, 1995

Perkins, J., *The Suffering Self: Pain and Narrative Representation in Early Christianity*, London, Routledge, 1994

Perren, R., *The Meat Trade in Britain 1840–1914*, London, Routledge & Kegan Paul, 1978

Peters, J. D., *Speaking into the Air: A History of the Idea of Communication*, Chicago, University of Chicago Press, 1999

—— 'Witnessing', *Media, Culture and Society*, vol. 23 (November 2004)

Petrenko, Y., *Public Opinion Fund, 1993–5, Television and Public Opinion*, Moscow, Carnegie Endowment, 1996

Petronius, *Satyricon*, trans. P. G. Walsh, Oxford, Clarendon, 1996

Pigshead and Pease Pudding, Waltham Forest, Waltham Forest Workshop, Oral History Project, 1985

Pimlott, B., *Harold Wilson*, London, HarperCollins, 1992

—— *Hugh Dalton*, London, Cape, 1985

—— 'The Media and the Monarchy', in J. A. Seaton (ed.), *Politics and the Media: Harlots and Prerogative at the Turn of the Millennium*, Oxford, Blackwell, 1998

—— *The Queen: The Jubilee Edition*, London, HarperCollins, 2001

—— 'Should the Arts be Popular?', Lloyds TSB Forum, Royal Academy lecture, 2001

Plass, P., *The Game of Death in Ancient Rome: Arena Sport and Political Suicide*, Madison, Wis., University of Wisconsin Press, 1995

Plath, S., 'The Scope of Writing', *Triquarterly*, no. 7 (fall 1966)

Plato, *The Last Days of Socrates: Euthyphro; The Apology; Crito; Phaedo*, trans. H. Tredennick & H. Tarrant, London, Penguin, 1993

—— *The Republic*, ed. T. Irwin, London, Everyman, 1993

Pliny the Elder, *Natural History: A Selection*, trans. and intro. J. F. Healy, London, Penguin, 1971

Politkovskaya, A., *A Dirty War: A Russian Reporter in Chechnya*, trans. and ed. J. Crowfoot, London, Harvill, 2001

—— *Putin's Russia*, London, Harvill, 2004

—— *A Small Corner of Hell: Dispatches from Chechnya*, trans. A. Burry, Chicago, University of Chicago Press, 2003

Pork Rearing, London, HMSO, 1995

Potter, D. S., *Literary Texts and the Roman Historian*, London, Routledge, 1999

Price, M. E., 'The Market for Loyalties in Electronic Media', in R. G. Noll & M. E. Price (eds.), *A Communications Cornucopia: Markle Foundation Essays on Information Policy*, Washington, DC, Brookings Institution Press, 1998

—— *Television, the Public Sphere and National Identity*, Oxford, Clarendon, 1995

Pushkin, A., & Lermontov, M., *Narrative Poems*, trans. C. Johnston, London, Bodley Head, 1984

Putnam, R., *Bowling Alone: The Collapse and Revival of American Community*, New York, Simon & Schuster, 2000

Quigley, C., *The Corpse: A History*, London, McFarland & Co., 1996

Quintilian, *The Institutio Oratoria*, vol. 3, trans. H. E. Butler, London, Heinemann, 1922

—— *Oration*, ed. H. E. Butler, London, Haskins, 1971

Radcliffe-Brown, A. R., 'On Joking Relationships in Africa', *Journal of the Institute of African Language and Custom*, vol. 13 (1940)

Rantanen, T., *Foreign News in Imperial Russia: The Relationship between International and Russian News Agencies, 1856–1914*, Helsinki, Suomalainen Tiedeakatemia, 1990

Rawls, J., *A Theory of Justice*, Oxford, Oxford University Press, 1999

Reith, J., *Broadcast over Britain*, London, Cassell, 1926

Report of the Committee on the Future of Broadcasting (the Pilkington Report), London, HMSO, 1962

'Report of the Committee on Modern Make-up for the Movie Industry', *Journal of the Society of Motion Picture Engineers*, vol. 10, no. 4 (1963)

Report of the Committee on the Use of Video Recordings in Identification, Manchester, National Police and Mortuary Practices Board, 1996

Report on Massacres in Afghanistan: A Human Rights Watch and Eyewitness Account, no. 2, London, Human Rights Watch, 1998

Reporting Chechnya, Russian American Press Information Center, Moscow, 1996

Reporting the Holocaust: Fifty Years of Press Stories, New Haven, Shorenstein Center for the Study of Press and Politics, Kennedy School of Government, Harvard University, 1999

'Reporting the World', Freedom Forum workshop, 17 October 2001

Rey, R., *The History of Pain*, Cambridge, Mass., Harvard University Press, 1995

Richardson, J., *Death and its Signs*, London, Macmillan, 1974

Richardson, R., *Death, Dissection and the Destitute*, London, Penguin, 1989

Ries, N., *Russian Talk: Culture and Conversation during Perestroika*, Ithaca, NY, Cornell University Press, 1997

Riesman, D., *The Lonely Crowd: A Study of Changing American Character*, New Haven, Yale University Press, 1951

Rifkin, J., *Beyond Beef: The Rise and Fall of the Cattle Culture*, New York, Dutton, 1993

Ritvo, H., *The Animal Estate*, London, Penguin, 1987

Rixon, D., *The History of Meat Trading*, Nottingham, Nottingham University Press, 2000

Roberts, S., Smith, S., & Bryce, C., *Children at Risk? Safety as a Social Value*, Buckingham, Open University Press, 1995

Robins, K., *Beyond Imagined Community*, London, Goldsmith's College, 2001

Robins, K., & Aksoy, A., 'Thinking across Spaces: Transnational Television from Turkey', *European Journal of Cultural Studies*, vol. 3, no. 3 (2000)

Rochat, F., & Mogdigliani, M., 'Captain Greunnengerr', in T. Blass (ed.), *Obedience to Authority: Current Perspectives on the Milgram Paradigm*, Mahwah, NJ, Lawrence Erlbaum Associates, 2000, pp. 15–32

Roeder, G., *The Censored War: American Visual Experience during World War Two*, New Haven, Yale University Press, 1993

Romano, C., 'The Grisly Truth about Bare Facts', in R. K. Manoff & M. Schudson (eds.), *Reading the News*, New York, Pantheon Books, 1987

Ross, E., *The Grief of God: Images of the Suffering of Jesus in Late Medieval England*, Oxford, Oxford University Press, 1997

Rothschild, M., *Animals and Man*, Oxford Romanes Lecture, Oxford, Oxford University Press, 1986

Russia and the Chechen Wars, Moscow, Carnegie Foundation for Peace, 2000

Russia/Chechnya Mortality during Sweep Operations, London, Human Rights Watch, 2002

Sabato, L., *Feeding Frenzy*, New York, Free Press, 1991

Sabato, L., & Simpson, G., *Dirty Little Secrets: The Persistence of Corruption in American Politics*, New York, Times Books, 1996

Sahlins, M., *Culture and Practical Reason*, Chicago, University of Chicago Press, 1977

Saleci, R., *The Spoils of Freedom: Psychoanalysis and Feminism after the Fall of Socialism*, London, Routledge, 1994

Sandberg, S. (ed.), *Hyperactivity Disorders in Childhood*, Cambridge, Cambridge University Press, 1996

Saunders, C., *Hospice and Palliative Care*, Sevenoaks, Edward Arnold, 1990

Scannell, P., *Broadcast Talk*, London, Sage, 1991

—— *Radio, Television and Everyday Life: A Phenomenological Approach*, Oxford, Blackwell, 1996

Scarry, E., *The Body in Pain: The Making and Unmaking of the World*, Oxford, Oxford University Press, 1985

Schell, J., *The Real War: The Classic Reporting on the Vietnam War*, London, Corgi, 1989

Schlesinger, P., *Reporting Crime*, Oxford, Clarendon, 1994

Schönbon, C., *God's Human Face: The Christ Icon*, San Francisco, Ignatius, 1994

Schudson, M., *Advertising: The Uneasy Persuasion, its Dubious Impact on American Society*, New York, Basic Books, 1984

—— *The Good Citizen, a History of American Civic Life*, Cambridge, Mass., Harvard University Press, 2000

—— *Origins of the Ideal of Objectivity in the Professions: Studies in the History of American Journalism and American Law*, New York, Garland, 1990

—— *The Power of News*, Cambridge, Mass., Harvard University Press, 1995

—— *The Sociology of News*, New York, Norton, 2003

Schyler, T., 'Iraq: Why We Went to War', *New York Review of Books*, 2 October 2004

Scott, R., *War in Iraq*, London, Profile, 2002

Seaton, J. A., 'The BBC and the Holocaust', in J. A. Seaton & B. Pimlott (eds.), *The Media in British Politics*, London, Longman, 1987

—— 'A Fresh Look at Freedom of Speech', in J. A. Seaton (ed.), *Politics and the Media: Harlots and Prerogative at the Turn of the Millennium*, Oxford, Blackwell, 1998

—— 'The Holocaust', in J. A. Seaton & B. Pimlott (eds.), *The Media in British Politics*, London, Longman, 1987

—— 'Is Impartial News an Endangered Species?', in J. Lloyd & J. Seaton (eds.), *What Can be Done? Making Politics and the Media Better*, Oxford, Blackwell, 2005

—— 'Public, Private and the Media: Where Do We Draw the Line?', *Political Quarterly*, vol. 74, no. 2 (2003)

Sell, M., *Preparing Meat for the Family*, London, Pearson Press, 1921

Sen, A., & Drèze, J., *Hunger and Public Action*, Oxford, Clarendon, 1989

Seneca, *Moral and Political Essays*, trans. and ed. J. M. Cooper & J. F. Procope, Cambridge, Cambridge University Press, 1995

—— *Seneca in English*, ed. D. Share, London, Penguin, 1998

Sennett, R., *The Fall of Public Man*, New York, Vintage, 1973

Serpell, J., *Animals and Human Society*, London, Routledge, 1994

—— *In the Company of Animals: A Study of Human–Animal Relationships*, Cambridge, Cambridge University Press, 1996

Seton-Watson, H., *The Russian Empire: 1801–1917*, Oxford, Clarendon, 1988

Seymour-Ure, C., 'Are the Broadsheets Becoming Unhinged?', in J. A. Seaton (ed.), *Politics and the Media: Harlots and Prerogative at the Turn of the Millennium*, Oxford, Blackwell, 1998

—— *The Political Impact of Mass Media*, London, Constable, 1974

Shawcross, W., *Allies: The US, Britain and Europe and the War in Iraq*, London, Atlantic, 2004

Shils, E., *The Calling of Education*, Chicago, University of Chicago Press, 1997

Silverman, L., *Tortured Subjects: Pain and Truth in France*, Chicago and London, University of Chicago Press, 2001

Simpson, A. W. B., *Cannibalism and the Common Law: The Story of the Tragic Last Voyage of the Mignonette and the Strange Legal Proceedings to which it Gave Rise*, Chicago, University of Chicago Press, 1984

Smith, A., *The Theory of Moral Sentiments*, ed. D. D. Raphael & A. L. Macfie, Oxford, Clarendon, 1976

Solzhenitsyn, A., *The Gulag Archipelago: An Experiment in Literary Investigation*, London, Collins, 1986

—— 'One Word of Truth', in *Collected Works*, Sphere Books, London, 1972

Sorokin, P., *The Crisis of Our Age*, London, One World, 1992

Southern, R. W., *Saint Anselm: A Portrait in a Landscape*, Cambridge, Cambridge University Press, 1990

—— *The Making of the Middle Ages*, London, Hutchinson, 1953

—— *Robert Grosseteste: The Growth of the English Mind in Medieval Europe*, Oxford, Clarendon, 1986

Sparks, C., 'Post-Communist Media in Transition', in J. Corner, P. Schlesinger & R. Silverstone, *International Media Research: A Critical Survey*, London, Routledge, 1997

Spivey, N., *Enduring Creation: Art, Pain and Fortitude*, London, Thames and Hudson, 2001

—— *Understanding Greek Sculpture: Ancient Meanings, Modern Readings*, London, Thames and Hudson, 1996

The Standardization of Motion Picture Make-up, Hollywood, Max Factor, 1937

Stannard, D. E., *The Puritan Way of Death: A Study in Religion, Culture and Social Change*, New York, Oxford University Press, 1997

Starr, D. P., *Blood: An Epic History of Medicine and Commerce*, London, Little, Brown, 1999

Steinberg, O., *The Sexuality of Christ in Renaissance Art and the Modern Oblivion*, New York, Pantheon, 1983

Strack, S., (ed.), *Death and the Search for Meaning*, Northvale, NJ, Aronson, 1997

Stull, D., & Broadway, M., *Anyway You Cut It: Meat Processing in Small Town America*, Lawrence, Kan., University Press of Kansas, 1995

Tacitus, *Dialogue on Oratory*, trans. and ed. R. Mayer, Cambridge, Cambridge University Press, 2001

Tertullian, *Apologeticus; De spectaculis*, trans. T. R. Glover, London, Heinemann, 1931

—— *Apologia*, trans. A. Souter, intro. J. Mayor, Cambridge, Cambridge University Press, 1917

—— *Disciplinary and Moral Works*, trans. M. Massey, Cambridge, Cambridge University Press, 1982

—— *The Octavius of Minucius Felix*, trans. G. H. Rendall, London, Heinemann, 1931

—— *Tertullian English Selections: Christian and Pagan Witness in the Roman Empire*, ed. R. P. Sider, Washington, DC, Catholic University Press, 2001

Thompson, J. B., *The Media and Modernity*, Cambridge, Polity, 1995

—— *Political Scandal*, Cambridge, Polity, 2000

Thompson, J. M., *Robespierre* (1935), Oxford, Blackwell, 1988

Thompson, W. F., *The Image of War: Pictorial Reporting of the American Civil War*, London, Louisiana State University Press, 1996

Titmuss, R. M., *The Gift Relationship: From Human Blood to Social Policy*, London, Allen & Unwin, 1970

Tolstoy, L., 'The Woodfelling: A Cadet's Story', in *How Much Land Does a Man Need? and Other Stories*, London, Penguin, 1993

Tsagarousianou, R., *Cyberdemocracy*, London, Routledge, 1998

Tumber, H., *Media Power, Professionals and Policies*, London, Routledge, 2000

Turner, J., *Filming History: The Memoirs of a Newsreel Cameraman*, London, British Universities and Film and Video Council, 2002

Twitchell, J. B., *Dreadful Pleasures*, Oxford, Blackwell, 1985

Urban, J. B., & Solovei, V., *Russia's Communists at the Crossroads*, Boulder, Col., Westview, 1997

Vachnadze, G. N., *Secrets of Journalism in Russia: Mass Media under Gorbachev and Yeltsin*, Commack, NY, Nova, 1992

Van Creveld, M., *On Future War*, London, Brassey's, 1991

Van Gennep, A., *Rites of Passage*, trans. M. Vizedon & G. L. Caffee, London, Routledge & Kegan Paul, 1909

Van Os, H., *The Art of Devotion in the Late Middle Ages in Europe, 1300–1500*, London, Merrel Holberton, 1994

Van Zoonen, L., *Feminist Media Studies*, London, Sage, 1994

Veyne, P., *Bread and Circuses: Historical Sociology and Political Pluralism*, trans. B. Pearce, London, Allen Lane, 1990

Virilio, P., *War and the Cinema: The Logistics of Perception*, London, Verso, 1989

Walsh, J., *The Meat Machine: The Inside Story of the Meat Business*, London, Columbus, 1986

Walters, R. C., *Broadcast Writing: Principles and Practice*, 5th edn, New York, McGraw-Hill, 1994

Webb, B., *The Diary of Beatrice Webb*, vol. 1: *Glitter Around and Darkness Within, 1873–1892*, ed. N. & J. MacKenzie, London, Virago, 1982

—— vol. 4: *1924–1943, The Wheel of Life*, ed. N. & J. MacKenzie, London, Virago, 1985

Weitzmann, K., *Art in the Medieval West and its Contacts with Byzantium*, London, Variorum Reprints, 1982

Wenders, W., *Emotion Pictures*, London, Faber, 1989

Whelan, R., *Robert Capra: The Defiant Photographer*, London, Phaidon, 2001

Whetham, E. H., *Beef Cattle and Sheep, 1910–1940: A Description of the Production and Marketing of Beef Cattle and Sheep in Great Britain from the Early Twentieth Century to the Second World War*, Cambridge, University of Cambridge Department of Land Economy, 1976

White, T., *How to Write News*, Boston, Mass., Focal, 2002

Wills, G., *Foreign News in America*, Cambridge, Mass., Shorenstein Center for the Study of Press and Politics, Kennedy School of Government, Harvard University, 2003

Winner, D., *Peter Benenson*, London, Exley, 1991

Winston, B., *Damn Lies and Documentaries*, London, British Film Institute, 2000

Woolf, V., 'On Being Ill', in *Collected Essays*, vol. 4, London, Chatto & Windus, 1967

Writing News, New York, CNN, 2000

Wyman, M., *Public Opinion in Post-Communist Russia*, London, Macmillan, 1996

Yates, F., *The Art of Memory*, Harmondsworth, Penguin, 1978

YouGov, *Public Trust*, London, YouGov, 2003

Zimbardo, P. G., *The Stanford Prison Experiment*, Stanford, Stanford University Press, 1985

Index

Page numbers in italics refer to illustrations.

Aberfan disaster 228
advertising, media pressures of 81
Afghanistan
  1998 massacre report 82
  Coalition war 230
  Soviet war 155, 163
  US operations 143
Agatha, St, martyrdom 127
Aids
  mortality from 276
  political will needed 276–7
Allen, Tim 147
Amnesty International
  Chechen War 156
  information dissemination 82
  precepts 81–2
Androcles, and the lion 60
Anselm, St, nature of the divine 112–13
anti-globalization demonstrations 266
anti-hunt demonstrations *104*
anti-war reporting 222
Arafat, Yasser 27, 28
architecture, as public expression 108
Arena chapel, Padua, Giotto's frescos
  107–8
Arendt, Hannah 179, 247, 292
Ariès, Philippe, 182, 209, 228
Aristotle 251, 284
Ash, Timothy Garton 146, 195
Asquith, Herbert 210
attention
  crisis of public 253
  news requirements 249–51

attention disorders 247
attention spans, audiences 246–8, 289
audience research, media consumption
  10–11
audiences
  assumed consent 240–41
  attention of 246–8
  judgements by 230
  media trust by 280
  passive listening 247
  shocking of 219–21
Auguet, Roland 68
Augustine of Hippo, St 52, 191
Austen, Jane, *Mansfield Park* 243
authority, acceptance of 278–80

'bad' death 183, 192–3, 195–6, 229
  media reactions 204–5
Bakhtin, Mikhail 177
Baldwin, Stanley, 'power without
  responsibility' speech 42
Bali, funerals 213
Balkan atrocities (1880s), public
  attitudes to 43, 45
Barish, Jonas 243
Bart, St, effects of cold 116
Barton, Carlin 55, 69
BBC
  attacks on 45
  programme commissioning 133
  religion within 87
  reporters 188
Bedford, John Russell, 6th Duke of 7

beef
  consumption of 5–6, 8–9, 9
  livestock breeding 6–8, 7
Bell, Martin 217, 218
Belsen liberation 45
Belting, Hans 92, 93, 107, 109
Benedict, St 107
Benenson, Peter 81
Bernard of Clairvaux, St, on Christ's
    humanity 109
Beslan school siege 165, 179, 242
Bieber, Martin 62
Binski, Paul 188
Binyon, Lawrence, To the Fallen 210
blame culture 44
blood
  child's attitude to 29
  film industry 20–21, 21
  hiding 18
  in meat industry 18–19
  newspaper portrayal 19, 20, 22–3
  pathology 26
  symbolism of 26–8, 29
blood donation 23–5, 24
Blunkett, David 33
'body bags', effect of images 143, 201–2
Boltanski, Luc 281
Bonaventure, St 110
Borg, Alan 205
Bourdieu, Pierre, 8, 14, 15
Bourke, Joanna 187
Braudel, Fernand 8
'breaking news' xviii
Bridget of Sweden, St 120
Brighton, hotel bombing 215
British Medical Association 240
broadcast journalists, public attitudes
    towards 34
broadcasting see television
Brothers, Caroline 223
Brown, Peter 69
BSE crisis 17
burial rituals
  Christianity 191–2
  funerals 192
Burke, Peter 213
Buruma, Ian 186

butchers
  children of 36
  code of honour 45
  historical attitudes towards 35–8
  historical standing 39
  skills 3–6, 5
  social standing 11, 38
butcher's shop, model 30
butchery
  see also meat
  adolescent attitudes 2
  anonymity of modern 38–9
  'assembly line' 39–40, 40
  beef 5–9, 7, 9
  blood 18–19, 29–30
  childhood attitudes 1–2, 29
  hygiene 29–30
  meat rationing 9–10
  metaphor for violence 2
  Royal Smithfield Show 11
  slaughtering 40–41, 40
  supermarkets 38
Butler, Lady Elizabeth 206
Bynum, Catherine Walker 113
Byzantine Empire
  see also icons
  fall of 99
  Orthodox tradition 95–6

cancer, palliative care 130
Cannadine, David 209–10
cannibalism, public attitudes to 273–4
Capra, Robert 231
car accidents, children 276, 277
Carnegie Foundation 171, 175
casualty levels
  acceptable 212
  anxiety over 144
  Chechen wars 170, 171
  government attitudes to 141
  public acceptance of 141
  World War I 193
Catherine of Siena, St 120
celebrity reputations 32
Cenotaph, Whitehall 207–8, 209
censorship
  decreasing 262–3, 262

and emotions 252
and Freedom of Information 252
impact on military 261
Indonesian defence 252
Chechen wars
armaments in 162–3
casualty levels 170, 171
causes 167–8
Chechen successes 166
dangers to journalists 168–9
executions 128
first 155, 157–8, 162–3, 171, 174
Grozny bombings 161, 164
human rights in 164
public opinion 167
real-time news 164–5
reporting 163–5
and Russian media 158–9
second 155, 167–9, 171
Western reporting 176
Western views of 155–6
Chechnya
anarchy in 160–61, 168
Beslan school siege 165, 179
criminal gangs from 162
deportations from 161
deportations to 160
geopolitics of oil 161
hospital siege 165
internal conflict 168
Russian isolationist policies 161–2
topography 160
'chequebook' journalism 46
children
attention disorders 247
attitudes to blood 29
attitudes towards butchers 36
attitudes to butchery 1–2
compassion for 257–8
informed medical consent 240
Iraq War 100, 132
road-accident mortality 276, 277
Vietnam War 131, 131
in wars 100, 131–2, 131
World War II evacuees returning 236
Christ
see also Crucifixion

case against representation 98
evolution of images 93–5
in majesty 106
Man of Sorrows 112
reverence to images of 97
as 'The Good Shepherd' 90, 91
'true' images 94, 95, 96–7, 98
Christian martyrs
accounts of 72
Agatha, St 127
Catherine of Siena, St 120
and divine comfort 114
Dorothy of Mantua, St 121
Erasmus, St 119
Forty Martyrs of Sebaste 116,
117–18, 117
George, St 114, 116
Henry Suso, St 120–21
imagery 85, 86–7, 89–92
impact of 73–4
intercessionary powers 100
Perpetua, St 72–3, 73
Polonius, St 75
resurrection 74–6, 127–8
Roman games 71, 72–4, 78,
84
self-punishment 120–21
torture 114, 116
Christianity
see also Crucifixion; icons;
Nonconformists
burial rituals 191–2
and classical statuary 97
depictions of suffering 84–5
martyrology 72, 88
salvation 105, 107
scriptural authority 87, 88
spiritual understanding 107
suffering in 87, 88–9, 105, 108–9
Cicero, M. Tullius 56, 67
civilians
see also children
and combatants 222
increased risks to 141
war casualties 141, 193
Claudius I, Roman games 60
clichés, news 230–31

CNN
  Iraq War 248
  style sheets 251
Cold War, behavioural constraints 135,
  145
Coleman, Katherine 62
Colosseum, Rome 54, 59, 67
combatants, and civilians 222
commercial pressures, news production
  81
Commodus 65
common man, death of 211, *211*
communication
  and globalization 266–7
  and loss of distance 269
  telegraph 269
compassion
  and democracies 129–30
  emotional response 258
  and empathy 285–6
  fatigue 277
  and sense of self 265
competition, within media xvii
computer games
  anxieties about 248
  as comparative material 272
conflicts *see* wars
Connell, Ian, 32
Constantine V, iconoclasm 96–7
controls on journalism and television
  240–41
Cooper, Sir Frank 142, 144
corpses
  exhumation 227
  media depictions 225
  persons present with 225–6, 227
  unburied 191–2
  viewing traditions 203–4
couch-potato syndrome, death 220
Crapanzano, Vincent 48
Crouch, Colin 293
Crucifixion
  centrality of 86, 109
  depictions of pain 109–110
  'Doubting' Thomas 127
  early depictions 105, *106*
  imagery 84–5, 100–101, 105, *106*

imago pietus 109
  Mary's reactions to 113–14, *115*, 129
  passionate responses to 113
  salvation through 85–6
  symbolism of 99
  understanding of 107–8
  voluntary nature of 113
cruelty, culture of 51
cultural differences
  entertainment choices 137–8
  erosion of 134

Daily Mail 15, 44
Darnton, Robert 140, 244, 270
Darwin, Charles, pain experiments
  122–3
David, King 188–9
Day, Robin 187
Dayan, Daniel 138
De spectaculis, Martial, M. Valerius 59,
  60–61, 64, 67
De Waal, Thomas 163, 168
deadlines, media coverage 252
death
  see also news deaths
  'bad' 183, 192–3, 195–6, 204–5, 229
  of common man 211, *211*
  couch-potato syndrome 220
  and fear of mortality 183–4
  first-world view of third world 193–4
  'good' 182–3, 228–9
  heroic 205–6
  incorporation rites 190
  media representations 223–4
  medical definitions 192
  and the medical profession 182
  nature of 190–91
  objectivity of reporting 197–8
  political messages 211–12
  public 52
  and religious rituals 190–91
  risks to viewer of 220
  rites of separation 190
  and ritual 186
  social attitudes to xx
  transition rites 190
  violent 184–5, *184*

Death of General Wolfe on the Heights of Abraham, The, West, Benjamin 205, 206
Death of Nelson, The, Maclise, Daniel 207
democracy
    and communications 238
    and compassion 129–30
    and famines 151
    and free press xvii–xviii
    imposition of 148
    and journalism 34
    and news xv, 289
    and party allegiances 140–41
    universality of Western liberal 157
Derbes, Anne 113
Descartes, René 235
Diana, Princess of Wales, funeral 211, 216–17, 216, 238, 239
Dickens, Charles, *Hard Times* 258
diet, meat 9–10
Dimbleby, Richard, Belsen liberation 45
divine, nature of 112–13
documentaries, fixed 244
Domitian 61–2
Dorothy of Mantua, St 121
Douglas, Mary 32
drama
    deception within 243
    and news 139
    tragedy 241
Dudayev, Dthokar 163
Dunkirk evacuation, Churchillian account 172
Dürer, Albrecht, *Sudarium of St Veronica* 95

Eastern Bloc, speed of changes 140
Eden, Sir Anthony 7, 7
editing
    reality events 80–81
    selective 81
editorial judgements, and journalists 199–200
El Salvador conflict 192–3, 198
elephants, Roman games 59

Eliot, George 258
Elizabeth II, Remembrance Day 270
Ellis, Frank 157
emotional genres, creation of 232–3
emotional manipulation, journalism 237–8
emotional responses
    compassion 258
    moulding of 140
    rating 242–3
    restricting 230
    routine stories 235
emotional ties 257–8
emotions
    see also empathy; sympathy
    distrust of 255, 259
    etymology 251
    expressions of 236–7, 257
    fundamental nature of 235
    Mill, J. S. on 253–4
    as needs 257
    Nussbaum, Martha on 256–7, 258
    performed 243
    and photojournalism 231
    purposes 257
    universality of xxi
empathy
    and compassion 285–6
    and the 'feel-good factor' xxii
    protective response 258
    and understanding 286
entertainment
    news as xvii, 80
    preferences 137–8
Erasmus, St, martyrdom of *119*
Ethiopia, famine 150, 183, 237
Etruscans, Roman games origins 53
Euphyne 97
Euripides, *Medea* 241, 256
evacuees returning 236
Evans-Pritchard, Edward 188
executions 128
exhumations 226, 227

Falklands War 142, 144
    burial of casualties 204

famines
  Ethiopia 150, 237
  and a free press 151
  international aid 237
  Soviet Union 170–71
Feifel, Herman 209
fiction, attitudes to 248–9
fictionalized reality events 245
Figes, Orlando 153, 160
film industry, blood effects 20–21, 21
First World War see World War I
'floral fascism', funerals as 238, 239
foetus photographs 277–81
food price control, and Roman games 67, 68
Ford, Henry 39
Forty Martyrs of Sebaste 116, 117–18, 117
Foucault, Michel 70
France
  foreign policies 281
  judicial torture 114
Francis of Assisi, St 109, 110–11, 111
Franciscans, art patrons 110–112
free press, and democracy xvii–xviii
Freedom of Information, UN Charter 252
freelance reporters
  economic situation 219
  risk-taking by 269–70
freezing, torture by 116
Freud, Sigmund
  on attitudes to death 220
  on newspaper sellers 250
  on World War I 187
friendly fire 141, 232
Fukuyama, Francis 157
funerals 192
  Bali 213
  Diana, Princess of Wales 210–211, 216–17, 216, 238, 239
  early New England 194
  as 'floral fascism' 238, 239
  political functions 212–13
  ritual 210
  royal 210–211, 213, 216–17, 216

  as social need 208–9
  spiritual aspects of 214
  Victorian 209–210
Fussell, Paul, 186

G8, anti-globalization demonstrations 266
Gaidar, Yegor 177
Galbraith, J. K. 140
Galen 55
games, Roman see Roman games
Geertz, Clifford 83, 213
gender differences, media consumption 12–13, 178
General Strike, news during 248
genocide, Holocaust 185, 212, 271–3
geopolitics, of oil 161
George, St, martydom 114, 116
George VI, death of 12
Germany
  attitude to history 186
  war propaganda 221
Gibbon, Edward, Decline and Fall of the Roman Empire, The 51, 66, 74
Giotto, frescos in Arena chapel, Padua 107–8
gladiators 57
  as celebrities 57, 58
  cost of 55–6
  defeat of 57–8
  empathy with 69
  noblemen as 57
  origins 58
  racial origins 56–7
  sacramentum gladiatorium 55, 56
  suppliers of 56
  weapons 56–7
Glasnost Defence Foundation 164, 166
global understanding, lack of 270
globalization
  and communication 266–7
  media consumption 133–4
  news 127
  witness phenomenon 142
Glover, Jonathan 273, 277
Goldberg, Jonathan 213
Gombrich, Ernst 289

'good' death, managed 182–3, 228–9
Goody, Jack 37, 244
Gover, Geoffrey 208–9
gossip, tabloid journalism 283
Gowing, Nick 195
Grass, Günter 121
Greco, El, *Laocoön* 122, 123
Greeks, statuary 97
Gregory I, Pope, Christian imagery 99
Grey, John 35
grief 188–9
Grossman, Vasily 152, 165
Grozny 161, 164, *166*
Guernica 222
Gurevitch, Michael 18

Hallin, Daniel 197, 199
Hanrahan, Brian 218
Hardy, Barbara 259
Hastings, Sir Max 148
Henry Suso, St 120–21
Henry V, William Shakespeare 213
heroic deaths 205–6
Herrin, Judith 96, 97, 99
hierarchy of pain 125
Hippolytus of Carthage, St 74
Hiroshima, atomic bomb 212
Hirst, Paul 148
Hobsbawm, Eric 8, 42
Hogarth, William
    The Harcot's Progress 204
    O! The Roast Beef of Old England 8,
        9
Holocaust 212
    media taboos 185
    reports of 271–3
Homer, *The Iliad* xvi, 53
Horace, Q. 66
Hosking, Geoffrey 176
hostage-taking, Iraq War 213
'hot news' 31
human rights
    see also Amnesty International;
        Human Rights Watch; Red Cross;
        War and Peace Reporting
    in Chechnya 164
    debates xx–xxi

'fifth estate of politics' 82
    as minority rights 136
Human Rights Watch
    Chechen Wars 156
    precept 82
Hume, David, on reason 284
Hynes, Samuel 186

icons
    emotional responses to 96
    intercessionary powers 100
    Mandylion 94
    private uses 96, 97
    public uses 95–6
    role of 90
    spread of 99
    as true images of Christ 96–7
Ignatieff, Michael 145
illness, portrayal *122*
imagery
    Christian martyrs 85, 86–7, 89–92
    Christian reverence 97
    Islamic attitudes 96
images
    influence on understanding 92, 93
    managed 27–8, 202
    manipulation by 92–3
incorporation rites, death 190
Indonesia, censorship defence 252
    informed consent, medical treatment
        240
insurgent terrorist attacks 271
intelligence failures, Iraq War 142
international aid, famines 237
Iraq War
    children in *100*, 132
    executions 128
    friendly fire 232
    hostage-taking 213
    intelligence failures 142
    and local politics 146–7
    news broadcasts 248
    and public concentration span 138
    return of casualties 204, *205*
    US casualties 201–2
    US justifications 136, 137
    and US public opinion 137

Islam, attitude to imagery 96
ITN, innovation 46

Jagger, Charles Sergeant, 208
James, William 121, 265
Japan
  Hiroshima bombing 212
  partial histories 186
al-Jazeera 172, 248
jeremiad format 194, 195–6
Jerome, St 97
John of Damascus 99
journalism
  see also news; photojournalism
  'chequebook' 46
  controls on 240–41
  democratic role 34, 237
  emotional manipulation 237–8
  forces on 148–9
  moral imperatives 283–4
  objectivity 197–8, 231–2, 260
  quality 43, 246, 293
  in Russia 157–60, 177
  in Soviet Union 159
  subjectivity 177–8
  tabloid 32, 246, 283, 292–4
journalists
  see also reporters
  butchery analogy 31–2
  crisis of public attention 253
  dangers to 164, 168–9, 223
  and editorial judgements 199–200
  factual interpretation 43
  and grief 189
  misreadings by 234–6
  need for self-examination 295
  Nonconformists as 43, 45, 87–8
  as outsiders 200
  public attitudes towards 34
  values 232
Judaism
  see also Holocaust
  attitude to Incarnation 112
Juvenal, D. Junius 57, 64, 69

Kaldor, Mary 142
Katz, Elihn 138

Kehoe, Vincent 21
Kieckhefer, Richard 121
known lives
  preference for 274–5, 274, 275
  and statistical lives 273
Kosovo conflict
  Loyn, David reports 196–7
  mass graves 226–7, 227
  Muslims murdered 201
Kouchner, Bernard, Médecins Sans
    Frontières 192, 281
Kraus, Karl 288

Laocoön, El Greco 122, 123
Latey, Mark 144
Lawrence, D. H., on sympathy 254
Layard, Richard 158
League of Nations 136
Lecky, William 52–3
legal evidence, news as 231
Leontius 98–9
Lermontov, Mikhail 160
Lieven, Anatol 157–8, 159, 168
Lifton, Robert J. 209, 212
lions, Roman games 60, 61
Lithuania, Russian suppression in 163
lives, known and statistical 273
Lloyd, John 82, 154, 159–60, 164
London, 2005 bombings xxiii
Loyn, David, 196–7, 197
Luddolph of Saxony, images of pain
    110
Lukács, Georg 42
Lutyens, Sir Edward 207, 209
Lutz, Catherine 253, 256

McAuley, Mary 157
McCormack, Robin 105
Macedonia, potential conflict 234–5
MacGregor, Neil 129
Maclise, Daniel, Death of Nelson, The
    205, 207
Manchester Guardian 87
Mandylion 94
Mango, Cyril 98
Mannheim, Karl 42
Marguerite of Oingt 113

marketing pressures, news production
291
Martial, M. Valerius, 59, 60–61, 64, 67
martyrology, Christian 72, 88
martyrs
  see also Christian martyrs; suicide
    attackers
  concept of 72
Marvin, Carolyn 27
Mary the Virgin, representations at
    Crucifixion 113–14, 115
Mass-Observation 261
Massacre of the Innocents, changed
    attitudes to 118
Mazower, Mark 136
Mazzini, Giuseppe 52
meat
  see also butchery
  additives 17–18, 20
  age at slaughter 16
  artificial colourings 17, 19–20
  beef 5–9, 7, 9
  BSE crisis 17
  diet 9–10
  hanging 16
  importation 15
  media analogies 14–15
  public choices 14
  public tastes 16–17
  rationing 9–10
  Smithfield Market 37, 38
Medea, Euripides 241, 256
Médecins Sans Frontières
  interventions by 281–2
  Kouchner, Bernard 192, 281
media consumption
  audience research 10–11
  emotional responses 140
  gender differences 12–13, 178
  globalization 133–4
media controls
  see also censorship
  Russia 154, 159–60, 175, 177,
    180–81
media conventions, purposes 265
media coverage
  deadlines 252

and national interest 179
and public perceptions 147
and social change 268–9
media organizations
  local incitement by 233–4, 234
  public contact with 108
  selective editing 81
  in Soviet Union 159
media sensationalism 46–7
medical treatment, informed consent
    240
Melzack, Robert 124, 125–6
memorials
  Cenotaph, Whitehall 207–8, 209
  Royal Artillery, Hyde Park Corner
    208
  tomb of the unknown warrior 206–7
  World War I 207, 208
Merridale, Catherine 158, 175, 176,
    179, 180
Meyrowitz, Joseph 267
Mickiewicz, Ellen 158
Mignonette, sinking of 273–4
Milgram, Stanley, obedience
    experiments 278–80
Mill, John Stuart
  Autobiography 254
  On Liberty 233
minorities
  attitudes to local television 264–5
  public hatred for 233
  Russian hostility to 167
minority rights, as human rights 136
misreadings, by journalists 234–6
mobile phones, use in disasters xxiii,
    132, 175–6, 267
Montesquieu 294
moral imperatives, journalism 283–4
morality
  and the news 32
  political 294
mortality
  Aids 276
  child road accidents 276, 277
  fear of 183–4
  twentieth century 200
Moscow theatre siege 165, 175–6

Mozambique floods, rescue 274, 275
mutual sympathy 255

Nash, John 264
Nash, Paul, *The Void of War* 264
Nast, Thomas, *The Power of the Press*
    36
national interest, and media coverage
    179
NATO, Serbian operation 141, 143
Neil, Ron 216
Nero, Roman games 65–6
neutrality, news 288, 290
news
    attention spans 249–50
    clichés 230–31
    as a commodity 47
    competitive nature of 213, 237
    conflict bias 142
    as cultural product xxii
    and democracy xv
    and drama 139
    emotional changes 259–60
    as entertainment xvii, 80, 138–9
    feminization of audiences 178
    globalization 127
    'hot' 31
    impartiality 288
    as legal evidence 231
    market pressures on xvii
    moral stance 30–31, 32
    neutrality 288, 290
    personal values 2
    political impact xix, xx, 78–9
    pre-planned events 71
    psychological aspects xv
    public taste 288
    real-time 132
    ritualization of 49–50
    and satire 239
    sequential analysis 139–40
    shocks in 219–21
    simplifications within xxi
    social effects of 47–8
    as social reconstruction 34
    and tragedy 241–2, 242
    and vicarious risk 50–51

violence in 33–4
news deaths
    political implications 214–15, 215
    public participation 214
    violent 184–5, 184
news formats, universality 139
news production
    commercial pressures 81
    continuity 217–18
    integrity of 218–19
    marketing pressures 291
    as morality play 31
    partisanship 133
    rules of 189
    selective 83
    sound bites 291
news values 139
    see also tabloid journalism
    commercial pressures 291–2
    emotional mobility 238
    justice 255
    local encoding 263
    maintenance of 219
    as reflection of public values 83
    shifts xix–xx
    as simplifiers xxii–xxiii
news-gathering
    cost of wars 145
    and public tastes xvi
    and security 50
news-ordering, importance of 33
newspaper proprietorship, 'power
    without responsibility' 42
newspapers
    decline in readership 15, 288
    portrayal of blood 19, 20, 22–3
    and profit element 42–3
NGOs *see* Amnesty International;
    Human Rights Watch; Red Cross;
    War and Peace Reporting
Nilsson, Lennart, foetus photographs
    277–8
Nonconformists, as journalists 43, 45,
    87–8
Northern Ireland troubles
    Omagh bombing 219
    revenge punishments 147

Russian versions 174
Scandinavian coverage 174, 225
United Kingdom coverage 225
Nussbaum, Martha 255–6, 256–7, 258

obedience experiments
Milgram, Stanley 278–80
Stanford Prison Experiment 279
objectivity
journalism 197–8, 231–2
and reality events 231
oil, geopolitics of 161
Omagh bombing 219
O'Neil, Oonora 282, 284
Origen 98
Ostrovorsky, Arkady 177
Oswald, Lee Harvey, murder of 267, 268

paedophiles, media-led campaigns
against 233, 234
pain
communication of 102, 103, 121, 124
conventions for depiction of 108–9
Crucifixion 109–110
describing 121–2, 125–6
hierarchy of 125
McGill Questionnaire 125
media depictions 80, 103, 131–2
medieval representations 128–9
perception of 123–4
quantification of 124–5
relief of 123–4, 126
representing 122–4
Roman attitude to 49
palliative care 130–31
paparazzi photographers 35, 36
parochialism, dangers of 181
Passion, the see Crucifixion
passive listening 247
Pasternak, Boris, Dr Zhivago 152
Paxton, Frederick 191
Peacock, Florence 204
Pedelty, Mark 193, 198
performed emotions 243
Perkins, Judith 88

Perpetua, St, martyrdom 72–3, 73
personal values
maintenance of 83
and news 2
Petronius 59
photojournalism
and emotions 231
paparazzi 35, 36
powers of 101
as record 224
still pictures 102–3
trade in images 141
pietà 114, 115, 129
Pimlott, Ben 238
Piranesi; Giambattista, Colosseum, Rome 54
Plath, Sylvia 260
Plato, on poets 284, 285
Plutarch 61
political manipulation, of suffering 153
politics
of human rights 82–3
morality of 294
need for self-examination 295
and news xix, xx,
news deaths 214–15, 215
party allegiances 140–41
public involvement 108
and public pleasure 52
and Roman games 67–9, 69, 70, 79, 290
and violence 118–20
of wars 131–2
Politkovskaya, Anna 156
Putin's power consolidation 156, 178
state controls 154–5
Polonius, St, martyrdom 75
post-conflict commitments 148
poverty
child road accidents 277
twentieth-century attitudes to 140
poverty gap, Western nations 259
Power of the Press, The, Thomas Nast 36
'power without responsibility' speech, Stanley Baldwin 42
precision bombing, target selection 223

prejudices, media responses to 83
private voyeurism 80
propaganda
    Iraq War executions 128
    Spanish Civil War 224
    wars 221–2
public opinion
    assessments of 108
    Chechen wars 167
    and wars 144
public perceptions, and media coverage
    147
public punishment, Roman games
    70–71
public sensitivity, changes in 46
public taste
    meat 16–17
    media sensationalism 46–7
    news 288
    trivia 148, 294
    and violence xvi, 287, 294
public voyeurism 80
public-service broadcasting
    decline of 45–6
    ITN 46
    support for 294–5
Pushkin, Aleksandr 160
Putin, Vladimir
    Chechen wars 155, 169–70
    power consolidation 156, 178
Putnam, Robert 249

quality journalism 43, 293
    truth and 245
Quintilian, M. Fabius, violence 118–20

Rabbit, Chaïm Soutine 3
Rabelais, François 177
radicalism, red symbolism in 26–7
'Rambo Loop, The' 146, 146
rationality xv–xvi
Rawls, John xxii
reading, gender divisions 12
real-time news
    Chechen wars 164–5
    claims of 243
    limitations 132

murder of Lee Harvey Oswald 267,
    268
realism, and accuracy 289
reality events
    doctoring 18
    editing 80–81
    fictionalized 245
    and objectivity 231
    violent deaths 185
reason
    Hume on 284
    and sentiment 133
Red Cross, precepts 81
religious rituals, death 190–91
reporters
    BBC 188
    freelance 219, 269–70
    role of war 186–7
    women war 178
reporting
    determinants xviii–xix
    World Trade Center attack 218
representation, opposition to 243–4
Reservoir Dogs, blood effects 21
resurrection, Christian martyrs 74–6,
    127–8
revenge killings 82
revenge punishments, Northern Ireland
    147
Riesman, David 247
Rifkin, James 41
righteous indignation, tabloid
    journalism 246
risk, news portrayal 50–51, 142
rites of separation, death 190
Ritvo, Harry 6
road accident mortality, children 276,
    277
Robespierre, Maximilien 292–3
Roman emperors
    and games 65–7, 66
    political standing 67–8, 69
    public popularity 69
Roman Empire
    later politics 76
    religions 87
Roman games

see also gladiators
attendance 56
audiences 51–2, 64–5, 103
Christian martyrs 71, 72–4, 73, 78,
   84
cost of 55–6, 67
emperors and 65–8, 66
and food price control 67, 68
frequency 54–5
history 53–4
imagery 58
munus sine missione shows 56
place of 78
politics of 67–9, 69, 70, 79, 290
popularity 51–2
programmes 62
public punishment at 70–71
purposes 49, 52
as reflection of morals 52–3
sacred elements 54
spread of 64
and the theatre 62
theatrical performances at 62–4
wild animals 58–62, 61
Romans
  attitude to pain 49
  manners 76–7
  statuary 97
  torture and 70–71
Romer, Alan 175
Rothschild, Miriam 41
Royal Artillery Memorial, Hyde Park
   Corner 208
royal funerals 210–11, 213, 216–17,
   216
Royal Smithfield Show 11
rumours, reporting of xviii, 195, 238,
   252, 283, 291
Russia
  see also Soviet Union
  attitudes to violence 165
  Chechen wars 143, 155, 158–65
  foreign press as opposition 175
  Glasnost Defence Foundation 164,
   166
  hostility to minorities 167
  journalism in 177

Lithuanian suppression 163
  media controls 154, 177, 180–81
  military expenditure 173–4
  mortality in 170–71
  Moscow theatre siege 165, 175–6
  national characteristics 180–81
  political control of media 172–3
  post-Communist social problems
   153–4
  predicament of 157–8
  societal changes 154
  and Soviet legacy 151–2
  Western media domination 175
Russian journalism 157–60
  control 154–5
  media organizations 159–60
  Vietnam model 163–4
Rwanda, death in 281, 285

Sabato, Larry 283
sacramentum gladiatorium 55, 56
Sahlins, Marshall 10
saints
  see also persons by name
  imitation of Christ's suffering 120–21
  men as 121
  resurrection 127–8
  women as 121
satire, and news 239
Sayle, Murray 231
scandal, tastes for 270
Scandinavia
  Northern Ireland troubles 174
  violent deaths 184–5
Scarry, Elizabeth 126
Schudson, Michael xiv, 42, 198–9, 231,
   245
Sebaste, Forty Martyrs of 116, 117–18,
   117
Sebastian, St 116
Second World War *see* World War II
selective editing 81
selectivity, in news production 83–4
Sen, Amartya 151
Seneca, L. Annaeus (the Younger) 77
  on emotions 238
  Roman games 55, 56, 60, 62, 67, 69

Sennett, Richard 13
sensationalism, media 46–7
sensitivity, public 46, 48
sentiment
    media-aroused 293
    and reason 133
Serbia, NATO operation 141, 143
Serpell James 39, 41
Seton-Watson, Hugh 160
Shakespeare, William, *Henry V* 213
Shawcross, William 145
Shils, Edward 42
shocks, to audiences 219–21
Simpson, John 232
Sinclair, Upton, *The Jungle* 39
slaughtering, public attitudes to 40–41
Smith, Adam, *Theory of Moral
    Sentiments* 254, 265
Smithfield Market 37, *38*
soap operas 138
social attitudes
    changing xx
    Romans 76
social changes
    media-led 268–9
    in USA 249
social effects, news 47–8
Socrates 86
Solon 243
Solzhenitsyn, Aleksandr 161, 263
Somali wars *115*
Sorokin, Pitirim 152
Southern, Richard 107
Soutine, Chaïm, *Rabbit 3*
Soviet Union
    see also Russia
    Afghan war 155, 163
    Chechen deportations 161
    domestic crises 158
    Gulags 263
    independent media in 159
    mortality in 170–71
    oppression in 151–2
    suffering in 152–3
    World War II heroism 152, *153*
Spain, distrust of fiction 248
Spanish Civil War 223–4

Stanford Prison Experiment 279
Stannard, David 194
state controls, Russia 154
statistical lives
    and known lives 273
    as political mortalities 276–7
Steinbeck, John 231
still photography, power of 102–3
Strack, Steven 209
Strong, Sir Roy 213
style sheets, television 251–2
subjectivity, journalism 177–8
Sudan War, 'burying' of 137, 281–2
Sudarium of St Veronica, Dürer,
    Albrecht 95
suffering
    broadcast portrayal 149–50
    in Christianity 87, 105, 108–9
    imagery of 89, 129
    media hierarchies 130
    moralizing about 282–3
    overexposure to 103
    political manipulation of 153
    public demand for 103–4
    salvation through 85–6
    societal differences 127
    in Soviet Union 152–3
suicide attackers 75
supermarkets, butchers 38
Symmachus, Q. Aurelius 59–60
sympathy 254–5

tabloid journalism
    gossip 283
    judgemental 32
    morals 292
    objectivity claims 198
    righteous indignation 246
    targeted 283, 293
Tacitus, P. 64
target selection, precision bombing 223
taste
    see also public taste
    origins 13–14
    social changes 28
telegraph, development 269
television

censorship 262–3
confrontational *135*
controls on 241
documentaries 244
entertainment preferences 137–8
globalization 267
minority attitudes to 264–5
public exposures on 244
real-time news 132
representations of wars 145
Russian, political control 172–3
soap operas 138
style sheets 251–2
twenty-four-hours news 289
war coverage costs 145
World Trade Center attack 128, 224
Tertullian, Q. Septimus
capital punishment 63
Christian martyrs 74, 86, 87
Roman games 51, 58
theatre, and Roman games 62
Thomas, 'Doubting' 127
Titmus, Richard, 8, 23–5
Tolstoy, Leo 160
tomb of the unknown warrior,
symbolism 206–7
torture
by freezing 116
Christian martyrs 114, 116
France 114
Roman Empire 70–71
and truth 114
Toynbee, Polly 15
tragedy
acceptance of 284–5
Aristotle on 284
and news 241–2, 242
transition rites, death 190
Trumbull, John 206
truth, questioning 245
tsunami victims, Thailand *194*
Turkey, television reports from 264–5

Ukraine, democracy 148
UN Charter, Freedom of Information
252
understanding, and empathy 286

unknown warrior, tomb of 206–7
United Kingdom
see also Northern Ireland troubles
Aberfan disaster 228
broadcasting coverage 148–9
fiction in 248
General Strike 248
war propaganda 221–2
universality of Western liberal
democracy, impending 157
USA
Afghan operations 143
'assembly-line' butchery 39–40, *40*
broadcasting coverage 148–9
casualty censorship 201–2
El Salvador conflict 198
foreign-news broadcasts 288
hostility to 134
international interventions 134
Iraq War justifications 136, 137
partisan news production 133, 232
return of casualties 204
social changes within 249
USSR see Soviet Union

values see news values; personal values
Van Creveld, Martin 146–7
Van Gennep, Arnold 190
Veronica, St 94, *95*, 101
Veyne, Paul 58, 68
victimhood 145
victims
compassion for 245
innocence of 281
media characteristics 280–81
passivity 282
victories, and wars 143–4
Vietnam War
children in 131, *131*
documentaries 185
reporting conventions 128
and Russian journalism 163–4
violence
politically necessary 118–20
and public taste xvi, 287
re-examining 185–6
reporting 33–4

violence – *cont.*
  revenge killings 82
  voyeurism and 50
violent deaths *184*
violent news
  broadcasting 184–5
  public reactions 290–91
  reality demand 185
  Scandinavia 184–5
voyeurism
  private 80
  public 80, 270
  and violence 50

war artists 264, *264*
War and Peace Reporting, Chechen wars
  156
wars
  'body-bag' images *143*
  burial of fallen 203
  casualty levels 141, 144
  children in *100*, 131–2, *131*
  civilian casualties 141
  costs to media 145
  definitions 147
  hostility to 142
  leaders' positions 137
  media bias 142
  media-created 233
  political realism 142
  politics of 131–2, 135
  post-conflict commitments 148
  propaganda 221–2
  and public concentration span 138
  and public opinions 144
  role of reporters 187–8
  target selection 223
  trade in images 141
  victimhood 145
  and victories 143–4
Washington Post 87
Webb, Beatrice 248, 250, 254
Weitzmann, Kurt 99, 118
Wenders, Wim 246

West, Benjamin, *Death of General Wolfe on the Heights of Abraham, The* 205, 206
Western liberal democracy, universality
  of impending 157
Western media domination 133–4
  Russia 175
Western nations, poverty gap 259
wild animals, Roman games 58–62, *61*
Wollen, W. B. 206
women
  fiction-reading 248–9
  media audience 178
  as saints 121
  war reporters 178
Woolf, Virginia 121
World Health Organization
  pain 121, 130
  palliative care 130
World Trade Center attack
  changing reports xxi
  managed images of 27–8, 202, 263
  news analysis 139–40
  planning 71
  as 'reality game' 137
  reporting 218
  television observers 251
  and US foreign politics 134
  varying reportage 128, 224
World War I
  Freud on 187
  literature of 186–7
  memorials 207
  military casualties 193
World War II
  Belsen liberation 45
  civilian deaths 193
  declaration of 250
  Dunkirk evacuation 172
  evacuees returning 236
  military censorship 262–3
  Soviet heroism 152, *153*

Yeltsin, Boris 162–3, *164*, 167